*Oracle Press*™

Oracle Database 10g Linux Administration

Edward Whalen

D1275651

McGraw-Hill/Osborne

New York   Chicago   San Francisco
Lisbon   London   Madrid   Mexico City   Milan
New Delhi   San Juan   Seoul   Singapore   Sydney   Toronto

The McGraw·Hill Companies

McGraw-Hill/Osborne
2100 Powell Street, 10th Floor
Emeryville, California 94608
U.S.A.

To arrange bulk purchase discounts for sales promotions, premiums, or fund-raisers, please contact
McGraw-Hill/Osborne at the above address.

Oracle Database 10*g* Linux Administration

234567890 IBT/IBT 0198

ISBN 0-07-223053-3

Acquisitions Editor
    Lisa McClain

Project Editor
    Carolyn Welch

Contributing Authors
    Robert Bryan Thomas
    Fraser Talbot
    Dan Hotka

Technical Editors
    Michael New
    James Petts
    Greg Marsden
    Joel Becker

Copy Editor
    Bob Campbell

Proofreader
    Susie Elkind

Indexer
    Claire Splan

Composition
    Apollo Publishing Services

Cover Series Design
    Damore Johann Design, Inc.

Series Design
    Jani Beckwith, Peter F. Hancik

This book was composed with Corel VENTURA™ Publisher.

About the Author

Edward Whalen is the founder of Performance Tuning Corporation (www.perftuning.com), a consulting company specializing in database performance, administration, and backup/recovery solutions. Prior to starting Performance Tuning Corp., Mr. Whalen worked at Compaq Computer Corporation as an OS developer, and then as a database performance engineer. He has extensive experience in database system design and tuning for optimal performance. His career has consisted of hardware, OS, and database development projects for many different companies. Mr. Whalen has written three other books on the Oracle RDBMS and four books on MS SQL Server. He has also worked on numerous benchmarks and performance tuning projects with both Oracle and MS SQL Server. Mr. Whalen is recognized as a leader in database performance tuning and optimization. In addition to his experience in Oracle on many different OS platforms, such as Solaris, AIX, HP-UX, and Windows, he has recently spent significant time working with Oracle on Linux, including the deployment of some of the first RAC clusters on Linux. He works closely with both Red Hat and Novell/SUSE with many different flavors of Linux.

About the Contributing Authors

Robert Bryan Thomas is a Senior Performance Consultant at Performance Tuning Corporation. He has a diverse background in database performance, Oracle RAC, data warehousing, and SAN storage. He currently specializes in Oracle10*g* RAC on multiple OS platforms. Robert Thomas graduated from Texas A&M University with a degree in Computer Science.

Fraser Talbot is a Senior Performance Consultant at Performance Tuning Corporation. His background includes several years of database administration, exclusively Oracle and Oracle E-Business Suite. He and his wife, Virginia, and three daughters, Margaret, Susan, and Elizabeth, reside in Houston, Texas.

Dan Hotka is a Training Specialist, who has over 27 years of experience in the computer industry and over 22 years of experience with Oracle products. He is an internationally recognized Oracle expert with Oracle experience dating back to the Oracle V4.0 days. He is also the author of *Oracle9i Development by Example* and *Oracle8i from Scratch* by Que and has co-authored six other popular books. He is frequently published in Oracle trade journals, and speaks regularly at Oracle conferences and user groups around the world. Visit his website at www.DanHotka.com. Dan can also be reached at dhotka@earthlink.net.

Contents

PART I
Oracle on Linux Overview

PART II

Deploying Oracle 10*g* on Linux

PART III
Oracle RAC on Linux

PART IV

Administering and Tuning Oracle Database 10*g* on Linux

PART V

Oracle Products on Linux

Acknowledgments

I t is not easy acknowledging all the people who have made this book possible. Not only is there the work that went into the book itself, but there is the support and encouragement of friends and family who helped move the book forward.

I would like to thank the following: contributing authors Robert Bryan Thomas, Fraser Talbot, and Dan Hotka; Lisa McClain and Carolyn Welch at McGraw-Hill/Osborne; and technical editors James Petts and Michael New. This book would not be what it is without the help of a great team of editors from Oracle Press.

I would also like to thank Larry Ellison. Without him Oracle would not be what it is today. Thanks to Jim Enright, who helps me when I need help. I would also like to thank Wim Coekaerts, who puts out a great product, and Ken Jacobs, whom I have had the pleasure of knowing and from whom I have gained a new appreciation of Oracle's RDBMS.

Writing a book involves a lot of time and effort. I would like to thank my wife, Felicia, for putting up with the sacrifices necessary to write this book.

Introduction

he popularity of Linux is growing at an astounding rate. But it was only a few years ago that Linux did not even exist. To understand what makes Linux tick, it is necessary to look at the history of Linux. Linux is fashioned after the UNIX operating system, so to completely know the history of Linux you must also know the history of UNIX.

History of UNIX

It was in the late sixties that development of the UNIX operating system began at AT&T Bell Labs to create a new operating system that ran on the PDP-7 computer. This development was done by Ken Thompson and Dennis Ritchie and culminated in the first release of the UNIX operating system in 1971. Subsequently, several other releases were done in somewhat quick succession, but the next major release was release 4 in 1973. Release 4 was significant in that it was the first release of the UNIX operating system written using the "C" programming language. It is interesting to note that the "C" programming language was being developed in parallel with the UNIX operating system; however, it was not until the "C" language was stable enough that the UNIX operating system was rewritten in "C".

In 1975 the 6th edition of UNIX was released. This was the first edition that was released outside of Bell Labs. This began the initial popularity and proliferation of UNIX to other companies and to different development communities. Following this, several different flavors or brands of UNIX-like operating systems were released. These operating systems had a command set and programming API in common, but because of trademark and ownership issues, many of these different varieties of UNIX came out under different names and with slightly different variations and market focus.

For example, in 1980, Microsoft released a UNIX-like operating system called Xenix. Xenix was designed to work on PC computers that used the Intel processor. In 1982 and 1983 AT&T UNIX System Group (USG) released System III and then System V (the first supported UNIX release). Both of these were intended for minicomputers. In 1984 the University of California released its own UNIX operating system UNIX 4.2BSD. This variety of the UNIX operating system became popular with computer system manufacturers such as Digital Equipment Corporation and Sun Microsystems.

After several years of competition between the different varieties of UNIX, UNIX System V release 4 was released. This release took features of USG UNIX, BSD UNIX, and Xenix and incorporated them into one UNIX specification. Soon after that, AT&T spun off the UNIX System Group into an independent group known as the UNIX Systems Lab or USL. It was at this time that the first version of Linux was released.

In 1993 Novell purchased the UNIX Systems Lab and transferred the rights to the UNIX trademark and specifications to the X/Open group. To this day, there are still many varieties of UNIX and UNIX-like operating systems being developed and used throughout the world. With many of these varieties the only difference between a UNIX operating system and a UNIX-like operating system is the use of the UNIX trademark.

How Linux Began

In 1991, at the University of Helsinki, Finland, Linus Torvalds began working on a new operating system that looked and worked similarly to the UNIX operating system, but with none of the baggage of patents and trademarks associated with it. Mr. Torvalds wanted to develop an operating system that could be put into the public domain, where source code could be distributed without licensing fees and without violating other people's trademarks. Thus, the Linux operating system was born.

The Linux operating system was based somewhat on the principles of the GNU project in which all software and source code should be held in the public domain. The GNU project began work on a public domain "C" compiler in 1994. By 1991, when Torvalds began working on his operating system, the GNU C Compiler (GCC) was available and free to be used for his project.

The GNU project came out of the Free Software Foundation. The Free Software Foundation (FSF) is a non-profit organization founded in 1985. Its goal was to support the free software movement, and specifically the GNU project. The GNU General Public License (GPL) was designed to promote and protect free software. The FSF holds most of the copyrights for GNU software and enforces those copyrights. The GNU project is still very popular today.

This was soon followed by the release of Linux to the world. But the first releases of Linux were used primarily as development and desktop systems. The first releases of Linux were not suitable for server systems because of the lack of support for larger systems. In order for Linux to be supported on servers, it was necessary to have support for multiprocessors, large amounts of memory, and a variety of hardware components and applications such as Oracle. This support for more robust and larger system support began with the later Linux kernels.

In 1994 the 1.0 version of the Linux kernel was released. Although this gave desktop users and developers something to work with, it did not provide the support that was needed for a server. In 1996 this kernel was finally released. The 2.0 kernel supported multiprocessor systems and included a more robust I/O subsystem. In 1999 the 2.2 kernel enhanced this support and in 2001 the 2.4 kernel provided a stable, high performance operating system. This OS support enhanced the support in the 2.2 kernel. With the 2.6 kernel (note that only even versions are released), the I/O subsystem was greatly enhanced and provided larger amounts of memory.

With the current version of the Linux server, most hardware vendors provide drivers and support. It is possible to build Linux systems with large amounts of memory (64GB) and many TB (terabytes) of disk storage using SCSI or SAN storage. Along with this robustness and extensive hardware support is extensive support from vendors such as Oracle. Today, Oracle supports all of its mainstream products on the Linux operating system, and many complementary products to Oracle support Linux as well.

Linux and Unix Timelines

The following is a summary of the history presented in the previous sections:

- **1969**   Ken Thompson and Dennis Ritchie at AT&T Bell Labs started development of the UNIX operating system using a PDP-7.

- **1971**   1st edition was released.

- **1973**   4th edition was rewritten in "C" and released along with the "C" language itself.

- **1975**   6th edition was released outside of Bell Labs.

- **1980**   Microsoft released Xenix.

- **1982**   AT&T's Unix System Group (USG) released System III.

- **1983**   UNIX System V, the first supported UNIX, was released.

- **1984**   FSF started work on the GNU "C" compiler.

- **1984**   University of California, Berkeley, released 4.2BSD.

- **1989**   UNIX System V release 4 was released, unifying System V, BSD, and Xenix.

- **1991**   USL (Unix Systems Lab) was spun off.

- **1991**   Linus Torvalds began work on Linux at the University of Helsinki in Finland and the first version was released.

- **1993**   Novell bought USL.

- **1993**   Novell transferred the rights to the UNIX trademark and specifications to X/Open.

- **1994**   Linux Kernel 1.0 was released; Red Hat Linux made its debut.

- **1996** Linux Kernel 2.0 made its debut, supporting multiprocessors.

- **1996** Los Alamos National Lab used 68 PCs running Linux to create a parallel processing supercomputer.

- **1999** Linux version 2.2 kernel was released.

- **2001** Linux version 2.4 kernel was released.

- **2004** Linux version 2.6 kernel was released.

As you can see, Linux has come a long way in a short amount of time.

Linux Varieties

Once the popularity of Linux became apparent, a number of companies began commercially distributing Linux. Even though the hard-core Linux followers still might have preferred to download source code and build the Linux operating system by hand, this was not a practical way for software to be distributed to the masses. In addition, companies began to explore the idea of deploying Linux in their companies, running mission-critical applications. In addition to the need to have a more stable and tested Linux distribution, these companies also needed something that could be easily deployed and supported.

Among the first distributions of Linux was the MCC Interim Linux, which was available from the University of Manchester in 1992. Around the same time was a Linux distribution from Texas A&M University called TAMU. However, neither of these distributions was really of commercial quality. In response to his own frustration about software updates, Patrick Volkerding created the Slackware distribution. This distribution became available in July of 1993 and is the oldest Linux distribution in use today. Slackware Linux is also known as one of the more pure Linux distributions because it does not add on applications and GUI tools that are not available in other Linux distributions.

Today, there are literally hundreds of Linux distributions available. However, in order to properly support the Linux operating system with the quality that Oracle support is known for, Oracle has selected a few Linux distributions from which you can choose. Oracle's selection is based on the quality of the distribution, its popularity, and the availability and quality of support from the OS vendor. Of the Linux distributions available today, Oracle supports Red Hat and United Linux.

Red Hat Linux was founded in 1993 and is one of the largest Linux companies. Much of the popularity of Red Hat Linux is derived from its partnerships with various hardware vendors. Dell, HP, and IBM all support Red Hat Linux. Red Hat Linux Enterprise 3.0 and Red Hat Linux Advance Server are excellent platforms for Oracle Database 10*g*.

SUSE Linux became a very popular version of Linux mainly in Europe and Asia, but its popularity quickly spread worldwide. In 2003 Novell purchased SUSE Linux, putting them back into the forefront of the UNIX/Linux operating system arena. SUSE Linux Enterprise Server 9 (SLES 9) was the first large-scale commercial distribution of the 2.6 kernel. Dell, HP, and IBM also support SUSE Linux. As with Red Hat Linux, SUSE Linux Enterprise Server (SLES) is an excellent platform for Oracle Database 10*g*.

What is important to remember when you purchase a Linux distribution to run on Oracle is that you find one that offers the support you need. Many of these distribution companies have arrangements with your hardware vendor so that you only have to make one phone call if you have a problem and it will be resolved, whether it is hardware or software at fault. It is important that you find a vendor that will offer the type of support you require for your company and your requirements.

History of Oracle

Compared to the Linux operating system, Oracle has a very long and rich history. In this section, you will learn the history of Oracle, and in the next section you will learn the history of Oracle on Linux.

- **1977** Larry Ellison, Bob Miner, and Ed Oates formed a company called Relational Software Inc. (RSI). Here, they decided to build an RDBMS called "Oracle," using the "C" programming language whenever possible and the SQL interface. Soon after, version 1 (prototype only) was released.

- **1979** RSI delivered the first product to customers. The "Oracle" RDBMS version 2 ran on the Digital PDP-11 running the RSX-11 operating system and was soon ported to the DEC VAX system.

- **1983** Version 3 was introduced touting changes in the SQL language as well as performance enhancements and other improvements. Unlike earlier versions, version 3 was written almost entirely in the "C" programming language. At this point RSI changed its name to the Oracle Corporation that we know today.

- **1984** Oracle version 4 was released. Oracle RDMBS version 4 supported both the VAX system and the IBM VM operating system. Version 4 was the first version to incorporate read-consistency.

- **1985** Oracle introduced version 5 of the Oracle RDBMS. Version 5 was a milestone because it introduced client/server computing to the market with the use of SQL*Net. Version 5 was also the first MS-DOS product to break through the 640K barrier.

- **1988** Oracle introduced version 6. Version 6 introduced low-level locking as well as a variety of performance improvements and functionality enhancements including sequence generation and deferred writes. In addition, PL/SQL and hot backups were introduced. I was first introduced to Oracle6 back in the days when we used to run the TP1, TPC-A, and TPC-B benchmarks. At this point, Oracle was running on a large variety of different platforms and operating systems.

- **1991** Oracle introduced the Oracle Parallel Server option on version 6.1 of the Oracle RDBMS on the DEC VAX platform. Soon the Parallel Server option was available on a variety of platforms.

- **1992** Oracle introduced Oracle7. Oracle7 included many architectural changes in the area of memory, CPU, and I/O utilization. Oracle7 is the full-featured RDBMS that you are all used to and have been using for many years. Oracle7 introduced many advances in the area of ease of use such as the SQL*DBA tools and database roles.

- **1997** Oracle introduced Oracle8. Oracle8 added object extensions as well as a host of new features and administration tools.

- **2001** Oracle introduced Oracle9*i* release 1. This was the first release of the Oracle9*i* product and included features such as the Oracle RAC (Real Application Clusters) product.

- **2002** Oracle introduced Oracle9*i* release 2. This release built on Oracle9*i* release 1 and included new features such as the cluster filesystem for Oracle9*i* RAC.

- **2004** Oracle released Oracle10g for grid computing. This release takes Oracle to a new level of features, stability, and performance.

History of Oracle on Linux

As you have seen in the last section, Oracle has been around for quite a while. In fact, Oracle has been around much longer than Linux. It was only a few years ago that Oracle started shipping products for Linux. The first Oracle RDBMS for a Linux product was version 8.0.4. However, this was not the first Oracle RDBMS that would actually work on Linux. In July of 1998 Oracle announced that it would support Oracle7 for SCO UNIX running on Linux. In late 1998 Oracle released Oracle8 version 8.0.4 for Linux.

This was a significant move for Oracle, since now there was a low cost operating system that Oracle could use to compete with the Windows operating system. Several major companies such as Dell, HP, and IBM all jumped on the Linux bandwagon. At the same time Oracle was developing the latest releases of the Oracle RDBMS, they were also working with the Linux vendors to put improved support into their products. There were a number of things that Oracle requires from an operating system in order to become a viable platform for performance and stability. These features include:

- **Asynchronous I/O** Asynchronous I/O is an operating system feature that allows I/Os to be queued without the calling process having to block (wait) on the I/O to complete.

■ **Multiprocessor support** Oracle performs very well with two or more
processors. Linux had Multiprocessor (MP) support in version 2.0 of the
kernel, but it was much improved in version 2.4.

■ **Large memory support** The Intel/AMD 32-bit systems are based on 32-bit
memory addressing. This allows the system to support up to 4GB of RAM.
Recent modifications have allowed workarounds that provide memory
higher than 4GB to be used. Of course, 64-bit systems can access terabytes
of data natively.

■ **Robust I/O subsystem** In order for large systems to use Oracle, it is
necessary to support an I/O subsystem that is scalable, powerful, and
robust. This requires RAID controllers, SAN, and NAS storage to be
supported.

■ **Wide support of hardware** There must be a lot of choices in terms of
network hardware, I/O subsystems, tape backup, etc.

So, even though Oracle officially had a version of the RDBMS that worked
on Linux, there was still some catch-up to do on the OS side. As the Linux kernel
improved, so did the Oracle RDBMS and support from hardware vendors.

Oracle's clustering product Oracle Parallel Server (OPS) required the hardware
vendor to supply an Operating System Dependent layer or OSD. This did not work
well with the Linux model, where the OS was not developed by the hardware vendor.
In 2001 when Oracle9*i* was released, so was Oracle's new clustering technology—
Oracle Real Application Clusters or Oracle RAC.

Oracle RAC allows sets of commodity Linux computers to work together as one
system. This set of computers allows multiple Oracle instances to access the same
database. This is known as a cluster. Oracle9*i* and RAC clusters on Linux have
become very popular in the last few years. In fact, I have personally been involved
in a large number of Linux RAC clusters.

In May 2002, Oracle9*i* R2 was released on Oracle. This was yet another big step
for Oracle on Linux because of the improvements in both Oracle and with Oracle
RAC clusters. Oracle9*i* R2 provided additional security features geared toward
Internet computing.

The biggest gain for Oracle on Linux came on June 5, 2002, when Larry
Ellison announced that Oracle on Linux was a strategic direction for Oracle.
This announcement thrust Linux into the spotlight and increased the popularity
of Linux among the Oracle community. Oracle increased the marketing efforts
on the Linux operating system, and the number of customers running Oracle
RAC on Linux began to increase.

This year, Oracle has taken RAC clusters a step forward with Oracle10*g*, the grid
computing model. Grid computing is a number of Oracle RAC clusters connected
together to provide large amounts of capacity by allowing large numbers of computer
systems and storage systems to work together to provide the capacity you need.

With Oracle10g on Linux you now have the most state-of-the-art RDBMS running on the most state-of-the-art operating system. That is, until the next version comes out.

Oracle Product Overview on Linux

Oracle now supports the full range of products on Linux. In fact, Oracle now runs their own business on Linux using the Oracle eBusiness Suite. In this section, you will see an overview of the different Oracle products that are now supported on Linux.

The Oracle RDBMS

Of course, the Oracle RDBMS is supported on Linux. The Oracle RDBMS (Relational Database Management System) is the Oracle database product. The Oracle RDBMS allows you to manage large amounts of data quickly and safely. The Oracle RDBMS has but one job: to manage data. The Oracle RDBMS has one responsibility: to protect that data from loss. The Oracle RDBMS was originally designed for a UNIX operating system, and thus its architecture is perfectly suited for Linux. Although Oracle runs on architectures other than UNIX-like operating systems, it is best suited for them as you will see in Chapter 3.

The Oracle RDBMS includes many features and add-ons that make up the complete RDBMS package. Included with the Oracle RDBMS is Oracle Real Application Clusters (Oracle RAC) as well as a number of other features:

■ **Scalability** The Oracle RDBMS scales; that is, as you increase the number of CPUS and amount of memory, you can support more users and processors. Oracle scales over a large number of operating systems and hardware platforms.

■ **Performance** Oracle performance is record setting. Over the years Oracle has held many of the highest performance ratings on many of the standard database benchmarks.

■ **Business continuance features** Oracle supports a robust backup and recovery feature set as well as standby database features.

■ **Clustering technology** Oracle RAC clustering is the most advanced clustering technology available today. Oracle RAC clustering is scalable and supports a variety of hardware platforms as well as any number of cluster nodes. Oracle RAC clusters provide both scalable performance as well as failover capabilities. Oracle RAC clusters make up the foundation of grid computing.

■ **Application development** Oracle supports many interfaces into the database including XML, which is tightly integrated with the Oracle JVM.

- **Security**   Oracle has many security features designed to keep your data safe and secure. This includes a robust data encryption system and virtual private database.

- **Grid computing**   New in Oracle10g, grid computing allows many Oracle databases using RAC clusters to act as a grid of computers. Grid computing provides capacity when it is needed and failover capabilities if they are ever needed.

The Oracle database is a full-featured product that not only provides the performance and scalability that you would expect, but also provides a feature set that is unequalled in the industry. In addition to the Oracle database product, Oracle also can provide you with a full-featured web server suite and a complete business application suite as described in the following sections.

OracleAS

Oracle Application Server is a set of tools designed to provide you with a robust high performance Internet server to complement the Oracle database server. The Oracle Internet Application Server includes the following tools and servers:

- **Oracle HTTP Server**   The Oracle HTTP Server is an Apache web server that is 100 percent Apache compatible with Oracle enhancements. The Oracle HTTP Server includes plug-ins for Microsoft Internet Explorer and Netscape. Also included is a Perl interpreter and dynamic monitoring of the Apache web server.

- **J2EE**   Oracle J2EE is a Java server environment that supports web services such as SOAP, UDDI, and WSDL. It also supports JSPs and servlets.

- **JDeveloper**   JDeveloper is Oracle's Java design, development, optimization, and deployment tool. JDeveloper is used to quickly deploy enterprise ready J2EE applications.

- **Dynamic content**   Oracle Internet Application includes support for the PHP dynamic web content language. With PHPs and the Oracle database, dynamic content and applications can be deployed.

- **Portal**   The Oracle iAS portal product provides an environment for easily deploying an e-business portal.

- **Single Sign-on**   Oracle Single Sign-on provides an infrastructure for accessing applications, portals, and web services via a single sign-on. This alleviates the need to keep track of multiple sign-ons for each application.

- **Forms Service**   The Oracle Forms Service allows you to easily deploy Oracle Forms via web applications. You can move your forms applications to the Web quickly and easily.

- **Reports Service** This tool allows you to utilize Oracle reports service via a web interface.

- **Wireless** Oracle iAS includes wireless support, thus allowing you to easily deploy your data and applications to wireless devices.

- **Web Cache** The Oracle Web Cache allows you to cache not only Internet content but database information as well. This is provided to make your applications perform better.

Oracle Collaboration Suite

The Oracle Collaboration Suite is a relatively new product for Oracle. Oracle Collaboration Suite is a complete office management suite that is designed to be a replacement plug-in for other office suites such as Microsoft Exchange. Oracle Collaboration Suite contains a full-featured set of applications that can be used to run your entire company infrastructure as described here.

- **Email** This is a full email management system that supports protocols such as Internet Message Address Protocol (IMAP4), Post Office Protocol (POP3), and directory services using the Light-weight Directory Access Protocol (LDAP).

- **Calendar** Collaboration Suite provides a full-featured calendaring program that includes individual and group schedules and a robust search feature. Included in calendaring is conflict checking and resolution.

- **Filesharing** Oracle Files is a robust and scalable filesharing application. Oracle Ultra Search is incorporated into filesharing, thus enabling terabytes of data to be searched quickly and effortlessly.

- **Voicemail and fax** Oracle voicemail and fax allow important business information to be centrally and securely stored by Oracle. This provides security, performance, and the ability to access this information anywhere within your company.

- **Web conferencing** Oracle Web Conferencing allows two or more people to collaborate online efficiently and inexpensively. Oracle Web Conferencing allows online discussions as well as the ability to share applications over the network.

As you can see, Oracle Collaboration Suite provides a full-featured set of applications that can make your business more efficient.

Oracle E-Business Suite

The Oracle E-Business Suite is what was formerly known as Oracle Applications. The Oracle E-Business Suite consists of over 100 modules with everything from financials to supply chain management to procurement. In fact, one of the main benefits of running Oracle E-Business suite is the number of integrated modules. A few of the main modules are described here:

- **Financials**   Oracle Financials consists of a set of modules based on the Oracle General Ledger module. Some of these modules include Accounts Payable, Accounts Receivables, Cash Management, Assets, Budgets, and Financial and Sales Analyzers.

- **Human Resources**   Oracle Human Resources consists of a number of modules such as Human Resources, Payroll, Time and Labor, Recruiting, and Advanced Benefits.

- **Manufacturing**   Oracle Manufacturing contains a number of modules including Bills of Materials, Cost Management, Inventory, Order Management, Warehouse Management, Order Fulfillment, and a number of other modules.

- **Marketing**   Oracle Marketing is based on Oracle CRM foundation and includes modules on Customer Intelligence, Marketing Intelligence, and Trade Management.

- **Sales**   Oracle Sales contains a number of modules including Customer Intelligence, Quoting, Sales Analyzer, and Telesales.

In addition, Oracle E-Business Suite contains modules relating to Advanced Planning, Business Intelligence, Contracts, e-Commerce, Learning Management, Professional Services, Product Development, Projects, and Treasury.

The Oracle E-Business Suite is a full-featured suite of applications that can be used to run your business.

Since Oracle E-Business Suite version 11.0.5, the E-Business Suite has been available on Linux. In fact, Oracle is now running its own business on the Oracle E-Business Suite on the Linux operating system. Linux has become a popular platform for the E-Business suite not only because of the flexibility of Linux and its price, but because of the variety of hardware platforms that are available for Linux and its performance.

In fact, Oracle E-Business Suite on Linux RAC clusters has become a very popular platform in the last few years. The use of the RAC cluster provides a scalable and stable platform for the E-Business Suite, and Linux is the perfect platform for Oracle RAC clusters. This is why this combination has become so popular.

Summary

The Linux platform is somewhat new, but is quickly gaining in popularity. Linux has evolved from an idea to a major contender in the operating system arena in a short fifteen years.

Even though Oracle has only embraced Linux for a short time, they have done so with gusto. I believe that the future of the Oracle Database lies with Linux and commodity hardware. This combination has provided a highly competitive marketplace where hardware improvements are being made very quickly and the market is evolving. In the next few years you will see the emergence of 64-bit Oracle running on Linux and larger and larger systems and storage being used with Linux.

As you will see in the next few chapters, Linux is still evolving, but so is Oracle. Linux is an ideal platform for Oracle, since changes necessary for Oracle to perform and run better can easily be incorporated into the operating system quickly and efficiently. Even now, changes such as the Oracle Cluster File System (OCFS) and Automatic Storage Management (ASM) are being incorporated into the Linux operating system. In the next few years you will see the relationship between Oracle and the Linux community grow closer together as they work together to make both the Oracle Database and the OS better.

PART
I

Oracle on Linux
Overview

CHAPTER
1

Linux Architecture

n order to properly set up, configure, and administer Oracle on Linux, you should have some idea of how the Linux operating system works, how it is architected, and how to configure it. Administering the Linux system and configuring options varies, both by vendor and by version of the operating system. In this chapter, you will learn about the Linux kernel, how it works, and how it is configured. Later, in Chapter 4, you will learn more about how to tune specific parameters.

By understanding the architecture of Linux, you will be better equipped to monitor, configure, and tune the operating system. In addition, you will better understand how the operating system and Oracle work together (as well as against each other sometimes). In Chapter 2, you will learn about how Oracle is architected and specifics of what parts of the operating system Oracle depends on. This chapter will begin with the Linux kernel, the I/O subsystem, processes, and threads. Later in this chapter, you will learn about devices and filesystems and how to rebuild the Linux kernel.

Unlike proprietary UNIX operating systems of the past, where you would get your UNIX operating system from your hardware vendor, there are a number of different distributions of Linux. Although Linux source code is freely available on the Internet, most companies that are deploying Linux with Oracle demand a higher level of support than can be achieved by downloading source code off of the Internet and compiling it yourself. Once Linux started becoming more popular, companies such as Red Hat and SuSe began commercializing Linux. In order for Linux to be adopted by commercial users, things like pre-packaged software and support became more of an issue.

Two of the most popular Linux offerings are from Red Hat and SuSe. Red Hat was founded in 1993 and since then has grown to be one of the most dominant Linux vendors. SuSe was founded in 1992 and has recently been acquired by Novell. Both of these companies offer enhancements to the Linux operating system that make it more robust and more suited for Enterprise applications and offer support programs which are a necessity for Enterprise customers.

Both Red Hat Enterprise Linux and SuSe Enterprise Server support features that assist the Enterprise customer with the smooth operation of their system, including the following:

- Kernel upgrade procedures that allow for patching of kernels without having to recompile the entire operating system

- Supported configurations and kernels that are tested and validated

- A guaranteed upgrade path

Obtaining your Linux distribution from a reliable vendor that provides world-class support has many advantages. Many vendors that provide and support Linux are very good. Because of the dominance of the Linux market by Red Hat and SuSe, this book focuses on these two vendors.

Operating System Overview

An operating system exists to allow the user to run programs. The Operating System consists of a number of different types of programs and layers that handle different types of functions. As with most terminology, the initial architects of the early operating systems used analogies in order to illustrate their point. The innermost core of the operating system became known as the kernel, and the outer layers of the operating system were appropriately labeled the shell. The shell is used by the user to interact with the operating system, and between the shell and the kernel lie the system utilities.

The kernel is responsible for operating systems services such as processes management, scheduling time on the CPU, memory management, and system calls. System calls allow the shell to communicate with the kernel and perform functions like accessing disks.

Several different types of kernels are very popular today, some of which may be familiar to you. The first of these is known as a monolithic kernel (shown in Figure 1-1), and is made up of only three layers.

The second type of kernel that is popular uses a microkernel. The microkernel architecture (shown in Figure 1-2) can have many more layers than the monolithic architecture.

The Monolithic Kernel

A monolithic kernel is the simplest kind of kernel, and is created as one single executable, where each part of the kernel accesses the same memory structures. Monolithic kernels have a long tradition of use in operating systems such as UNIX, Windows, and DOS. Though some people believe the trend in more modern operating systems is not to use a monolithic design, Linux does use a monolithic kernel, and integrates its advantages without its traditional disadvantages.

The advantage of the monolithic kernel is that since it is one executable, all of the memory is available everywhere within the kernel. This means that data does not need to be passed between different layers of the operating system, thus improving

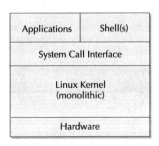

FIGURE 1-1. *The monolithic kernel model*

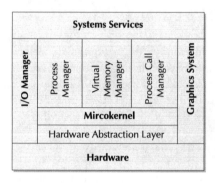

FIGURE 1-2. *The microkernel model*

performance. Traditionally, the disadvantage of monolithic kernels is that whenever you want to add another device driver or kernel addition, the entire kernel must be rebuilt. This can be quite painful, especially for novices.

Unlike traditional monolithic operating systems, Linux uses a hybrid monolithic kernel that supports Kernel Loadable Modules, known as KLMs. Kernel Loadable Modules allow for device drivers and kernel layers to be dynamically loaded and unloaded from the kernel. This offers several advantages. Loadable modules only utilize memory when they are used. Loadable modules are used for several areas of the operating system, including

- **Device drivers** These are programs designed to communicate with and operate a specific hardware device.

- **Filesystem drivers** Filesystem drivers allow many different filesystems to be used in the operating system. Unused filesystems are not loaded into the kernel.

- **System calls** System calls are communication channels between the users and the kernel. By permitting loadable system calls, custom-made system calls can be developed and added into the kernel.

- **Network drivers** Loadable network drivers allow for the addition of new and custom network protocols.

- **Executable interpreters** Various executable interpreters can be loaded and unloaded from the kernel as necessary.

By supporting loadable modules, the kernel has a level of functionality that is available in microkernels while offering the features of a monolithic kernel. There are several commands that can be used to list, view, and manage KLMs. These commands are listed here:

Command	Description
lsmod	Used to list the modules currently loaded in the kernel
insmod	Used to install a KLM (load a module)
modprobe	Used to manage KLMs
rmmod	Used to remove KLMs from the kernel
depmod	Used to handle module dependencies
ksyms	Used to display kernel symbols and which modules they belong to

Loadable modules can be quite useful and convenient, since kernel recompiles are not required to add modules.

The Microkernel

In a microkernel architecture, a very small kernel interacts with the hardware and is surrounded by layers of operating system code that perform different functions. The microkernel performs kernel functions such as thread management and some memory management in interprocess communication, but many other OS services (such as I/O processing) run outside of the kernel. This is also true of device drivers, which can be used even though they haven't been linked into the kernel. These device drivers just need to be able to communicate with the other OS functions as well as the kernel.

Many modern operating systems use a microkernel model, including Microsoft Windows server products like Windows NT, Windows 2000, and Windows 2003. Other operating systems that use the microkernel architecture include AIX and Mach.

Linux Overview

The Linux operating system consists of a hybrid monolithic kernel (as mentioned earlier), system calls and utilities, and shells used to access the OS. As with most UNIX-like operating systems, with the exception of the kernel, you have your choice regarding use of utilities and shells. In fact, most Linux varieties come with at least three shell programs you can choose from. The most popular are sh (the Borne shell), ksh (the Korn shell), and bash (the Borne-Again shell).

In addition, the Linux operating system comes with a huge variety of utilities and applications that can assist you with data manipulation, word processing, computing, and other tasks. The shell, like most Linux programs, can be used in both an interactive mode or in a batch mode. Creating shell programs, or scripts, is a great way to perform maintenance tasks over and over again. A good rule of thumb is that if you are going to do something more than once, make a shell script out of it. They can be very powerful and perform a number of tasks, thus saving you from having to write a compiled program.

In this section, we will explore some of the Linux utilities provided with your Linux distribution (as well as the development environment), the Linux architecture, and how to configure Linux. Later in this chapter, we will explore the Linux kernel configuration, how to rebuild a Linux kernel, and also discuss the boot process.

The Linux Directory Structure

The Linux operating system directory structure uses a tree-like structure. The top level of this tree structure is known as the root directory. From the root, the directory structure branches out into different branches, which in turn branch out into other branches. From the top level, there are a number of core directories that contain configuration information, programs and utilities, user data, and system data. The main directory branches are shown next.

Directory	Usage
bin	The bin directory contains programs or binaries used by the operating system.
boot	The boot directory is used to boot the system.
dev	This directory contains the device nodes or files that link to hardware devices.
etc	The etc directory contains system configuration information.
home	This directory contains user home directories.
lib	The lib directory contains libraries needed by the operating system.
mnt	This directory is used to temporarily mount other filesystems such as CD-ROMs and floppies.
proc	This pseudo filesystem contains Linux configuration and operational information. The pseudo filesystem looks like a filesystem, but is actually a view into the running kernel. The /proc filesystem is used to configure the kernel as well as to get information from the kernel.
sbin	The sbin tree is used for system binaries used during the system startup process.
tmp	The tmp directory tree contains temporary files.
user	The user tree contains user programs and utilities and includes subdirectories such as /usr/bin, /usr/sbin, and /usr/local/bin.
var	The var directory tree contains information that varies as the system runs, such as log files and print spool files.

These directories are crucial to the operation of the Linux operating system. However, they do not necessarily exist within the same filesystem. It is your choice when configuring the system whether directory trees such as /home, /usr, and others are part of the / filesystem or whether they are a mounted filesystem. You will learn more about this later in the chapter when filesystems are covered.

Linux Utilities and Directories

Linux operating systems include a wealth of utilities. Even the most experienced UNIX and Linux guru most likely has not used all of them. These utilities and applications provided with Linux perform a number of different tasks and can be used standalone or with other applications. In this section, you will learn about what types of utilities are provided within the Linux operating system and what they can be used for.

The Linux utilities can be broken down into a number of different areas that perform various general functions. At the highest level, these utilities can be divided into administrative (system) utilities and user utilities. The system utilities can typically be found in the directory /sbin, /usr/sbin, /bin, and /usr/bin. An overview of utilities is described next in terms of this directory structure.

Utilities in /sbin

The utilities in the /sbin directory are reserved for those utilities required for booting, as well as the core functionalities necessary to run Linux itself. There are over 250 utilities in this directory. They provide a wide variety of support functionality relating to the I/O subsystem, filesystem, and network. A short sample of these utilities is given next.

Filesystem and I/O Utilities   The following utilities are used in configuring, querying, and starting up the I/O subsystem and filesystems. These utilities exist in the /sbin directory. This list is only a sample and is not all-inclusive.

Utility	Function
badblocks	Used to find bad blocks on a device
bevlabel	Keeps symbolic links consistent even if device names change; used in conjunction with Oracle RAC and RAW devices
blvtune	Used for elevator sorting; an important filesystem tuning tool
bdisk	Formats and partitions a disk drive
bsck	Filesystem checker
bdparm	Gets hard-disk parameters
bwapon/swapoff	Enables and disables swapping on a device

Network Utilities   The following utilities are used in configuring, querying, and starting up the network. These utilities exist in the /sbin directory. Again, this list is only a sample and is not all-inclusive.

Utility	Function
arp	Address Resolution Protocol
ethtool	Used to manage and monitor the network adapters at the hardware layer
ifconfig	Used to configure and manage network adapters
route	Manipulates IP routing tables

General OS Utilities   The following utilities are used in running the operating system. These utilities exist in the /sbin directory. This list is only a sample and is not all-inclusive.

Utility	Function
date	Used to print or set the system time
clock	Determines processor time
chkconfig	Query and update system services runlevel information
grub	The bootloader
init	Starts and controls system processes
lsmod	List loaded modules
poweroff	Shuts down and powers off the system
service	Starts a service

As you can see, there are a number of very critical services used during the system startup process that exist in the /sbin directory. This directory is critical during the boot process and is part of the / filesystem. This is used as part of the boot process before the /usr filesystem is mounted (if /usr is a separate filesystem).

Utilities and Daemons in /usr/sbin
The utilities in /usr/sbin, though system utilities, are not necessarily needed to boot the system. They contain administrative tools used for the system to function once it is

up and running. There are over 300 utilities in the /usr/sbin directory. A sample of
some of these tools is given here.

Utility	Function
useradd	Used to add new user accounts to the system
groupadd	Used to add groups to the system
lpadmin	Used to administer the line printer service

In addition, the /usr/sbin directory is where many of the daemon executables are
found. Daemons are programs that perform services for the system. Some daemons
run in the background all the time, while other daemons are run only when needed.
Daemons are very important to the operation of the system. Some of the most important
ones that reside in /usr/sbin are listed next.

Daemon	Function
atd	The atd runs jobs that have been submitted to run at a later date (a scheduled time).
crond	The crond runs regularly scheduled jobs submitted by cron. These might be regular system or user programs that run every hour, every day, every week, and so on.
smbd	The Samba daemon serves SMB/CIFS services to clients.
smtpd	The smtpd is the simple mail transfer protocol daemon.
sshd	This is the secure shell server. SSH clients connect through this daemon.
tcpd	This is a network server for TCP traffic.

As you can see, the /usr/sbin directory contains many utilities used by the system
and by the system administrator. This directory is very important to the operation of
the system, in conjunction with the system utilities in the /sbin directory.

Utilities in /bin

The utilities in the /bin directory are similar to /sbin in that they are mostly administrative
in nature; however, the /bin utilities might be used by regular users as well, hence
they are separated from /sbin. The reason these files are in /bin rather than /usr/bin is
that it is possible that some of these utilities might be needed by the system administrator

during boot, thus they will be available before /usr is mounted. Some of the utilities in /bin include the Linux shell programs, as listed next.

Shell	Description
bash	The GNU Borne-Again shell. This is the newest shell, incorporating features of both sh and ksh. Bash is the default shell program.
csh	csh was the first shell program that provided the ability to create shell programs resembling their C language cousins. It therefore allowed shell programmers to create sophisticated shell programs.
ksh	The Korn shell is a more sophisticated version of the basic Borne shell. You can create complicated shell programs using ksh.
sh	sh is the original Borne shell. This shell provides basic shell functionality as well as basic shell programming abilities.
tcsh	The tcsh is an enhanced csh that allows for command-line editing and completion.
zsh	zsh is a new shell that provides many of the features of ksh but has been enhanced to include spell checking, history, and so on.

As you have heard before, Linux and UNIX are all about choices. You are free to use whichever shell you prefer.

Utilities in /usr/bin

The utilities in /usr/bin are the utilities most likely to be used by the end user. These utilities are used for browsing directories, editing files, sending e-mail, and performing other tasks. The /usr/bin directory contains almost 1500 utilities that can be used by both the administrator and end user. These utilities also include many of the development environment utilities mentioned in the next section. A sample of some of the files in /usr/bin are shown next.

Utility	Function
at	Used to run programs at a time in the future
awk	A pattern scanning and processing language
compress	Used to compress and expand files
cut	Prints selected parts of a file
diff	Compares files and prints differences
df	Displays available disk space
ftp	File Transport Protocol tool
ghostscript	Postscript and PDF interpreter

Utility	Function
gzip	Used to compress and decompress files
lLess	Used to view the contents of files
lpr	Lineprinter interface; used to print files
mysql	The optional mysql database
perl	A sophisticated programming language interpreter
rsh	The remote shell processor
ssh	The secure shell processor
sudo	Used to run a program as root
tail	Reads from the end of a file
top	Displays top CPU processes
who	Displays a list of users on the system
zip	Used to compress and uncompress files

I have not covered all of the utilities in detail because there are so many of them. As you become more familiar with Linux, you will become comfortable with a subset of these utilities that suit your needs and experience. You will find that you can use different utilities and applications to perform the same tasks with different levels of complexity and functionality. For example, you can write shell programs with any of the shells mentioned in the previous section, but you can also create sophisticated scripted programs using PERL. PERL is a sophisticated language that can easily call other applications, such as SQL*Plus.

The Development Environment

The Linux development environment is quite sophisticated and full featured. It's mostly made up of the GNU compilers and libraries, as well as a wealth of system routines and libraries. The development environment supports C++, C, and assembly language programs, and thus it's heavily focused on C++ and C. Because Linux source code is written in C and is readily available for developers to modify and recompile, it is crucial that a robust C development environment be available within the Linux operating system.

The Linux development environment consists of the GNU compiler collection, the debugging tools, and the associated utilities, including

- ■ The GNU compiler collection (gcc)
    - ■ cpp, the C preprocessor
    - ■ as, the assembler
    - ■ ld, the linker

- The GNU Debugger (gdb)
- The binutils, a set of binary utilities used by developers:
  - ar, the archiver—creates, modifies and extracts files from code archives
  - nm—used to list symbols within object files
  - objcopy—used to copy and convert object files
  - objdump—used to display the contents of a binary file
  - ranlib—generates index to archive contents
  - size—lists section and total sizes of object files
  - strings—lists printable strings within files
  - strip—discards symbols from files
  - readelf—displays information about ELF format files

The development environment is very important to the Linux system, just as it is to UNIX systems. Linux is a dynamically configurable system which does not require the kernel to be relinked; however, Oracle does require a relink as part of its installation and configuration. It is necessary for the linker to be installed in order for Oracle to be installed.

The development environment available within Linux is similar to that offered on many UNIX platforms. In fact, the GNU compiler collection is available on many UNIX platforms. However, this development environment is very different from the development environment you would find under Windows. It is also unlike the graphical development environment you would get from Oracle, such as with JDeveloper.

Let's look at some of the components of the Linux development environment.

GCC, the GNU Compiler Collection

The GNU compiler collection consists of the C preprocessor, the assembler, and the linker. These components are all needed in order to process programs. Although the GNU compiler collection is typically invoked by using the command **gcc**, the individual components can be called separately.

You might wonder about the difference between C programs and C++ programs. The GNU compiler collection contains only one compiler, but will compile both C and C++ programs. The GNU compiler collection also compiles Objective C programs as well. The **gcc** command contains optimizations for different processors and systems and is considered one of the best performing compilers available today. In fact, many benchmarks use the GNU compiler collection.

cpp, the GNU preprocessor, performs functions such as macro expansion, conditional compiler directives, inclusion of header files, and line control. The preprocessor is the first step in creating binary executables from source code.

as, the GNU assembler, is used to create object files from assembly code files. The object files it creates are appended the .o suffix and are binary object files. Once you have created object files from C source files, they must be linked together with system object files.

ld, the GNU linker takes object files and links them together with system libraries and object files in order to create binary executable files or programs. Since the linker takes object files and combines them together to make executable files, it is not always necessary to have source code to all of your programs. Oracle ships with a set of object files that are taken and linked with system libraries and object files in order to create the Oracle executable. You don't have access to Oracle source code, but at times you might need to create assembly language programs to replace some of Oracle's functions. For example, in order to change the base address where Oracle runs, it is necessary to create an assembly language file called ksms.s and relink the Oracle binary. This is all done without having access to Oracle source code.

The GNU Debugger

The GNU debugger allows you to create programs with special debug information included. This allows you to set breakpoints within the code and step through the code as it is executing. This is valuable in that it allows you to examine the contents of variables while the program is running. This might help you to determine where the problem is in the program itself—for instance, where a variable is being overloaded or where memory is not properly being released.

In addition, the debugger allows you to examine a program after it has terminated. The debugger may be able to help you determine where the program has terminated so you can fix it. For those of you who have done any type of system development, you will appreciate the debugger utility.

The Binutils

The binutils are a collection of utilities used by developers to assist with the development, deployment, and debugging of Linux applications. They are simply a set of various GNU utilities that are packaged together, and consist of the following applications:

- **ar, the archiver**   Creates, modifies, and extracts files from code archives. Code archives are libraries of object files used to organize these object files. Although an archive can be made up of any type of file, we are mostly concerned with object libraries. The ar utility is used to maintain object files within these libraries.

- **nm**   Used to list symbols within object files. This is a very useful debug tool that can help you find symbols within object files.

- **objcopy**   Used to copy and convert object files. objcopy is used to convert object files from one type to another, such as from bdf to elf.

- **objdump**   Used to display the contents of a binary file. This is useful for developers who are concerned about the actual contents and format of their object files, as well as the function of their code.

- **ranlib**   Generates an index to archive contents. The ranlib utility will take an object library and create an index of symbols so you can find which object in the library has the symbol you are looking for.

- **size**   Lists the section and total sizes of object files. The output displays the various sizes of different parts of your code, such as text and data segments, as well as the size of the bss section of the code.

- **strings**   Lists printable strings within files. This is very helpful if you are looking for a particular object file that has displayed an error message.

- **strip**   Discards symbols from files. It can be used both for size considerations as well as for security.

- **readelf**   Displays information about ELF format files. This is similar to objdump except that it works with ELF files.

Though the binutils may be of no use to many of you, they serve an important purpose when it comes to software development and debugging. This is especially true if you are only planning on running Oracle.

The make Utility

The make utility is used to create binary files from source files and object files based on a template, or makefile. The makefile is used to define dependencies between source files, object files, and executables. These relationships, as well as methods of creating various dependent files, are used to create binaries. For example, the following relationships can be set up within a makefile:

    test relies on test.o
    test is created by linking test.o with lib.a
    test.o relies on test.c
    test.o is created by running gcc on test.c

This is just a description and does not represent the actual syntax of the makefile and the make utility.

Once these relationships are set up, all that is necessary is to run make against the makefile. If test.o is newer than test.c, make understands and will not recompile test.c. If test is newer than test.o and lib.a, it also will not relink test.

Because of the sophistication of make and makefiles, you can set up complicated relationships and when a file or files have been changed, it is not necessary to recompile and relink everything. Make will understand the relationships and will only compile and link what is necessary. This is important for programs such as the Linux kernel, which contain hundreds of programs. If everything needed to be recompiled and relinked every time a single change was made, it would take hours.

The Linux User Interface

Linux has a number of different user interfaces available for use. Among these user interfaces are the command-line interface using the shells mentioned earlier in this chapter and the graphical user interface that uses the X Windows user interface. In many systems I see, the system administrators prefer to only run the graphical environment when needed, since it uses more memory and CPU resources than the character interface. However, some tasks, such as installing Oracle, require the GUI interface.

X Windows

In 1984, MIT formed Project Athena in order to develop a compatible graphical user interface (GUI) that would work on their many different brands of workstations, thus allowing for continuity among those systems. The X Windows system was designed as a graphical user interface that could run both remotely and locally equally well, while relying on either local or remote resources. X Windows has been a part of the Linux operating system since the first release.

The X Windows system is available on almost every operating system and supports a large number of different computer architectures. X Windows is the standard graphics protocol for Linux, but is also supported on Microsoft Windows as well.

The X Windows architecture is divided into two components: the server, which serves graphical images, and the client, which serves the application. To many, the terminology seems backwards. If I were to run an application on a server with the graphics being displayed on my workstation, the workstation is actually the X client, and the server where the application is running is considered the client. This might take a little getting used to for those of us who work with other client/server type applications.

The X Windows system is designed to display things on a screen. It is not designed to provide a look and feel. That's the job of the window manager. The window manager (such as Motif) is designed to provide the look and feel of components such as titlebars, buttons, sliders, and so on.

GUI Environments

Like most things in Linux, you have a choice. Linux comes with many different graphical environments. The two most popular ones are Gnome and KDE. There are other environments available today, but these are currently the ones most people choose. This is partly due to the fact that these two environments ship with the two largest Linux distribution versions. If you want to use another graphical environment for yourself, feel free to. Since Oracle's GUI utilities are written in Java, they run directly using X Windows, irrespective of window manager.

Overview

The graphical user interface (GUI) desktop is the graphical environment that you can log into in order to use the Linux system. For those of you familiar with the Microsoft Windows operating system, it is a similar concept. The GUI desktop provides you easy access to system tools and applications without having to traverse the operating system in a command-line mode. GNOME and KDE, the major desktop environments, both serve the same function, but have a different look and feel. The GNOME desktop environment comes out of the GNU Project and has been around since 1997. GNOME stands for the GNU Network Object Model Environment. KDE, which appeared in 1996, stands for the K Desktop Environment.

The Oracle Java utilities will run equally well regardless of whether you are using the GNOME or KDE desktop environments, or even if you are not running them. In order for these utilities to work, you must have an X Windows server that supports Java.

Remember that the graphical desktop environment can be a useful tool, but it is not a necessity. These days it doesn't matter whether OEM is completely web-based. Web-based administration is simply an option; it's not the only way to do it.

In fact, most users who utilize the system as an Oracle Database server will never see this environment since both system and database administrators will most likely be administering the OS and database remotely over the network. However, for tasks such as installing software, and using tools like the Oracle Enterprise Manager, GNOME and KDE can be very convenient.

By having the ability to use this tool when necessary, you might find some tasks much easier. Others, however, can be done just as simply through the command-line interface. Which interface you use, or whether you actually need one is really up to you.

GNOME

The GNOME desktop began as a free alternative to KDE, which started out mired in licensing issues. GNOME was seen as a free and open way to enable the non-technical user to utilize the Linux operating system.

The GNOME desktop is made up of a number of different development tools and APIs that allow developers to both enhance the GNOME environment as well as develop native applications. While you can develop applications specifically for GNOME, it is not necessary. X Windows and Java applications work as well.

KDE

K Desktop Environment (KDE) predates GNOME and was originally fashioned after the Common Desktop Environment (CDE), a commercial product developed by several major UNIX vendors. While KDE and GNOME are similar in nature, there is some licensing controversy surrounding KDE. If you want to commercially distribute a KDE application, you must purchase a KDE development license before you start coding your application.

KDE is also made up of a number of development tools and applications specifically developed for the KDE environment. Both GNOME and KDE have been ported to other operating systems besides Linux.

Linux Web Server Utilities

Linux first became popular as a web server, even before administrators considered it an excellent Oracle server.

Linux includes one of the best web servers ever designed, the Apache web server.

The Apache Web Server

The Apache web server is an open source HTTP web server that runs on many platforms including Linux, UNIX, and the Windows operating system. The Apache web server is available with the Linux operating system as well as from Oracle as part of Oracle's Internet Application Server (IAS) product and IBM's WebSphere product. The Apache web server is known for its configurability, the ability to interface into multiple database products including Oracle, DB/2, and others. The Apache web server's performance is comparable to any other commercial web server and as of 2003, 62 percent of all web servers were running on the Apache HTTP server.

The Apache HTTP server contains a number of modules, including a PERL module, an authentication module, and a proxy module. In addition, many utilities are available to analyze Apache log files.

There are a number of ways to develop applications that use both the Apache web server and the Linux operating system. These include languages such as Java and PHP. PHP has become a very popular way of creating web applications that include database content.

CGI Programming in Linux

In order for web users to access the Oracle Database, it is necessary to use a CGI or common gateway interface. The Apache HTTP server supports several CGI languages including mod_perl and PHP. mod_perl is an optional module for the Apache web server that embeds the PERL interpreter into the Apache server itself in order to avoid restarting the PERL interpreter every time it is called. By having this as a module within the HTTP server itself, significant overhead can be avoided.

More recently, PHP (a recursive acronym for PHP Hypertext Processor) has become a very popular CGI for Linux and Apache. PHP is one of the preferred tools for creating web applications using Oracle Internet Application Server. Applications for using PHP to access Oracle will be discussed in more detail later in this book.

The Linux Boot Process

The boot loader is responsible for starting up and booting the Linux operating system. Linux has available to it several different boot loaders. Among these are Lilo and Grub. Grub is the newest boot loader and is most often used. It's a state-of-the-art boot loader and supports features such as the use of configuration files. The boot process is a multiphase process

Stage 1—The Primary Boot Loader

In the first stage, the primary boot loader is called by the hardware's BIOS. This primary boot loader is a very small piece of code that is only responsible for invoking the secondary boot loader. The system BIOS simply starts running code from a specific place on the disk. This is the primary boot loader. Once the primary boot loader has been invoked, it will begin running the much larger, secondary boot loader.

Stage 2—The Secondary Boot Loader

The secondary boot loader is where more operating-system specific code exists. This code exists on the /boot partition. The GRUB boot loader will display a menu of available operating systems that can be booted. Here you can select the operating system or kernel you want to boot and GRUB will continue with the next stage, which is loading the OS.

Stage 3—Loading the OS

In this stage, the OS loads. In some cases, a RAM disk is created in order to load drivers needed during the installation process. This RAM disk, known as the initrd or initialization RAM disk, is necessary to load SCSI device drivers. Because of this, whenever you create a new Linux kernel, you must also create a new initrd image.

Once enough of the OS has been started, control is passed to the /sbin/init program. The /sbin/init program in turn starts services and tools. The /sbin/init program also mounts filesystems needed for normal operation of the OS. Once this stage has completed, the Linux system is ready to be used.

Linux Source Code

One advantage of Linux is that the source code is available freely on the Internet, as well as with the Linux distribution. If you choose to install the kernel source "package," it will be installed in the /usr/src directory. Under this directory, you will see a directory named for the version of the Linux source code stored there, such as /usr/src/linux-2.4. Under this directory, you will find the source code for the Linux kernel as well as device drivers. With the Linux source code installed, you not only can rebuild the kernel, you can add additional device drivers as well.

In many cases, it is not necessary for you to rebuild the Linux kernel by hand since the rpm or installation package will rebuild the kernel for you. However, under certain special circumstances you may want to rebuild the Linux kernel. This is covered in the next section.

Rebuilding the Linux Kernel

Rebuilding the Linux kernel is typically unnecessary; however, you might find that you want to make some changes that require a kernel rebuild. In this case, follow these instructions in order to build your own kernel.

1. Make sure you have the Linux source code package installed. Alternatively, you can download this off http://www.kernel.org/. You would not do this for Enterprise Linux.

2. Run the command **make mrproper**. This command cleans up the source tree and removes any remnants of previous kernel builds, thus ensuring you are creating the kernel from scratch.

3. Create the .config file. A good starting point for the .config file are the files in the /usr/src/linux-2.4/configs directory. You will find a number of files in this directory with names like kernel-2.4.21-i686.config, kernel-2.4.21-i686-smp.config, and kernel-2.4.21-i686-hugemem.config. Pick the kernel config template that best represents your system. If you have more than one processor, pick the kernel config file with smp in the name. If you have more than 4GB of RAM, pick the one with hugemem in the name.

4. Customize the configuration file. This can be done by editing the file, or by using the command **make menuconfig** in order to run the Linux kernel configuration utility (shown in Figure 1-3). You could also use **make config**, **make xconfig**, or **make oldconfig** to create the kernel configuration file.

5. There are three ways to modify the .config file before building your custom kernel: **make config**, **make menuconfig**, and **make xconfig**.

6. Once you have created the configuration file, run **make dep**. This will create the kernel dependencies.

7. Run **make clean** in order to clean the kernel tree.

8. Build the kernel by running **make bzImage**. This will create the Linux kernel. It's not a bad idea to modify the makefile to make sure the default kernel

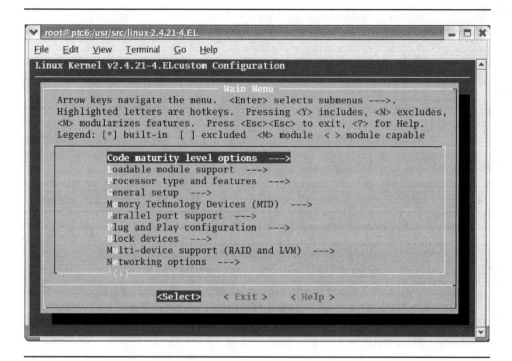

FIGURE 1-3. *The kernel configuration utility*

isn't overwritten. With Red Hat, the line beginning with EXTRAVERSION tags custom on the end of the kernel name.

9. In order to create the Linux modules, run the command **make modules**.

10. Once you have created the Linux modules, you will install them by running the command **make modules_install**. This will install the modules into the proper directories. The directory where the modules are installed includes the kernel version number. For a custom kernel, the directory might be something like /lib/modules/2.4.21-4ELcustom/kernel/drivers.

11. In order to install the Linux kernel, run the command **make install**. This command performs a number of functions including copying the kernel to the boot partition, building a new initrd image, and adding the entry to the bootloader configuration file.

Once you have concluded these steps, the kernel is ready to be booted.

Processes and Threads

Within the Linux operating system, there are many programs simultaneously running on the system. In the operating system, these "programs" are commonly known as processes. Each process has its own virtual memory space and runs independently of other processes. As you will see in the next chapter, Oracle depends on many different processes to perform different functions. Threads are concurrent "threads" of instructions which run within a single process, like having concurrent programs within a single larger application. The way that Linux is architected there is little benefit from running with threads instead of processes, as they take the same types of kernel accounting structures, and most kernel programmers strongly recommend against using threads. See the following section for more details.

What Is a Process?

A process has memory and CPU cycles associated with it since it's a program that performs a function and runs on the processor.

Processes are used throughout the operating system. The Linux tasks scheduler is responsible for scheduling all of the processes running on behalf of the users. Each process runs for a few milliseconds and is then taken off of the CPU before another program is loaded in . This operation, known as a task switch or context switch, ensures that all running programs get some amount of processor time. Within the kernel, a process is made up of a number of different components; code ("text"), data, stack variables, file I/O information, and signal tables. These components must all be copied in and out of memory as the process switches in and out.

The context switch operation occurs tens of thousands of times per second on your system. Although this is an integral part of the Linux operating system, it is an expensive operation. In order to minimize the expense of the context switch, the Light Weight Process or Thread was developed.

Oracle's Use of Processes

Oracle's architecture takes advantage of the use of many processes. As you will learn in the next chapter, the Oracle instance is made up of a number of different processes that perform different functions. By using a number of different processes on different CPUs, Oracle can achieve very good scalability.

What Is a Thread?

A thread minimizes the cost of the context switch by allowing several processes to share some of the same information. If you have many users utilizing the same program, the program can be loaded into memory and the same memory and stack variables can be used by different incarnations of the same program by just moving the stack pointer to where that instance of the program happens to be running. This cuts down on context switches, since only the stack pointer is changing.

These threaded operations only work within the larger context of a process, thus different processes that are running different programs still require a context switch. This is known as a user-space thread.

In addition to user-space threads, there are kernel-space threads that are used to run the operating system itself. This allows the kernel itself to be threaded and thus very efficient.

Devices

The Linux operating system is made up of many devices. A device can be seen as a file that is used to send input and output through. Some files represent a piece of hardware and some are software components. Regardless of whether the file is a hardware or software component, I/O can be directed to it in essentially the same manner.

Many hardware devices exist on the system, such as the floppy drive, the fixed disk, network devices, and so on. Devices are divided into two categories: character or raw devices and block devices.

Character Devices

A character device is a device where the user process transfers data directly to the device in a sequential manner, rather than block devices which can be accessed in a more random fashion. Some examples of raw or character devices are

- Tape devices
- Floppy disk drives
- Terminal devices
- Parallel print devices
- Sound devices

In addition, character devices can be accessed by programs that would normally use block devices. Oracle can actually use raw devices for its data storage. However, Oracle must use a block interface to this character device. This will be explained in more detail in subsequent chapters.

Block Devices

Block devices allow buffered I/O and can handle more specific requests for data. Block devices can be accessed randomly. Unlike a character device that can receive any size request, block devices will access the underlying data only in certain block size requests. This is why they are known as block devices. Block devices include the following:

- RAM disks
- SCSI disk devices
- CD-ROM devices

The devices we normally use for Oracle utilize block device–based filesystems.

Logical Volume Managers

An Oracle database can use raw devices or filesystems, but it can also use an LVM for its storage. A Logical Volume Manager, or LVM, is a software product that manages storage by combining physical disk blocks from different physical disks into a logical disk volume. This allows you to manage your storage in an orderly manner for both performance and ease of use. Features of an LVM include

- **Storage aggregation**   Many individual disk drives can be combined together into a single logical disk drive.

- **Storage virtualization**   The storage can be reconfigured, added to, and resized even while that storage is being used. You can add additional storage to a volume while you are using it.

- **Snapshots**   With an LVM, you can take snapshots of the data, thus creating faster and more efficient backups.

LVMs have been used with Oracle for storage for many years. Linux LVMs are becoming much more common, with several types available for use.

Automatic Storage Management

Automatic Storage Management (ASM) is Oracle's answer to LVMs. ASM is an LVM which has been developed specifically for Oracle, working with it to provide an Oracle storage virtualization layer. In essence, ASM simplifies Oracle storage management by allowing disk groups to be formed that can be used to hold the Oracle data and logs. By using ASM, the actual physical placement of the data within the file group is done automatically as well as tablespace management. ASM is designed to both simplify and optimize data storage within the Oracle database and is another option that you might choose.

Filesystems

Most storage within the Linux system is done via a filesystem. A filesystem is the layer above the block devices that allows user access to the disk devices. It permits structures such as directories and files. The filesystem is created on top of the disk device, has its own cache, and is used to manage access to the disk drive.

Filesystems provide features such as directories, which are abstractions that allow for a hierarchical storage structure. A directory is a structure that can hold other directories or files. These files, in turn, can hold data.

Another feature of a filesystem is its ability to place properties on directories or files in order to provide security by allowing permissions to be put on files and directories.

Filesystems may have other features, such as the ability to work within a cluster and the ability to journal the data being written to the filesystem. Some specific filesystems and their features are discussed in the next sections.

ext3

The primary filesystem used within Linux is ext3, which is based on ext2 with filesystem journaling. Journaling reduces the amount of time needed to recover changes to the filesystem if the system is uncleanly rebooted, which can take hours on a multiple-gigabyte storage device. In a journal led filesystem, changes that are constantly being made to the disk are written to a special file called the "journal." This journal is similar to the redo log on Oracle and is used to fix inconsistencies that might have occurred during a power failure or some other loss of processing. Journal led filesystems have been in use for many years and are extremely fast and stable.

OCFS

OCFS is the Oracle Cluster Filesystem. The Oracle Cluster Filesystem is an Oracle filesystem that allows multiple systems to use the same filesystem. This overcomes the problem of accessing shared storage for Oracle RAC (Real Application Cluster) systems.

The advantage of OCFS is that you can build a cluster using a filesystem. This makes the management tasks involved in handling data files used in an RAC system much easier. With OCFS, you can create data files as you would under any other filesystem. Files can be set with auto growth on and additional files can be added as needed.

RAW Devices

RAW devices are also supported by Oracle. With RAW devices, Oracle does not use a filesystem. The Oracle RDBMS manages the storage entirely itself. RAW devices have been very popular for Oracle because of performance. By bypassing the filesystem code, CPU usage can be reduced since there is no filesystem processing being done. However, managing Oracle on RAW devices can be complex and difficult.

Until the introduction of OCFS, Oracle RAC databases were required to be built on RAW devices.

By using RAW devices, Oracle is responsible for the data storage, and since the Oracle RAC cluster manages the storage as well as the cluster, the system coordination problems are solved. RAW devices are limited and difficult to manage. With Oracle 10*g* we now have several options for a RAC cluster: RAW devices, OCFS, or ASM.

Summary

This chapter has introduced you to the Linux operating system. You have learned a bit about the directory structure, the tools available to you, and how to configure some of the key components. It is important to understand the OS in order to properly manage the Oracle database on this OS. Of course, this chapter is not a complete administration guide for Linux. There are plenty of good books on the market for that.

In this chapter, we attempted to give you a flavor of the Linux architecture, so that in the next chapter when you learn about the Oracle architecture, you will begin to understand how the two work together. There, you will find out about the Oracle Database architecture and afterward begin to learn more of the specifics of administering the Oracle Database on Linux.

CHAPTER
2

Oracle Architecture

he basic fundamentals of the Oracle architecture have remained constant since Oracle's modern versions (8*i*, 9*i*). That architecture has a lot of history, and with it a respected record of stability and performance. This is not to say that there aren't significant improvements in Oracle 10*g*, there are. However, the base architecture has not changed significantly and that is also true of changes between Oracle10*g* and Oracle10*g* R2.

The Oracle Database is defined by Oracle to be a collection of data treated as a unit. The purpose of the database is to store and retrieve data. All other components are simply additional features designed to aid in that task. Thus, the Oracle Database server is the set of programs and utilities that work together to help you retrieve that data in a secure and efficient manner.

The Oracle Database Server

The Oracle Database server is made up of both physical and logical components that provide an abstraction layer allowing you to efficiently access the data in the database. The Oracle Database server is architected in such a way that it not only offers optimal performance, but is scalable as well. A scalable architecture allows you to add additional system components to achieve greater system performance.

The Oracle Database 10*g* server consists of the database (the information) and the instance (the embodiment of the system). The database consists of both the physical files that reside on the system and the logical pieces such as the database schema. These database files take various forms, as described in the following section. The instance is the method used to access the data and consists of processes and system memory.

The Oracle server architecture is made up of the following components, which will be covered in this chapter:

- The database

- The Oracle instance

- Additional Oracle utilities

This chapter will introduce you to those components as well as explain how the Oracle server works to provide access to your data.

The Oracle Instance
The Oracle Instance is a term that will be used throughout this book and is explained in detail later in this chapter. The Oracle Instance is defined as the processes and shared memory that is necessary to be able to access the database. The instance itself is not part of the database. In fact, with the Oracle 10*g* RAC (Real Application Clusters) system multiple instances can share the same database.

The Oracle Database has both a logical and a physical layer. The physical layer consists of the actual files that reside on the disk, while the components of the logical layer map the data to these physical components.

This chapter will begin by providing an overview of the Oracle architecture, followed by details of how certain operations such as transaction processes, reading and writing, and other operational tasks are done. Also included in this chapter is an overview of some of the things that affect Oracle performance.

The Oracle Database

The Oracle Database is made up of both physical and logical components. The physical components are things you can view from outside the database server itself and are made up of files or other storage components on the OS. The logical data structures represent how data is stored in those datafiles, and can only be viewed from within the Oracle Database server. In this section, you will learn about both the physical and logical data structures. Later, you will see how they are used by the Oracle Database server.

Physical Data Structures

The physical layer of the database consists of several types of files:

- One or more datafiles

- One or more control files

- Two or more redo log files

- Archive log files (optional, but recommended)

- Parameter files

- Alert and trace log files

- Backup files

All of these files are crucial to the optimal and stable operation of the Oracle Database server. If any of these files are lost or damaged, data may be lost and the Oracle instance might crash.

Datafiles

The datafiles contain the information stored in the database. A datafile can only belong to one database, but as you will learn later, a database can be accessed by more than one Oracle instance. You can have as few as one datafile or as many as hundreds. The maximum size of a datafile is OS- and Oracle-dependent. With Linux, the maximum size of a datafile is 4 million data blocks in size; thus for a smaller block size, the maximum datafile size is smaller than for a larger block size.

The information for a single table can span many datafiles, or many tables can share a set of datafiles. As you will see later in this chapter, the datafiles make up a logical object called a tablespace—the container that holds the database objects. Spreading tablespaces over many datafiles might have a significant positive effect on performance, as discussed later in this book.

In addition to Oracle datafiles, Oracle10g has introduced ASM (Automatic Storage Management). ASM is essentially an Oracle managed filesystem that can only be used by Oracle objects. ASM is assigned a group of disk drives (raw devices) and Oracle manages those devices. ASM takes a group of disk drives and creates an ASM group. An ASM group is similar to a filesystem in that the ASM group can hold a variety of Oracle data storage objects, such as tablespaces, redo log groups, archive logs, backups, etc.

ASM is different from a typical Linux filesystem in that you cannot use OS commands such as ls to view the contents of an ASM group. In addition to storing Oracle tablespaces, redo logs, etc., ASM can do disk striping and fault tolerance. However, I do not recommend software (ASM) fault tolerance when you can use hardware fault tolerance. This is due to both fault tolerance and performance.

ASM uses a small Oracle instance called the "ASM Instance" to manage the ASM devices. The ASM instance must be up and running before you can use ASM devices. ASM limitations are very high, and they include

- 10,000 ASM disks in a storage system

- 4 petabytes maximum for each ASM disk

- 1 million files for each disk group

- 2.4 terabyte maximum storage per each file

These limits shouldn't be reached any time soon (at least not until Oracle 11 is available).

In order to use an ASM when creating Oracle storage objects simply specify the ASM group name prefixed with a + instead of the filename (i.e., '+diskgroup1' instead of the file name). It is not necessary to specify a location within an ASM group.

NOTE
I always recommend that redo logs, archive logs, and data files be physically separated. This is true of ASM groups as well. If you use ASM, separate these components into a minimum of 3 ASM groups. In the unlikely occurrence that your storage were to fail you might save two of the three components. ASM is covered in more detail in Chapter 6: Installing Oracle10g on Linux.

Control Files

The control files are used to store information such as the name of the database and the locations of data and redo log files. Oracle needs this information to start up the database instance. It is essential that the control files be protected. Oracle provides a mechanism for storing multiple copies of the control files. In a clustered environment, the control files must be accessible by all members of the cluster.

Redo Log Files

The redo log files, collectively known as the redo log, store a record of all changes made to the database. This information is used in the event of a system failure to reapply changes that have been made and committed but may not have been made to the datafiles. It is essential that the redo log files have good performance and are protected against hardware failures (either through software or hardware fault tolerance). If redo log information is lost, you cannot fully recover the system in the event of a failure.

Oracle provides a method for multiplexing redo log files by creating a duplicate of each redo log file. Depending on the amount of redo log activity, you may or may not want to use this. In most cases, by using hardware RAID technology you can avoid the Oracle and OS overhead by doing redo log fault tolerance in hardware, rather than using Oracle mirroring. However, if you do this, it is recommended that caching be disabled on that disk volume because of the criticality of the redo information. In some extreme cases where redo activity is very high, you can enable caching on the I/O subsystem if the Oracle mirrored caches are on different RAID systems with independent caches.

The redo log is used for media recovery, which is necessary when a backup of the database must be restored, as well as for instance recovery. In the event of a power failure, the information in the redo log files is used to restore the database to the point of failure. This is why the redo log files are so important.

In a clustered environment, each instance has its own set of redo log files, but they must all be accessible from every system. In the event of a loss of one of the nodes in a cluster, one of the other nodes can use the failed node's redo log files to recover the portions of the database that were in use by the failed node. This will be covered in more detail in the Real Application Clusters (RAC) chapters.

Archive Log Files

The archive log files are essentially backups of the online redo log files described earlier. When running in archivelog mode, these backups of the online redo log files are done automatically. The archive log files are essential for restoring the Oracle database from a media failure. Archive log files are also used in Oracle Data Guard. Later in this chapter, where Oracle logging is described, the archive log process is covered in more detail.

Parameter Files

The Oracle parameter files are used to store system configuration information. These parameter files exist in one of two forms. The pfile is an ASCII text file that can be modified in a text editor and is used during system startup. The spfile (server parameter file) is an Oracle readable file that is modifiable only within the Oracle server and is the currently recommended method of configuration. The spfile is the default method of starting up an Oracle database. When the startup command is issued, the instance will search for a server parameter file named $ORACLE_HOME/dbs/init*SID*.ora. In a RAC environment, this file simply contains a link to the shared spfile (either on a shared file system, such as OCFS, or on a raw device). The main difference between a pfile and an spfile is that the pfile is a client-side file, while the spfile is a server-side file.

An spfile can be created from a pfile and vice versa. An spfile is created using the following command:

```
CREATE SPFILE = '/u01/ORCL/spfileORCL.ora'
FROM PFILE = '/opt/oracle/admin/ORCL/pfile/initORCL.ora';
```

Conversely, a pfile can be created from a pfile using a similar command:

```
CREATE PFILE = '/opt/oracle/admin/ORCL/pfile/initORCL.ora'
FROM SPFILE = '/u01/ORCL/spfileORCL.ora';
```

At times, it is convenient to reconfigure the Oracle instance by following these steps:

1. Create a pfile.

2. Modify the Oracle system by editing the pfile.

3. Start the instance using the pfile.

4. Make any changes you need to, such as setting up archiving, and so on.

5. Create an spfile.

6. Restart the instance using the spfile.

Alert and Trace Files

The alert and trace files store information generated by the Oracle Database server and background processes. The alert log contains information about startup and shutdown operations, the configuration of the system, the state of the system, and errors that have occurred. The trace files store specific information about problems that have occurred in the system. These trace files can help to determine what has gone wrong and how to fix problems with the system.

Backup Files

The backup files may exist in a number of forms based on the type of backup that you are doing. The backup files might be managed by you, or might be managed by a backup program. This is completely dependent on the type of backup and the type of backup software you are using.

Many Oracle users depend on third-party backup solutions. These backup products utilize the underlying Oracle APIs, but provide additional features such as the ability to use tape libraries and multiple devices.

Logical Data Structures

Whereas the physical data structures consist of OS files, the logical data structures represent the way that data is stored within the Oracle Database server. The logical data structures are designed for efficiency as well as performance.

The logical data structures consist of the following components:

■ Tablespaces

■ Segments

■ Extents

■ Data blocks

Within these logical data structures reside the Oracle schema objects. The schema objects will be covered later in this chapter.

The Oracle data structures are made up of a number of different components, some logical and some physical. The smallest element of the database is the data block, which is a fixed size and is used to store row pieces. Data blocks are stored in contiguous sets, known as extents. The set of extents that make up a database object are known as segments.

The blocks, extents, and segments are stored in datafiles. One or more datafiles makes up a tablespace, as shown in Figure 2-1. Tablespaces are storage containers for database objects. When an object, such as a table or index is created, it is assigned to a tablespace. Once that assignment is made, and its properties are set, the RDBMS handles extent management automatically.

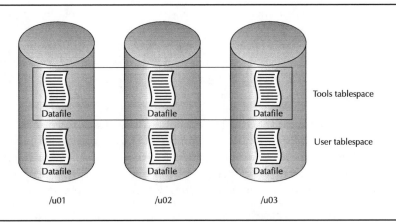

FIGURE 2-1.   *Tablespaces and datafiles*

In this chapter, you will learn how blocks, extents, segments, tablespaces, and datafiles are managed and the properties associated with them. In the next chapter, you will learn about the additional Oracle data structures, the redo log, control files, and the system undo mechanism.

By understanding the Oracle data structures, you will better understand how the Oracle RDBMS functions, and therefore will better understand how to administer and tune it. By understanding the basic building blocks, you will better be able to understand the rest of this book.

Tablespaces

The Oracle tablespace is the repository of database objects in the Oracle Database. The tablespace is made up of one or more datafiles, which can be either files on the operating system filesystem, files on an Oracle Cluster Filesystem (OCFS), a RAW device, or files managed using Automatic Storage Management (ASM). Datafiles can be made to be of a fixed size or they can be extended automatically or manually. Once the tablespace has been created and objects are assigned to a tablespace, the handling of the physical storage of the objects is done automatically.

Typically, tablespaces are set up for users or groups of users that share a common set of data. For example, Accounts Receivable might have its own tablespace and Accounts Payable a different tablespace. The two groups might share a general ledger tablespace. This allows space and user management to split up the data based on function. Within the tablespace, the data is managed automatically.

Dividing groups into different tablespaces simplifies the administration of these groups. Tablespaces are made up of one or more datafiles. By using more than one datafile per tablespace, you can spread the data over many different disks to distribute the I/O load out and improve performance. It is also easy to extend the size of a tablespace by adding additional datafiles.

An Oracle tablespace can be made up of as few as one datafile, or as many as 1024 datafiles. This allows you to create very large tablespaces, and thus, very large database objects.

The tablespace is important in that it provides the finest granularity for laying out data across datafiles. Once the tablespace is created, you'll have significant control over how the actual tables are distributed within the tablespace. By carefully configuring the tablespace, you have some coarse configuration options (which you will see later in this chapter), but for the most part it is done automatically.

Every Oracle Database is required to have at least one tablespace. By default, when you create a database, the SYSTEM tablespace is created. The SYSTEM tablespace is where the Data Dictionary is kept. By default, a user will be assigned to the SYSTEM tablespace, but this is not necessary or recommended. Users can, and should, be assigned a tablespace based on the function that this particular user will be doing. Quotas can also be placed on these users, specifying how much space they can use.

Tablespaces can hold any one of four types of segments. These segments are

■ **Data segments** These are the basic type of segment. The data segment can be used to hold tables and clusters.

- **Index segments**   Index segments are used to hold indexes.

- **UNDO segments**   UNDO segments are special types of segments used to store undo information. UNDO segments will be covered in more detail in the next chapter.

- **Temporary segments**   Temporary segments are used for storing temporary data.

In addition, there are several different types of tablespaces available within the Oracle9*i* database. These various tablespace types serve different purposes and are therefore handled differently by the database.

- **Normal tablespace**   The default or standard tablespace type is used to store Oracle objects and is created with a **CREATE TABLESPACE** command.

- **Temporary tablespace**   The temporary tablespace is used to hold temporary segments and is created with a **CREATE TEMPORARY TABLESPACE** command.

- **Undo tablespace**   The undo tablespace is a special tablespace used to hold undo data and is created with a **CREATE UNDO TABLESPACE** command.

- **Read-only tablespace**   The read-only tablespace is a normal tablespace with read-only attributes. Changes cannot be made to a read-only tablespace. Read-only tablespaces are created as a normal tablespace and made read-only later.

Tablespaces are made read-write by default but can be altered to become read-only (as shown later in this chapter in the section "Read-Only Tablespaces"). Read-only tablespaces can be very useful in a number of situations.

A tablespace can either be managed via the Oracle Data Dictionary (Oracle8 and earlier) or via locally managed tablespaces. Locally managed tablespaces were a feature added in Oracle9*i* and have several advantages.

Dictionary Managed Tablespaces   Dictionary managed tablespaces are the previous standard way of managing space within the database. The extent management is done via tables in the Data Dictionary. Whenever an extent is created or released, this information is updated within the Data Dictionary. Extent management has been done this way for a long time.

With dictionary managed tablespaces, the tablespace and objects are defined with an initial extent size, the size of the next extent, and then the size of each additional extent via the PCTINCREASE parameter. This would specify how much bigger each additional extent is over the previous extent that was created. This is a very nice system, but Oracle has improved upon this with locally managed tablespaces.

Locally Managed Tablespaces   Oracle8*i* introduced the locally managed tablespace. With Oracle9*i* Locally Managed Tablespaces became the default and preferred tablespace type. This is the default tablespace type within Oracle 10*g*, and a new tablespace will be created with the locally managed option unless otherwise specified.

Locally managed tablespaces manage the extents within the tablespace itself. This allows for a more scalable solution by reducing the contention on the Data Dictionary. Within locally managed tablespaces, the extents can either be created in a uniform size or in a progressively larger size. With locally managed tablespaces a bitmap is used to manage the extents within the tablespace. In addition, when modifying extents, no rollback information is created, as was done with dictionary managed tablespaces.

With a locally managed tablespace, the extent size can either be determined automatically on a per tablespace basis or it can be specified in the storage clause for a given database object. If you specify the extent size, it will be uniform throughout the tablespace.

Manual or Automatic Space Segment Management   Within the tablespace, the freespace in the segments can either be managed via freelists or with a bitmap. Using freelists is the traditional method of managing segments within a tablespace and uses the PCTUSED and PCTFREE parameters, as described later in this chapter. Freelist segment management is configured by specifying MANUAL in the segment management clause. New with Oracle9*i* is the bitmap method of managing free space within segments. This is known as automatic space segment management and is the preferred method of managing segments. Bitmap extent management is enabled by specifying AUTO.

Creating Tablespaces   Creating a tablespace consists of specifying one or more datafiles and storage parameters. The datafiles can be either filesystem files or raw

Tablespace Size

A normal tablespace can consist of up to 1024 datafiles. An Oracle datafile has a limit of 4 million blocks; thus, the Oracle size limit is 4 million blocks x block size. The maximum size of a OS datafile is OS-dependent; therefore, the maximum size of a datafile is either the size of the maximum OS file, or the Oracle limitation, whichever is smaller.

Oracle10g has introduced the Bigfile Tablespace. The bigfile tablespace allows you to create one large datafile that is 4 billion blocks in size. The bigfile tablespace is designed to be used with RAID systems that support large datafiles or with ASM. In order to create a bigfile tablespace, use the command CREATE BIGFILE TABLESPACE instead of CREATE TABLESPACE.

devices. The storage parameters specify how the tablespace is used. They are very important and will be discussed in greater detail later in this chapter.

Creating tablespaces is done with the **CREATE TABLESPACE** command using various options. Not every option will be covered here, since there are so many of them, and since you can easily look them up, but let's look at a few of them. The basic commands to create a tablespace are

```
CREATE [UNDO] TABLESPACE tsname
DATAFILE data_file_name data_file_size
[storage clause]
[BLOCKSIZE size [K]]
[TEMPORARY]
[EXTENT MANAGEMENT DICTIONARY]
[EXTENT MANAGEMENT LOCAL [AUTOALLOCATE]]
[EXTENT MANAGEMENT LOCAL [UNIFORM SIZE size [K/M]]
[SEGMENT SPACE MANAGEMENT AUTO]
[SEGMENT SPACE MANAGEMENT MANUAL]
```

Let's look at these key parameters in a little more detail.

Parameter	Use
UNDO	The undo parameter specifies that the tablespace you are creating is an undo tablespace. Undo tablespaces are covered in detail in the next chapter.
Storage clause	The storage clause specifies the filename, size, and so on.
BLOCKSIZE	The BLOCKSIZE parameter is used to allow you to create a nonstandard block size tablespace.
TEMPORARY	Specifies that the tablespace is used as a temporary tablespace.
EXTENT MANAGEMENT	The EXTENT MANAGEMENT clause allows you to specify whether the tablespace is locally or dictionary managed.
SEGMENT SPACE MANAGEMENT	The SEGMENT SPACE MANAGEMENT clause is used to specify AUTOMATIC (bitmap) or MANUAL (freelist) management of freespace within segments.

There are many more optional parameters that can be used to create tablespaces. These optional parameters can be found in the Oracle documentation. Here are a few examples of creating tablespaces.

A locally managed simple tablespace

```
CREATE TABLESPACE ts1
DATAFILE '/u01/app/oracle/oradata/orac/ts01.dbf' SIZE 10M;
```

Same as the previous, but specifying the details

```
CREATE TABLESPACE ts2
DATAFILE '/u01/app/oracle/oradata/orac/ts02.dbf' SIZE 10M
EXTENT MANAGEMENT LOCAL UNIFORM SIZE 1M
SEGMENT SPACE MANAGEMENT AUTO;
```

A dictionary managed tablespace

```
CREATE TABLESPACE ts3
DATAFILE '/u01/app/oracle/oradata/orac/ts03.dbf' SIZE 10M
DEFAULT STORAGE (INITIAL 1M NEXT 1M PCTINCREASE 10)
EXTENT MANAGEMENT DICTIONARY
SEGMENT SPACE MANAGEMENT MANUAL;
```

A locally managed undo tablespace

```
CREATE UNDO TABLESPACE undo01
DATAFILE '/u01/app/oracle/oradata/orac/undo01.dbf' SIZE 10M;
```

There are a number of optional parameters in the **CREATE TABLESPACE** command. The Oracle docs will list all of these options.

Coalescing the Tablespace   With local management of extents, it is unnecessary to coalesce extents, but with dictionary management it is sometimes necessary. Since the Data Dictionary managed tablespace allocates space to schema objects in extents of various sizes, it is possible that over time this space may become fragmented. As extents are allocated, Oracle looks for free space that is closest in size to the space needed for the new extent. As the tablespace ages, and extents are added and freed, you may find there are many small free extents located next to each other.

By coalescing the tablespace, the adjacent free extents are coalesced into larger free extents, thus making the free space more flexible to new extent allocations.

The SMON process automatically will coalesce tablespaces if this feature has not been disabled. It is rarely necessary to coalesce a tablespace by hand, but it is important to know how and why this operation is performed.

System Tablespace

If your SYSTEM tablespace is locally managed, you cannot create any dictionary managed tablespaces and the preceding example will fail. If you want to create dictionary managed tablespaces, the SYSTEM tablespace must be dictionary managed.

Adding Datafiles to a Tablespace

It can be faster to add datafiles to a tablespace than to specify them at tablespace creation since adding datafiles can be done in parallel. Datafile creation at tablespace creation time is done serially, one at a time. For a large tablespace creation, this can save significant time.

Adding Datafiles   It is often necessary to add more datafiles to a tablespace if you need more space or want to spread out I/Os among more disk drives. It is also faster to add datafiles to a tablespace than to create them at database creation time. The CREATE TABLESPACE command works serially, that is, it creates one datafile at a time. By adding datafiles, this operation can be parallelized; thus, multiple datafiles can be added to a tablespace simultaneously.

Datafiles are added by using the **ALTER TABLESPACE** command, as shown in this example.

```
ALTER TABLESPCE ts1
ADD DATAFILE '/u01/app/oracle/oradata/orac/ts01b.dbf' SIZE 10M;
```

This command will add an additional 10MB datafile to the tablespace named ts1.

Altering Tablespace Properties   Other properties of the tablespace that can be changed via the **ALTER TABLESPACE** command are

- Add or rename a datafile

- Bring it offline or online

- Coalesce the extents in a dictionary managed tablespace

- Begin or end backup mode

- Change from permanent to temporary or temporary to permanent

- Change the storage clause, size, or put it into autoextent mode

As you can see, there are a number of options.

Read-Only Tablespaces   As described earlier, it is possible to alter a tablespace to make it read-only. Read-only tablespaces are similar to read-write tablespaces with the restriction that no changes can be made to the schema objects residing on those tablespaces. When a tablespace is made read-only, the need to back up this tablespace is eliminated.

Since the data is guaranteed not to change, it is unnecessary to perform regular backups on the read-only data. If a backup has been performed at some time in the past, this backup should be good for the life of the tablespace.

Since the read-only tablespace is not modified by Oracle, it is possible to place the tablespace on read-only media such as a CD-ROM or a WORM drive. If this data is archival in nature but must be available, a CD-ROM is an excellent choice.

Creating Read-Only Tablespaces   All tablespaces are created read-write and must have data populated in them before they are useful. Once the data and indexes have been created to your specification, the tablespace can be made read-only either via the **ALTER TABLESPACE** command or within the Oracle Enterprise Manager.

The tablespace can also be made read-only with the **ALTER TABLESPACE** command, as shown here. The syntax used will look something like this:

```
ALTER TABLESPACE "ts1" READONLY;
```

There are several uses for the read-only tablespace, but they are fairly specific. Whether or not you can take advantage of them depends on your applications.

If you have a large amount of static data that can be put on slower media, the read-only tablespace may be advantageous for you. Also, if you want to guarantee that archival data is not modified, this may also work for you.

Temporary Tablespaces   Temporary tablespaces are used in order to perform sort operations that cannot fit into memory. By allocating a tablespace specifically for sorting, it is unnecessary to allocate and deallocate space in tablespaces that are used for other purposes, thus causing fragmentation.

When a sort operation cannot fit in memory, it must create and use a temporary segment. This temporary segment allocates extents and will continue to allocate extents until it has enough room to perform the sort. With large DSS queries these temporary segments can become quite large.

By having tablespaces specifically for this type of operation, not only will the sorts be more efficient, but there will be less temporary usage on your data tablespaces.

Creating Temporary Tablespaces   A tablespace can be made temporary when it is created with the **CREATE TABLESPACE** command, or it can be changed from a permanent tablespace to a temporary tablespace by using either the GUI tools or the **ALTER TABLESPACE** command. A tablespace can be changed to temporary using a syntax similar to this:

```
ALTER TABLESPACE "ts2" TEMPORARY;
```

It is rare that you will ever be changing a tablespace from permanent to temporary or temporary to permanent. Typically, temporary tablespaces will be created one way or the other, and remain that way for the duration of their existence.

Tablespace Tricks and Tips   The tablespace is the resource from which the schema objects obtain their space. It can be thought of as similar to a filesystem on a set of disk drives. The space is there and allocated, but is not used until somebody creates a file or saves some data. This is also true of the Oracle tablespace.

As schema objects are created, extents are allocated from the tablespace. These extents are allocated based on the storage parameters of the schema creation, or in lieu of them, the tablespace's default storage parameters.

Oracle tries to balance space within the tablespace based on the percentage of freespace available. This can cause some problems, however.

If you have two 18GB disk drives and create an Oracle tablespace with two datafiles—one of 10GB on the first disk drive and one of 5GB on the second—Oracle will proportionally fill the datafiles such that the larger one has twice as much data. This is all fine and good, but will typically cause more I/Os to be done on the disk drive with the larger tablespace. This imbalance is not good. If you need multiple datafiles, it is better to spread them equally among disk drives.

Other ways to better balance the I/O load are to take advantage of hardware features or OS features, such as disk striping. By striping your disk drives either with a disk array or software striping, the load will be fairly well balanced among all of the disk drives in the stripe.

Configuring and managing tablespaces can be a time-consuming task, requiring a lot of up-front planning. This planning is well worth it, however. Time spent planning now can mean much less time spent fixing problems later.

Tablespace Maintenance   Once the tablespaces have been created, your job is not over. It is necessary to monitor both the space used and the load balancing of your tablespaces. Capacity planning and sizing are very important duties. By anticipating problems and solving them before they become critical, you will avoid costly problems. By monitoring the system and planning for the future, you can also avoid costly downtime.

Monitoring the Tablespaces   Tablespaces can be monitored via the Enterprise Manager or a variety of third-party applications that are very good at graphically

Use RAID Rather than Tablespace Load Balancing

Disk striping can be an easy way to balance the I/O load between disk drives. A hardware or software disk array will evenly distribute the data among all of the disk drives in the stripe.

The old-fashioned way of laying out Oracle Databases was to create tablespaces with many datafiles and spread them among individual disk drives. This has been replaced with the more modern standard of creating large RAID stripes and fewer, large datafiles in a tablespace.

Perform Regular Tablespace Monitoring
Try scheduling several days during the month to monitor system performance.
Put it on your calendar at the beginning of the month. Designate several different
days of the week and times of day so you get some different samples.

showing tablespaces, extents, and segments. Although it is a good idea to monitor
your tablespaces regularly, locally managed tablespaces has made tablespace
management much easier.

The most important task in tablespace management is space management. It is not
unusual for databases to grow much faster than you initially anticipated. This can cause
serious space problems if you are not prepared.

Load Balancing   It is very important to monitor the physical I/O usage of your
disk drives in order to make sure you are not experiencing performance problems.
Periodically look at the physical disk statistics during peak and non-peak usage
periods. Don't rely on anything staying the same. The performance characteristics
of your system are constantly changing and must be monitored.

Data Blocks
Within Oracle, the space used to store data is controlled by the use of logical structures.
These structures consist of segments, extents, and data blocks. A segment is a set
of extents used to store a particular type of data. Segments, in turn, are made up of
collections of pieces called extents, which are themselves composed of data blocks
(see Figure 2-2). A block is the smallest unit of storage in an Oracle Database. The
database block contains header information concerning the block itself, as well as
the data.

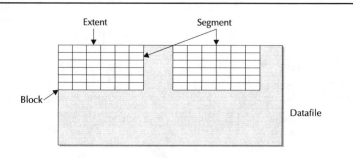

FIGURE 2-2.   *Segments, extents, and data blocks*

Nonstandard Block Sizes
Prior to Oracle9*i*, all blocks in the database were the same size. The block size was determined at database creation and was fixed. From Oracle9*i* forward, the initial database is still created with a single block size, but additional tablespaces can be created with different block sizes. This allows a single database to be optimized for both OLTP and data warehousing applications. This can be useful for different types of database activity. Small block sizes are very efficient for OLTP type activity, whereas large blocks are great for data warehousing and decision support applications.

Data blocks are the smallest pieces that make up an Oracle Database. Every I/O operation to disk and Oracle data operation in memory is done at the block level, although multiple blocks can be written or read at a time. Oracle data is stored on disk, and in memory in blocks. The block size of a tablespace is determined at tablespace creation time. The size of a data block can vary depending on what you choose and can be as small at 512 bytes or as large as 64KB.

Oracle9*i* introduced the concept of nonstandard block sizes. With Oracle9*i* and Oracle Database 10*g* servers, you can now have a database with different tablespaces utilizing different block sizes.

The Oracle block is the basic building block of all the data stored within the Oracle Database. The Oracle block holds row pieces within the block. A row piece is either an entire row, a part of a row, or a pointer to a row. If only a part of a row is stored in the block, then this is said to be a chained row. If a pointer to a row is stored in the block, then this is a migrated row. Chained and migrated rows are discussed later in this section.

The block itself consists of several parts. The beginning of the block is made up of the block header. Next is the table directory, followed by the row directory. The rest of the block is made up of free space and row data. How the block is allocated between free space and row data is determined by the block allocation parameters PCTFREE and PCTUSED, which are described later in this section. The block header, the table directory, and the row directory are considered overhead and usually take up 84 to 107 byes of space. The different parts of the block are described here:

Block Header   The block header contains information about the block, such as the block address and the type of segment that the block is a part of. As you will learn later in this chapter, there are several different types of segments, such as data segments and index segments.

Table Directory   The table directory contains information about the table data that is stored in the block.

Row Directory	The row directory contains information about each row or row piece that is stored in the block, including that row piece's address.
Free Space	The free space is simply that—space that is free for usage by the database. How much free space is reserved is discussed later in this section.
Row Data	The bulk of the block is made up of table or index data that is stored within the block as a row piece.

An Oracle block is shown here in Figure 2-3.

The block is the basic container that all other components of the Oracle data structure is made up of. Data is stored both on disk and within the buffer cache in blocks. Efficient storage of blocks is essential for good system performance and for minimizing waste. One of the bad things that can happen to blocks is to have them become migrated or chained rows.

Migrated and Chained Rows   There are two cases where the row pieces do not reside in the data block, or when the row pieces do not entirely reside in the data block. These are the cases of migrated and chained rows. Oracle has created these mechanisms to account for both modifications to data and to support very long rows. Let's look at these cases.

Migrated Rows   When data is updated and the updated row piece cannot fit in the block that it is updated from, that row is moved in its entirety to a different data block. Since indexes rely on the rowid or location of the row in the block where it is updated from, that address must be maintained. In order to maintain this address, the data is moved to a new block and a pointer to the new location is left in its place.

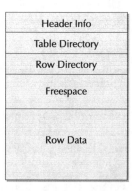

FIGURE 2-3.   *The Oracle block structure*

This is essentially a forwarding address. Although this is an efficient way to avoid having to update indexes, it can be inefficient in the long run.

Migrated rows cause overhead in the system because Oracle must spend the CPU time to find space for the row and then copy the row to the new data block. This takes both CPU time and I/Os. Therefore, any UPDATE statement that causes a migration incurs a performance penalty.

Chained Rows   If a row is inserted into a block and cannot fit, the row is broken down into several row pieces that are inserted into different blocks. These row pieces are considered chained rows. Although migrated rows can be avoided or fixed, chained rows usually can only be avoided by creating a database with a larger block size, and even that can't handle every case.

If you want to change the block size, you can export the data and rebuild the database with a larger block size. With Oracle9*i*, you can now create a new tablespace with a larger block size and copy your data to the new tablespace.

You may not be able to avoid having chained rows, especially if your table has a LONG column or long CHAR or VARCHAR2 columns. If you are aware of very large columns, it can be advantageous to adjust the database block size before implementing the database.

A properly sized block ensures that the blocks are used efficiently and I/Os are kept to a minimum. If you create blocks that are too large, you will not make efficient use of space in the SGA. If you make the blocks too small, you might not be able to fit an entire row into a block. The block size should be determined by your application and your data.

Chained rows cause overhead in the system not only when they are created but each time they are accessed. A chained row requires more than one I/O to read the row. Remember that Oracle reads from the disk data blocks; each time the row is accessed, multiple blocks must be read into the SGA.

Listing Migrated and Chained Rows   You can check for migrated and chained rows with the **LIST CHAINED ROWS** option of the **ANALYZE** command. In order to analyze for chained and migrated rows, you must first create the CHAINED_ROWS table. This is done by running the SQL script utlchain.sql, which is found in the RDBMS/admin directory of your Oracle release.

```
SQL> @utlchain
Table created.

SQL> Rem
SQL> Rem Analyze the Table in Question
SQL> Rem
SQL> ANALYZE
  2   TABLE scott.emp LIST CHAINED ROWS;
```

```
Table analyzed.

SQL> Rem
SQL> Rem Check the Results
SQL> Rem
SQL> SELECT * from chained_rows;

no rows selected
```

If any rows are selected, you have either chained or migrated rows. To solve this problem, copy the rows in question to a temporary table, delete the rows from the initial table, and reinsert the rows into the original table from the temporary table.

PCTUSED and PCTFREE   When you create a tablespace, you can specify whether the tablespace is locally managed or dictionary managed (as you will learn in the next few sections). In addition, you will learn that you can have segment management be manual or automatic. If you choose to have segment management be manual, you can use the PCTUSED and PCTFREE parameters to specify how the data blocks are allocated. With segment management automatic, these options are not available.

When you create a table, index, or tablespace in manual segment management mode, you have the option of setting the behavior of the data blocks within that table

PCTFREE–PCTUSED Example
Assume that you have the following values for PCTFREE and PCTUSED:

    PCTFREE = 20
    PCTUSED = 40

In this example, you can add new rows to the data block until the data block becomes 80 percent full (100 percent - 20 percent free). When this occurs, no more rows can be added to this data block; the space is reserved for growth of the existing rows. However, updates can use that additional space.

You can add new rows to the data block only when the percentage of available space in the block has been reduced to 40 percent (used). This effectively saves space in the data blocks for growth of rows and avoids chaining.

The defaults for PCTFREE and PCTUSED are as follows:

    PCTFREE = 10
    PCTUSED = 40

or index by using the storage parameters PCTUSED and PCTFREE. These storage parameters determine how the data blocks are filled up and used to reserve space in data blocks for updates. By using PCTFREE and PCTUSED, you have more exact control over the use of the data blocks themselves. In many cases, knowing your application and your data can help you improve overall system performance.

Earlier in this section, you have seen the effect of chained and migrated rows, which occur when an insert or update doesn't have sufficient room in the current block. The storage parameters PCTUSED and PCTFREE are used to reserve space in blocks for updates so that migrated rows do not occur.

Think of PCTFREE as a *high water mark* and PCTUSED as a *low water mark*. If the space in a data block is such that there is less space left than PCTFREE, no new rows can be added in that block until the amount of space in the table is less than PCTUSED.

The sum of PCTFREE and PCTUSED cannot exceed 100. Because PCTFREE actually represents a high water mark of 100 PCTFREE, if the sum of the two exceeds 100, there is an inconsistency in the formula and PCTFREE would be less than PCTUSED.

PCTFREE   PCTFREE has the effect of reserving space in the data block for growth of existing rows. New rows can be added to the data block until the amount of space remaining in the data block is less than the PCTFREE value.

A high PCTFREE value has the following effects:

■   There is a large amount of space for growth of existing rows.

■   Performance is improved because blocks have to be reorganized less frequently.

■   Performance is improved because chaining is reduced.

■   Typically requires more space because blocks are not used as efficiently. There will always be a moderate amount of empty space in the data blocks.

A low PCTFREE value has the opposite effects:

■   There is less space for growth of existing rows.

■   Performance is reduced because reorganization may become more frequent.

■   Performance is reduced because rows may have to be chained more often, increasing CPU use as well as causing additional I/Os.

■   Space is used more effectively. Blocks are filled more completely, thus reducing waste.

Using PCTFREE can help if you have an application that frequently inserts new data into rows. Because the PCTFREE option is used in the **CREATE CLUSTER**, **CREATE TABLE**, **CREATE INDEX**, and **CREATE SNAPSHOT** commands, it is worth the effort to look at each of your tables, clusters, and indexes individually and decide on an effective PCTFREE value for each.

PCTUSED   Once PCTFREE is reached, no new rows can be inserted into the data block until the space in the block has fallen below PCTUSED. Another feature of PCTUSED is that Oracle tries to keep a data block at least PCTUSED full before using new blocks.

A high PCTUSED value has the following effects:

■ It decreases performance because you usually have more migrating and chained rows.

■ It reduces wasted space by filling the data block more completely.

A lower value for PCTUSED has the following effects:

■ Performance is improved because of the drop in the number of migrated and chained rows.

■ Space usage is less efficient because there is more unused space in the data blocks.

Just as with PCTFREE, it is worth the effort to look at each table individually and determine a value for PCTUSED that more accurately fits your application. Doing so can improve your system's performance.

Here are a few guidelines to follow when adjusting PCTFREE and PCTUSED:

■ **Update activity, high row growth**   If your application frequently uses updates that affect the size of rows, set PCTFREE fairly high and PCTUSED fairly low. This arrangement allows for a large amount of space in the data blocks for row size growth. For example:

    PCTFREE = 20–25
    PCTUSED = 35–40
    (100 - PCTFREE _) - PCTUSED = 35 to 45

■ **Insert activity, small row growth**   If most inserts are new rows and there is very little update with row growth, set PCTFREE low and set a moderate value for PCTUSED to avoid chaining of new rows. This arrangement allows new rows to be inserted into the data block until the point at which more insertions are likely to cause migration or chaining. When this point is reached, no more insertions occur until there is a fair amount of space left in the block. Afterward, inserting can resume.

```
PCTFREE = 5–10
PCTUSED = 50–60
( 100 - PCTFREE _) - PCTUSED = 30 to 45
```

■ **Performance primary, space abundant**   If performance is critical and you have plenty of space available, you can ensure that migration and chaining never occur by setting PCTFREE very high and PCTUSED extremely low. Although this can waste quite a bit of space, all chaining and migration should be avoided.

```
PCTFREE = 30
PCTUSED = 30
( 100 - PCTFREE _) - PCTUSED = 40
```

■ **Space critical, performance secondary**   If you have very large tables or if you have moderate-sized tables and disk space is at a premium, set PCTFREE very low and PCTUSED very high. This arrangement ensures that you take maximum advantage of the available space. Note that you will see some performance loss caused by increased chaining and migration.

```
PCTFREE = 5
PCTUSED = 90
( 100 - PCTFREE _) - PCTUSED = 5
```

NOTE
PCTUSED and PCTFREE options are only available in manual segment management mode. It is recommended that you run in automatic extent management mode.

Using Multiple Block Sizes

One of the most exciting new features introduced in Oracle9*i* is the ability to mix multiple block sizes in the same database. This allows you to take advantage of both the DSS advantages of a large block size and the OLTP advantages of a small block size. This can be quite useful, but is very dependent on you knowing your system and your data.

In order to use multiple block sizes, you must do two different things. First, you must set up the Oracle buffer cache to be divided into different parts based on block size. Then you must create tablespaces using the nonstandard block sizes.

NOTE
By setting the parameter DB_CACHE_ADVICE to ON, statistics relating to the performance benefits of multiple block sizes are gathered and are available in the table V$DB_CACHE_ADVICE performance view.

Setting Up the Oracle Buffer Cache for Nonstandard Block Sizes   The amount of memory allocated for the default buffer cache is determined by the DB_CACHE_SIZE parameter. The standard block size is set by the DB_BLOCK_SIZE parameter and nonstandard cache sizes are set by the parameters DB_2K_CACHE_SIZE, DB_4K_CACHE_SIZE, and so on.

Set the parameter DB_CACHE_SIZE to be the amount of memory you wish to allocate to the default block size. Set DB_2K_CACHE_SIZE, DB_4K_CACHE_SIZE, and the others to the amount of memory that you want each of those block sizes to have access to.

NOTE
Multiple buffer caches using the KEEP, RECYCLE, and DEFAULT cache settings only apply to the default block size.

Creating Tablespaces with Nonstandard Block Sizes   In order to create a tablespace with a nonstandard block size, you must use the BLOCKSIZE keyword when creating the tablespace. This keyword is followed by the block size you are setting for this tablespace. An example of this is shown next:

```
CREATE TABLESPACE oltp_ts
DATAFILE '/u/oracle/data/oltp1.dat' SIZE 100M,
'/u/oracle/data/oldp2.dat' SIZE 100M
BLOCKSIZE 2K
```

This example will create a 2K tablespace. Other size tablespaces can also be created.

Extents
In order for the Oracle RDBMS to achieve maximum flexibility while at the same time trying to maintain excellent performance, it was necessary to create a mechanism where contiguous sets of blocks are created and managed together. Imagine a situation where an entire Oracle disk subsystem is composed of individual blocks belonging to different objects. This would be very inefficient and slow. In order to achieve this efficiency, the extent was created.

An extent is a set of contiguous blocks that belong to an Oracle object. This set of blocks is created whenever additional space for an object is needed. The number of blocks in an extent is determined by what mode you are running extent management in, as well as the storage parameters.

Dictionary Managed Tablespace Extent Management   The traditional method of managing extents is specifying the extent size within the storage clause of the CREATE TABLE or CREATE TABLESPACE statement. Here, you specify the minimum size, the size of the second extent, and the percentage of growth of each additional extent. This allows for larger and larger extents to be created as more space is needed in the object. Although this was very efficient, because of the fact that the tablespace extent information was stored in the data dictionary, there is a lot of overhead associated with it. Because of that, locally managed tablespace extent management was invented.

Locally Managed Tablespace Extent Management   Locally managed tablespace extent management manages the tablespace extents within the tablespace itself. Depending on how it is configured the extents are created in either a uniform size or a progressively larger size. This is determined by the UNIFORM or AUTOALLOCATE clauses, which allow the extents to be managed within a bitmap instead of within a table in the Data Dictionary. Although this might lead to the creation of more extents than you would have within dictionary managed tablespaces, the management is simpler and faster. In addition, if the extents are of uniform size, there is not the type of fragmentation experienced in dictionary or autoallocated managed extents. Locally managed tablespaces with autoallocated extents are recommended.

Segments

A segment is simply a collection of extents that make up a particular Oracle object, such as a table, index, and so on. There are several different types of segments as described next:

Segment Type	Purpose
Data Segments	These are the basic type of segment. The data segment can be used to hold both tables and clusters.
Index Segments	Index segments are used to hold indexes.
Rollback Segments	Rollback segments are special types of segments that are used to store undo information. Rollback segments have been replaced by undo tablespaces and system managed undo tablespaces. The use of UNDO tablespaces is highly recommended.
Temporary Segments	Temporary segments are used for storing temporary data generated during Oracle operations. Temporary segments might be used for sorts or joins.

These segments can be thought of as the data objects themselves. There are a few exceptions though. An Oracle cluster actually contains multiple objects within a segment and a portioned table is actually an object made up of multiple segments. However, with these few exceptions, the segment is the collection of extents that makes up an object.

The Oracle Instance

The Oracle Database server consists of the database and an Oracle instance. The term Oracle instance has already been mentioned in this chapter and is the most important component of the Oracle Database server. You will hear the term Oracle instance mentioned throughout this book.

The Instance Defined

The Oracle instance consists of the Oracle processes and shared memory necessary to access information in the database. The instance is made up of the Oracle background processes, and the shared memory used by these processes, as illustrated in Figure 2-4.

This combination of Oracle background processes and memory defines the Oracle instance. The combination of the Oracle instance and the database makes up the Oracle Database server.

The Oracle instance is made up of the Oracle background processes and the memory used by those background processes. The definition of an Oracle instance does not involve the actual database; however, a database is needed for the startup of the Oracle instance.

Components of the Instance

As defined in the previous paragraph, the Oracle instance is made up of the Oracle background processes and the memory used by these processes. The background

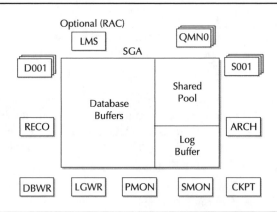

FIGURE 2-4. *The Oracle instance*

Real Application Clusters

The Oracle instance is made up of the Oracle background processes and the shared memory used by those processes. That shared memory is known as the System Global Area, or SGA.

An Oracle instance can connect to one and only one database to form the Oracle Database server. However, multiple instances can connect to the same database. This is the basis for the Oracle Real Application Cluster known as Oracle RAC. Those of us who use RAC systems on a regular basis tend to refer to it as an RAC cluster. Even though cluster is defined in the acronym, it sounds better that way.

processes are a number of Oracle processes that are started when the instance is created. These processes are used to maintain the Oracle Database as well as allow users to perform their desired tasks.

In addition to the background processes, there is memory that is allocated for these processes and user processes that should be utilized in order to access the Oracle Database. This memory is known as the System Global Area, or SGA. In this section, you will learn about both the background processes and the SGA memory.

Background Processes

Background processes are the Oracle processes used to perform various tasks within the Oracle instance. These tasks vary from communicating with other Oracle instances and performing system maintenance and cleanup, to writing dirty blocks to disk. Here are brief descriptions of the Oracle background processes:

Background Process	Duty of the Background Process
DBWR The Database Writer Process	The DBWR is responsible for writing dirty data blocks from the database block buffers to disk. When a transaction changes data in a data block, it is not necessary for that data block to be written to disk immediately. Because of the sophisticated mechanisms that Oracle has developed, changed data does not need to be written out immediately, but in the event of a failure, no data will be lost. Because of this, the DBWR can write this data out to disk in a manner that is more efficient than writing when each transaction completes. Usually, the DBWR writes out data on a regular schedule, unless data buffers need to be cleaned out and the DBWR writes out data more quickly. When data is written out, it is done in a least-recently-used fashion. For systems in which asynchronous I/O (AIO) is available, only one DBWR process is necessary. For systems in which AIO is not available, performance can be enhanced by adding more DBWR processes.

Background Process	Duty of the Background Process
LGWR The Log Writer Process	The LGWR process is responsible for writing data from the log buffer to the redo log. Since the COMMIT operation relies on the LGWR to write out the log record, the performance of the system can be very sensitive to the performance of the LGWR.
PMON The Process Monitor Process	The PMON process is responsible for keeping track of database processes and cleaning up if a process prematurely dies (PMON cleans up the cache and frees resources that may still be allocated). PMON is also responsible for restarting any dispatcher processes that may have failed.
SMON The System Monitor Process	SMON performs instance recovery at instance startup. This includes cleaning up temporary segments and recovering transactions that have died because of a system crash. SMON also defragments the database by coalescing free extents within the database.
CKPT The Checkpoint Process	The CKPT process is responsible for signaling the DBWR process to perform a checkpoint and to update all the data and control files for the database to indicate the most recent checkpoint. A checkpoint is an event in which all modified database buffers are written to the datafiles by the DBWR. The CKPT process is optional. If the CKPT process is not present, the LGWR assumes these responsibilities.
ARCHn The Archiver Process(es)	The ARCH process is responsible for copying the online redo log files to archival storage when they become full. ARCH is active only when the RDBMS is operated in ARCHIVELOG mode. When a system is not operated in ARCHIVELOG mode, it may not be possible to recover after a system failure. You should always operate in ARCHIVELOG mode. There may be up to ten archivers.
RECO The Recovery Process	RECO is used to clean up transactions that were pending in a distributed database. RECO is responsible for committing or rolling back the local portion of the disputed transactions.
Dnnn The Dispatcher Processes	When the Multithreaded Server option is used, at least one Dispatcher process is used for every communications protocol in use. The Dispatcher process is responsible for routing requests from the user processes to available shared server processes and back.
Snnn The Shared Server Processes	The Shared Server processes are used when the shared server configuration or MTS is used. These processes act like a dedicated server process, but are shared among many users.
LMS The ORACLE RAC (Real Application Clusters) Lock Manager Service	When RAC is used, this service is used to manage locks between the different nodes in the cluster.
QMNn The Queue Manager Process(es)	The Queue Manager processes are used to manage job queues with the Oracle advanced queueing option. You can have up to ten queues; QMN0–QMN9.

As you can see, there are a number of background processes. With some operating systems, such as Microsoft Windows, the background processes are actually threads running within one process. This can be problematic, since all of the threads in a process must share the same virtual memory address space.

With Linux, the background processes are actually processes, not threads. This provides us with a very flexible, high-performing, and scalable system.

The SGA

The SGA is a shared memory region Oracle uses to store data and control information for one Oracle instance. The SGA is allocated when the Oracle instance starts; it is deallocated when the Oracle instance shuts down. Each Oracle instance that starts has its own SGA. The information in the SGA is made up of the database buffers, the redo log buffer, and the shared pool; each has a fixed size and is created at instance startup.

Database Buffer Cache   The buffer cache stores the most recently used data blocks. These blocks can contain modified data that has not yet been written to disk (sometimes known as dirty blocks), blocks that have not been modified, or blocks that have been written to disk since modification (sometimes known as clean blocks). Because the buffer cache keeps blocks based on a most-recently-used algorithm, the most active buffers stay in memory to reduce I/O and improve performance.

The buffer can be split up into several different pieces known as the Keep Cache, the Recycle Cache, and the Default Cache. These caches have different purposes and can be used to increase the performance of the system.

In addition to the three pieces of the buffer cache just described, since Oracle9*i* you can now have buffer caches of a non-default block size. This allows you to create buffer caches for several different block sizes. However, you can only split the default block size cache into Keep, Recycle, and Default.

Redo Log Buffer   The redo log buffer of the SGA stores redo entries or a log of changes made to the database. The redo log buffers are written to the redo log as quickly and efficiently as possible. Remember that the redo log is used for instance recovery in the event of a system failure.

Shared Pool   The shared pool is the area of the SGA that stores shared memory structures such as shared SQL areas in the Library Cache, and internal information in the Data Dictionary.

Large Pool   The large pool is an optional area that can be used instead of the shared pool for certain functions. The large pool can be used for I/O operations, backup and recovery, the shared server processes, memory for the XA interface, and memory for parallel message queues for the parallel query option.

The Shared Pool is very important, since an insufficient amount of memory allocated to the Shared Pool can cause performance degradation. The Shared Pool is made up of both the Library Cache and the Data Dictionary Cache.

The Library Cache   The Library Cache is used to store shared SQL. Here is cached the parse tree, and the execution plan for every unique SQL statement. If multiple applications issue the same SQL statement, the shared SQL area can be accessed by each of them to reduce the amount of memory needed and to reduce the processing time used for parsing and execution planning.

The Data Dictionary Cache   The Oracle Data Dictionary contains a set of tables and views Oracle uses as a reference to the database. Oracle stores information here about both the logical and physical structure of the database. The Data Dictionary contains information like the following:

- User information such as user privileges

- Integrity constraints defined for tables in the database

- Names and data types of all columns in database tables

- Information on space allocated and used for schema objects

The Data Dictionary is frequently accessed by Oracle itself for the parsing of SQL statements. This access is essential to the operation of Oracle since performance bottlenecks in the Data Dictionary affect all Oracle users. By making sure that you have allocated a sufficient amount of memory to the Shared Pool, you should see no performance problems.

User Processes

In addition to the Oracle background processes, there are processes that are created on behalf of the user. These are known as the server processes. It is this server process that is responsible for retrieving data requested by the user and returning it to them. In addition, the server process is responsible for modifying data in the buffer cache on behalf of the user.

User, or client, processes are the user's connections into the Oracle Database server. The user process manipulates the user's input and communicates with the Oracle server process through the Oracle program interface. The user process is also used to display the information requested by the user and, if necessary, can process this information into a more useful form.

Server Processes

When a user connects into the Oracle Database server, a server process (sometimes known as shadow process) is created on behalf of the user. The server processes communicate with the user and interact with Oracle to carry out the user's requests. For example, if the user process requests a piece of data not already in the SGA, the shadow process is responsible for reading the data blocks from the datafiles into the SGA. There can be a one-to-one correlation between the user processes and the shadow processes (as in a dedicated server configuration). Although one shadow process can connect to multiple user processes (as in a multithreaded server configuration), doing so reduces the utilization of system resources.

PGA Memory

The PGA is a memory area that contains data and control information for the Oracle server processes. The amount and content of the PGA depends on the Oracle server options you have installed. This area is made up of the following components:

- **Stack space**   This is the memory that holds the session's variables, arrays, and so on.

- **Session information**   If you are not running the multithreaded server, the session information is stored in the PGA. If you are running the multithreaded server, the session information is stored in the SGA.

- **Private SQL area**   This is an area in the PGA where information such as binding variables and runtime buffers are kept.

It is important to keep the user's memory in mind when you are sizing your system, since there might be hundreds of users simultaneously connected to the Oracle Database server. It is the sum of the memory of all of these users that will add up to the total memory used by the user processes. Later in this book, you will see how to configure the memory for both the SGA and PGA memory areas.

MTS vs. Dedicated Server Processes

With a dedicated server process, there is a one-to-one correlation between the user process and the server process. Each server process is dedicated to one user process. With large systems, you could potentially have huge numbers of users connected into the Oracle Database server, and thus huge numbers of processes. In order to reduce the number of processes, you can use some sort of transaction monitor or multiplexer, or you can use the Oracle multithreaded server option. MTS allows multiple user connections to share the same server processes.

How MTS Works The multithreaded server allows many user processes to share a number of shared server processes by queuing user requests in a queue in the shared pool. These requests are taken off the queue and processed by shared server processes. The connections to the users, and the queuing of the requests are handled by dispatcher processes. These dispatcher processes are responsible for receiving the request, placing it on the queue and returning the data to the user once the request has been completed.

MTS vs. Dedicated The main advantage of using the multithreaded server is the reduction of server processes. This can greatly reduce CPU usage as well as memory usage. As you might guess, however, the multithreaded server does add additional overhead to the system. This is why, for long running batch jobs, a dedicated server process is recommended.

For each individual user, a dedicated server process would be more efficient and faster, but for the Oracle Database server as a whole, it might be more efficient to run with shared server processes. This is both because of the overhead involved in creating a new server process, as well as the memory and system resources each server process consumes. I have found that you can easily run hundreds of users via dedicated server processes on a Linux system, but when you get to the range of 600–700 users, it is time to look into the Multithreaded Server model.

Oracle 10*g* New Features

Oracle 10*g* brings with it a host of new features designed to improve performance, scalability, administration, and development, as well as to enable grid computing. New features have been added to almost every component of the Oracle Database server.

Performance and Scalability Features

Oracle 10*g* performance and scalability features include the following new features and improvements:

- **Configurable network parameters** With Oracle 10*g*, you can now configure the TCP/IP send and receive buffers in order to optimally configure for your particular application and network.

- **InfiniBand network support** Oracle has added on support for the InfiniBand network Sockets Direct Protocol (SDP) standard, thus allowing for use of the new InfiniBand network.

- **Single set-aggregation in RETURNING clauses** In cases where transactions process many rows in the same table, this can be a big win.

■ **Data Pump** For those of you who have used export and import in the past, the Oracle Data Pump provides similar functionality, but with much higher performance and a rich feature set.

The performance and scalability features of Oracle 10*g* alone are worth upgrading, but as you will see, there are many more features that make this a great release.

Clustering

With Oracle 10*g*, RAC has been greatly improved and enhanced and several new features added, including the following:

■ **High Availability Extensions** With Oracle 10*g* RAC, you can now enhance your applications by using RAC extensions that are available at the application level.

■ **Cluster Workload Scheduling** Scheduling can now be done at the cluster level, rather than at the instance level, without the need to modify applications.

Oracle 10*g* RAC is the key component to the grid computing architecture and has been greatly enhanced to support that task.

Availability

Oracle has done a great job of enhancing the availability features (in addition to Oracle 10*g* RAC). Included in this release are

■ **Rolling Upgrades** From this release on, it is possible to perform rolling upgrades using logical standby databases. This is done using Data Guard and SQL apply.

■ **Enhanced Online Redefinition** Oracle has enhanced the ability to redefine schema objects while the database is up and running.

Manageability

A number of manageability features have been added to make manageability easier and more intuitive. These new features include

■ **Java Monitoring Tool** A new tool has been added to monitor various aspects of the Java Virtual Machine and its interaction with the Oracle SQL engine.

■ **Enhanced Wait Monitoring** In addition to wait statistics, Oracle now is able to keep a history of waits and what caused them.

- **End-to-end application tracing** Enhanced tracing is now able to trace applications, as well as J2EE, end-to-end.

- **Database Features Statistics** Oracle can now keep track of which features are being used.

- **Automated Scheduling** A unified scheduler can now be used to automate administrative tasks.

As you can see, a large number of new administrative features have been added.

Business Intelligence

Oracle has added several features that improve the performance and usability of the Oracle Database server in business intelligence environments. Included in this feature set are the following:

- **Bioinformatics** Oracle has added native support in the database for DOUBLE and FLOAT data types. This greatly enhances performance for applications that perform intense computational analysis, such as bioinformatics customers.

- **Statistical functions** This new feature places statistical functions into the database, thus eliminating the need to extract data only to perform these functions external to the database.

- **Document functions** A number of new features for document handling have been added into the database.

These and several other features not mentioned here have been added to the Oracle SQL engine to enhance business intelligence processing.

Application Development

Several new features have been added for application development. These features include

- **Expanded local coverage** This feature adds new territories and languages as well as enhances those that already existed.

- **Unicode 3.2** Oracle now supports the Unicode 3.2 standard.

- **Globalization Development Kit** The Oracle GDK helps to deploy Internet applications that work in a global environment.

Oracle has added several new features aimed at assisting the developer in running applications in a global environment.

Linux 64-Bit Support

Oracle has added native support for 64-bit Linux. This support allows for the configuration and management of large amounts of RAM and very large SGAs. The feature is covered in detail later in this book.

Grid Computing

Introduced in Oracle 10*g*, grid computing takes low-cost servers running both Oracle 10*g* and Linux and clusters them together into a grid. This grid is highly available because of the redundancy of the cluster. In addition, it is high-performing and scalable because of the ability to add extra nodes as needed. At the database layer, grid computing is based on the Oracle RAC cluster which will be presented in detail later in this book. At the application layer, Oracle has added new load balancing and redundancy grid controls to enable application grids.

Summary

This chapter introduced you to the Oracle architecture. In the next chapter, transaction processing and schema objects, an integral part of that architecture will be presented. This will form the basis of the rest of the book where the concepts and architecture of Oracle are deployed and tuned with the Linux operating system.

In addition to discussions of the Oracle architecture, this chapter discussed grid computing and presented some of the new features available with Oracle 10*g*. In the following chapters you will learn how the Oracle architecture depends on the Linux operating system and how it should be configured in order to optimally support Oracle.

CHAPTER
3

Transaction
Management and the
Oracle Schema Objects

n the previous chapter, you learned about the Oracle data structures (both physical and logical) and the Oracle instance. In addition, you were briefly introduced to the Oracle server processes and how they worked. In this chapter, we continue exploring the Oracle architecture, showing how it works. You will learn how the server process retrieves data from the Oracle Database and how data is inserted into the database or modified within it. This process is a combination of both the server processes and the Oracle background processes.

This chapter also covers transaction management, an integral part of the operation of the Oracle Database server. Lastly, we'll discuss the Oracle schema objects.

Oracle Functionality

In exploring the Oracle architecture, let's first look at how Oracle processes read and write from, and to, the database. Understanding these processes is key to comprehending some of the performance topics covered later in this book.

This section starts by examining how users both read data from the database and write to it. Other topics such as read consistency and locking will also be introduced, followed by checkpoints and undo.

Reading from the Database

Reading from the RDBMS is completely handled by the user's server process. The server process first determines if the data is in the SGA, and if not, the data is copied by the server process from the datafile into the SGA. Once there, the data is manipulated within the SGA. By having the server processes manipulate the data in the database, a large amount of concurrent processing can be done since there are potentially many server processes running (at least one per user in dedicated server mode, or the configured number of shared server processes).

In general, the following steps are performed. I say "in general" because there are options, such as the parallel query option and shared server process, that work slightly differently. But let's just look at the basic case.

1. The request is passed from the user to the server processes. This might be a dedicated server process or a shared server process.

2. The server process checks to see if the desired data is in the buffer cache of the SGA.

3. If the data is in the buffer cache, it is retrieved and returned to the user, or manipulated as necessary.

4. If the data is not in the buffer cache, the server process reads the data out of the datafile and puts it into the buffer cache.

5. Once the data is in the SGA, it can be sent back to the user or manipulated as required.

This architecture, which allows each process to work independently when reading data, scales well with both the number of CPUs and the number of processes. In fact, this is a very scalable architecture.

Concurrency

Concurrency is the ability of Oracle to allow many users to access the database and the data within the database at the same time. Oracle has been designed to achieve maximum concurrency at optimal performance. Concurrency is achieved via several different mechanisms, the use of which depends on the type of concurrency.

Writing to the Database

When writing to the database the server process adds, updates, or deletes data from the buffer cache in the SGA. The server processes never write to the datafiles themselves. This is done by the DBWR (Database Writer) process. When modifying data in the database, the following steps are performed.

1. If an insert is being done, space is found in a block in the buffer cache and the data is inserted into that block buffer.

2. If an update or delete is being done, a read of that data is done, as previously described, and then the data is modified or deleted in the buffer cache. A copy of the original data is written into the UNDO tablespace in case it is needed for read consistency or a rollback operation.

3. Once the data has been modified in the buffer cache, a log record is written into the redo log. Once the redo log entry has been written out, the change is considered completed.

4. At a later time, the DBWR process will take the data that has been changed and write it out to the datafiles. The DBWR process is the only process that writes to the datafiles, but the server processes can read from the datafiles.

The method for writing to the database simplifies the writing process while optimizing performance.

Locking

When modifications are being made to the database, the undo records allow for other processes to read the data; however, in order to keep multiple processes from modifying data at the same time, locking is used. Oracle uses row level locking to achieve this attribute with minimal effect to other processes accessing the database. Only the row or rows being modified are locked. Other rows in the same database or buffer can be modified simultaneously.

Read Consistency

Read consistency is the attribute that allows multiple processes to read from the database and achieve a consistent view of the data. When a process begins to read the data from the database, the data it gets is consistent as of the point of time when the statement began.

For example, if a statement begins to read data from a table, and in the middle of the action to read that data, some of that data is modified from within a different process, the original unmodified data is read. This provides a consistent view of the data. Within the Oracle RDBMS, this is achieved via the undo records. When data is modified, the original data is saved within the undo records until both the statement that has modified the data has been committed and all other processes that might read that data have completed.

Since this view is consistent as of the start time of the statement, there might be several different versions of the same data stored in the undo records. This provides a high-performance method of achieving read consistency.

Data Integrity

Certain functions are absolutely essential for the proper functioning of the database server. Among these is data integrity, recovery from failure, error handling, and so on. The following sections list and describe some of these functions.

Checkpoints

When writing to the database, changes are made in the buffer cache within the SGA and written out to the database files later by the DBWR process. This is done using an LRU (Least Recently Used) list algorithm. Because recently used data might never go to the end of the LRU, Oracle must somehow make sure that dirty or modified buffers eventually get written out. This is to assure the integrity of the database and shorten the recovery time (in the event of a failure). Oracle does this with a mechanism called a checkpoint.

LRU Algorithm

An *LRU* (*Least Recently Used*) is a list of items that has the most recently used item at the top of the list. As new items get added to the top of the list, older items are moved down the list. If an item on the list is used, it is moved back to the top of the list. If resources need to be reclaimed, the items to be discarded are taken from the bottom of the list. This way, items that are used frequently will stay near the top of the list. LRUs are used for caching and other resources both within Oracle and the Linux operating system.

The checkpoint process makes sure that the dirty buffers are eventually written out to disk. Oracle uses either the CKPT background process or the LGWR process to signal a checkpoint. But what is a checkpoint and why is it necessary?

Because all modifications done to data blocks are done on the block buffers, there are changes to data in memory that are not necessarily reflected in the blocks on disk. Because caching is done using a least-recently-used algorithm, if a buffer is constantly modified, it is always marked as recently used and is therefore unlikely to be written out by the DBWR.

A checkpoint is used to ensure that these buffers are written to disk by forcing all dirty buffers to be written out on a regular basis. This does not mean that all work stops during a checkpoint; the checkpoint process has two methods of operation: the fast checkpoint and the normal checkpoint.

In the normal checkpoint, the DBWR merely writes out a few more buffers every time it is active. This type of checkpoint takes much longer but has less of an effect on the system. In the fast checkpoint, the DBWR writes a large number of buffers at the request of the checkpoint each time it is active. This type of checkpoint completes much quicker and is more efficient in terms of I/Os generated, but it has a greater effect on system performance at the time of the checkpoint.

You can use the time between checkpoints to improve instance recovery. Frequent checkpoints reduce the time required to recover in the event of a system failure. A checkpoint automatically occurs at a log switch.

The Redo Log

The Redo Log files are used to store redo information. Each time data is changed in the database, a log record is written describing these changes. With this information, the database can be recovered in the event of a system failure, by replaying committed transactions and rolling back noncommitted transactions.

If a catastrophic system failure occurs, as with a power failure, component failure, and so on, the Oracle instance will be aborted. Thus, it will either immediately be cut off, or in the event of a disk failure, the instance may crash. If this occurs, all changed data in the buffer cache will be lost; only changes that have been written out to disk will be saved.

When Oracle is restarted, the information in the redo log file is used to replay all changes that have been made to the database since the last time the datafiles were written to. All previously committed transactions will be recovered, something known as *rolling-forward*. All transactions that had modified data but have not been committed will be backed out. This is known as *rolling-back*. Rolling-back is similar to the operation that would be executed if you were to issue a ROLLBACK statement rather than a COMMIT at the end of a transaction.

This redo log file is necessary for proper recovery. If the redo log file is lost, due to a disk failure, you will not be able to recover in the event of a system failure. Because of this, the redo log file must be protected against this kind of failure. I recommend that disk mirroring or RAID1 be used on all redo log files.

Protect the Redo Log

If you use a write-cache on the controller that has the redo log files and it is not battery backed-up, you are in danger of losing data. In the event of a power failure, you will lose redo information and may not be able to recover.

Since the redo log files are so critical to the recoverability of the system, it is recommended that you do not use a caching disk controller with write-caching unless that cache is battery backed-up. In the event of a power failure, you must make sure no redo information is lost. It is often recommended that write-caching not be used at all on the redo log, but I feel that if the write cache is protected by battery back-up, your risk is reduced and write-caching is acceptable.

How the Redo Log Works

Each change to the database is logged into the redo log. Because of this, in the event of a failure, all changes made since the last backup can be recovered with the use of these redo log files. If the instance should fail, due to a power failure or other system failure, the redo log files can recover all changes done since the last checkpoint.

When a COMMIT operation is performed, the redo information is written into the redo log buffers. The LGWR process writes the redo log files with the information in the redo log buffer. The COMMIT operation is not completed until the redo log has been written. Once this has occurred, that transaction is irrevocable and will be recovered in the event of a system failure. Thus, you can see how important the redo log file really is.

The redo log is made up of two or more redo log files or log file groups. A log file group is a set of files that Oracle uses for redundancy. A redo log group is treated as if it were one redo log file; however, it is redundant. In this manner, the redo log is protected against disk failure. A redo log group is made up of one or more redo log files and must be protected against disk failure. If you are using disk mirroring to protect the redo log, it is not necessary to use redo log file groups. Since the disk is protected, single log files are sufficient. Most people choose to take advantage of a hardware

Checkpoints

A checkpoint causes all in-cache data blocks that have been modified and not been written out to disk to be written to the disk. These unwritten changed buffers are called <I>dirty buffers.<M> Dirty buffers are what cause the system to be recovered since data might have been changed in memory and committed, but not written out to disk. In addition, there might be changes that have been written out to disk, but not yet committed.

RAID system rather than use Oracle mirroring due to the performance benefits of hardware RAID over Oracle mirroring.

The redo log has two or more log files or log file groups that are used in an alternating fashion. Once the first log file has filled up, the logging operation moves to the next redo log file in the chain. If archiving is enabled, when it fills up and the log switch occurs, this file is copied to an *archive log file*. These archive log files are very important for the recoverability of the system in the event of a catastrophic failure.

Operations on the redo log files are done with the **ALTER DATABASE** command. Using the **ALTER DATABASE** command, you can add redo log groups and redo log files, rename redo log files, and perform other tasks.

Log Switches and Checkpoints

Each time a redo log file or log file group fills up, it switches to the next redo log file in the sequence. This switch, called the *log switch,* causes several automatic events to occur. They consist of:

- **The checkpoint**   A log switch always causes a checkpoint to occur, which flushes all dirty buffers from the Oracle buffer cache. This reduces the amount of time a recovery will take, if needed.

- **Archiving**   If archiving is turned on, and it should be, the log switch causes the redo log file that was just active, to copy its contents to an *archive log file*. This archive log file is used in recovery if needed.

- **The log sequence number**   Each time a redo log file is reused, it is given a *log sequence number*. This *log sequence number* is also given to the associated archive log file.

Archiving and checkpointing are integral parts of the Oracle RDBMS functionality and are critical to system recoverability and stability.

Log Switch and Checkpoint Intervals

The initialization parameters LOG_CHECKPOINT_INTERVAL and LOG_CHECKPOINT_ TIMEOUT can be used to control the checkpoint interval. The parameter LOG_ CHECKPOINTS_TO_ALERT is used to print a message into the alert log whenever a checkpoint occurs. This is nice for seeing when checkpoints are happening, but can easily create extremely large amounts of alert log space.

LOG_CHECKPOINT_INTERVAL

The LOG_CHECKPOINT_INTERVAL is set to a number of operating system blocks that are used before the log switch occurs. For most operating systems, the size of the blocks is 512 bytes. So, this parameter will set the number of 512-byte blocks used in the redo log before a checkpoint occurs.

If your redo log files are 10MB in size and you want the checkpoint interval to be one-tenth of the redo log file, use the following formula to determine the value of LOG_CHECKPOINT_INTERVAL.

```
LOG_CHECKPOINT_INTERVAL = 1MB / 512 (bytes/block) = 2048 blocks
```

To accomplish this, set LOG_CHECKPOINT_INTERVAL=2048 in the parameter file. To have the checkpoint only occur at log switches, set the value of LOG_CHECKPOINT_INTERVAL to be very high.

LOG_CHECKPOINT_TIMEOUT
The parameter LOG_CHECKPOINT_TIMEOUT specifies a time interval in seconds in which the checkpoint will occur. This will automatically run the checkpoint process at this interval.

To set the checkpoint to occur every ten minutes use the following equation:

```
LOG_CHECKPOINT_TIMEOUT=600
```

By setting the checkpoint interval on a timer, you can be assured that checkpoints happen regularly, even if there is not much activity at the time.

Forcing a Checkpoint
A checkpoint can also be forced by hand. If you want to force a checkpoint, use the following command:

```
ALTER SYSTEM CHECKPOINT;
```

Occasionally, you may want to do this if you think your system is in risk of some sort of failure, perhaps from a thunderstorm or other natural phenomena.

Forcing a Log Switch
As with the checkpoint, a log switch can be forced by hand. If you want to force a log switch, you can do so with the following command:

```
ALTER SYSTEM SWITCH LOGFILE;
```

It is rare, however, that you will need to switch logfiles.

Sizing the Redo Log Files
Typically, the redo log files are sized in order to manage the size of the archive log files. In the past, the redo log files would be kept small so that they could easily be written to tape. With today's tape sizes, however, this is no longer a major concern. If you do not have a particular medium in mind for archiving, or the space is unlimited, you should make the redo log file a manageable size.

There is no rule of thumb for the size of the redo log files. Your own preference should help you decide on this. Remember, if you make them too big you could potentially go all day without performing a log switch (thus causing an archive log file to be created). This can be dangerous since the longer you go without creating an archive log file, the less recoverability you will have in the event of a media failure, as described in the next section.

Archiving the Redo Logs

When a log switch occurs, the log records in the filled redo log file are copied to an archive log file if archiving is enabled. This archiving is usually done automatically. Since the redo log file cannot be reused until the archive process has completed, you should make certain you don't try to reuse that log file before the operation is complete. There are several ways to ensure the archiving process happens quickly. They are

- **Archive to Disk**   You can archive to disk and then copy those archive log files to tape later. This will keep the archiving process from waiting on a tape drive or other slower medium from completing.

- **Use Multiple Log Files**   By having more than two redo log files (two is the minimum requirement), you can be simultaneously archiving two or more log files while a third is being used for logging. If the redo log has not completed archiving by the time it is needed, transactions will stop until it is available.

Archiving is very important to maintain recoverability in the database.

Adding Additional Redo Log Files and Groups

As with many of the other functions we have seen in this book, there are several ways to add to the redo log. Most of these utilities have an option of using either a graphical or command-line utility. Redo log files can be added with the Oracle Enterprise Manager, with SQL statements, or with a number of third-party tools. In this section, you will learn how to add additional redo log files using SQL statements.

Adding to the Redo Log with the ALTER DATABASE Command

Logfiles or logfile groups can be added or modified with the **ALTER DATABASE** command or via the Oracle GUI utilities. I really prefer the command-line utilities since they can be scripted, and as such, are a permanent record, capable of being used over and over again.

```
ALTER DATABASE
ADD LOGFILE GROUP 3
( '/u01/data/log3a.log', '/u01/data/log3b.log' )
SIZE 10M;
```

To add a new logfile to an already existing group, you can use the command:

```
ALTER DATABASE
ADD LOGFILE MEMBER '/u01/data/log3c.log' TO GROUP 3;
```

Or if you don't know the group name, you can use the same command and specify the other members of the logfile group as in:

```
ALTER DATABASE
ADD LOGFILE MEMBER '/u01/data/log3c.log'
TO GROUP ( '/u01/data/log3a.log', '/u01/data/log3b.log');
```

As I have said before, by using an SQL script and the **ALTER DATABASE** command, you can preserve a permanent record of the change, and use this file as a template for other similar operations. If you are running a command, you might as well put it into a SQL script and save it.

Modifying Redo Log Files and Groups

As with many of the other functions we have seen in this book, there are several ways to add to the redo log. Most of these utilities have an option of using either a graphical or command-line utility. Here are the methods for modifying the redo log with SQL statements.

Modifying the Redo Log with the ALTER DATABASE Command

Logfiles or logfile groups can be modified with the **ALTER DATABASE** command, as shown earlier in this book. Again, I really prefer the command-line utilities since they can be scripted, and as such, are a permanent record, capable of being used repeatedly.

For example, a redo log file can be renamed with the command:

```
ALTER DATABASE
RENAME LOGFILE '/u01/data/log1.doc' TO '/u01/data/log2.doc';
```

Or you can delete a logfile with the command:

```
ALTER DATABASE
DROP LOGFILE '/u01/data/log1.log';
```

Or with a logfile group, you can drop the entire logfile group with the following command:

```
ALTER DATABASE
DROP LOGFILE GROUP 3;
```

Or if you don't know the number of the logfile group, you can drop the logfile group by specifying the names of the logfile group members, as shown next:

```
ALTER DATABASE
DROP LOGFILE GROUP ('/u01/data/log3a.log', '/u01/data/log3b.log');
```

If necessary, you can drop just a logfile group member with this syntax:

```
ALTER DATABASE
DROP LOGFILE GROUP MEMBER '/u01/data/log3b.log';
```

NOTE
You cannot drop or alter an active log file. In order to perform an operation on a specific log file you should perform an ALTER SYSTEM SWITCH LOGFILE command to make the next log file in the sequence be the active log file. Then you can work on the log file that was previously active.

Characteristics of the Log Files

The redo log files are one of the few files in the Oracle Database that is always written to in a sequential manner. Since redo records are only read during recovery, it is also a write-only file during normal operations.

Because of the sequential nature of the redo log files, by isolating these files onto separate disk volumes you can take advantage of the fact that sequential I/O is much faster than random I/O. Keep in mind that the archival operation reads from the redo log file, so if you have two redo log files on the same disk volume, the archive process in conjunction with the redo log operation will not be sequential in nature.

NOTE
I use the term disk volume to refer to either a disk drive or a set of disk drives in a RAID array.

In most cases, the performance of the redo log operation is not usually a problem. However, if you are running in a high transaction rate environment, you may need to separate each redo log file to its own disk volume.

NOTE
The redo log files should be protected, either by using log file groups or with a RAID array. When using a RAID array (either hardware or software), use RAID1 for the redo log files. RAID1 offers the most protection and the fastest write performance.

The performance of the archive log volume is not as important as that of the redo log volume, but it is still fairly important. It is necessary that the archival operation be completed before the redo log file needs to be reused.

In many cases, archival information can be kept on another system and restored when necessary. If you are doing this, or are keeping your archive log files on tape, you may want to archive to disk first and then copy to tape or to the network. In this way, you can restore that data quicker. If you are copying your data to a backup system, you can use RAID5, which is slower but less costly. In any case, archiving to a temporary area first frees up the redo log file in the fastest possible time.

The danger of archiving to a disk area is that if this disk were to fail, your archive log files would be lost, thus leaving your system vulnerable. If you are archiving to disk, this should never be on the same disk volume as your database or log files. In the event of a disk failure, you would lose everything if they were on the same disks.

Undo

When data is modified in the database, Oracle records this transactional information so it may be used in the event that the transaction needs to be rolled back. Undo tablespaces and rollback segments are also used to provide read consistency and enable database recovery. Undo tablespaces and rollback segments contain the undo information used in *rollback* operations. Remember, a transaction can be finished either by issuing a COMMIT or ROLLBACK statement. These statements perform completely opposite operations.

A COMMIT operation finishes a transaction by finalizing all of the changes that have been made. Once the COMMIT operation has finished, all changes are finalized and cannot be undone. In the event of a system failure, all changes made in this transaction will be recovered.

A ROLLBACK causes all of the changes made during the transaction to be undone. Once the rollback operation has finished, you must resubmit the transaction in order to reproduce the changes that were made. After the rollback, it is as if the transaction never occurred.

Read consistency allows a long-running transaction to always obtain the same data within the query. During the transaction, the data presented to the user is consistent as of a single point in time and does not change. Even though the data may have changed, and perhaps the DBWR may even have written it out, other transactions do not see those changes until a COMMIT has occurred. In fact, only transactions that start after this transaction has been committed see those changes.

This is accomplished by the long-running transaction reading its data from both the database buffers and the undo information as necessary. This is why undo space cannot be deallocated until all transactions that were running at the time of the undo data creation have completed. With Oracle9*i*, either undo tablespaces or rollback segments can be used.

Read consistency has traditionally been handled in Oracle by rollback segments. New to Oracle9*i* is the use of system-managed undo (SMU), which handles read consistency, rollbacks, and recovery.

With *Oracle9i*, the recommended method of managing undo information is to use the system-managed undo (SMU) scheme. Using this method of undo, you do not need to put the level of effort into configuring and tuning rollback segments that you do when using the rollback segment undo (RBU) scheme.

The system-managed undo (SMU) scheme is enabled by setting the initialization parameter UNDO_MANAGEMENT to AUTO, and by setting the initialization parameter

UNDO_TABLESPACE to the name of the tablespace to be used. This, in conjunction with creating an undo tablespace, will enable SMU.

For those of you who still wish to configure rollback segments by hand, you can do so by setting the initialization parameter UNDO_MANAGEMENT to MANUAL. For those of you opting to use the SMU scheme, there is very little to fine-tune. To properly configure a system's rollback segments, you must create enough rollback segments, and they must be of a sufficient size.

Undo Tablespaces or System-Managed Undo (SMU) Mode

As mentioned earlier, SMU mode is enabled by setting the UNDO_MANAGEMENT parameter to AUTO. In SMU mode, there are very few initialization parameters to adjust. An undo tablespace must be created and then that tablespace assigned to undo information. With this new scheme of managing undo information, you can now specify how long undo information is retained. This, in conjunction with sizing the undo tablespace, is all that is required to manage undos.

Creating an Undo Tablespace

Undo tablespaces are created with the **CREATE UNDO TABLESPACE** command. The undo tablespace is created just like any other tablespace and requires you to specify the location and size of the tablespace. It can be made up of one or more datafiles and is similar to the temporary tablespace in that it can serve only one function.

In addition to setting the UNDO_MANAGEMENT parameter to AUTO, you must also assign the tablespace to undo by using the UNDO_TABLESPACE initialization parameter.

The undo tablespace should be created large enough to hold the required amount of undo information. This can be roughly calculated using the UNDO_RETENTION parameter as discussed later in this section. That parameter specifies how long undo information is retained.

If you know how long the undo information is retained, along with how much undo information per second is being generated, you can calculate how much undo tablespace is needed. Use the formula:

```
Undo space needed = Undo retention time * Undos/time
```

For example, if the undo retention was 300 seconds and the system generates 1000 undo blocks per second, the number of blocks required is

```
Undo blocks required =
(300 seconds) * (100 undos blocks/sec) = 30,000 blocks
```

Thus the space required is 30,000 times the block size.

Monitoring the Undo Tablespace

In order to find out what the undo rate is, you can monitor the dynamic performance view, V$UNDOSTAT. Some of the data that is of particular interest is

Parameter	Meaning
BEGIN_TIME	The time when the measurement interval began.
END_TIME	The time when the measurement interval ended.
TXNCOUNT	The total number of transactions committed during the measurement interval.
UNDOBLKS	The number of undo blocks that were consumed during the measurement interval.
SSOLDERRCNT	The number of OER errors that have occurred during the measurement interval. If this is high, the undo retention period should be re-evaluated.
NOSPACEERRCNT	Specifies the number of OER errors that have occurred for this instance. If this is high, the size of the undo tablespace should be reevaluated.

If you are seeing non-zero values for the error counts, you can do one of two things: lower the retention period or increase the size of the undo tablespace.

Tuning the Retention Period

The retention period allows you to specify how long undo information is retained. The parameter UNDO_RETENTION is specified in seconds. The length of time that undo information is retained is 30 seconds, by default. This is probably sufficient. If you feel that undo information needs to be retained longer, you can increase this value.

Increasing the retention periods allows undo information to be kept longer so that long-running transactions that require a consistent view of data have a better chance of finishing. If you receive the error message "snapshot too old," increasing the undo retention period will reduce this.

Rollback Segments or Rollback Segment Undo (RBU) Mode

Rollback segments record transactional information that may be used in the event that the transaction should be rolled back. They are also used to provide read consistency and enable database recovery. Since rollback segments were made obsolete in Oracle9*i*, they will not be covered here.

Introduction to Transaction Management

Earlier in this chapter, you were introduced to how Oracle performs read and write operations. In essence, any write operation is considered a transaction, since data is being changed. A transaction is defined to be a logical unit of work that contains one or more SQL statements. A transaction is atomic, in that either the entire transaction succeeds or the entire transaction fails. This is accomplished via the COMMIT or ROLLBACK statement on the user's part, or a system failure that automatically initiates a rollback operation.

Some of this section is a review from earlier in the chapter when writing to the database was covered; however, because of the importance of transaction management, this topic will be covered in more detail, and some new features of transaction processing will be introduced.

Transactions

To give you a better idea of how Oracle operates, this section analyzes a sample transaction. Throughout this book, the term transaction is used to describe a logical group of work. This group of work can consist of one or many SQL statements and must end with a commit or a rollback. This example assumes a client/server application using Oracle Net; however, the process is similar for local client applications. The following steps are executed to complete the transaction:

1. The application processes the user input and creates a connection to the server via Oracle Net.

2. The server picks up the connection request and creates a server process on behalf of the user.

3. The user executes an SQL statement and commits the transaction. In this example, the user changes the value of a row in a table.

4. The server process takes this SQL statement and checks the shared pool to see whether there is a shared SQL area that has this identical SQL statement. If it finds an identical shared SQL area, the server process checks to see whether the user has access privileges to the data. If the user has access privileges, the server process uses the shared SQL area to process the request. If a shared SQL area is not found, a new shared SQL area is allocated, the statement is parsed, and then it is executed.

5. The server process retrieves the data from the SGA (if present) or retrieves it from the datafile into the SGA.

6. The server process modifies the data in the SGA. Remember that the server processes can only read from the datafiles. Because the transaction has been committed, the LGWR process immediately records the transaction in the redo log file. At some later time, the DBWR process writes the modified blocks to permanent storage.

7. If the transaction is successful, a completion code is returned across the network to the client process. If a failure has occurred, an error message is returned.

While transactions are occurring, the Oracle background processes are all doing their jobs, keeping the system running smoothly. Keep in mind that while this process is going on, hundreds of other users may be doing similar tasks. It is Oracle's job to keep the system in a consistent state, to manage contention and locking, and to perform at the necessary rate.

This overview is intended to give you an understanding of the complexity and amount of interaction involved in the Oracle Database server. As we look in detail at the tuning of the server processes and applications later in this book, you can use this overview as a reference to the basics of how the Oracle Database server operates. Because of the differences in the various Linux operating systems, minor variances in different environments will be discussed individually.

COMMIT

The COMMIT operation is used to finalize a transaction and make any changes that have occurred within the transaction permanent. Once a transaction has committed,

Transaction Note

A transaction is not considered committed until the write to the redo log file has been completed. This arrangement ensures that, in the event of a system failure, a committed transaction can be recovered. In the event of a system failure, uncommitted transactions are rolled back, and committed transactions are rolled forward using the redo log files. Without the redo log files, the database would be left inconsistent in the event of a system failure.

The redo log is used for recovery in the event of a system failure. If the system were to crash, any committed transaction will be rolled forward (replayed) and uncommitted transactions are rolled back (undone). This guarantees the consistency of the database. This makes the redo log very critical. It is because of this that many people decide not to use hardware write caches on the redo log disk volume. I feel that a battery backed-up write cache is safe and can be used.

it cannot be undone without performing an additional operation to manually change the data back. The COMMIT operation makes sure that the entire transaction has completed successfully before the COMMIT statement returns success to the user.

In order for this COMMIT operation to complete, several steps must occur.

1. The unique System Change Number (SCN) for the transaction is written into the transaction table in the undo tablespace.

2. The Log Writer (LGWR) writes out the redo log information and the SCN to the redo log file. Until this has actually been written out, the transaction cannot complete. This is why the performance of the redo log files and the LGWR is very important.

3. Locks are released.

4. The COMMIT statement returns a successful return code to the user process.

The COMMIT operation is very important both to the stability of the data, and to the performance of the system. In order to facilitate in transactions, the savepoint operation has been introduced.

Savepoints

The savepoint allows you to save your work several times during a long and complex transaction. By creating several savepoints, you can roll back to a specific savepoint without having to roll back to the beginning of the transaction. This allows you to correct data problems in a long transaction without having to start over.

A transaction can be rolled back to any savepoint within the transaction; however, all SQL statements that have occurred since that savepoint will be rolled back as well. Take the following example:

1. Transaction begins

2. SQL

3. Savepoint A

4. SQL

5. Savepoint B

6. SQL

7. Savepoint C

8. SQL

The transaction can be rolled back to savepoint A at any time. When this occurs, all SQL statements from savepoint A to the end of the transaction are rolled back. It is not possible to roll back only between savepoint A and savepoint B.

Savepoints are created using the SAVEPOINT SQL statement as follows:

```
SAVEPOINT my_savepoint_a;
```

In order to roll back to a savepoint, use the SQL statement ROLLBACK TO SAVEPOINT, as shown next:

```
ROLLBACK TO SAVEPOINT my_savepoint_a;
```

The savepoint operation can be quite useful in complex transactions.

Rollback

The rollback operation rolls back, or undoes, all of the SQL statements that have been processed. Changes that have been made to data blocks are changed back to the original data. Rollbacks can be done on the entire transaction, or to savepoints as described earlier. When a rollback operation occurs, the data blocks are changed back to their original values using data in the undo tablespace and locks are released. Rollbacks can be called via the ROLLBACK statement or it will occur automatically during the database recovery.

Flashback Operations

Introduced in Oracle9*i* and improved upon in Oracle 10*g*, the undo retention period of transactions in the undo tablespace allows for several features that allow you to take a point-in-time view of data in the database. These include flashback query, flashback table, and flashback database. Features like this can be very valuable to both the DBA and the end user, who might need to recover some recently lost data. Flashback operations can be done as far back as the undo retention period, so don't waste any time.

Flashback Queries

Flashback queries use the read consistency feature of the Oracle Database server and the undo retention period of the undo tablespace in order to allow you to perform a point-in-time query. This is done by using the AS OF extension to the SELECT statement. The AS OF clause can take either a timestamp or an SCN, or using the BETWEEN clause can provide the data as it existed between those two events.

Here is an example of a SELECT statement that will retrieve the data that existed one hour in the past.

```
SELECT salary
FROM employees
AS OF TIMESTAMP (SYSTIMESTAMP - INTERVAL '1' hour)
WHERE last_name = 'Ellison';
```

This is a fairly useful query in retrieving a single item; however, it can become more useful in recovering an entire table that has been incorrectly modified, as shown next:

```
SELECT *
FROM employees
AS OF TIMESTAMP (SYSTIMESTAMP - INTERVAL '1' hour);
```

This data could then be used to reconstruct the table as it should be. Another way to do this would be the FLASHBACK TABLE statement; however, you would have row level control here.

FLASHBACK TABLE

The **FLASHBACK TABLE** command takes an entire table and flashes it back to a point in the past. This can be very useful for reverting a table to an earlier state, but remember, all data in that table is reverted. As with the flashback query, the FLASHBACK TABLE statement can use either a timestamp or SCN. In order to flash a table back, use the **FLASHBACK TABLE** command, as shown next:

```
FLASHBACK TABLE employees
TO TIMESTAMP (SYSTIMESTAMP - INTERVAL '1' hour);
```

Again, be careful. Since this reverts an entire table back to the original data, all changes will be lost.

FLASHBACK DATABASE

The **FLASHBACK DATABASE** command is similar to the **FLASHBACK TABLE** command except that it reverts an entire database back to its previous state. As with the two previous commands, the **FLASHBACK DATABASE** command can take either a timestamp or SCN.

Introduction to the Oracle Schema Objects

So far, you have been introduced to the Oracle data structures, both physical and logical, as well as the Oracle instance. In this chapter, both the Oracle functionality and transaction processing have been explained. So, to finish our discussion of the Oracle architecture, we'll now explore the Oracle schema objects. Even with the discussion of the schema objects, you will have learned everything about the Oracle architecture. There is still plenty more information to come, but that will be introduced later in conjunction with the specific administrative tasks that work with those components.

Tables

Tables are the basic storage object in Oracle. A table holds records or rows of data that are defined by the various fields or columns that have been defined for that table. Each table has a table name associated with it, as does each column. In this book, components of tables will be referred to as rows and columns since this is the way Oracle refers to them. Though other products may use different terminology, the components are the same. An illustration of a table is shown in Figure 3-1.

Each column is defined by a column name, a data type, and a width. The width can be either a fixed value or a variable length value for some data types. Tables are created via the CREATE TABLE statement, which defines the table name as well as the column names and widths for each. In addition, a constraint can be put on a column specifying that the data meet a particular specification. An example of a table creation is shown next.

```
CREATE TABLE demo_table
(     id          NUMBER(8) CONSTRAINT demo_id_nn NOT NULL,
      lname       VARCHAR2(40) CONSTRAINT demo_lname_nn NOT NULL,
      fname       VARCHAR2(20) CONSTRAINT demo_fname_nn NOT NULL,
      phone       VARCHAR2(20),
      email       VARCHAR2(20)
);
```

The first three columns are defined with a constraint that forces values to be non-NULL if values are inserted into those columns. The use of the CONSTRAINT clause is optional, but can be very useful to specify certain data criteria. In this case, it wouldn't make much sense to have a row inserted into the table without a first name, last name, and ID.

Partitioning

In Oracle8, the partitioning option was introduced into the database server. Partitioning allows a single table to be divided into multiple segments, thus distributing one table

Name	Age	Breed
Teller	10	Border Collie
Ada	4	Border Collie
Roz	4	Border Collie
Oliver	2	Border Collie
Bgosh	1	Akbash

FIGURE 3-1. *An Oracle table*

across them. The partitioning option allows you to spread out partitions by placing each into its own tablespace, or you can put all of the partitions into the same tablespace. Regardless of whether you split the partitions into different tablespaces or if they are all placed in the same place, they have the same advantage.

Partitioning has several different variations, as listed next:

- **Range partitioning**   Data is partitioned by defining upper and lower ranges of data for each partition.

- **Hash partitioning**   Data is partitioned using a hash function that hopefully will uniformly distribute data when there is no good manual way to do so.

- **List partitioning**   Data is partitioned by a list of values.

- **Composite partitioning**   Data is partitioned by using two of the preceding methods.

By partitioning, the amount of data accessed during certain operations might be reduced (depending on several factors). This will increase the performance of the system and reduce the load upon it.

Why Partition?

Partitioning provides a major advantage over monolithic tables. Partitioned tables can reduce the amount of data accessed during some operations, such as with aggregates and tablescans. As with any type of operation, this requires proper use of partitioning. If the data in a table were partitioned into different pieces based on a data range— such as months, for example—only the partitions needed in a SQL statement would be accessed. Let's look at an example:

If a table were partitioned into one partition per month, and a SQL statement were issued that performs an aggregation function for a set of months, only the partitions that held data for the months required in the query would be accessed. This can reduce the amount of data accessed.

Indexes

Indexes are optional structures used to help speed access to table or cluster data. Indexes are both logically and physically independent from table data. This means that the data is not affected by whether there is, or is not, an index. However, the performance of accessing data in the index is affected by the use of indexes.

Indexes are designed to speed the access of data. An index, like the index in this book, is designed to help find data in a table quickly by using structures that store information about the column or columns indexed, and what row or rows that data exists in.

With Oracle 10*g*, there are several different types of indexes. These indexes are designed differently and serve unique purposes that work well with various types of data. These indexes are

■ **B-tree indexes** The B-tree index uses a tree structure to traverse the index while zeroing in on the requested data.

■ **Bitmap indexes** A bitmap index keeps a bitmap of each unique column or set of column values.

■ **Bitmap join index** This is a bitmap of join values on two or more tables.

■ **Function index** This is an index built on a user-specified (manual) index function.

Indexes are covered in more detail in Chapter 17.

Views

Views are an abstraction of data in one or more underlying tables or views in the Oracle Database. A view is a representation that appears to SQL statements as a table, but in fact is a definition of the representation of that table or tables that was created with a SQL statement. A view can be a subset of an underlying table, or a superset made up of a join between two or more tables. A view takes the output of a query and treats it as a table. There are two different types of views that Oracle supports: the standard view and the materialized view.

Standard Views
Normal views are SQL statements that define a subset or superset of data within a table. These views don't actually store any data. When the view is used within a query, the SQL statement that defines the view is merged with the calling SQL statement in order to create a merged SQL statement allowing the underlying data to be accessed.

Materialized Views
A materialized view is also made up of a SQL statement on underlying table and/or view data; however, a materialized view actually stores data and takes up space on the system. This type of view can be used to store aggregate data such as sums, products, and so on. When these types of functions are run against a materialized view, the aggregate data can be quickly accessed.

Sequences

Oracle includes a built-in sequence generator that automatically provides a sequence of numbers. This feature has been provided by Oracle to enable faster performance and better concurrence for applications that need a sequence of numbers. Because of the way Oracle has created the sequence, it has high performance. Also, because of the design, the sequence allows for many processes to get sequence numbers simultaneously with no duplications.

Clusters

The term cluster is very overused these days. The Oracle table cluster is a structure within Oracle that allows for multiple tables to be stored together based on a join key. This object allows for quick access to the joined table data, since it is stored together. In addition, within the cluster you can reference and access the clustered tables independently.

Synonyms

A synonym is simply an alias for another object in the database. A synonym can be an alias for a table, view, materialized view, or other Oracle object including packages and procedures.

Summary

This chapter began where the previous chapter left off, discussing the way Oracle works internally to perform reads and writes and transaction processing. Along the way, read consistency and the Oracle schema objects were also explored.

Now that the basics of Oracle and Linux have been covered, this book will proceed to explain more of the administrative and design tasks required of the Oracle / Linux DBA.

PART
II

Deploying Oracle 10g
on Linux

CHAPTER
4

Sizing Oracle 10g
on Linux Systems

ne of the most important tasks that you must perform when designing an Oracle system is sizing. *Sizing* is the act of determining the amount of hardware resources you must configure for your system. It is closely related to another subject: *capacity planning*. This chapter will begin by introducing these topics and will explain a bit of the mathematics behind sizing and capacity planning. Some of the basic performance characteristics of different components of your computer system will be covered as well.

Although sizing and capacity planning are closely related, there are some significant differences in their end goal. Sizing is the estimation of the hardware requirements necessary to process a workload within specified parameters. These parameters are often known as the *service-level agreement* (*SLA*). The service-level agreement is a contract between the customers of the system and the department that is in charge of managing the system. It is usually written in such a way that the response times of certain transactions must fall within a designated limit. Service-level agreements will be covered in more detail later in this chapter.

Capacity planning is different from sizing in that capacity planning is the art and science of determining when an existing system will reach its capacity and what new hardware might need to be added to avoid the consequences of reaching that limit. This chapter is different from other chapters in this book in that you will finally get to use some of the mathematics you learned in high school and college.

An Introduction to Sizing

In any system, there are basic fundamental limits. As the utilization of the system nears those limits, the way things operate starts to change. This is mainly due to the fact that as you near a fundamental limitation of a resource, queuing begins to occur. When you have reached the fundamental limit of the resource, queuing is guaranteed. Once queuing is happening, response times will increase. In this section of the chapter, we will look at capacity and queuing as well as service-level agreements and performance metrics.

Sizing for Peak Utilization and Steady-State Utilization

When sizing a system, you must look at both peak utilization and steady-state utilization. The *peak-utilization period* refers to the period of time that causes the most stress on the system. The peak-utilization period might occur at a certain time of day, or at a certain time of the week, month, or quarter. In many financial systems, the peak utilization period comes at the end of month, quarter, and year. It is often necessary to size a system for the peak-utilization period, since that is when the most response time problems will occur.

The *steady-state period* is the time of day when the load on the system is fairly constant. By definition, the load on the system during the steady-state period is less than the load on the system during the peak-utilization period.

The Peak-Utilization Period

The *peak-utilization period* is the time of day when the system is experiencing its highest level of load. It is normal that there are one or more times during the day when the utilization of the system exceeds the normal utilization of the system. This can be due to several factors, including the following:

- **Work habits**   Employees tend to arrive at work around the same time, log into the system, and begin their work. This occurrence happens at specific times during the day, such as in the morning and after lunch.

- **Scheduled tasks**   This might include batch updates, backups, and daily reports.

- **Nonscheduled tasks**   Many times users will submit large reports when you least expect them.

If you were to size your system to perform optimally during the steady-state period, you might find that during the peak-utilization period the acceptable response times for operations are exceeded. Whether or not this violates your service-level agreement depends on the particular agreement.

The Steady-State Utilization Period

The *steady-state period* is the time of day when the load on the system is fairly constant. This does not necessarily mean that the load is always constant at this particular time, but typically it is. During steady-state, the utilization of the system is less than the utilization during peak periods and should be much less than the capacity of the system. The performance during steady-state is not usually an issue if the system is tuned to handle the load during peak utilization.

One of the goals of grid computing is to redeploy systems into different tasks when it is necessary to achieve the required capacity. Grid computing is beginning to address this and will improve on it as the technology improves.

Service-Level Agreements

A *service-level agreement* (*SLA*) is a contract or agreement between the provider of the service(s) (the IT department) and the customer(s) (the user community). This SLA is used to define an acceptable level of performance for the system. The service-level agreement can take many forms, but the purpose of the SLA is always the same, to guarantee a level of service to the users and supply a metric to the IT department so they know if they are providing acceptable service.

Although many companies have implemented service-level agreements, many have not. Even among those with a service-level agreement, often there isn't sufficient monitoring—or enough analysis of that monitoring—to know if the SLA is being met. When no SLA is present, or the current SLA is not being monitored, there are frequently performance problems.

The SLA Customer Point of View

The SLA should be carefully negotiated by both sides. From the customer point of view, the SLA should define uptime requirements and response time criteria that are required to complete the necessary work. In addition to these criteria, the SLA will also usually include requirements. This is the customer's chance to specify the minimum requirements that the system must meet.

The term customer is used to describe the users of the system. Thus, a customer of the IT department might actually be another department within the same company.

The SLA IT Point of View

The IT department should negotiate an SLA that is both feasible and that can be implemented within budgetary constraints. The SLA should include scheduled and some unscheduled downtime, as well as peak and nonpeak response time criteria. It is up to the IT department to build in enough downtime for upgrades and periodic maintenance.

SLA Samples

An example of an SLA would include requirements that certain transactions be completed within a designated period 90 percent of the time, and within a longer period 100 percent of the time. It would also include uptime requirements, scheduling requirements, and special event requirements. Let's look at a few items that might be included in an SLA.

Response Time Criteria   Your SLA might include a table such as the following:

Transaction	90% Response Time	100% Response Time
Trans 1	1 sec	1.5 sec
Trans 2	3 sec	5 sec
Drop-down menus	1 sec	1.2 sec
Reports	10 sec	15 sec

This is purely a sample of what you might have within the SLA. Notice that both individual transactions and transaction types can both be represented here.

Notification Schedules   Your SLA might also include notification schedules such as the following:

All planned downtime will be reported to the call center 14 days in advance. All emergency downtime will be reported to the call center 15 minutes before the system is shut down (if possible).

From the IT department perspective, you might require the following:

The number of users added to the system will be provided to the IT department 30 days before those increases in users begins.

This will allow you to plan ahead.

Uptime Requirements   The SLA might also include uptime requirements such as:

The system will be up except for 4 hours of planned downtime during which maintenance will be performed between 1:00 A.M. and 5:00 A.M. on the first Sunday of the month.

NOTE
Don't forget to plan some downtime for maintenance. I have found that if the user community is aware of the downtime and is properly notified, they don't usually mind too much.

SLA Notes   The service-level agreement can be a very useful tool, both from a customer and a provider standpoint. By agreeing ahead of time and documenting the level of service required, it is much easier to achieve that level of service. If you don't have a goal, you can never reach it.

System Resources, Capacity, and Queuing

Computer systems, like most things, have fundamental resource limitations. Resources such as CPU time have very specific limitations that cannot be exceeded. When you get to 100-percent CPU utilization, it is obvious that you cannot use any more CPU time. Other resources, such as I/O operations, do not have a limitation that is quite so obvious as CPU resources, but they do have one. Network utilization also has limitations that are similar to those involving I/O.

As this fundamental maximum utilization of a component is neared, queuing begins to occur. Once you have reached the maximum capacity of the resource, queuing is a certainty.

Why is queuing important? It's important because the response time of an access to a resource is equal to the service time (how long it takes to process) of the resource, plus the time the job spends in a queue waiting (wait time) on the resource to service your request. In mathematical terms, the following equation applies:

```
Response Time = (Queue Length * Service Time) +
Service Time
```

Thus the response time is equal to the time it takes for your job to be serviced plus the time it takes for all the jobs ahead of you to be serviced. As you get closer to the physical limitations of the resource, the chance of queuing increases. Once you reach the physical limitation of the resource, you are guaranteed to have queuing, thus your response time increases. In fact, as you get close to the physical limit of the resource, the chance of queuing increases exponentially, as shown in Figure 4-1.

You can see that as the utilization nears the limitation of the resource, the queue length can increase greatly. The point where the response time begins to increase dramatically is called the *knee of the curve* and is at about 80 percent of maximum. Try to use your system so as not to exceed this knee of the curve. This can be accomplished by adding more hardware in order to increase the maximum capacity.

CPU Performance and Queuing

As every CPU cycle begins to be taken up, your particular thread of execution is more and more likely to have to wait for resources to become available. As you reach 100-percent utilization, you are guaranteed to have to wait. As mentioned earlier, this will increase the time it takes for your job to run since it must wait for the processor to become available before it can run your task. This queuing increases exponentially, as shown in Figure 4-1.

CPU utilization is an interesting component to watch for several reasons, which are described next:

- CPU has a finite limit. In a second, a fixed number of CPU cycles are available for processing.

- The amount of work done by the CPUs will vary based on the clock speed, bus speed, and caches available in the CPU.

- Many systems allow you to have more than two CPUs. This allows you to scale your system by adding more resources.

CPU utilization is a great performance metric because of its finite limits and its representation of the workload on the system. It is great for comparing the same system over time, but difficult for comparing unlike systems.

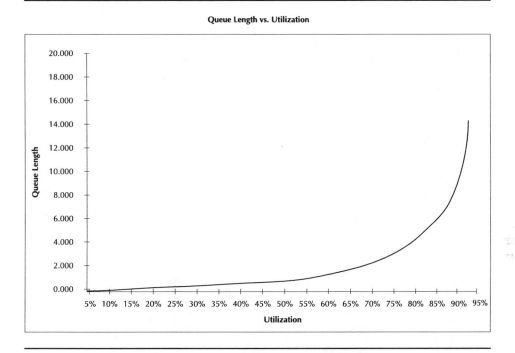

FIGURE 4-1. *Queue Length vs. Utilization*

I/O Performance and Queuing

So what does this mean in the real world? For a 15K RPM SCSI disk drive, the theoretical maximum random access performance is about 165 IOPS (I/Os per second). In order to run at a rate that offers good response times (< 20ms), you should operate at no more than 75 percent of maximum performance, or at about 125 IOPS.

As you can see from Figure 4-2, the I/O response time or *latency* increases as you reach the maximum capacity of the disk drive. By overdriving the I/O subsystem, you can actually see very high I/O latencies. I have personally seen systems where the I/O latency is over 500ms (1/2 second). These response times can cause significant performance problems in your Oracle database such as slow response times, blocking, and latching problems.

When running at normal levels (< 75-percent utilization), you might expect latencies to be anywhere from 6ms to 20ms. Let's assume 10ms for our case. If the disk drives are overtaxed and latencies are at 100ms, the total query time could be ten times the query time at the lower rate. Thus, a decision support query that takes a minute to run might actually take ten minutes due to overdriving the I/O subsystem. Hopefully, you can begin to see now why sizing is so important.

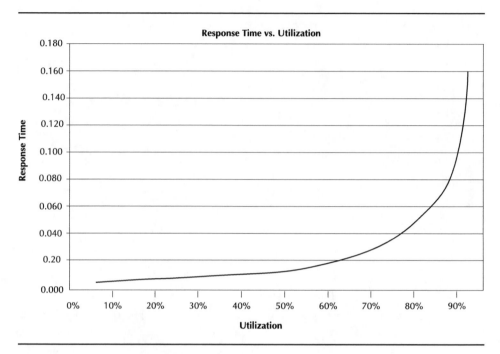

FIGURE 4-2. *Response Time vs. Utilization*

Network Performance

Unlike the I/O subsystem, the network does not queue. When a network packet is sent, if another packet is sent at the same time, they both must be re-sent. This is known as a collision. Like the I/O subsystem, as you get closer to the physical limitations of the network, the number of collisions increases, as well as the queuing. As with many components of the computer system, as you reach the limits, the response time increases exponentially.

Memory

Memory is a little different in that there is no queuing and there are no collisions, but as you overdrive the system it will run out of physical memory. The more you push the memory subsystem, the less RAM you have available. Once you have used up all of the physical RAM, some of the pages in memory are moved off to disk. This is known as paging. Paging and swapping are similar, but not quite the same. In some operating systems, an entire process is moved in and out of memory for execution. This is known as swapping. Linux uses paging, where 4K pages are moved in and out of memory as needed. Because of the history of Linux and UNIX, the area that is used for this paging activity is known as the swap partition, even though it is used for paging rather than swapping.

Paging in a Virtual Memory System

You probably don't realize it, but if you use a PC running Windows, you are using a virtual memory system. If you have ever wondered why an application that has already been run, but hasn't been accessed in a while, seems to take a long time to respond, take a look at the disk drive LED. You might see that there is a great deal of disk activity going on.

If you see this disk activity, then you are probably experiencing paging. PC applications typically use much more memory than you actually have on the system. So, the next time you are experiencing slow performance, take a look at the disk light.

The kernel process, kswapd, is the daemon used to move pages in and out of memory. If you were to run ps or top, you would see the kswapd process. This process is also known as the pageout daemon. When performing system and Oracle tuning, paging should be avoided at all costs. If your system is paging, most other performance problems should be considered secondary until the paging situation is resolved. In a normally running system, you should see little or no paging/swapping.

Although technically the process of moving pages in and out of memory as needed is called paging, because of history and tradition, this process is referred to as swapping. In order to keep with standard Linux terminology, I will refer to it as swapping as well.

Since physical memory is hundreds of times faster than disk I/O, you can understand why performance drops off dramatically when swapping occurs. From a performance standpoint, it is very important to configure your system's memory so that swapping does not occur. This is one reason we prefer not to run other applications on Oracle database server systems.

Metrics

When monitoring a system, it is important to put metrics in a place that can be used to measure the system. Metrics are the measurable values you have chosen to gauge how well the system is working. Many different metrics can be used. What type of metrics you choose will vary based on what your concerns are about the system and how it is working. Some examples of different types of metrics include the following:

Metric	Description
CPU utilization	CPU utilization is a great metric to use if you're concerned about reaching the capacity of your system. CPU is good because there is a set maximum. You can only use 100 percent of the system's CPU capacity.
I/O utilization	I/O utilization in IOPS (I/Os per second) is a good measurement because you can calculate the maximum value you don't want to exceed. Our rule of thumb is that you should not exceed 125 IOPS per disk drive.

Metric	Description
Online users	Knowing the number of online users will not necessarily tell you if you are exceeding the capacity of your system or not, but it is a good measurement of what load is being put on the system. It is also a very useful variable for calculating future load.
Response Time	If you have the capability to measure the response time of transactions on your system, you will find it to be the most useful metric. However, response time often varies with respect to the number of simultaneous users, so you want to make sure you are taking scaling into account here. This can also be used to judge how well the service-level agreement is being met.

There are only a few metrics that can be used to measure the utilization of your system. Some examples are shown in Figures 4-3 and 4-4.

By determining which metrics are right for you and monitoring those metrics, you will be able to monitor how the system is doing as well as interpolate when the system might run out of resources in the future. Metrics are also a great way to report to management on the state of the system.

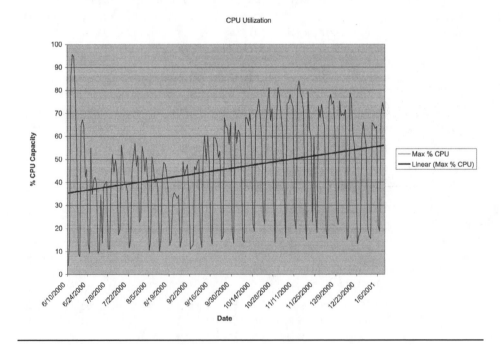

FIGURE 4-3. *CPU utilization as a performance metric*

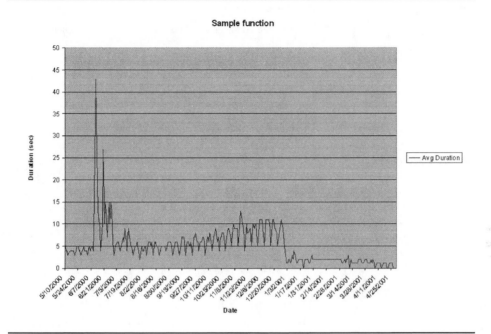

FIGURE 4-4. *Response time as a performance metric*

Oracle Sizing

Oracle sizing involves setting tunable parameters in such a way that Oracle resources allow separate operations to function at various levels of users, processes, and activity. Two different types of Oracle parameters are used to size the Oracle instance. The first type of parameter sets absolute limits that cannot be exceeded and affects how the Oracle instance uses resources. The second type of parameter might affect Oracle performance, but it is not a set limit that cannot be exceeded.

Limitation Parameters

The parameters that limit resources are usually fairly easy to size with the needs of the system, since they affect things such as maximum number of sessions, maximum number of processes, and so on. Let's look at a list of some of the most common of these parameters.

Parameter	Description
CIRCUITS	The maximum number of virtual circuits available for network sessions.
DISPATCHERS	This parameter can be used to specify the maximum number of dispatchers.

Parameter	Description
DB_FILES	The maximum number of database files that can be opened for an instance.
LICENSE_MAX_SESSIONS	Specifies the maximum number of sessions that have been licensed, and thus the maximum number of sessions allowed to run on the system.
LICENSE_MAX_USERS	Specifies the maximum number of users that are allowed to exist in the database.
LICENSE_SESSIONS_WARNING	This is the value where alerts are issued indicating that you will soon reach the maximum number of sessions allowed.
MAX_DISPATCHERS	Specifies the maximum number of dispatchers that can be running simultaneously. You should use DISPATCHERS instead since this is only maintained for backwards compatibility.
MAX_SHARED_SERVERS	The maximum number of shared server processes that can run simultaneously.
OPEN_CURSORS	The maximum number of cursors that can be open at any one time.
OPEN_LINKS	The maximum number of connections to remote databases that can be opened in one session.
PARALLEL_MAX_SERVERS	The maximum number of parallel query servers that can run simultaneously.
PROCESSES	Specifies the maximum number of OS processes that can attach to the Oracle instance.
SGA_MAX_SIZE	Specifies the maximum size of the SGA for the life of the instance.
TRANSACTIONS	Specifies the maximum number of concurrent transactions.

These parameters set hard limits that cannot be exceeded and do not offer much in the way of tuning for performance. However, they are very useful in setting limits so that Oracle does not allow more resources to be used than are allocated.

Resource Parameters

Unlike the parameter that set the hard limits for adding users, the resource parameters are tunables that can limit system resources. These can dramatically affect system performance. They include parameters such as:

Parameter	Description
DB_nK_CACHE_SIZE	The size of the various nonstandard buffer caches.
DB_BLOCK_BUFFERS (obsolete)	The number of database block buffers in the buffer cache. This parameter has become obsolete sinceOracle9i.
DB_CACHE_SIZE	The size of the default buffer cache.
DB_KEEP_CACHE_SIZE	The size of the keep cache in the buffer pool.
DB_RECYCLE_CACHE_SIZE	The size of the recycle cache in the buffer pool.
JAVA_POOL_SIZE	Memory used for Java stored procedures.

Parameter	Description
LARGE_POOL_SIZE	The size of the large pool. This is used for shared session memory, parallel execution memory, and disk I/O buffers.
LOG_BUFFER	The size of the redo log buffer. The redo log buffer is used for caching redo entries until the log writer process can write them out.
PGA_AGGREGATE_TARGET	This specifies the target size for PGA memory and thus makes SORT_AREA_SIZE and HASH_AREA_SIZE obsolete.
SESSION_CACHED_CURSORS	This parameter specifies the number of session cursors that can be cached in memory.
SHARED_POOL_SIZE	The size of the shared pool. The shared pool contains the library cache and the data dictionary.

These parameters will affect how the system performs based on a particular workload. Parameters such as the DB_CACHE_SIZE will help some applications perform better, and with other applications it will not help much at all. This chapter is not about performance tuning, but about sizing.

These parameters directly affect the size of the system that you must configure. When the value of these parameters are increased, more system resources are consumed, thus it is necessary to properly size both the parameters as well as the system. Setting parameters too high can often be worse than setting them too low. This is especially true where memory is involved. If Oracle tries to use more than the available physical memory, swapping will occur, thus adversely affecting system performance. In addition, if some parameters are set too high, the Oracle instance might even fail to start.

In Chapter 2, the Oracle architecture was presented to you. Within the Oracle architecture there are two main areas of memory usage: the SGA and the PGA. The SGA memory allocation is determined by many of the Oracle initialization parameters such as DB_CACHE_SIZE, SHARED_POOL_SIZE and LOG_BUFFER, as well as a number of other parameters. With 9*i* and above the SGA can grow from the startup size, determined by DBA_CACHE_SIZE, etc., up to MAX_SGA_SIZE if this is set, and it is important to make sure that this is the value used for sizing, since it can push a non-paging system to start paging.

In addition to the SGA, there is memory used by each individual process, including the shared server processes and parallel query processes. This memory is variable, based on how much memory is needed at any time. This is the primary area where you can run into problems. It is because of this that Oracle has changed the way PGA memory is allocated.

In the past, you would set parameters such as SORT_AREA_SIZE and HASH_AREA_SIZE, which would define the maximum amount of memory that each individual user process could use. Depending on how much memory each process needed and how many processes there were, this memory could vary and sometimes become quite large.

With Oracle9*i*, a new parameter was introduced. PGA_AGGREGATE_TARGET sets the optimal amount of memory for all user processes to use. When more processes are running, each one is allocated less memory. This greatly reduced the difficulty in sizing Oracle memory.

With Oracle 10*g*, you can simply take the amount of system memory available, subtract the size of the SGA, and allocate the remainder of the memory to the PGAs. This is much easier than it was with previous versions of Oracle.

Hardware Sizing

Hardware sizing involves choosing the right amount of hardware for your Oracle system. Sizing is not an exact science, but is part science, part art, and part intuition. When sizing the system, it is necessary to look at the use of the system, the amount of resources necessary to perform well and the amount of growth that the system should be able to sustain without requiring additional hardware. There are several main areas of hardware sizing that must be done. They include CPU sizing, memory sizing, and sizing the I/O subsystem.

CPU Sizing

The number and speed of CPUs have an effect on how fast tasks complete in the system. Increasing the number of CPUs that you put in your system will increase the performance of tasks if there is sufficient concurrency. If there is only one thread of processing happening in the system, it can only run on one CPU. Adding CPUs will not cause that one task to complete faster, however, it will only allow multiple concurrent tasks to finish in a faster time.

As you learned earlier in this chapter, queuing can occur on CPUs when processes must wait on other processes to complete before the CPU is available. By adding more CPUs, you create more opportunity for processes to run. If one CPU has 100 percent of CPU time available for processing, a system with four CPUs has 400 percent time available.

Systems where there is a lot of concurrency or many processes running at the same time can greatly benefit from multiple processors. In addition, systems where queries can be parallelized with the Oracle parallel query option can also benefit from multiple CPUs.

In addition to the number of CPUs, you should also look for the size of the CPU cache. In multiprocessor systems, a larger cache can help avoid cache misses, and therefore reduce bus utilization. This will help performance. When running Oracle, it is usually better to opt for a CPU with a larger cache, even if it means getting a slower chip.

Memory Sizing

The amount of memory available to Oracle in a system determines how many and which types of user processes and queries can run efficiently. The amount of memory needed and the amount of memory utilized at any particular time is very dependent on the type and number of operations being done during that period, and as such is very difficult to predict.

So, what do you do in order to size the memory for the type of application that you are running? Well, there are several ways to do this. The easy way out is to simply get as much memory as you can afford and allocate it to the Oracle processes and SGA. On one hand, this is cheating, since you haven't really sized the memory subsystem at all. However, since memory is relatively cheap compared to memory prices a few years ago, this is now a practical thing to do.

Remember that the memory Oracle uses can actually be thought of as two separate pieces. The SGA is kept in shared memory, which is governed by Linux kernel parameters that limit the size of shared memory. Shared memory is allocated out of a special pool of memory and is not swappable. The Oracle processes memory, however, can be swapped out. When considering how big to make the SGA, remember that the Oracle processes can require a large amount of memory. The more processes you have running, the more memory they will consume.

Keep in mind that with 32-bit processor-based systems, it is not usually very efficient to purchase more than 4GB of RAM since this is all the memory that a 32-bit processor can use without using memory extensions that have a lot of overhead. Going from 4GB to 5GB of RAM might be slower, due to the overhead involved in using memory above 4GB, but using 8GB of RAM will be faster than 4GB of RAM.

In addition, with the PGA_AGGREGATE_TARGET parameter you can now dial in the amount of memory used by all of the processes, thus taking advantage of available memory without running the risk of paging.

If you are not using Oracle9*i* or later, the manual method of sizing memory is to monitor the system and try to interpolate the amount of memory necessary with additional processes being used. For example, take a snapshot of the memory being used with 100 users connected and then again with 200 users connected. This should allow you to estimate the amount of memory used per user. However, the PGA_AGGREGATE_TARGET parameter will nullify use of this method, since the sum of all PGA memory should remain constant regardless of the number of users.

I/O Subsystem Sizing

The I/O subsystem has unique sizing characteristics due to the nature of the makeup of the components. Why is this important? A properly configured I/O subsystem will allow Oracle to perform optimally. A poorly configured I/O subsystem can easily become a bottleneck and can severely affect performance. Let's look at the I/O subsystem starting with the basic component—the disk drive—and then look at RAID controllers and RAID levels.

The Disk Drive

The basic component of the I/O subsystem is the disk drive, also commonly known as the hard disk drive or hard disk. Anyone who has anything to do with computers knows what a disk drive is. In this section, you will be given a brief overview of how the disk drive operates and what the limiting factors are.

Later in this chapter, you will see how disk drives are used to create RAID arrays and how the disk drive performance limits interact with the RAID controller performance characteristics. By understanding these limitations, you can determine if you have a properly sized and configured I/O subsystem and how to solve any problems you might have.

The disk drive is one of the few mechanical components in your computer's system. Being a mechanical component presents several challenges. Since the disk drive is made up of several motors and servos, some of which are running at very high speeds, it can and does generate a great deal of heat. Because of this and various frictional forces, the disk drive is one of the most likely components to fail in your system. In fact, all disk drive specifications tell you the mean time between failures (MTBF).

Since it is a mechanical component, there are certain laws of physics involved in its operation that cannot be broken. This results in certain performance limitations that cannot be altered. Before we get into these limitations, let's review how a disk drive works.

Disk drives are made up of one or more disks, which we refer to as platters. A platter is a round disk that actually holds the data magnetically. Data is written around the platter in tracks just like a CD or LP (anyone remember those?). A data track is in turn made up of individual chunks of data called sectors. A typical sector is 512 bytes. A platter is shown in Figure 4-5.

A disk armature rides above the disk drive and has a component on the end of it called the head. The head is used to read data from the sectors. This armature can only move radially across the surface of the platter. The disk drive relies on the rotation of the platter to move the requested data under the disk head. The movement of the armature and head over the platter is referred to as disk seeks. The movement of the sectors under the head is referred to as rotation.

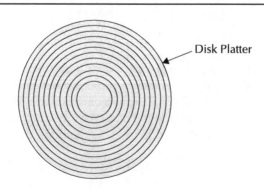

FIGURE 4-5. *A disk platter*

In order for a requested sector to be read, the armature must first seek to the proper track. Once it is at the correct track, the disk must wait for the requested sector to rotate under the head. The time it takes for the drive to seek is called the seek time. The time it takes for the data to rotate under the head is known as rotational latency. Seek time and rotational latency are shown in Figure 4-6. Later in this section, both of these concepts will be covered in greater detail.

A typical disk drive is made up of more than one platter and both sides of the platter are used. These platters are stacked on top of each other and have multiple heads connected to a single armature. Since all of the heads are stacked on top of each other and can read and/or write simultaneously, it is more efficient to do this. Thus, a disk drive will read and/or write multiple sectors simultaneously. Remember that both sides of the platter are used.

The stack of tracks used to store data is called a cylinder. By allowing all of the heads to be used at once, a disk drive can access and write data much faster than moving to each sector individually. Disk cylinders are shown in Figure 4-7.

In order to understand the performance of a disk drive, you must understand the performance of seeks and rotational latency.

Seek Time   A seek is the motion of the disk armature to move from one track to another, and the seek time is the time it takes for the armature to move from one track to another. Seeks can be divided into three different types: full disk seeks, track-to-track seeks, and random seeks. Although functionally the same, they are categorized separately due to the different performance characteristics.

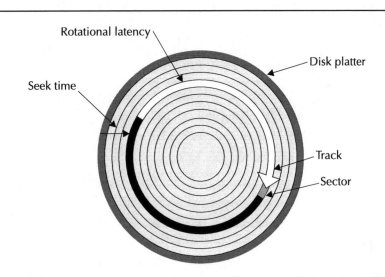

FIGURE 4-6.   *Seek time and rotational latency*

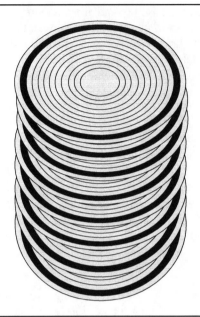

FIGURE 4-7. *Disk cylinders*

Full disk seeks occur when the armature must move from the outermost track to the innermost track or vice versa. Track-to-track seeks involve the armature moving from one track to an adjacent track, hence the name track-to-track seek. Random seeks are somewhere between the other two. This is the type of seek that we are most concerned about, since full disk seeks rarely, if ever, occur.

The full disk seek time of a high performance SCSI disk drive is approximately 7.5 ms for reads and 8 ms for writes. Although full disk seeks rarely occur, the full disk seek time is provided in order to give you a worst-case scenario.

The random seek time for a high performance SCSI disk drive is approximately 3.9 ms for reads and 4.5 ms for writes. This is the type of seek that is very likely to cause performance problems.

The track-to-track seek time for this same SCSI disk drive is 0.5 ms for reads and 0.7 ms for writes. You can see that the track-to-track seek time is considerably less than the random seek times.

Rotational Latency   Once the armature has completed, the seek to the track where the data resides must then wait for the platter to spin underneath it to where the data resides. The time it takes for the data to move under the head is called the rotational latency. The rotational latency primarily depends on how fast the disk drive is spinning. Thus, a 15,000-RPM disk drive has a smaller rotational latency than a 10,000-RPM disk drive.

The average rotational latency is approximately half of the maximum rotational latency. The maximum rotational latency can be derived from the rotational velocity. For a 15,000-RPM disk drive, the maximum rotational latency is

$$\text{Max Rotational Latency} = (1 / 15{,}000\text{-rpm}) \times (1 \text{ min} / 60 \text{ sec})$$
$$= 1.11 \ \mu \ (\text{usec})$$

As you can see, even the maximum rotational latency is minute compared to the random, or even the track-to-track seek time. In fact, in the entire I/O subsystem, nothing comes close to the random seek time in terms of latencies. If we estimate the average rotational latency as half of the maximum rotational latency, we get about 0.55 μ.

Disk Drive Performance
The time it takes to read data from a disk drive is made up of the accumulation of several different functions. These functions are

- The seek time
- The rotational latency
- The transfer time

In addition to the disk drive latencies, the data must then be transferred across the I/O bus to the controller, and controller latency will be incurred as well. The latencies external to the disk drive will be covered later in this chapter in the section on RAID controllers.

In order to get a more accurate estimate of the performance of various disk drives, let's do some calculations. Once we know the specification of a disk drive and know a little about the type of I/Os being done, we can get a pretty good idea of the performance of the disk drive.

Reading the Disk Spec Sheet
The first step in determining the performance of a particular disk drive is to look at the disk drive specification sheet. This specification will provide the information you need

to calculate the maximum and optimal performance of the disk drive. The specific performance depends on what types of I/Os are being performed.

A typical disk drive specification sheet will contain the following information and looks something like that seen in Table 4-1.

In addition, there is a wealth of information about operating conditions, such as min and max temperature, humidity, and so on, as well as power requirements. This example is not intended as a complete disk drive specification, only a sample.

From the information we have about this disk drive, we can make some calculations on I/O rates and the maximum and optimal performance. This will be divided into performance for both random and sequential I/Os.

Specification	Value	Specification	Value
Manufacturer	Acme disk	Sectors per track	345
Model name	Big disk	MTBF (mean time between failures)	1,200,000 hours
Model number	12345	Internal transfer rate (min)	385 Mbits/sec
Physical characteristics	Height, width, weight	Internal transfer rate (max)	508 Mbits/sec
Formatted capacity	18GB	External (I/O) transfer rate (max)	160 Mbytes/sec
Interface type	Ultra SCSI 160	Average seek time, read	3.9 msec
Buffer cache size	4096 Kbytes	Average seek time, write	4.5 msec
Rotational speed	15,000 RPM	Track-to-track seek, read	0.5 msec
Number of disks (physical)	5	Track-to-track seek, write	0.7 msec
Number of heads (physical)	10	Full disk seek, read	7.5 msec
Total cylinders	10,377	Full disk seek, write	8 msec
Total tracks	103,770	Average rotational latency	2 msec
Bytes per sector	512		

TABLE 4-1.   *The Disk Drive Specification of a Fictitious Disk Drive (courtesy of the Seagate web site)*

Disk I/O Capacity

As a database performance consultant, I see a number of different types of performance problems. One of the commonest problems is insufficient I/O capacity. It is quite common for the number and size of disk drives to be chosen purely by the amount of space needed. This is a common mistake.

As you see from this chapter, a physical disk drive can only perform a certain number of I/Os before it becomes overloaded and latencies begin to increase. Increased latencies can be the root cause of excessive resource contentions and slow response times.

In most cases, it will provide better overall performance to configure your system with four GB disk drives rather than one GB disk drive. I say most cases, since there are situations where the I/O subsystem is simply not a problem, regardless of the number of disk drives. By sizing your system for both performance and space, you can achieve optimal performance.

Sequential I/O Performance

When accessing data sequentially, seek time is not as much of an issue as when you are accessing data randomly. The time it takes to do a sequential I/O can be determined by the following formula:

Seconds per I/O = (Track-to-Track Seek Time)+(Average Rotational Latency)+(Transfer Time)

= (0.6 msec)+(0.5* msec)+(apx0.010µsec)

= 1.1 msec (apx.)

* The value of 0.5 msec was given for rotational latency rather than the 2 msec specified in the spec sheet because with sequential I/O adjacent sectors, read and rotation latency only come into effect occasionally.

Here we are assuming that there is a track-to-track seek between each I/O. Since the specification sheet tells us that there are, on average, 345 sectors per track, this is unlikely if you are doing truly sequential I/O. However, when depending on the Oracle block size and multiblock I/O, the effects of this are unknown.

Assuming our calculation is correct and it takes approximately 2.6 msec to perform one sequential I/O, the maximum number of sequential I/Os that can be performed on this disk drive is calculated by the following formula:

I/Os per second or IOPS = 1 / (seconds per I/O)

= 1 / (2.6 msec / 1000 msec per sec)

= 384 IOPS

This number is approximate, since we don't really know how many I/Os require the track-to-track seek. So we can say that at least 307 IOPS can be performed sequentially.

Random I/O Performance

The calculation for random I/Os is more important, since random I/O performance is one of the commonest performance problems that occurs in an Oracle system. We know that random seeks occur during random I/O operation, and most I/O operations done by Oracle are random in nature. As with the sequential I/O, the time it takes for a random I/O to occur is determined by the same formula:

Seconds per I/O = (Random Seek Time)+(Average Rotational Latency)+(Transfer Time)
= (4.3 msec)+(2.0 msec)+(apx0.010μsec)
= 6.3 msec (apx.)

Here we are assuming that there is a random seek between each I/O. In addition, we are assuming a mixture of reads and writes where 4.3 msec is used rather than 3.9 msec for reads and 4.5 msec for writes.

Assuming our calculation is correct and it takes approximately 6.3 msec to perform one random I/O, the maximum number of random I/Os that can be performed on this disk drive is calculated by the following formula:

I/Os per second (IOPS) = 1 / (seconds per I/O)
= 1 / (6.3 msec / 1000 msec per sec)
= 158 IOPS

But this doesn't give us the entire story. If you have ever studied queuing theory, you will remember that as you get close to reaching the bandwidth limit of a device, the chances of queuing will increase. So, what does this mean? As you get closer to the limit of 158 IOPS per second, even though this number is the maximum rate that the drive can do without queuing, there is a greater chance of queuing and thus the I/Os will begin to take longer and longer.

This queuing is illustrated in the chart in Figure 4-8.

You can see that the closer you get to the maximum theoretical performance, the longer the disk latencies get. Since Oracle performance is very sensitive to I/O latencies, it is important to not overdrive the I/Os.

NOTE
A disk drive only handles one I/O at a time. If the disk drive is busy handling an I/O when a request for another I/O comes into the controller, this request is queued until the first I/O is completed. Thus it is possible, and common, to experience queuing even at low I/O rates.

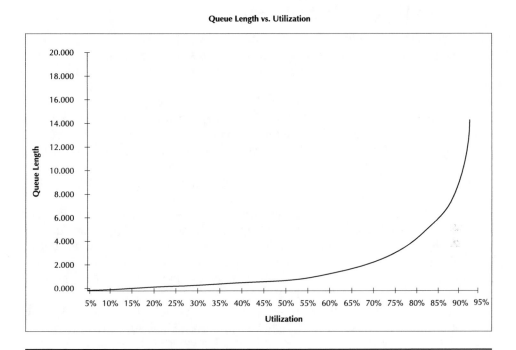

FIGURE 4-8.   *I/O queuing*

In order to achieve this, we would optimally want to run the disk drives at the point on the chart known as the knee of the curve. This is the point where the slope of the curve starts to move sharply upwards and occurs at about 80 percent of capacity. Thus, random I/Os should optimally not exceed 126 I/Os per second in this example.

Additional Considerations   In the previous two sections, you have seen that theoretically a disk drive can access data at the following rates:

- Sequential I/Os: 384 IOPS
- Random I/Os: 158 IOPS

In addition to the latencies incurred by the disk drive itself, other latencies can be incurred by the I/O controller and the operating system device driver. This additional latency can be small or large depending on how busy the device is. Since this additional latency is dependent on specifics of the I/O subsystem, it will not be covered here; however, you should be aware of it.

RAID Disk Subsystems

There are several different types of I/O subsystems you can use with your computer systems. For database servers, RAID systems are probably the most popular. RAID systems come in a variety of different types and configurations, as you will see in this section.

The acronym RAID stands for Redundant Array of Inexpensive Disks. RAID I/O subsystems serve two main purposes. The first is to provide a fault-tolerant I/O subsystem. A fault-tolerant I/O subsystem is one that can survive the failure of a component in the system (usually a disk drive) without incurring any loss of data. The second purpose of a RAID subsystem is to allow multiple individual disk drives to be configured into a larger virtual disk drive. This is done for both the ease of administration and performance reasons.

The RAID subsystem can combine two or more disk drives into one larger logical disk drive by using disk striping. Disk striping takes the logical disk layout, and using different algorithms, places that data on two or more disk drives. Disk striping does not make a logical disk drive fault-tolerant, but it can improve disk access times by spreading I/Os among multiple disks. In addition, disk striping can be combined with fault-tolerant features of the controller.

Most RAID controllers offer a number of different options for configuring logical disk volumes using different striping options and different fault-tolerant RAID types. The different RAID configurations are commonly known as RAID levels and define how the data is striped across the different disks in the I/O subsystem. These different RAID levels offer different levels of fault-tolerance, different performance characteristics, and different costs. Some RAID levels involve disk striping and some RAID levels do not.

Hardware vs. Software RAID

A RAID I/O subsystem can be formed either by purchasing a hardware RAID subsystem or by using software RAID. Both of these options have advantages and disadvantages.

The hardware RAID subsystem will have greater performance since other processes running on the system CPU will not affect it. In addition, hardware RAID subsystems can support features that software RAID subsystems may not be able to, such as hot-swappable disk drives and prefailure alerting. However, a hardware RAID subsystem can only be configured to stripe the drives that are attached to that controller, so the number of drives in a logical disk volume is limited to the number of drives that the controller can support. In addition, a hardware RAID subsystem can have a battery backed-up cache, whereas a software RAID system can't.

Software RAID subsystems have a price advantage, since it is not necessary to purchase additional hardware. In addition, a software RAID subsystem can be configured to stripe across all of the disk drives in the system and is not limited by controllers. Thus, you can create a software RAID volume across disk drives that are attached to many I/O controllers.

It is also possible to use software striping to stripe hardware disk volumes that are logical RAID volumes on a hardware RAID controller. Thus, the two can be combined in order to create massive logical disk volumes. This is something I do not recommend due to the overhead involved in software RAID.

For the purposes of this book, since it is performance and stability focused, we will assume a hardware RAID device.

Striping

Striping involves spreading data across multiple disk drives in order to create a logical disk drive that is larger than any individual disk drive in the system. Disk striping involves dividing the logical disk drive into pieces referred to as either stripes or chunks. Typically, these stripes are distributed to the individual disk drives in a round-robin fashion, as shown in Figure 4-9.

As mentioned previously, to the OS and to the users, the logical RAID volume appears as one large disk drive. If you are using a hardware RAID controller, the OS does not even know the difference. Striping is used in several of the different RAID levels supported by most RAID subsystems. In this section, we will examine the different RAID levels and how they operate.

RAID0

RAID0 is disk striping with no fault-tolerance. Thus, RAID0 is not redundant. With a RAID0 configuration, you can stripe data across multiple disk drives in order to create a large logical disk volume. However, a failure of any of the disk drives in the volume will result in the loss of the entire logical volume.

RAID0 is disk striping only and typically works in a round robin fashion. RAID0 is the most economical of the RAID levels and provides the highest performance, as you'll discover later in this section. You will see that, as in most things, there are tradeoffs. For instance, RAID0 provides high performance and value at the expense of no fault-tolerance.

Disk Stripe

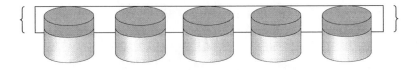

FIGURE 4-9. *Disk striping*

RAID1

RAID1 is also known as *disk mirroring*. In RAID1, all the data stored on a disk drive is duplicated on another disk in the array, as shown in Figure 4-10. Each time a write occurs to the logical disk, the data must be written to *both* physical disks before the logical write is considered completed. With disk mirroring, a single disk is mirrored to another disk; these disks can also be striped with other disks to form a larger logical volume. This combination of disk striping and mirroring is known as RAID10, RAID1+0, RAID0+1, or RAID 1/0 (depending on the manufacturer).

Because the mirroring is on a one-to-one basis, half of the disk drives in the system could actually fail (depending on which disks they are), and the system can still be operational. With most disk array controllers, you can split the mirror across SCSI busses. This arrangement allows for the failure of an entire SCSI bus (for example, a cabinet failure) without affecting operations.

With disk mirroring, you can use only half the disks in the system (the other half are used for the mirrors). In other words, if you use disk mirroring with two 18GB disk drives, you can use only 18GB of space. When writing, you get the benefit of only one disk in terms of performance because a logical write invokes two physical writes.

You may see a benefit from reading from a mirrored drive. Some disk array controllers support split seeks, in which reads can occur simultaneously on different mirrored drives to different data. The disk with the heads closest to the requested data retrieves the data. Depending on the data access methods, this feature may or may not provide any benefits.

If you can afford the cost of disk mirroring, RAID1 is the best choice when fault tolerance is required. With disk mirroring, you achieve the highest level of protection as well as the fastest disk access possible for a fault-tolerant volume.

RAID10

RAID10 is a combination of RAID0 and RAID1. With a RAID10 volume, each disk drive has its contents mirrored onto another disk drive and at the same time these mirrored disks participate as part of a stripe set, as shown in Figure 4-11.

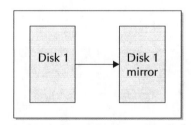

FIGURE 4-10. *A RAID1 configuration*

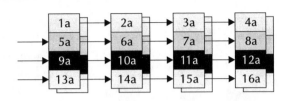

FIGURE 4-11. *A RAID10 configuration*

The advantage of a RAID10 volume is that you can achieve the administrative and performance advantages of a RAID0 volume coupled with the fault-tolerance of a RAID1 volume. The downside is that RAID10 volumes are the most expensive, since half of the usable space is lost to the mirror.

For database operations, RAID10 is the most preferable, as you will see later in this chapter.

RAID2
RAID2 is a parallel access RAID level where an error correction scheme called Hamming Code is used to correct errors. With RAID2, since all disk drives are used for all I/O operations, it can provide high throughput at the speed of one disk drive. RAID2 is shown in Figure 4-12.

While RAID2 can provide for a great deal of throughput, it takes three disk drives to provide the fault tolerance.

RAID3
RAID3 is a parallel access fault-tolerant method, similar to RAID2. The difference is that RAID3 only requires one disk drive for fault-tolerance. This is due to the fact that RAID3 uses a bit-wise parity rather than error correcting code. RAID3 is shown in Figure 4-13.

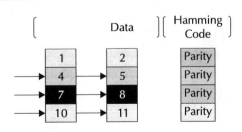

FIGURE 4-12. *A RAID2 configuration*

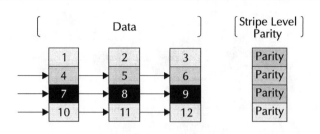

FIGURE 4-13. *A RAID3 configuration*

RAID3 can achieve a high transfer rate, but as with RAID2, only one I/O can be processed at a time. For small random I/Os, this can be a liability. RAID2 and RAID3 are both good for large sequential transfers, such as streaming video feeds.

RAID4

RAID4 is known as *drive parity,* or *data guarding* (not to be confused with Oracle Data Guard). In RAID4, one of the drives in the volume is used for data parity, as shown in Figure 4-14. If any one of the disks fails, the other disks continue running by reconstructing the missing data from the parity drive. The space available in a RAID4 volume incurs the loss of one disk drive's worth of space.

Unlike RAID2 and RAID3, RAID4 uses an independent access technique where multiple disk drives can be accessed simultaneously. This is good for random I/Os since they can be accessed in parallel. Thus the number of I/Os per second can reach the sum of the individual disk drive limits.

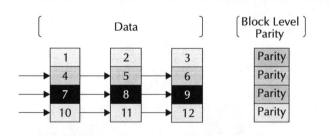

FIGURE 4-14. *A RAID4 configuration*

When you write to a RAID4 volume, extra I/Os are incurred in order to keep the parity up-to-date. In fact, since the parity must be kept up-to-date whenever data is added, the following process occurs:

1. Both the old data and old parity stripes are read.

2. An XOR is performed on old data and old parity.

3. The value and XOR are taken with new data to get the new parity.

4. Both the new data and new parity drives are written out.

Thus, for a single RAID4 write, four physical I/Os are incurred. For a RAID4 read, no additional I/O overhead is incurred.

The greatest disadvantage in RAID4 is the dedicated parity disk. Since the parity drive is involved in every write operation, only one write to the volume can be performed at a time. Other writes will begin to queue up under heavy write activity, and reads which depend on those writes will also begin to queue. Add this to the expense of the additional physical operations for each logical write, and you quickly build to a huge performance bottleneck on one disk.

RAID5

RAID5 is also known as distributed data guarding. RAID5 is similar to RAID4 except that the parity is not isolated to one disk drive. Rather, the parity is distributed across all the disk drives in the system, as shown in Figure 4-15.

As with RAID4, there is a penalty associated with RAID5 writes. For each write to disk, two reads take place, a calculation of the parity is done, and then two writes are done. Although a read generates only one I/O, a write generates four I/Os. This is done to maintain the parity.

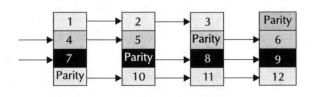

FIGURE 4-15. *A RAID5 configuration*

RAID5 will not suffer from the same write contention to a single disk as RAID4 does. Since the parity is distributed among all drives in the volume, more than one write operation can be in progress at a time. Potentially, there can be half as many writes occurring as there are disks in the volume.

RAID4 and RAID5 are both very economical, since you only lose one disk drive's worth of space in order to provide fault-tolerance; however, they pay the price in terms of performance.

Parity Overview

RAID3, RAID4, and RAID5 use a parity in order to maintain fault-tolerance. A parity is a binary method where the sum of the individual pieces add up to either an even or an odd value. The bits are added up using binary arithmetic and either a 0 or a 1 is added as a parity bit. The value of this parity bit depends on what is needed to maintain the proper parity of the sum of all of the bits.

Parity Example

Let's look at an example using three different bits and one parity bit. For our example, we will select even parity, thus the sum of all of the bits must add up to an even number. Taking the following three values:

```
A=1
B=0
C=1
```

These values add up to 2, thus the sum of A+B+C+Parity will equal an even number (2) if the value of the parity bit is 0.

In another example, let's take the following values:

```
A=0
B=1
C=1
```

In order for the sum of these values A+B+C+Parity to equal an even number (2), the value of the parity bit must be 1. In this manner, parity is created on every disk drive in the RAID controller—byte by byte, bit by bit.

Creating Parity

In order to create a RAID3, RAID4, or RAID5 volume, each data stripe must be read off of each disk drive and the parity calculated. This is sometimes known as data scrubbing. If you have created one of these RAID volumes, you may have noticed it taking a long time to create. This is why. Every disk in the volume must be read, parity created, and the parity must be written out. This can be quite time-consuming, depending on the size of the disk drives and the number of disk drives in the array.

Maintaining Parity

Once the volume has been created, it is unnecessary to recalculate the parity each time. Since the parity has already been calculated, it is possible to modify the parity based on the changes made by the insertion or modification of data. For example, if a data bit does not change, the parity bit does not need to change. If the data bit changes, then so must the parity bit. This is done using a bitwise exclusive "OR" operation (or XOR) on both the data and the parity bits.

Thus, to modify parity data, the following steps should be performed:

1. Read the data and parity stripes.

2. XOR the old data and parity.

3. Calculate a new parity using an XOR operation and new data.

4. Write out both new data and new parity.

Thus, for a parity write, four physical I/Os and two XORs are incurred. Not only are the additional I/Os important due to disk drive limitations, but their order is as well. Since there are two I/Os, two calculations, and two additional I/Os, the latency is, at minimum, twice the latency of a non-parity I/O (assuming infinitely fast parity calculation). This is important considering how sensitive Oracle is to I/O latency.

RAID Performance Overview

Now that you have seen the different RAID levels, let's look at how they perform. From this section until the end of the chapter, we will only look at the commonest RAID levels: RAID0, RAID1, RAID10, and RAID5. Although you may encounter other RAID levels, it is rare.

First, let's review a few facts.

- **Individual I/O operations occur at the speed of one disk drive** No matter how many disk drives are in the RAID volume, the I/O is going to one of them, thus you cannot exceed that speed. It is the fact that multiple I/O operations can occur at the same time on different disks that gives us better performance in a RAID system.

- **If you do exceed the physical performance limitations of the disk drive, queuing will occur and latencies will increase.**

- **The optimal performance rate for random I/Os is 128 IOPS (in these examples)** Exceeding this rate may cause increased latencies. Additional drives will allow for additional concurrency and more performance. If one drive can do 128 IOPS, a ten-drive RAID volume can do 1280 IOPS.

- **Almost all I/O operations are random in nature** Even if you are doing a sequential table scan, if someone else is accessing the same disk, the I/Os will become random.

Now let's look at the performance of some of the common RAID levels.

RAID0   RAID0 is the most straightforward RAID level to calculate performance characteristics. Assuming access to the RAID0 volume is random, and assuming 175 IOPS per disk drive, the optimal number of IOPS to the volume is calculated using the following formula:

```
(# of reads) + (# of writes) = (175 * n)
```

where *n* is the number of disk drives in the array. Thus, a ten-disk drive array could handle 1750 reads and writes per second.

RAID1 and RAID10   RAID1 and RAID10 volumes incur the write penalty of two physical writes for each write to the logical volume. This is due to the fact that all of the data on a disk drive must be duplicated on its mirror. Thus, the optimal number of reads and writes on a RAID10 and RAID1 volume is calculated using the following formula:

```
(# of reads) + (# of writes * 2) = (175 * n)
```

where *n* is the number of disk drives in the array. For a RAID1 array, $n = 2$.

RAID5   RAID5 volumes incur a penalty of four physical I/Os for every logical write. The old data and parity must be read, two XOR operations performed, and the new data and parity written. The optimal number of reads and writes on a RAID5 volume can be calculated using the following formula:

```
(# of reads) + (# of writes * 4) = (175 * n)
```

where *n* is the number of disk drives in the array.

RAID Level Performance Comparison
Let's compare the different RAID levels.

- RAID0 is the highest performing RAID level, since there is no fault-tolerance overhead. However, the fact that there is no fault tolerance renders RAID0 unacceptable for most database operations.

- RAID1 and RAID10 incur a 2x penalty on writes. They have the best level of fault tolerance, but are also the most expensive.

- RAID5 has the worst write penalty, incurring four physical I/Os for each write operation. RAID5 provides fault-tolerance, but can only tolerate the loss of one disk drive in the volume. However, it is the most economical of the RAID levels.

None of the above mentioned RAID levels incur any penalty for reads.

RAID Performance

As you have seen from this section, there are different performance characteristics for different RAID levels. RAID5 is very popular because of the economics involved, since you only lose one disk drive's worth of space while achieving some level of fault-tolerance. However, in most cases, RAID5 is not appropriate for use with Oracle.

My rule of thumb is not to use RAID5 unless the read/write ratio is 90/10. In other words, unless 90 percent of the I/O operations are reads, RAID5 is inappropriate. Of course, your mileage may vary, and if the I/O rate is sufficiently low, then this shouldn't be an issue.

When calculating how many IOPS per disk drive are being done at the physical level, remember to multiply the RAID5 writes by four. This can drastically change your resulting data. For fault-tolerance and performance, I prefer RAID10.

As you can see, there are several factors to consider when selecting a RAID level. In the next chapter, you will see how Oracle I/O considerations should also be taken into account when selecting a RAID level.

No matter what your hardware vendor tells you, I/O sizing is a big issue. Though state-of-the-art I/O subsystems have many features, such as large caches and multiple busses, it doesn't change the fact that if you don't have enough disk drives, your performance will suffer.

One of the commonest performance problems encountered is a lack of sufficient I/O capacity. As disk drives become larger and less expensive, there is a tendency to replace several smaller disk drives with one larger one. While this is a good value, your performance might suffer. Be sure you do proper I/O sizing before ordering your new I/O subsystem.

Capacity Planning

Capacity Planning refers to a complex, ongoing performance study of hardware and software resource consumption on an existing system in order to prepare for the growth of the system's workload. These studies are prepared primarily to maintain the service-level agreement (SLA) as system resource usage increases. In other words, capacity planning is the art of sizing an already existing system in order to determine when you might run out of capacity.

In addition to projecting resource utilization, capacity planning allows you to project what-if scenarios on workloads. In a typical capacity planning study, the technician performing the task will have historic performance data stored in the database and will be able to project trends in the following areas:

- Normal growth of CPU utilization
- Disk usage
- Memory usage

The technician will also be able to project sudden rises in CPU, disk, and memory utilization caused by the addition of new users to the system.

These studies can be extremely detailed and can involve profiling the activities of specific users. This is valuable information because not only can you add hypothetical generic users to the system for resource projection purposes, but you can add specific users as well, such as General Ledger users, Accounts Payable users, and so on.

By performing capacity planning studies, IT management can have sufficient time to plan the addition of new hardware in order to maintain the service-level agreements currently in place. In some cases, tuning ideas can come out of capacity planning studies as well.

Summary

This chapter has covered the basics of sizing and capacity planning, and has touched on many of the main areas of these fields. Sizing and capacity planning is a difficult science, as you can see from the various discussions in this chapter.

Sizing is very important, since incorrect sizing early in your hardware acquisition can result in a poorly configured system, and thus bad performance later on down the road. It is much more economical to properly size a system than it is to fix a poorly performing system already in use.

CHAPTER
5

Configuring the Linux System for Oracle

I n order to run Oracle on Linux, it is first necessary to install and configure Linux in such a way that Oracle has sufficient resources. These resources might consist of things like sufficient memory, sufficient disk space, proper tuning, and so on. Once this has been completed, the Oracle installation can commence. After Oracle is installed, there are some specific choices you can make regarding your Oracle configuration in order to optimize performance on Linux.

In this chapter, both the Linux configuration for Oracle, and the Oracle configuration for Linux will be covered. As with many of the operating systems that Oracle supports, there are some Linux specifics you should be aware of. At the end of this chapter, you will be prepared to properly install and configure Linux and Oracle on Linux.

Preinstallation Procedures for Linux

Several steps are required to properly configure your Linux system for Oracle. Some of these steps involve configuring the Linux kernel parameters correctly, while some involve setting up hardware devices correctly. Others determine storage setup, as well as how to size the system properly. In this section, all of these steps will be covered.

Only a few parts of the Linux configuration have to be carefully thought out before installing the operating system. The most important of these is the configuration of the Linux filesystems. Once this decision has been made and the operating system has formatted both the partitions and filesystems, it is impossible to change. In fact, in order to redo the basic Linux partitions, the OS must be reinstalled. Since this is quite unlikely in a production environment, typically you will have to live with your initial choices for quite a long time.

Other important components must be configured as part of the OS installation, but things like the Linux tunable parameters, networking, and other configuration parameters can always be changed later without having to reinstall the operating system.

In addition to the initial filesystem configuration, it is also important to choose the right Linux components. When prompted to install groups of packages for things like OS or software development, these should be chosen. During the initial installation it is easy to install groups of packages, whereas later it is more difficult, since the individual packages must be picked.

Before beginning the Linux installation (and subsequently the Oracle installation), you must verify that you have met certain minimum requirements. These requirements are necessary for the proper installation and configuration of the Oracle Database Server and must be taken into account when installing and configuring the Linux operating system.

Minimum Requirements

The following minimum requirements must be met for the successful installation and configuration of the Oracle Database Server. If you cannot meet these requirements, your system should be reinstalled or your hardware upgraded so you can.

- **512MB of physical RAM**   This is necessary for the proper operation of the Oracle Database Server; however, this is a minimum requirement. For optimal operation, you really should have significantly more RAM than this.

- **1GB of swap space**   The amount of swap space is typically set to two times the amount of physical RAM. For systems where RAM is greater than 2GB, the amount of swap space can be more in the range of one to two times the amount of RAM. The more RAM you have, the less likely it is you will use the swap space.

- **/tmp must have at least 400MB of space**   If the /tmp partition is created as a separate partition, it must be at least 400MB in size. If the /tmp directory is part of the / (root) filesystem, there must be at least 400MB in addition to the space you will use for other usage.

- **Oracle file space**   You must allocate at least 1.5GB of space for the most basic Oracle install. This amount varies depending on the components you have chosen to install.

- **Oracle data files**   In order to install the basic sample database, you must have at least 1.2GB of space. This space can be either on a filesystem, an NFS partition, or on an Oracle ASM (Automatic Storage Management) disk group. In an Oracle 10*g* RAC environment, this storage must be shared between all of the nodes in the cluster.

These requirements should be considered when creating your Linux installation. It is quite painful to have to rebuild partitions in order to fit the Oracle installation, and the time required could make your installation take much longer.

Configuring the Filesystems

The Linux filesystem layout can consist of as little as three partitions, or as many as you want. The minimal requirements for a Linux configuration consist of the following two partitions:

- **/, the root partition**   This is the initial partition. All other partitions are mounted on subdirectories of the root partition.

- **swap, the swap partition**   The swap partition is not mounted as a regular filesystem, but is required by the Linux partition in order to function. The swap partition (or partitions) must be configured according to the minimum requirements listed earlier.

In addition to the minimal filesystem requirements, you can create separate partitions for different functions. Typical partitions that might be created during the installation process include the following:

Partition	Description
/home	The /home partition is used for the home directory of Linux user accounts. The Oracle user account is created in the /home directory tree, but the $ORACLE_HOME directory is not usually stored here.
/tmp	The /tmp partition is used for temporary files. Oracle uses this directory during the installation process, and the OS uses it in normal operation. If this is created as a separate partition, make sure it meets the minimum requirements listed earlier.
/usr	The /usr directory structure is used for programs; however, this is not where the Oracle programs reside. The Oracle programs reside in the $ORACLE_HOME directory, which is typically in the /opt directory tree.
/var	The /var directory structure is used for variable length files, such as log files, print spool files, and others.
/usr/local	The /usr/local directory tree is used for local programs and configuration files. Oracle uses this directory structure for some programs, but the bulk of the Oracle programs reside in the $ORACLE_HOME directory tree.
/opt	The /opt directory tree is used for optional programs. This is typically the location for the $ORACLE_HOME directory tree. In addition, Oracle data files might also be stored in this directory tree on some systems.

When configuring your system, take into account the minimum requirements listed earlier, as well as your own specific needs. If you are going to be creating a RAC cluster, give consideration to the shared storage requirements for the Oracle data files.

Choosing Linux Components

Choosing the right Linux components is another important part of planning your operating system installation. It is possible to load required components after the initial installation, but it is much easier to configure them during the initial installation.

As of the initial release of Oracle 10*g* for Linux, the following Linux distributions were supported:

Oracle 10*g* Release 1 (10.1.0)

- Red Hat Enterprise Linux 2.1 or 3.0

- SUSE Linux Enterprise Server 8.0 or 9.0 (SLES8 or SLES9)

Oracle 10g Release 2 (10.2.0)

- Red Hat Enterprise Linux EL 3 or EL 4

- SUSE Linux Enterprise Server 9.0 (SLES9)

Within these Linux distributions, it is necessary to first install the software development packages in order to have the gcc compiler and libraries installed. If you might need to upgrade the Linux kernel, you should install the kernel development package as well. It is recommended that the following packages be included in the list of packages you choose to install.

Red Hat Linux Packages

When installing Red Hat Linux, it is recommended you install the following packages in addition to the default packages and any other packages you have chosen. This is not a complete list and does not imply that other packages should not be installed.

- **Development Tools**   This set of packages includes the gcc compiler, PERL, python, and debuggers.

- **Kernel Development**   This is not specifically required for installing Oracle, but it is a requirement if you ever need to update the Linux kernel.

The minimum set of components required by the Oracle 10g installation is listed next:

System Components for Oracle 10g R1

System	Components
Red Hat 2.1 and 3.0	make-3.79 binutilss-2.11.90.0.8-12
Red Hat Enterprise Linux 2.1 (x86)	gcc-2.96.108.1 openmotif-2.1.30-11
Red Hat Enterprise Linux 3	gcc-3.2.3-2 compat-db-4.0.14.5 compat-gcc-7.3-2.96.122 compat-gcc-c++-7.3-2.96.122 compat-libstdc++-7.3-2.96.122 compat-libstdc++-devel-7.3-2.96.122 openmotif-2.2.2-16 setarch-1.3-1

System Components for Oracle10g R2

System	Components
Red Hat 2.1 and 3.0	make-3.79 binutils-2.11.90.0.8-12
Red Hat Enterprise Linux 2.1 (x86)	gcc-2.96.108.1 openmotif-2.1.30-11
Red Hat Enterprise Linux 3	make-3.79.1 gcc-3.2.3-34 glibc-2.3.2-95.20 compat-db-4.0.14-5 compat-gcc-7.3-2.96.128 compat-gcc-c++-7.3-2.96.128 compat-libstdc++-7.3-2.96.128 compat-libstdc++-devel-7.3-2.96.128 openmotif21-2.1.30-8 setarch-1.3-1

SUSE Linux Packages

When installing SUSE Linux, it is recommended you install the following packages in addition to the default packages and any other packages you've chosen. This is not a complete list and does not imply that other packages should not be installed.

- **Development Tools**   This set of packages includes the gcc compiler, PERL, python, and debuggers.

- **Kernel Development**   This is not specifically required for installing Oracle, but it is a requirement if you ever need to update the Linux kernel.

The requirements for SUSE Linux are slightly less than for Red Hat Linux due to the fact that more of the required components are installed by default. The following components are required for the Oracle installation. The minimum set of components required by the Oracle 10g installation is

Oracle 10g R1

- gcc-3.2.2-38
- openmotif-2.2.2-124

Oracle10g R2

- gcc-3.3.3-43
- gcc-c++-3.3.3-43
- glibc-2.3.3-98

- libaio-0.3.98-18

- libaio-devel-0.3.98-18

- make-3.80

- openmotif-libs-2.2.2-519.1

Summary
As long as you have met the minimum requirements, the Oracle installation will complete correctly. Without the minimum required software packages installed on your system, the portion of the installation where the binaries are relinked will fail.

Post-Installation Procedures for Linux
Once you have successfully installed the Linux operating system, there are a number of steps that must be taken in order to prepare for the Oracle 10*g* installation. These steps consist of adding Oracle user and group accounts, creating directories for the Oracle programs and database files, configuring Linux kernel parameters, and setting up environment variables. These steps are necessary in order to properly install the Oracle Database 10*g* server. In the next few sections, you will see how to perform these tasks.

Configuring Kernel Parameters
In order for the Oracle database server to function, there are certain OS resources that must be configured. These resources are set, by default, at levels too low for the Oracle Database 10*g* server to start and function properly. Fortunately, the Linux operating system allows these parameters to be changed dynamically, thus no reboot is required when kernel parameters are modified.

There are several ways to modify kernel parameters. The kernel parameters can be modified dynamically by modifying the values in the /proc pseudo filesystem. As a review, the /proc filesystem contains kernel system performance and configuration information as well as a way to change kernel parameters.

The parameters that need to be configured for Linux involve semaphores, shared memory, the maximum number of open files, and the port range for IP. The semaphore parameters all exist in the /proc/sys/kernel/sem file and are semmsl, semmns, semopm, and semmni. It is required that the following minimum values must be met:

Parameter	Value	Description
semmsl	250	Maximum number of semaphores per ID
semmns	32000	Maximum number of semaphores in the system (must be equal or greater than semmni * semmsl)
semopm	100	Maximum number of operations per semaphore call
semmni	128	Maximum number of semaphore identifiers

The size of the SGA is dictated by the shared memory parameters found in /proc/sys/kernel/shmall, /proc/sys/kernel/shmmax, and /proc/sys/kernel/shmmni. These files are described next:

Parameter	Value	Description
shmall	297152	Maximum number of shared memory pages systemwide
shmmax	Half the size of memory	Maximum size of a shared memory segment
shmmni	4096	Maximum number of shared memory segments systemwide

The other parameters that need to be set for the Oracle installation are /proc/sys/fs/file-max and /proc/sys/net/ipv4/ip_local_port_range. These are described next:

Parameter	Value	Description
/proc/sys/fs/file-max	65536	Maximum number of file handles that Linux allocates
/proc/sys/net/ipv4/ip_local_port_range	1024 65000	The range of IP port numbers. By default, this is 1024 to 4999, only allowing 3975 outgoing connections. This is not sufficient for Oracle.

The first method of changing the kernel parameter is dynamic and can be changed at any time. This is accomplished by changing the value in the /proc pseudo filesystem. However, the values are reset with each reboot. The second method allows you to set up a configuration file which is read at boot time and is used to set kernel parameters each time the system is booted.

Configuring Kernel Parameters Using the /proc Pseudo Filesystem
To view the current settings for the SHMMAX (Maximum Shared Memory Size) kernel parameter, enclose this in the font for UNIX commands:

    cat /proc/sys/kernel/shmmax

The value represents the amount of memory that can be allocated for shared memory. Since shared memory is used by the SGA, this also represents the maximum size of the Oracle SGA.

In order to modify the SHMMAX parameter, echo the new value to the /proc/sys/kernel/shmmax pseudo file, as shown here:

```
echo 2147483648 > /proc/sys/kernel/shmmax
```

This will set the maximum size of shared memory to 2147483648 bytes, or 2GB. This is sufficient for the installation of Oracle 10g, but might not be enough to run with the size of SGA you require for normal operations. For a 32-bit system, you can create an SGA up to 2.7GB in size. For SGAs larger than 2.7GB, there are some special tricks you can do (described later in this book).

One way to have these commands executed on every boot is to put them in the /etc/rc.local file, just as you would any shell script:

```
# Configuration parameters for Oracle
echo "250 32000 100 128" > /proc/sys/kernel/sem
echo "2097152" > /proc/sys/kernel/shmall
echo "2147483648" > /proc/sys/kernel/shmmax
echo "4096" > /proc/sys/kernel/shmmni
echo "65536" > /proc/fs/file-max
echo "1024 65000" > /proc/net/ipv4/ip_local_port_range
```

The /etc/rc.local file is run every time the system boots, thus the parameters will be reset each time the system boots. However, the preferred method is to change /etc/sysctl.conf.

Configuring Kernel Parameters Using the /etc/sysctl.conf File

The alternate method is to put the parameters into a file named /etc/sysctl.conf. This file sets the kernel parameters upon system boot. The /etc/sysctl.conf file contains the directory and value of the /proc file, as shown next:

```
kernel.shmall = 2097152
kernel.shmmax = 2147483648
kernel.shmmni = 4096
kernel.sem = 250 32000 100 128
fs.file-max = 65536
net.ipv4.ip_local_port_range = 1024 65000
```

Run the program /sbin/sysctl –p to load the values you put in this file, and verify that these parameters were set correctly. With Red Hat Linux, this file will be read on bootup by default. With SUSE Linux, use the following command to activate the sysctl.conf file:

```
/sbin/chkconfig boot.sysctl on
```

Adding Users and Groups

Before you can install Oracle on Linux, it is necessary to create an Oracle user account. This account must belong to the oinstall group and also be a member of the dba group. The groups are added with the **groupadd** command (/usr/sbin/groupadd):

```
groupadd oinstall
groupadd dba
```

The Oracle user account is created with the **useradd** command (/usr/sbin/useradd), as shown next:

```
useradd -g oinstall -G dba oracle (on Red Hat)
useradd -m -g oinstall -G dba oracle (on SUSE)
```

This will create the Oracle user account with the home directory as /home/oracle, a primary group of oinstall, and will generate it as a member of the dba group.

Configuring Shell Limits for the Oracle User

There are a few more optional tasks that must be done in order to allow the Oracle 10*g* installation to work. These tasks are related to increasing the shell limits so that Oracle can create and open large files. These steps involve editing the /etc/profile file to increase the ulimit. The following should be added to /etc/profile:

```
if [ $USER = "oracle" ]; then

if [ $SHELL = "/bin/ksh" ]; then
        ulimit -p 16384
        ulimit -n 65536
else
        ulimit -u 16384 -n 65536
    fi
fi
```

In addition, the following lines need to be added to /etc/security/limits.conf in order to change the number of processes and files that can be used by a single user:

```
* soft nproc 2047
* hard nproc 16384
* soft nofile 1024
* hard nofile 65536
```

The last step is to modify the /etc/pam.d/login file. Therefore, the following line should be added:

```
session    required    /lib/security/pam_limits.so
```

Once these tasks have been accomplished, you are almost ready to install the Oracle Database 10*g* server. All that's left is to create the directories where you will be putting the Oracle binaries and data files, and then setting the Oracle environment.

Creating Directory Structures

The Oracle installation requires three directories. These three directories serve different purposes and consist of:

- **Oracle Base**   Used as the base directory for the rest of the Oracle tree.

- **Oracle Inventory**   This location is used for the Oracle Universal Installer.

- **Oracle Home**   The Oracle Home directory is the directory where a particular software version is installed and is typically a subdirectory of Oracle Base.

The Oracle base directory might exist on several different mount points for different installations, and Oracle data files might reside on a different base tree than the Oracle binaries.

The I/O requirements in the directory structure where the Oracle binaries will be installed (the ORACLE_HOME directory) is fairly light. You must have sufficient space available, but you do not really need to worry about I/O performance. However, the location that holds the Oracle binaries should be configured with some fault tolerance. RAID1 is recommended.

For the Oracle data files, the directory naming structure follows the OFA naming convention of:

```
Mount_point/app/oracle
```

Typical mount points are /u01, /u02, /u03... for Oracle data files and /opt/oracle for the Oracle home directory.

The Oracle inventory directory has the path of *oracle_base*/oraInventory.

Oracle Directory Structure Example

A typical Oracle 10g system would have a directory structure similar to this:

/opt/oracle	Oracle Base
/opt/oracle/oraInventory	The Oracle inventory directory
/opt/oracle/product/10.1.0/db_1	The Oracle home directory for release 10.1.0
/opt/oracle/product/10.2.0/db_1	The Oracle home directory for release 10.2.0
/opt/oracle/product/10.2.0/client_1	The client software for Oracle 10.2.0
/u01/app/oracle/oradata/*SID*	The location of Oracle log or data files for the system identifier (SID) named *SID*
/u02/app/oracle/oradata/*SID*	The location of Oracle data files for an SID named *SID*

Setting Up the Oracle Environment

For those of you who have installed previous versions of Oracle in the past, you will notice that the Oracle environment setup has changed. Unlike the Oracle9*i* installation, the Oracle 10g installation does not require Oracle environment variables

Oracle Directory Permissions

The Oracle directories previously mentioned should be owned by the Oracle user with the group of oinstall that has permissions 755. In order to accomplish this, run the following:

```
mkdir /opt/oracle
chown -R oracle.oinstall /opt/oracle
chmod -R 755 /opt/oracle
```

to be set in the profile for installation. In fact, these variables should not be set in the profile before the system is installed. In the Oracle 10g installation, the only addition to the .bash_profile (or your appropriate shell profile file) is the following:

```
umask 022
```

This command sets the default file creation mask. The mask of 022 will create files with 644 or rw-r--r-- permissions.

If you do not have sufficient space in the temporary directories, the TEMP and TMPDIR environment variables should be set as follows:

```
TEMP=/u01/temp
TMPDIR=/u01/temp
export TEMP TMPDIR
```

The final step is to set the environment variables for ORACLE_BASE and ORACLE_SID. These are set in a similar fashion to those previously seen:

```
ORACLE_BASE=/opt/oracle
ORACLE_SID=orac
export ORACLE_BASE ORACLE_SID
```

Once these tasks are completed, the Oracle installation is ready to begin. Installing the Oracle Database 10g server is covered in the next chapter.

Installation Checklists

It is often quite valuable to have installation checklists. Checklists (shown next) are a reminder of the requirements and steps necessary to perform installations, and will help ensure that no steps are missed.

Installation Checklist for Oracle 10*g* R1

Step	Completed?
1. *Check hardware requirements.*	_____
512MB of RAM	_____
1GB of swap space	_____
400MB of temp space	_____
1.5GB of Oracle binary space	_____
1.2GB of Oracle data file space	_____
2. *Check Linux software for Oracle 10g R1.*	_____
Red Hat Enterprise Linux AS 2.1 or ES 3.0	
Software Development system installed?	_____
Kernel Development system installed?	_____
Red Hat Package Requirements	
Red Hat 2.1 and 3.0	
make-3.79	_____
binutils-2.11.90.0.8-12	_____
Red Hat Enterprise Linux 2.1 (x86)	
gcc-2.96.108.1	_____
openmotif-2.1.30-11	_____
Red Hat Enterprise Linux 3	
gcc-3.2.3-2	_____
compat-db-4.0.14.5	_____
compat-gcc-7.3-2.96.122	_____
compat-gcc-c++-7.3-2.96.122	_____
compat-libstdc++-7.3-2.96.122	_____
compat-libstdc++-devel-7.3-2.96.122	_____
openmotif-2.2.2-16	_____
setarch-1.3-1	_____
SUSE Linux Enterprise Server 8.0 (United Linux 1.0)	
Development Tools installed?	_____
Kernel Development installed?	_____
SUSE Package Requirements	
gcc-3.2.2-38	_____
openmotif-2.2.2-124	_____
3. *Set up kernel configuration parameters.*	
/proc/sys/kernel/sem "250 32000 100 128"	_____
/proc/sys/kernel/shmall "2097152"	_____
/proc/sys/kernel/shmmax "2147483648"	_____
/proc/sys/kernel/shmmni "4096"	_____

/proc/fs/file-max "65536"   _____
/proc/net/ipv4/ip_local_port_range "1024 65000"   _____

4. *Add groups and users.*
groupadd oinstall   _____
groupadd dba   _____
useradd –g oinstall –G dba oracle (on Red Hat)   _____
useradd –m –g oinstall –G dba oracle (on SUSE)   _____

5. *Configure shell limits and security.*
Modify /etc/profile   _____
Modify /etc/security/limits   _____
Modify /etc/pam.d/login   _____

6. *Create directories and set permissions.*

7. *Set Oracle environment variables.*
Only umask goes into the .bash_profile (or other profile)   _____
Set ORACLE_BASE and ORACLE_SID outside of profile   _____

Installation Checklist for Oracle 10*g* R2

Step	**Completed?**
1. *Check hardware requirements.*	_____
512MB of RAM	_____
1GB of swap space	_____
400MB of temp space	_____
1.5GB of Oracle binary space	_____
1.2GB of Oracle data file space	_____
2. *Check Linux software for Oracle 10g R2.*	_____
Red Hat Enterprise Linux AS or ES 3.0	
Software Development system installed?	_____
Kernel Development system installed?	_____
Package Requirements for Oracle 10g R2	
Red Hat Linux AS and ES 3.0	
make-3.79.1	_____
gcc-3.2.3-34	_____
glibc-2.3.2-95.20	_____
compat-db-4.0.14.5	_____
compat-gcc-7.3-2.96.128	_____
compat-gcc-c++-7.3-2.96.128	_____
compat-libstdc++-7.3-2.96.128	_____

compat-libstdc++-devel-7.3-2.96.128   _____
openmotif-2.2.3-4   _____
setarch-1.3-1   _____
SUSE Enterprise Linux 8.0 (United Linux 1.0)
    Development Tools installed?   _____
    Kernel Development installed?   _____
    SUSE Package Requirements
        gcc-3.3.3-43   _____
        gcc-c++-3.3.3-43   _____
        glibc-2.3.3-98   _____
        libaio-0.3.98-18   _____
        libaio-devel-0.3.98-18   _____
        make-3.80   _____
        openmotif-libs-2.2.2-519.1   _____

3. *Set up kernel configuration parameters.*
    /proc/sys/kernel/sem "250 32000 100 128"   _____
    /proc/sys/kernel/shmall "2097152"   _____
    /proc/sys/kernel/shmmax "2147483648"   _____
    /proc/sys/kernel/shmmni "4096"   _____
    /proc/fs/file-max "65536"   _____
    /proc/net/ipv4/ip_local_port_range "1024 65000" _____

4. *Add groups and users.*
    groupadd oinstall   _____
    groupadd dba   _____
    useradd –g oinstall –G dba oracle (on Red Hat)   _____
    useradd –m –g oinstall –G dba oracle (on SUSE)   _____

5. *Configure shell limits and security.*   _____
    Modify /etc/profile   _____
    Modify /etc/security/limits   _____
    Modify /etc/pam.d/login   _____

6. *Create directories and set permissions.*   _____

7. *Set Oracle environment variables.*   _____
    Only umask goes into the .bash_profile (or other profile)   _____
    Set ORACLE_BASE and ORACLE_SID outside of profile   _____

Summary

Unlike previous versions of Oracle, preparing for the Oracle installation is fairly straightforward. The biggest hurdles you will have to overcome with the Oracle 10*g* installation on Linux is the compatibility of versions of Linux. While it might be very uneventful to install Oracle 10*g* Release 1 on Red Hat Linux EL 3 or SUSE Linux Enterprise System 8.0, you might find it quite challenging to install Oracle 10*g* Release 1 on a version of those operating systems. These issues most likely will revolve around the libraries and versions of compilers that ship with these operating systems. My advice to you is to spend time carefully investigating the requirements to ensure you meet them. A checklist is always a good idea.

CHAPTER
6

Installing Oracle 10g on Linux

n some respects, installing Oracle 10*g* on Linux can be much easier than installing Oracle9*i*. In other respects, it can be more challenging. The degree of difficulty depends on the method of installation. Some of the new challenges revolve around the use of ASM—Oracle's Automatic Storage Management. Although ASM simplifies storage management, it involves some work to install and configure. Installing the Oracle database on Linux can be quite straightforward if installed on a standard filesystem.

The installation process can be broken up into preinstall, install, and postinstall/configuration steps.

Preinstallation Steps

Some of the preinstallation steps were covered in the previous chapter, so a brief review will be presented here along with the additional steps necessary to prepare for the Oracle installation. These steps involve creating and configuring the Oracle user, setting Linux kernel parameters, and preparing storage for the installation. All of these steps must be complete before the installation can proceed.

Kernel Configuration Parameters

There are a number of Linux kernel parameters that must be set. These are to make sure there are sufficient resources for Oracle to function properly during the installation, but might not be suitable for running your system in production. These parameters relate to the amount of shared memory that can be allocated for the Oracle SGA and semaphores that the Oracle processes use. The value of these parameters and how to set them were covered in the previous chapter. How to modify these parameters for your production system is covered near the end of this chapter.

Setting the Linux shared memory, semaphore, and shared memory parameters in conjunction with the configuration of the shell limits specified in the previous file will have configured the Linux system to where Oracle can now be installed. The final step is to configure storage for the Oracle installation.

Storage Requirements

Before Oracle is installed, the storage that the Oracle database server will be installed on should be configured. Unlike Oracle9*i*, in addition to filesystem and RAW devices, there is now a third option for the Oracle database files: ASM. Before the Oracle starting the installation, you should decide which type of environment you will be using, and then allocate and configure this storage. The bare minimum requirements for installing the Oracle home with a sample database are as follows:

Mount Point	Minimum Size	Purpose
/tmp	400MB	Used as a temporary area during the Oracle install. If /tmp is not sufficiently sized, the TEMP and TMPDIR environment variables can point to an alternate location.
SWAP	1GB	A 1GB swap space is required for the Oracle 10g installation.
ORACLE_BASE	1.5GB	The ORACLE_BASE directory or filesystem is the location of the Oracle binaries.
DATA	1.2GB	The Oracle datafiles for the basic sample database consume 1.2GB of space.
Archive Log		Sufficient space should be allocated for archive log files. There are no approximations for the space required for archive log files, since the amount of space required is based on the insert, update, and delete activity in your database.

NOTE
Since the amount of log data archived depends primarily on the number of changes and not the size of the database, the amount of data archived can be significant. It is not uncommon for a busy system to generate 10's of gigabytes of archive log data each day. The following SQL statement can be used to see how much archive data has been generated on a daily basis:

```
SELECT
TRUNC(completion_time) AS "Date"
, COUNT(*) AS "Count"
, (SUM(blocks * block_size) / 1024 / 1024) AS "MB"
FROM v$archived_log
GROUP BY TRUNC(completion_time);
```

This represents the bare minimum space requirements for the sample database installation. In order to create an Oracle database that is useful for you, the following considerations should be made.

- **Isolate the redo log files.** The Oracle redo log files should be separated into their own disks. This is both for performance and data protection, as noted in both Chapters 4 and 15.

- **Allocate sufficient I/O capacity for your data and indexes.** This does not mean allocate enough space, but rather allocate enough space and performance for your Oracle database datafiles. Remember that a single disk drive can only do a fixed number of I/O operations per second, as shown in Chapter 4.

■ **Isolate the archive log files.** As with the redo log files, the archive log files should be isolated from the data files. This is not only for performance reasons, but to protect them in the event of the loss of a single disk volume.

By allocating storage up front, changes and reinstallations might not be necessary. It is always better to plan ahead, rather than fixing problems later. As mentioned previously, the storage for the Oracle datafiles can be allocated on Linux filesystems, raw partitions, and on Automatic Storage Management volumes.

Filesystem Files

Using Linux filesystems is by far the easiest solution; however, it is also the solution with the weakest performance. The Linux filesystem adds additional overhead to Oracle I/O processing, thus utilizing more CPU and memory than necessary. This overhead and additional processing time is caused by two different issues: the filesystem cache and the limited block size available in the ext2 and ext3 filesystems.

Filesystem Caching When Oracle opens a datafile, it is opened in such a way that write-caching is disabled in the Linux filesystem. Even though write-caching is disabled, the filesystem cache is still used; however, writes are written into the cache and then written to disk.

As far as Oracle is concerned, the I/O has not completed until it has been fully written to disk, and since it has to be written into the cache first and then to disk, additional overhead is incurred. Thus, the Linux filesystem is very convenient and easy to use, but it is the worst performing of our three choices. Some filesystems are able to write directly to disk and completely bypass additional overhead. One example is the OCFS—the Oracle Cluster Filesystem—which has been used occasionally outside of clusters for this reason. However, OCFS is not a general purpose filesystem and can only be used by Oracle files. Other third-party solutions, such as the Veritas Volume Manager and Veritas Foundation Suite, have better performance than the standard Linux filesystems.

Filesystem Blocksize Along with concerns about the filesystem cache, when using the Linux filesystem there is an additional issue. The Oracle database is created with a standard block size that is often 8KB or larger. The problem with this is that the maximum block size on the ext2 and ext3 filesystem is 4KB. If you are using an 8KB Oracle block size on a 4KB filesystem, each Oracle I/O must use two filesystem blocks, since the 8KB request spans two 4KB blocks.

Creating Filesystems Creating filesystems for Oracle is fairly straightforward. The process involves creating the disk partitions, creating filesystems on those partitions, and then mounting those filesystems on the system.

A hard disk is divided into one or more logical partitions by using the fdisk command. Fdisk is used to divide the disk into these partitions. A Linux disk can be divided into as many as 15 partitions. The partition number of the disk drive is appended to the disk device name. For example, the first SCSI disk is /dev/sda with partitions /dev/sda1, /dev/sda2, and so on.

Each individual logical partition can have a filesystem created on it by using the mkfs command. The mkfs command can be used to create a number of different types of filesystems such as ext2, ext3, hpfs, OCFS, and others.

Once the filesystem has been created, it is mounted using the mount command. The filesystem must be mounted on a directory in the root filesystem. Once this is done, it is ready to be used by the OS and by the Oracle Database server. In order to see what filesystems are currently mounted on your system, simply type

```
mount
/dev/sda3 on / type ext3 (rw)
none on /proc type proc (rw)
usbdevfs on /proc/bus/usb type usbdevfs (rw)
/dev/sda1 on /boot type ext3 (rw)
none on /dev/pts type devpts (rw,gid=5,mode=620)
none on /dev/shm type tmpfs (rw)
/dev/sdb1 on /u01 type ext3 (rw)
```

In order to find the sizes of these filesystems, use the df command. This will show you the sizes, usage, and available space on each of the filesystems.

```
# df
Filesystem          1K-blocks     Used Available Use% Mounted on
/dev/sda3            3510364    2323220   1008824  70% /
/dev/sda1             101089      14231     81639  15% /boot
none                 127464          0    127464   0% /dev/shm
/dev/sdb1            4127076      32828   3884604   1% /u01
```

Linux has a very nice feature that can be used with many of the filesystem commands, such as df, du, and ls. The –h flag designates "human readable" format. This format displays the sizes in K, M, and G for kilobytes, megabytes, and gigabytes.

```
# df -h
Filesystem          Size  Used Avail Use% Mounted on
/dev/sda3           3.4G  2.3G  986M  70% /
/dev/sda1            99M   14M   80M  15% /boot
none                125M     0  125M   0% /dev/shm
/dev/sdb1           4.0G   33M  3.8G   1% /u01
```

Once you have created a sufficient number of filesystems with sufficient space, you're ready to begin the Oracle installation. Regardless of whether you intend to install the Oracle datafiles on Linux filesystems, raw partitions, or Automatic Storage Management, you still must have sufficient space available on the base filesystem for the Oracle binaries to install.

Raw Partitions

Raw partitions on Linux offer the best performance of any I/O option that you have, but they come at a price: they are complex and difficult to use. A raw partition is simply a slice of a disk drive. This slice is created using fdisk or parted and has no filesystem or volume manager associated with it. This raw partition can be accessed by Oracle, since Oracle datafiles don't need a filesystem. In fact, Oracle has had the capability to use raw devices for as long as I can remember.

Since Oracle cannot simply write to a raw device (/dev/sdb1, and so on) directly, there is an additional layer that must be used. This is the raw device file. The raw devices exist in the /dev/raw directory and are an additional interface into the physical device itself. This interface uses the rawdevices service and is configured in the /etc/sysconfig/rawdevices configuration file.

The rawdevices Service   The rawdevices service makes sure that each time the system boots the raw devices are pointing to the correct partition and disk drive. This allows configuration changes to be made without having to change the device that Oracle uses. For example, once an Oracle datafile is pointing to /dev/raw/raw1, that device will never change, even if the underlying device name has changed.

Device Names Might Change

It is possible that the physical device name might change. The name that the device is assigned by the operating system, such as /dev/sda, /dev/sdb, and others, is determined according to the scan order of the bus. If you were to configure partitions on the only SCSI device in your system, the names of the devices would be /dev/sda1, /dev/sda2, /dev/sda3, and so on.

If you were to add another SCSI controller into the system and it happened to be placed on a bus and slot that was scanned earlier than the original SCSI card, your existing devices would not be named /dev/sdb1, /dev/sdb2, /dev/sdb3, and so forth. One way to avoid this is to force the scan order of the controllers in your system by setting up aliases within the /etc/modules.conf file. By setting aliases that are increasing in order, the scan order of the controllers within the OS will be set as shown here:

```
alias scsi_hostadapter aic7xxx
alias scsi_hostadapter1 megaraid2
alias scsi_hostadapter97 qla2300
```

This will guarantee that the Adaptec adapter is listed first, then the MegaRaid adapter and finally the Qlogic adapter.

The /dev/raw devices allow you to account for this and modify the devices if the underlying device names were to change. This is configured in the /etc /sysconfig/rawdevices file and allows you to account for underlying device name changes without changing Oracle file names. This configuration is used by the rawdevices service. This should only be attempted with great care and adequate double-checking.

Each time the system boots, the rawdevices service checks the /etc/sysconfig /rawdevices file and makes any necessary changes. If you have added new hardware that has caused the device names to change, you must make these changes in the /etc/sysconfig/rawdevices file before you attempt to start up Oracle.

CAUTION
Be careful of device changes. Starting up Oracle with the incorrect raw devices can cause irreparable damages to your database. All data should be backed up before attempting to add any new devices to the system.

The /etc/sysconfig/rawdevices file is designed to help you avoid problems that could harm your system.

The /etc/sysconfig/rawdevices File The /etc/sysconfig/rawdevices file is used to associate raw devices such as /dev/raw/raw1, /dev/raw/raw2, and so on with physical devices such as /dev/sda1, /dev/sdb2, and their siblings. The /etc/sysconfig/rawdevices file has the following format:

```
<rawdev> <major> <minor>
<rawdev> <blockdev>
```

Either format is acceptable. The major device number indicates the device type (SCSI disk drive in our example), while the minor device number represents the partition. There are eight major numbers allocated to SCSI devices. These numbers are 8, 65, 66, 67, 68, 69, 70, and 71. There are 255 minor devices allocated to partitions on these SCSI devices, and each disk drive can have 15 partitions. The first 255 devices use major number 8, the next 255 devices use major number 65, and so forth. The following is a listing of some SCSI devices. Note the major and minor device numbers.

```
0 brw-rw----   1 root     disk      8,   0 Mar 19  2002 /dev/sda
0 brw-rw----   1 root     disk      8,   1 Mar 19  2002 /dev/sda1
0 brw-rw----   1 root     disk      8,   2 Mar 19  2002 /dev/sda2
0 brw-rw----   1 root     disk      8,   3 Mar 19  2002 /dev/sda3
0 brw-rw----   1 root     disk      8,   4 Mar 19  2002 /dev/sda4
0 brw-rw----   1 root     disk      8,  16 Mar 19  2002 /dev/sdb
0 brw-rw----   1 root     disk      8,  17 Mar 19  2002 /dev/sdb1
0 brw-rw----   1 root     disk      8,  18 Mar 19  2002 /dev/sdb2
0 brw-rw----   1 root     disk      8,  19 Mar 19  2002 /dev/sdb3
0 brw-rw----   1 root     disk      8,  20 Mar 19  2002 /dev/sdb4
0 brw-rw----   1 root     disk      8,  32 Mar 19  2002 /dev/sdc
0 brw-rw----   1 root     disk      8,  33 Mar 19  2002 /dev/sdc1
0 brw-rw----   1 root     disk      8,  34 Mar 19  2002 /dev/sdc2
0 brw-rw----   1 root     disk      8,  35 Mar 19  2002 /dev/sdc3
0 brw-rw----   1 root     disk      8,  36 Mar 19  2002 /dev/sdc4
```

In our example, the /etc/sysconfig/rawdevices file can have either of the following formats:

- /etc/sysconfig/rawdevices using major and minor device numbers:

```
/dev/raw/raw1 8 1
/dev/raw/raw2 8 2
/dev/raw/raw3 8 17
/dev/raw/raw4 8 18
```

- /etc/sysconfig/rawdevices using device names:

```
/dev/raw/raw1 /dev/sda1
/dev/raw/raw2 /dev/sda2
/dev/raw/raw3 /dev/sdb1
/dev/raw/raw4 /dev/sdc1
```

Either format is equivalent; however, I prefer to use the device name.

Using Raw Devices   There are two methods that can be used when creating an Oracle database with raw devices. The Oracle datafile itself can be the device name (for instance, /dev/raw/raw1), or you can create a symbolic link from an Oracle datafile name, such as system.dbf, to the raw device. Either method works fine.

The last method of creating an Oracle database is by using the Automatic Storage Management feature.

Automatic Storage Management

As mentioned previously, the final method of storage management is via the Automatic Storage Management feature, which is new in Oracle 10*g*. Automatic Storage Management is a set of tools that allows Oracle to manage datafiles on raw devices without having to assign each individual file to a raw partition. With ASM, a set of disks is assigned to a disk group and Oracle datafile needs are assigned to the same. Within the disk group, the storage is handled automatically by Oracle.

In addition to simplifying the storage needs of the Oracle Database, ASM can provide redundant storage, thus providing a layer of fault tolerance to your storage. ASM management is controlled via the ASM library driver and associated utilities. If you do not use the ASM library driver, you can still use ASM, but you must bind disk drives to raw devices as described in the previous section.

Installing the ASM Library Driver and Utilities   The ASMlib driver and utilities are available from Oracle in RPM format. Even if your Oracle installation CDs come with the ASMlib packages, it is always a good idea to check the Oracle Technology Network (OTN) web site and make sure you have the latest version of these rpms. At the time this book was written, you could find the latest OCFS software at www.ocfs.org. The list of RPMs should look something like this:

```
oracleasm-2.4.9-e-1.0.0-1.i686.rpm
oracleasm-2.4.9-e-enterprise-1.0.0-1.i686.rpm
```

```
oracleasm-2.4.9-e-smp-1.0.0-1.i686.rpm
oracleasm-2.4.9-e-summit-1.0.0-1.i686.rpm
oracleasmlib-1.0.0-1.i386.rpm
oracleasm-support-1.0.0-1.i386.rpm
```

The list can be broken down into three parts.

- The driver component that is used with the appropriate Linux kernel. Notice that the first four items in the list have the Linux kernel revision in the name of the file. These files support the Linux 2.4.9 kernel standard edition, enterprise, smp, and IBM summit kernels.

- The ASM library shared object file.

- The Oracle ASM support files. These are the programs used to configure and maintain the ASM volumes.

In order to install the proper files, select the driver component(s) suitable for your system, the Oracle ASM library module, and the support files using rpm, as shown next:

```
rpm -Uvh oracleasm-2.4.9-e-1.0.0-1.i686.rpm oracleasmlib-1.0.0-1.i386.rpm
oracleasm-support-1.0.0-1.i386.rpm
```

This will install all of the files you need to begin working with ASM. Next, the disk groups must be configured with ASM.

Configuring ASM Drives   There are two steps necessary to set up and configure ASM. First, ASM must be configured. This configuration is accomplished by running the command /etc/init.d/oracleasm configure, as shown next. The second step is to configure partitions to use ASM.

Configuring the ASM Library Driver

The ASM configuration script sets up the necessary configuration files and services in order to run ASM. The following specific tasks are done by running oracleasm configure:

- The /etc/sysconfig/oracleasm file is created. This file is used when the Oracle ASM service starts up.

- The /dev/oracleasm directory is created with the disks and subdirectories.

- The oracleasm kernel module is loaded. You can see this by running lsmod.

- The ASM library driver filesystem is mounted. You can see from the mount command that oracleasmfs is mounted on /dev/oracleasm.

The /etc/init.d/oracleasm configure command looks like this:

```
[root@ptc6 ASM]# /etc/init.d/oracleasm configure
Configuring the Oracle ASM library driver.
```

This will configure the on-boot properties of the Oracle ASM library driver. The following questions will determine whether the driver is loaded on boot and what permissions it will have. The current values will be shown in brackets ('[]'). Pressing ENTER without typing an answer will keep that current value. CTRL-C will abort.

```
Default user to own the driver interface []: oracle
Default group to own the driver interface []: dba
Start Oracle ASM library driver on boot (y/n) [n]: y
Fix permissions of Oracle ASM disks on boot (y/n) [y]: y
Writing Oracle ASM library driver configuration          [  OK  ]
Scanning system for ASM disks                            [  OK  ]
```

The oracle user account should own the driver interface with the dba group. Whether or not you want to start the ASM driver on boot is your decision; however, I would recommend you do start it on boot.

Setting Up ASM Drives

The next step in setting up ASM is to add drives or partitions to be used for ASM. In order to determine which drives are available for ASM, use the fdisk –l command. Fdisk –l lists all of the available partitions in your system, as shown next:

```
[root@ptc6 disks]# fdisk -l

Disk /dev/sda: 255 heads, 63 sectors, 14593 cylinders
Units = cylinders of 16065 * 512 bytes

   Device Boot    Start       End      Blocks    Id  System
/dev/sda1   *         1      3648    29302528+   83  Linux
/dev/sda2          3649      7296    29302560    83  Linux
/dev/sda3          7297     10944    29302560    83  Linux
/dev/sda4         10945     14593    29310592+   83  Linux

Disk /dev/hda: 240 heads, 63 sectors, 3883 cylinders
Units = cylinders of 15120 * 512 bytes

   Device Boot    Start       End      Blocks    Id  System
```

```
/dev/hda1    *          1        7     52888+  83  Linux
/dev/hda2               8     3779   28516320  83  Linux
/dev/hda3            3780     3883     786240  82  Linux swap

Disk /dev/hdb: 240 heads, 63 sectors, 7753 cylinders
Units = cylinders of 15120 * 512 bytes

   Device Boot    Start      End    Blocks  Id  System
/dev/hdb1    *          1       14    105808+  83  Linux
/dev/hdb2              15     7649   57720600  83  Linux
/dev/hdb3            7650     7753     786240  82  Linux swap
```

You might see several different types of disks, such as /dev/hdxx, which are IDE disks, /dev/sdxx, which are SCSI or SAN disks, and /dev/rd or /dev/ida disks, which are RAID disks. In addition, if you are running software such as EMC PowerPath or Veritas Volume manager, you will see different device names.

If you do not see the partition you want to use for ASM, you must use fdisk or parted to create those partitions before you can configure them with ASM. Once you see the partition you want to use, you can add that disk to ASM by using the /etc /init.d/oracleasm command with the createdisk parameter. All of the oracleasm parameters are listed in the next section.

NOTE
Although ASM disks can be created as a partition on a disk drive, Oracle recommends that an entire disk drive be used for ASM. This is accomplished by creating one partition that uses the entire disk.

In order to add /dev/sda3 to ASM, the following command is used:

```
[root@ptc6 root]# /etc/init.d/oracleasm createdisk VOL1 /dev/sda3
Marking disk "/dev/sda3" as an ASM disk                [  OK  ]
```

I can now query ASM to make sure that the ASM volume has been added for use with the ASM library driver.

```
[root@ptc6 root]# /etc/init.d/oracleasm listdisks
VOL1
```

Once you have one or more ASM disks available, you are ready to begin the Oracle installation process. Of course, ASM volumes are only necessary if you are going to create the Oracle database on ASM.

Oracleasm Optional Parameters   The Oracle ASM library driver supports a number of optional commands that are useful for administering ASM. You should be familiar with these commands if you intend to use ASM:

Command	Description
/etc/init.d/oracleasm configure	Used to configure the ASM module and ASM configuration file as well as set up the ASM mount point.
/etc/init.d/oracleasm [enable/disable]	These commands will change whether the ASM library driver starts on system boot. This command modifies the /etc/sysconfig/oracleasm file.
/etc/init.d/oracleasm [start/stop/restart]	These commands will stop, start, or restart the ASM library driver.
/etc/init.d/oracleasm status	Displays the status of the ASM library driver.
/etc/init.d/oracleasm createdisk name dev	This command takes the name of the volume to be created and a device name in order to associate a disk drive with ASM: /etc/init.d/oracleasm createdisk VOL1 /dev/sda3.
/etc/init.d/oracleasm deletedisk name	Removes a disk drive from its association with ASM.
/etc/init.d/oracleasm listdisks	Lists all of the disk names associated with ASM.
/etc/init.d/oracleasm querydisk [name/dev]	Used to determine if a disk name or disk device is associated with ASM. See the example that follows.
/etc/init.d/oracleasm scandisks	Used in RAC clusters in order to enable the cluster nodes to identify which disks have been associated with ASM on another node.

Here are a few examples of using the /etc/init.d/oracleasm commands: Checking the status of the ASM library driver:

```
[root@ptc6 root]# /etc/init.d/oracleasm status
Checking if ASM is loaded:                              [  OK  ]
Checking if /dev/oracleasm is mounted:                  [  OK  ]
```

Restarting the ASM library driver:

```
[root@ptc6 root]# /etc/init.d/oracleasm restart
Unmounting ASMlib driver filesystem                     [  OK  ]
Unloading module "oracleasm"                            [  OK  ]
Loading module "oracleasm"                              [  OK  ]
```

```
Mounting ASMlib driver filesystem                              [  OK  ]
Scanning system for ASM disks                                  [  OK  ]
```

Deleting an ASM disk:

```
[root@ptc6 root]# /etc/init.d/oracleasm deletedisk VOL2
Removing ASM disk "VOL2"                                       [  OK  ]
```

Adding an ASM disk:

```
[root@ptc6 root]# /etc/init.d/oracleasm createdisk VOL2 /dev/sda4
Marking disk "/dev/sda4" as an ASM disk                        [  OK  ]
```

Listing ASM disks:

```
[root@ptc6 root]# /etc/init.d/oracleasm listdisks
VOL1
VOL2
```

Querying ASM disks:

```
[root@ptc6 root]# /etc/init.d/oracleasm querydisk VOL2
Disk "VOL2" is a valid ASM disk
[root@ptc6 root]# /etc/init.d/oracleasm querydisk /dev/sda3
Disk "/dev/sda3" is marked an ASM disk
```

Scanning the ASM disks:

```
[root@ptc6 root]# /etc/init.d/oracleasm scandisks
Scanning system for ASM disks                                  [  OK  ]
```

NOTE
Whenever an ASM drive is added to a node in a RAC cluster, scandisk should be run on all other nodes in the cluster. This will validate that all nodes have refreshed all of the ASM information and are in sync.

Once the ASM drives are created, you are ready to begin installing Oracle. During the installation, you will be allowed to choose what type of datafiles you will be using for your database.

Using ASM Drives   ASM disks are used within the ASM instance, which is created as part of the Oracle 10g installation and is used for the sole purpose of managing

ASM disks. This instance uses the CREATE DISKGROUPS statement to create a disk group used in ASM. Using ASM drives is explained in more detail later in this chapter.

The Installation Process

The Oracle 10*g* installation process involves two steps. First, the installation medium must be staged. If you are copying the software from the Oracle technology network web site, the software must be uncompressed and extracted from the cpio file. The second step is to run the Oracle installer.

Several files are available for download, including:

- **ship.db.cpio.gz**   This is the Oracle Database binaries archive, containing all of the programs necessary to create the Oracle Database 10*g* server.

- **ship.ccd.cpio.gz**   The companion CD contains two separate installation types. The first consists of database components to go along with the database CD, including database examples, JPublisher, the Legato single-server version, Java libraries, and Oracle text supplied knowledge bases. The second installation type is made up of the companion components: the HTTP server and Oracle HTML DB.

- **ship.crs.cpio.gz**   The third image is the Oracle 10*g* Cluster Ready Services. This will be discussed in detail in subsequent chapters.

The first step in installing is to take the CD images you want to use, and stage them to a directory in your Linux filesystem.

Staging the Install

After creating an oracle_stage directory and changing the ownership of this directory to "oracle", copy the installation files to this directory. Make sure the Oracle user has permissions on this directory. Since the Oracle user will be performing the installation, the following steps should be run as the user "oracle".

The Oracle installation medium is staged by first uncompressing the file using gunzip (GNU Unzip). Simply run gunzip against each of the files you want to uncompress, as shown next:

```
gunzip ship.db.cpio.gz
gunzip ship.ccd.cpio.gz
gunzip ship.crs.cpio.gz
```

Once the files have been uncompressed, the installation medium needs to be extracted from the cpio files. Because each of these archives has a top-level directory that it unarchives to called Disk1, you should change this directory to another name before starting the next cpio command. This will avoid having all three CDs worth of programs in the same subdirectory. This is done using the cpio and mv commands, as shown next:

```
cpio -idmv ship.db.cpio
mv Disk1 db.Disk1
cpio -idmv ship.ccd.cpio
mv Disk1 ccd.Disk1
cpio -idmv ship.crs.cpio
mv Disk1 crs.Disk1
```

Once the CD or CDs are unpacked, you are ready to start the installation process.

Running the Installer

In order to invoke the installer, you will run the shell program runInstaller. Remember that there are a few prerequisites that must be done before you can run the installer. Here is a summary of those prerequisites.

- Kernel parameters must be set.

- Shell limits must be set.

- You must be logged in as the Oracle user account.

- You must be logged into a graphical session with X Windows for the Java installer to work.

- The environment variables ORACLE_BASE and ORACLE_SID should be set.

It is recommended that this program be run from the /tmp directory, so use the following commands to invoke the installer.

```
# cd /tmp
# /oracle_stage/db.Disk1/runInstaller
```

NOTE
In order for the Oracle installer to work, X-Windows must be up and running. If you are running the installer via an ssh shell, X-Windows should be running on your local PC and the option "ForwardX11 no" should be set in the .ssh/config file.

This will invoke a few checks and then the Oracle installer (Java application) will appear. The installation itself is fairly straightforward. One thing you will notice when you invoke the runInstaller program is that there are a few checks done before the Java application appears, as shown in Figure 6-1.

These checks include the following:

■ Making sure the operating system is Red Hat AS 2.1 (Oracle 10g R1), Red Hat AS or ES 3.0, or SUSE Linux Enterprise Server 8.0 (Oracle 10g R1) or 9.0.

■ Ensuring there is at least 80MB of temp space.

■ Making certain the system has at least 150MB of swap space.

■ Ensuring that the X Windows environment supports at least 256 colors.

If you are running on a test machine and do not meet all of the requirements, you can bypass the prerequisites checks by using the IgnoreSysPreReqs flag, as shown next:

```
# /oracle_stage/db.Disk1/runInstaller -ignoreSysPrereqs
```

Bypassing the prerequisite checks should only be done on a test system, and not on production systems. Once the checks have been done, or bypassed, the Java application is invoked and you should see the Oracle installer appear on your screen, as shown in Figure 6-2.

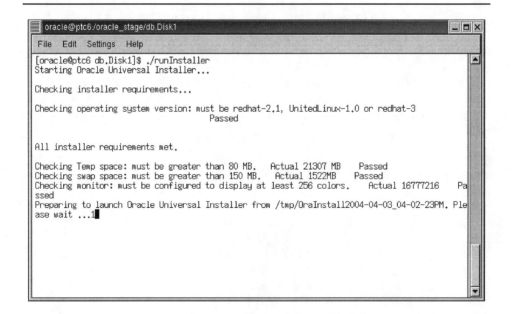

FIGURE 6-1. *Starting up the Oracle installer*

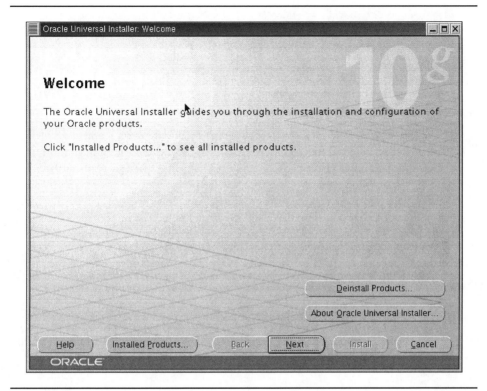

FIGURE 6-2.   *The Oracle Universal Installer*

A number of steps are needed to install the Oracle software on your system. The screens that appear will prompt you to make various decisions. The following are a few things you should be aware of during the installation process:

- The operating system group should be picked up as oinstall.
- In the file locations screen
  - The source file location should be in the stage directory underneath the staging directory you created. In our example, the source path should be /oracle_stage/db.Disk1/stage/products.xml.
  - The path should point to a subdirectory under *oracle_base*. This will look something like /opt/oracle/product/10.1.0/db_1 where *oracle_base* is /opt/oracle.
- The product prerequisite check should be successfully completed before continuing. If there are any errors, correct them and retry the test.
- Set the Oracle database name and SID correctly. It should have picked up the *oracle_sid* from the environment variable.

- Arrange the character set correctly. This is difficult to change later.

- Set the database management option. Here you can choose the new feature of allowing Grid Control for database management.

- Set the Database File Storage option. Here you can choose to use filesystems, or ASM or raw devices for the Oracle Database files (if a database is being created as part of the installation).

- Set backup and recovery options. New in Oracle 10*g* is the ability to schedule automatic backups. You can choose to do so as part of the installation, or you can set this up later.

- Once the installation has completed, take note of the URLs reported for Ultra Search, the Ultra Search Administration Tool, and iSQL *Plus. Typically, these include

  - **Ultra Search**   http://systemname:5620/ultrasearch

  - **The Ultra Search Administration Tool**   http://systemname:5620/ultrasearch/admin

  - **iSQL*Plus**   http://systemname:5560/isqlplus

  - **The Enterprise Manager database control**   http://systemname:5500/em

Once you have completed the installation, a few postinstallation tasks need to be done, as outlined in the next section.

Postinstallation Steps

Before you can begin to use your newly installed Oracle 10*g* database server, a few postinstallation tasks must be performed. These tasks include

- Downloading and installing patches

- Configuring Oracle products

- Testing and validating

It is important that these steps be accomplished before putting your database into production.

Downloading and Installing Patches

Patches for Oracle products can be found on the Oracle MetaLink web site at http://metalink.oracle.com. Once there, click Patches and search for patches for the Oracle product or products you have installed on your system. Each of these patches should be evaluated and, if you so choose, installed on your system. The steps necessary to install these patches are provided with the Oracle product patch set and vary based on the patch.

Configuration Steps

Configuration steps may or may not be necessary depending on your installation. Some of the configuration steps you might need to perform include the following:

- Backing up the Oracle database and binaries
- Configuring and tuning the database
- Adding user accounts
- Generating the Client Static Library

Whether or not these steps are needed depends on your configuration and your needs.

Documenting the System
Before going any further, you should document how your system is configured and how you performed the Oracle installation. If the system ever needs reinstalling, documentation might be the only way others know how things were set up.

Backing Up the Oracle Database and Binaries
The Oracle binaries and configuration files should be backed up once the original configuration is done. This allows you to restore things to a previous state if there are problems in the future. Later, you will concentrate on developing a schedule for backing up the Oracle database itself.

Initial Tuning of the Oracle Instance
The installation process uses the default Oracle parameters. Once you have installed the database and it is up and running, you will need to tune the Oracle instance to be able to perform as required.

Configuring the Database
Hopefully you have created the database with an idea of how it will look. For instance, once it has been created, you might need to add more tablespaces in preparation of importing your production data.

Recompiling Invalid PL/SQL Modules

Oracle recommends that the SQL script utlrp.sql be run in order to recompile all PL/SQL modules that might be invalid. This can be accomplished by setting your Oracle environment and connecting into SQL*Plus, as shown next:

```
[oracle@ptc6 oracle]$ . /usr/local/bin/oraenv
ORACLE_SID = [orac] ?
[oracle@ptc6 oracle]$ sqlplus "/ as sysdba"

SQL*Plus: Release 10.1.0.2.0 - Production on Sun Apr 4 14:58:24 2004

Copyright (c) 1982, 2004, Oracle.  All rights reserved.


Connected to:
Oracle Database 10g Enterprise Edition Release 10.1.0.2.0 - Production
With the Partitioning, OLAP and Data Mining options
```

Once you have connected into the Oracle Database 10*g* server, run the utlrp.sql script (assuming the database server is up and running).

```
SQL> @?/rdbms/admin/utlrp.sql

TIMESTAMP
----------------------------------------------------------------
COMP_TIMESTAMP UTLRP_BGN  2004-04-04 14:59:14


PL/SQL procedure successfully completed.


TIMESTAMP
----------------------------------------------------------------
COMP_TIMESTAMP UTLRP_END  2004-04-04 14:59:15


PL/SQL procedure successfully completed.


PL/SQL procedure successfully completed.
```

Generating the Client Static Library

Since the Client Static Library does not get created as part of the Oracle installation procedure, this will have to be done independently. In order to create libclntst10.a, follow this procedure:

```
[oracle@ptc6 oracle]$ $ORACLE_HOME/bin/genclntst
Created /opt/oracle/product/10.1.0/db_1/lib/libclntst10.a
```

This procedure assumes that the *oracle_home* environment variable has been set already. If it hasn't, you will need to set it or use the actual path name.

Setting Up Oracle Net

Another important task is to set up Oracle Net so your database server can be accessed by Oracle client systems. Oracle Net can be configured by editing the following files.

■ **Listener file** $ORACLE_HOME/network/admin/listener.ora

■ **Names file** $ORACLE_HOME/network/admin/tnsnames.ora

In addition to manually editing the network configuration files, the network can be configured by using the graphical Net Configuration Assistant or netca. netca is invoked by running the program $ORACLE_HOME/bin/netca. You will then see the Java application shown in Figure 6-3.

Once the network has been configured, you are ready to start testing.

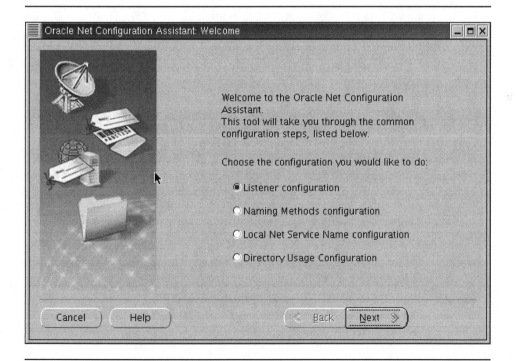

FIGURE 6-3.   *The Oracle Net Configuration Assistant*

Testing and Validating

Before putting any system or new database software into production it should go through a thorough testing phase. There are several methods for testing the database server. This can be as simple as validating that your application is returning the correct data or entail more sophisticated procedures such as load testing using enterprise load testing software. How and what you test will depend on your needs.

Additional Miscellaneous Configuration Steps

Depending on your configuration and requirements, you might need to configure or install other components, which might entail the following:

- Installing Java libraries
- Installing Oracle text supplied knowledge bases
- Configuring the Oracle messaging gateway
- Configuring Oracle precompilers
- Installing products from the companion CD

Installing and configuring these products is covered in detail in the Oracle installation documentation.

Summary

This chapter has covered the tasks required to install and set up storage for the Oracle Database 10*g* server. In the next few chapters, you will learn some variations on this with Oracle 10*g* RAC cluster, which allows multiple Oracle instances to access the same database, thus providing for scalability and fault tolerance at the same time.

The beginning part of this chapter focused on setting up storage for the Oracle Database 10*g* server. This is a very important task that must be accomplished before any database can be created. Here you learned about the three different methods of storage used by Oracle: filesystem files, ASM, and raw partitions. Which one you use will most likely depend on your experience, likes and dislikes, and individual needs.

The Oracle Universal Installer has been improved and is very easy to use. Once the installation and postinstallation tasks have been completed, you should be ready to move on to setting up and configuring your production database. As with any product, attention to detail is the key to success in installing Oracle 10*g* on Linux.

PART
III

Oracle RAC on Linux

CHAPTER
7

Oracle Real Application Cluster Concepts

ith most mission-critical systems there is a need for high-availability computing. If a mission-critical system is unavailable for days or even hours, your company might lose thousands or even millions of dollars. Many mission-critical systems cannot tolerate even a small amount of downtime where the database is unavailable.
There are many solutions available today to increase uptime and reduce system outages. Among these are: Oracle RAC, Oracle Data Guard, and other third-party utilities. Both Oracle RAC and Oracle Data Guard are part of the Oracle Maximum Availability Architecture (MAA). The MAA combines several high-availability, fault-tolerant, and Disaster Recovery solutions together in order to provide a system designed for maximum availability.

Today's mission-critical systems demand a high level of availability. Any downtime, if even for a few minutes, can be extremely costly. The cost of downtime can be in revenue from lost sales, which can be measured immediately, or in lost customers, which cannot be measured so readily. This cost could be thousands or even millions of dollars. It is not unheard of for companies to lose critical systems for hours or days.

By carefully designing your systems and taking advantages of high-availability features such as Oracle RAC and Data Guard, you can increase the availability of the systems. The concept of designing your system for maximum availability is outlined in the Oracle Maximum Availability Architecture (MAA). The MAA combines several high-availability, fault-tolerant and Disaster Recovery solutions together in order to provide a system designed for maximum availability.

NOTE
The Oracle Maximum Availability Architecture (MAA) is described in detail in the whitepaper "Oracle9i Maximum Availability Architecture." In addition, there is information on the MAA in the Oracle10g R1 documentation manual "High Availability Architecture and Best Practices" and the Oracle10g R2 documentation manual "High Availability Overview."

The Oracle Maximum Availability Architecture is made up of a complete standby data center where all levels of the application, infrastructure, and database layer are duplicated at a remote data center. This is shown in Figure 7-1.

By designing your system for maximum availability, you can reduce downtime, increase stability, and save your company from disaster. With the introduction of the Sarbanes-Oxley laws, some of this is not just a business requirement, but a legal requirement as well.

This chapter will cover one part of the maximum availability architecture; Oracle Real Application Clusters (Oracle RAC). Later, in Chapter 13, you will be introduced

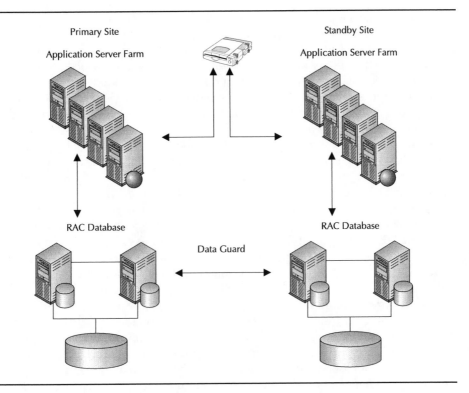

FIGURE 7-1.   *The Oracle Maximum Availability Architecture*

to Oracle Data Guard. This chapter will introduce you to general clustering concepts, followed by some specifics on what Oracle RAC does and how it works.

What Is Clustering?

In the most simple terms, a *cluster* is a group of independent servers that function as a single system. It can also be defined as multiple systems performing a single function, a black box.

Cluster Terminology

Let's go over some cluster terminology. A server that is connected to the cluster is known as a *node* in the cluster. If a node is currently processing data for the cluster, it is *active*. If a node is waiting for a failover before it starts working, it is a *passive* node in the cluster. A resource or a node is placed in a failed state after an unsuccessful attempt to bring it online.

When you create a cluster, you create an *alias* that users connect to. From the cluster's standpoint, the alias refers to the server that owns the service at a particular time. From the users' standpoint, the alias refers to the service they connect to regardless of which server the service resides on. When a failover occurs, users reconnect (unless the application or client operating system handles reconnection for them) to the alias (not to a server) and continue working. If users connect directly to the primary server rather than to the alias, they cannot reestablish their connections when the primary server fails.

Most clustering solutions employ cluster *objects* and *groups* (services). An application, a disk volume (for database volumes, files, or directories), an IP address, and so forth, are examples of cluster objects. A cluster group is a collection of related objects that make up a cluster resource such as an Oracle instance.

Failover occurs when an active node in the cluster or a component of the cluster configuration fails. Cluster services or resources from the faulty node relocate to the operational node. You can also trigger failover manually (e.g., by turning off a system to upgrade it), thereby taking one server offline and shifting the work to the secondary server. System failover capability means that only the entire system can fail over; individual objects (such as applications, disk volumes, etc.) cannot fail over. The secondary system assumes the identity and workload of the primary system (only on system failure) in addition to its own identity and workload. Application failover capability means that the system administrator can fail over one application or object at a time, keeping all other services and users intact on the nodes.

Failback switches the service or object from the secondary node back to the primary node after a failover has occurred, and resets ordinary operating conditions. Failback is usually a manual process, but it can be automatic. I would point out that the reason that failback is usually manual is that the condition that caused the failover in the first place may very well not be able to be cleared automatically but probably requires manual intervention to get it healthy again, thus potentially setting up a series of failovers/failbacks.

A *heartbeat* is the signal that the nodes in a cluster send each other to verify they are alive and functioning. The nodes transmit the heartbeat over direct LAN connections, through a hub or switch, or even via the SCSI bus. If the heartbeat ceases, one of the nodes has failed and the clustering software instructs the other node to take over. Employing more than one method to generate a heartbeat eliminates the problem of a minor failure triggering an unwanted failover.

The *interconnect* provides a communications link between the nodes in a cluster. Status information, heartbeat, and even lock information can travel over the interconnect. This connection can be over your LAN or directly from node to node, using Ethernet, 100Base-T, Fibre Channel, serial, SCSI, and so forth. Fault-tolerant clustering solutions typically use more than one interconnect path simultaneously to prevent unwanted failovers.

Cluster Definition

Now back to the definition of clustering. On a more complex level, clustering is taking a set of servers and running one to *N* number of applications on those servers. A cluster can be as simple as two servers clustered together in a simple failover configuration. If one server fails, the second server takes over processing for the application. Clusters can also be used to run very complex, distributed systems. One example of a complex cluster is the SETI@home project. The application takes the data and splits it into manageable chunks, which independent servers process. If one server fails, the others are not affected and the failed node's processes are redistributed to other nodes in the cluster.

There are several types of clusters: failover clusters, distributed database systems, and shared disk systems. A *failover cluster* is a set of servers where one server acts as a backup of the other server in case of a system failure. A *distributed database system* contains multiple servers running separate instances, where the data from the instances may be kept in sync by a variety of mechanisms. A *shared disk system* is a set of servers that share a disk system. The data that resides on the shared disk can be accessed by all servers in the cluster. Now let's review all three types of clusters in detail.

Failover Cluster

There are two types of failover clusters. One type is the active/passive cluster, and the other type is the active/active cluster. With an active/passive cluster only one server has a load at any given time. The second server is running in a passive mode, waiting for the other server to go down, but keeping in sync with the active server.

With an *active/passive* cluster configuration, only one of the servers uses its processing power for transaction processing, i.e., only one server actually runs an Oracle database. The applications connect to the Oracle database via a virtual IP address. This IP address will fail over to the other cluster if the Oracle database and database files fail over.

With increased functionality in Oracle Net 9*i* and 10*g*, you can also use the listener to provide failover functionality. The listener in conjunction with tnsnames and Transparent Application Failover functionality can be used to provide failover as well. The specific method of performing connectivity failover will depend on your failover solution.

The second type of failover cluster is the active/active cluster. In an *active/active* cluster configuration, both servers perform meaningful work all the time. Active/active clusters let you fully utilize your server resources and can support load balancing. Each server will run one instance and will be the failover database for the instance running on the other server.

With an active/active cluster, both servers are being used for processing. This type of cluster will generally run two different applications, one on each of the servers in the cluster. One of the disadvantages of this type of cluster is that you really need to size both servers in the cluster to be able to temporarily handle the processing of both nodes in the cluster in case of a failover. Both nodes in the cluster could be failed over to the other node at any time.

Distributed Database Systems

In a distributed database system, several database servers are kept in sync by one of several possible mechanisms. One type of distributed database system is a replicated database. Another type is a standby database.

A replicated database consists of multiple copies of the same database. Some replicated databases are read-only, and some are read/write. Oracle Advanced Replication is the one Oracle mechanism for keeping databases in sync.

Another type of distributed database system is the standby database. A standby database is a transactionally consistent copy of the active database. A standby database in Oracle 10*g* is part of the Oracle Data Guard product and is kept up-to-date using redo data. This standby database can be located on the same server, in the same server room, or in another state or country. The standby database is as current as the logs that are applied. The logs can be copied real-time using standby redo logs, they can be copied at each archive log switch, or they can be copied and applied with a delay.

There are advantages and disadvantages of each kind of distributed database. A true replicated database can consume a large amount of available resources keeping multiple copies of the database in sync. If two-phase commit is enabled, any change to the database is not fully committed until all the distributed databases have confirmed the update, and this can cause problems in a high-update environment. With a standby database configuration, however, the data in the standby database is only as current as the log files that have been applied. If a failure were to occur in the primary, all the unapplied log files would have to be applied to the standby before it was current and in an acceptable condition to begin to serve as the current active database.

Distributed databases are used in systems that require high availability. The most common type of distributed database is the standby.

Shared Disk System

Shared disk clustering employs a shared file system. Multiple systems access the same set of disks. All nodes in the cluster must have access to the shared disks. The Oracle shared disk system runs only one database with one or more instances accessing it. Oracle Real Application Clusters (RAC) is a true shared disk system, meaning that there are multiple instances accessing the same database files, which reside on the shared disk.With a shared disk system, multiple nodes in the cluster share a common set of disks. These disks are usually configured in some type of RAID configuration. Normally, there are a group of disks for the cluster information, often called the quorum. Actually, in RAC there is a quorum file, which is maintained on a shared disk by each of the participating nodes.

The main problem with a shared disk cluster has been keeping the nodes from interacting with each other in a negative way. Without proper control, each node could cancel out the other's updates. If control is too tight, application processing could slow down. Oracle has solved these problems with its RAC product. With 10*g* RAC, vendor clusterware is now nonspecific. The clusterware is the software that manages the interaction between the various systems in the cluster. The Oracle instance interacts with this clusterware to synchronize data within the nodes in the cluster. With 10*g*, the clusterware is called the Cluster Ready Services (CRS). CRS has to be up and running before an Oracle database can be installed and configured.

With 10*g*, Oracle has added a new feature for shared disk system: Automatic Storage Management (ASM). With ASM, DBAs no longer need to manage files and drives separately. Instead, DBAs will create disk groups consisting of disks and their assigned files. The combination of Oracle Managed Files (OMF) and ASM eliminates the need for a DBA to specify the filenames and locations for the physical database files when creating a new database, or adding files to an existing database. The DBA simply identifies the destination disk group, and Oracle takes care of the rest. ASM can also be extended to support other administrative tasks, including disk management, backups, and recovery. Although they are often employed with each other, OMF and ASM are separate features of Oracle and need not be used together.

ASM runs as a separate Oracle instance from the Oracle Database, but with less functionality than a normal instance. For a normal instance to take advantage of ASM, the ASM instance must be running before the normal instance starts. When the ASM instance starts, it identifies the various disk groups and the files they contain, mounts the disk groups, and then creates an extent map, which is passed to the database instance. The database instance itself is responsible for any actual input/output operations. The ASM instance is only involved during the creation or deletion of files and when disk configurations change.

RAC (Real Application Clusters)

In this section, we will review Real Application Clusters (RAC). We will start off with an overview of RAC, and then go into the components that make up a RAC database.

Overview of RAC

Real Application Clusters (RAC) is central to the Oracle product design for High Availability (HA). RAC is the product that will allow Oracle to fail over to another node when there is a problem. RAC employs a shared disk type of clustering. This allows all nodes in the cluster to have access to the data at the same time. There is only one set of data files that all of the nodes can use at all times. According to Oracle Corporation, the ultimate goal for Real Application Clusters is to provide manageability that is comparable to a single computer with a single instance of the Oracle database. In other words, for the common management tasks, the goal is to have the multinode system look and behave like a single system.

RAC clustering on Linux supports up to 64 clustered nodes. Each node in the cluster has a different physical Internet Protocol (IP) address. However, users (or clients) can connect to the database via a virtual database service name. Oracle can automatically balance the user load among the multiple nodes in the cluster, or the DBA can manually balance the user load. The RAC database instances on the different nodes subscribe to all or some subset of database services. This allows you to choose whether specific application clients that connect to a particular database service can connect to some or all of the database nodes. If more nodes are added to the cluster, the CPU and memory resources of the new node are immediately made available to the rest of the cluster. Data does not have to be repartitioned. This allows you to add nodes as you need them. Components of a RAC cluster are shown in Figure 7-2.

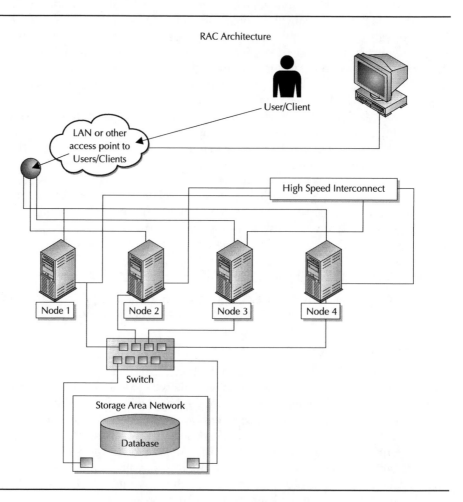

FIGURE 7-2. *Components of an Oracle RAC cluster*

In Oracle RAC, disk access and resources that manage data are shared. All instances have common data and control files. Each node has its own dedicated system memory, operating system, database instance, and application software. Each instance also has individual redo log files.

Each individual server runs its own oracle instance. These instances together make up one RAC database. Multiple RAC databases can be installed on one set of nodes. The instances for these databases can use all or some of the active nodes in the cluster.

Oracle RAC uses a shared cache system known as Cache Fusion. Cache Fusion uses the collective caches of all the nodes in the cluster to satisfy database requests (see Figure 7-3). Requests for a data block can now be satisfied by the local cache or any of the other caches (instead of having to go to disk). Extensive disk I/Os are performed only when none of the collective caches contain the necessary data, or when an update transaction performs a COMMIT operation that requires disk write guarantees. Cache Fusion enables nodes on a cluster to synchronize their memory caches efficiently using a high-speed cluster interconnect so that disk I/O is minimized. The key is that Cache Fusion enables shared access to all the data on disk by all the nodes on the cluster. Data does not need to be partitioned among the nodes. Oracle is the only open systems database with this capability.

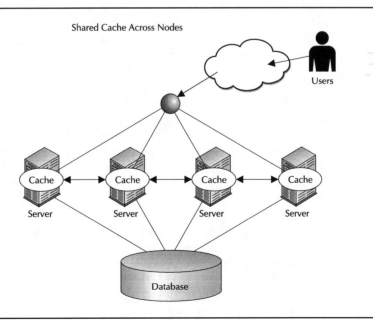

FIGURE 7-3.   *The Oracle RAC Cache Fusion architecture*

Oracle RAC 10*g* Components

Oracle RAC 10*g* is made up of several components. These components are the Cluster Ready Services, Services and Automatic Workload Management, Virtual Internet Protocol, and the Oracle Cluster Registry.

Cluster Ready Services (CRS)

Oracle Real Application Clusters (RAC) 10*g* introduces a complete, integrated clusterware management solution on all Oracle Database 10*g* platforms. This clusterware, called Cluster Ready Services (CRS), includes mechanisms for cluster connectivity, messaging and locking, and cluster control and recovery, as well as a workload management framework. Oracle 10*g* does not require third-party clusterware management software, although Oracle continues to support some third-party tools on certain platforms.

CRS is a core change in Oracle 10*g* from 9*i*. CRS provides a simple clusterware technology that is consistent across all platforms. In Oracle 9*i* on Linux, clusterware was a complicated piece that, if not configured properly at the start of the installation, could cause problems that would require reinstallation from scratch. CRS must be installed and running before RAC can be installed. With Oracle RAC 10*g*, up to 64 nodes are supported on all platforms. Users can also expect a consistent response across all platforms to high-availability challenges such as server node failures and cluster interconnect failures.

The CRS is made up of the following pieces: CRS home, a separate home directory for Cluster Ready Services; Oracle Cluster Registry (OCR); and the CRS voting disk. The CRS home directory should reside on a local drive. Since OCR and the voting disk need to be accessible before any of the Oracle instances in the RAC cluster start, you cannot use Automatic Storage Management (ASM) to store the two files. The CRS files must reside on a shared file system such as OCFS or RAW devices.

There are three daemons associated with the CSR: the Cluster Ready Services Daemon (CRSD), the Oracle Cluster Synchronization Server Daemon (OCSSD), and the Event Manager Daemon (EVMD). The CRSD performs high-availability recovery and management operations such as maintaining the OCR. It also manages application resources; that is, it starts, stops, and fails application resources. The CRSD runs as root and is restarted automatically upon failure. The CRSD keeps cluster state information and configuration profiles in the OCR.

The OCSSD manages cluster node membership and runs as the oracle user. This daemon maintains the heartbeat, and failure of this process will result in system reboot. This is a feature to prevent data corruption in the event of a split brain. It provides node membership, group access, and basic cluster locking. The OCSSD can operate with non-RAC systems. It can integrate with third-party clustering products or can be run without integration to vendor clusterware. OCSSD is also part of a single instance using ASM.

The EVMD is the event manager daemon that starts the RACGEVT process. This daemon will generate events when things happen to the cluster. It spawns a permanent child, evmlogger. EVMD scans the callout directory and invokes callouts. Like CRSD, this daemon is restarted automatically upon failure, but it runs as the oracle user.

There is a fourth daemon, OPRCD, which will only appear on platforms that do not use vendor clusterware with the CRS. OPRCD is the process monitor for the cluster. There is only one set of these daemons running on each node no matter how many Oracle instances are running.

Each daemon has a set of logfiles, which are found in the following locations:

Daemon	Logfile location
CRSD	$CRS_HOME/crs/log
EVMD	$CRS_HOME/evm/log
OCRD	$CRS_HOME/ocr/log

CRS is started automatically whenever the system is rebooted. The DBA or Systems Administrator can also stop and start the CRS manually by executing the following commands:

```
/etc/init.d/init.crs start
/etc/init.d/init.crs stop
```

The CRS requires both the voting disk and the OCR, and if either of these files is not available, CRS will not start. CRS must be up and running before the Oracle RAC instances can be mounted. Three network addresses are required for the CRS: a public IP address, a private interconnect IP address, and a virtual IP address (VIP). The VIP and public addresses must be set up in DNS prior to the CRS installation.

The command to see the status of the CRS is crs_stat. The format of the output of this command is difficult to read, so I recommend running a script to better format the output. Here is a sample script that will return the output from the crs_stat binary in a more readable form.

```
crs_stat.sh
#!/usr/bin/ksh

# Sample 10g CRS resource status query script
#
# Description:
# - Returns formatted version of crs_stat -t, in tabular
# format, with the complete rsc names and filtering keywords
# - The argument, $RSC_KEY, is optional and if passed to the script, will
# limit the output to HA resources whose names match $RSC_KEY.
```

```
# Requirements:
# - $ORA_CRS_HOME should be set in your environment
RSC_KEY=$1
QSTAT=-u
AWK=/bin/awk # if not available use /usr/bin/awk
# Table header:echo ""
$AWK \
'BEGIN {printf "%-45s %-10s %-18s\n", "HA Resource", "Target", "State";
printf "%-45s %-10s %-18s\n", "-----------", "------", "-----";}'
# Table body:
$ORA_CRS_HOME/bin/crs_stat $QSTAT | $AWK \
'BEGIN { FS="="; state = 0; }
$1~/NAME/ && $2~/'$RSC_KEY'/ {appname = $2; state=1};
state == 0 {next;}
$1~/TARGET/ && state == 1 {apptarget = $2; state=2;}
$1~/STATE/ && state == 2 {appstate = $2; state=3;}
state == 3 {printf "%-45s %-10s %-18s\n", appname, apptarget, appstate; state=0;}'
```

Services and Automatic Workload Management

With Oracle 10g, application workloads can be defined as services so that they can be individually managed and controlled. DBAs control which processing resources are allocated to each service both during normal operations and in response to failures. Performance metrics can be tracked by service. Thresholds can be set to automatically generate alerts should these thresholds be crossed. Resource consumption controls and CPU resource allocations are managed for these services using Resource Manager. Oracle facilities and tools such as Parallel Query, Job Scheduler, and Oracle Streams Advanced Queuing also use services to manage their workloads.

Workload sharing configurations can be defined in many different ways. For example, let's assume that you have a five-node RAC cluster with two instances, A and B, serving as the preferred instances for an OracleAS 10g application. This same cluster could have instances C, D, and E as the preferred instances for a Customer Relationship Management (CRM) application. Instances A and B are the available instances for CRM if one or more of CRM's preferred instances become unavailable. Instances C, D, and E are the available instances for AS 10g if one or more of the AS 10g preferred instances become unavailable. This configuration enables each service to use a group of instances that acts as both preferred instances and available recovery instances. After a failure, a client recovers its connections on another instance in the same group. With this configuration, during normal operations, RAC routes application sessions by service to separate groups of instances. If a preferred instance becomes unavailable, then CRS relocates connections among the remaining RAC instances that offer that service. Workload-managed configurations achieve the highest performance and availability by routing connections according to service. Planned and unplanned outages on one domain can be isolated from other domains, and the affected service can be recovered or upgraded in isolation.

The Automatic Workload Repository tracks service-level statistics as metrics. Server-generated alerts will be sent out when they exceed or fall below certain thresholds. The DBA has the option to then respond by stopping overloaded processes, changing the priority of a job, or by modifying a service-level requirement. This enables the DBA to maintain continued service availability despite service-level violations.

You can configure

- Priorities relative to other services

- The measurement of service quality

- Alert mechanisms and event notification to monitor changes to service quality

- Recovery scenarios for responses to service quality changes

The Automatic Workload Repository ensures that the CRS workload management framework and resource manager have persistent and global representations of performance data. Such information helps Oracle schedule job classes by service and to assign priorities to consumer groups. If necessary, you can rebalance workloads manually with a PL/SQL procedure. You can use this procedure to disconnect sessions but leave the service running.

When an instance goes offline due to a failure, CRS will relocate the service to another available instance. CRS relocates the service and reestablishes the connection without service interruption. The underlying service components on which the relocation relies must be enabled for relocation and restarted. Otherwise, the connections cannot be reestablished.

VIP: Virtual Internet Protocol

One of the new features of Oracle 10*g* RAC is the Virtual Internet Protocol, or VIP. This is a virtual IP address that is used for failover of the nodes in the cluster.

Let's go back and review the requirements for Oracle 9*i* RAC IP addresses. RAC used two addresses: one for the private interconnect network and one for the public network external to the cluster. To access the RAC database, you must specify the public IP addresses/hostnames in the tnsnames.ora file.

With 10*g* RAC, there is now a requirement for three IP addresses for each node in the cluster. The additional IP is for the virtual IP (VIP). You can now use the VIP in the tnsnames.ora file in place of the public IP. The VIP will fail over to a surviving node if a failure is detected.

Both the VIP and the public IP need to be defined in the DNS. The VIP is configured using the VIPCA (Virtual Internet Protocol Configuration Assistant) utility, which is invoked during the Oracle CRS installation procedure.

Oracle Cluster Registry (OCR)

The Oracle Cluster Registry (OCR) contains cluster and database configuration information for RAC Cluster Ready Services (CRS), including the list of nodes in the cluster database, the CRS application, resource profiles, and the authorizations for the Event Manager (EVM). The OCR can reside in a file on a cluster file system or on a shared RAW device. When you install Real Application Clusters, you specify the location of the OCR. The OCR contains configuration details for the cluster database and for high-availability resources such as services, Virtual Internet Protocol (VIP) addresses, and so on.

RAC Database Components

RAC databases are just like any other database, comprising control files, redo logs, datafiles, and one server parameter file (SPFILE) or one or more PFILEs, or client-side parameter files. Each instance is made up of the System Global Area (SGA) and the instance background processes.

The control file contains information on the state of the datafiles, redo logs, and recovery state. You cannot easily recover a database without at least one good control file or backup control file. For this reason, you should always multiplex your control files using the standard Oracle methods. For a RAC database, all control files must reside on the shared storage. Best practices dictate that you should have at least three control files that should reside on three different storage groups or LUNs. This way, if you completely lose a storage group, you can still recover the rest of the database with one of the other control files.

The next important piece of the RAC database consists of the redo log files. Redo log files have already been covered, but it is important to note the differences between the redo log of a RAC cluster and that of a stand-alone database. Each instance must have at least two groups of redo log files. The datafiles for these groups should reside on an individual storage group. Best practice specifies that each redo log file reside on an individual, mirrored pair for maximum performance. Each file accesses data synchronously, so if you put anything else on the RAID group, it could become asynchronous. Due to the large affect redo logfiles can have on database performance, I recommend placing them on individual RAID groups.

Datafiles are another essential part of an Oracle RAC database. In a RAC database, all of the datafiles must reside on shared storage. As with all Oracle databases, the placement of the datafiles can greatly affect performance. The current Oracle recommendation is to stripe and mirror everything (SAME); that is, to put the datafiles on a RAID 1+0 storage group. The data files are the physical files in which Oracle stores the data. These files must be accessible from all the nodes in the RAC. It is important to analyze and understand your application fully before you allocate your datafiles. If you have an I/O-intensive application and anticipate I/O stress being placed on your system, you will want to identify the tables that will have the most I/O access, and will likely want to place the datafiles associated with these tables on separate data groups or on RAID 1+0 storage groups that can handle I/O load that will be generated by the application.

Another component of an Oracle RAC is the server parameter file, or SPFILE, which is used in conjunction with the parameter file, or PFILE. Each instance in an Oracle RAC requires a PFILE to start the database up. The recommendation by Oracle is for the PFILE to simply point to the SPFILE, as in the following example.

```
pfile='/u01/PROD/spfilePROD.ora'
```

The SPFILE contains the startup parameters for the Oracle instance. In an Oracle RAC, all the instances share some parameter settings, but other parameters might be different for each instance. To ensure they are all started with the same parameter set, the SPFILE should reside on the shared storage. The parameters in the SPFILE are the same parameters that previously resided in the init.ora file. There are some additional parameters for RAC that will be described later. The SPFILE is stored in a non-editable format: although it looks like plain text, if you edit the file, you risk that it will no longer work. Therefore, if you want to change the location of the control files, for example to move them around to separate data groups, you will need to perform the following steps:

1. Create a PFILE from the current SPFILE.

2. Stop the database and/or all instances.

3. Copy the control files to the new locations.

4. Edit the PFILE to include the new locations for the control files.

5. Finally, start one of the databases using the new PFILE and create an SPFILE at the old location using the new PFILE.

At this point, the instances residing on the other nodes in the cluster can be started the normal way: they will all start using the new SPFILE.

You can always start an Oracle RAC instance if the init.ora file (PFILE) is identical to the existing SPFILE.

The last group of database components consists of the instance processes. These are the background processes for the Log Writer (LGWR), the Database Writer (DBWn), the System Monitor (SMON), the Process Monitor (PMON), the Recoverer (RECO), and the Archiver (ARCx), along with the Checkpoint process (CKPT).

The Log Writer, LGWR, writes log file entries. It reads from the log buffer in the SGA and writes to the redo log files. The Database Writer, DBWn, writes out dirty buffers from the database buffer cache. A *dirty* buffer is one that has been modified from the original data on disk and hasn't been written out. This is the only process that writes to datafiles; it uses a least recently used (LRU) list algorithm to determine which blocks to write to disk.

The System Monitor, SMON, performs instance recovery at database startup. It can recover another instance in a RAC system. SMON cleans up temporary segments and coalesces free extents. The Process Monitor, PMON, performs process recovery on failed user processes. It cleans up the database buffer cache and frees up resources. PMON checks on Dispatcher and Server processes, restarting them if necessary.

The Recoverer, RECO, recovers distributed processes. If a Server connection is lost, RECO attempts to reconnect it. RECO completes commits or rollbacks. The Archiver processes, of which there may be up to ten, named ARC0 to ARC*n*, archives redo log files after a log switch.

Archiver processes exist only when the database is operating in ARCHIVELOG mode.

CKPT, the Checkpoint process, signals DBWR and marks blocks for checkpoints. It assists the DBWR, but it does not write to datafiles.

There are other background processes running for Oracle RAC: The Dispatcher (DMNn) process is used with shared server processes; Lock is used with RAC; Job Queue (the coordinator, CJQ0, and the job queue slave processes, J*xxx*) and Queue Monitor (QMON) are used for batch processing and advanced queuing, respectively. Dedicated Oracle server processes also run in the background, spawned on behalf of the user processes. Dedicated server processes check, then read data the buffer cache. They also modify data in the buffer cache, but do not themselves write to the datafiles. Other processes include query servers, used for parallel queries; shared server processes, used with the shared server architecture; and dispatchers, used with shared servers.

RAC Configuration Files

Oracle 10*g* RAC has made several changes to configuration files and initialization parameters. Two of the main changes are the ocr.loc file, which replaces the srvConfig.loc file, and the GCS_Server_Processes parameter.

The ocr.loc configuration file specifies the location of the Oracle Cluster Registry, which contains the Cluster Ready Services configuration information. This file resides on each of the servers in the cluster and points to the shared storage location. If CRS will not start the first time, there is a good chance that this file on one of the servers has an incorrect location for the CRS configuration files. The CRS configuration is initialized from one node in the cluster, but it is accessed by all nodes when CRS starts on that node.

The GCS_SERVER_PROCESSES parameter specifies the initial number of server processes in Global Cache Service to serve the inter-instance traffic among RAC instances. This is a new parameter introduced in 10*g*. The default value for this parameter is 2 for RAC databases, but the value can range from 1 to 20. This parameter can also be set differently for each instance in the cluster.

The Cluster Interconnect

The *interconnect* is a vital part of the Oracle RAC configuration. It is composed of several pieces: the private network that connects all nodes in the cluster, the Oracle processes that communicate between the servers, and the communication protocol the network information passes on.

The purpose of the interconnect is to communicate the status of all nodes in the cluster as well as all the instances that reside on the cluster. The interconnect passes the locking information and global cache information between nodes. Realistically, this interconnect must be configured with Gigabyte Ethernet at a minimum, since even on an extremely inactive database, a 100 Mbps Ethernet connection very quickly becomes saturated. The interconnect and internode communication protocols can affect Cache Fusion performance. In addition, the interconnect bandwidth, its latency, and the efficiency of the IPC protocol determine the speed with which Cache Fusion processes block transfers.

Because Cache Fusion exploits high-speed IPCs, RAC benefits from the performance gains of the latest technologies for low-latency communication links used in cluster database interconnects. You can expect even greater performance gains if you use more efficient protocols, such as InfiniBand, TCP/IP, Virtual Interface Architecture (VIA), RDMA, and user-mode IPCs. Cache Fusion reduces CPU use with user-mode IPCs, also known as memory-mapped IPCs, for all platforms. If the appropriate hardware support is available, then operating system context switches are minimized beyond the basic reductions achieved with Cache Fusion alone. This also eliminates costly system calls and data copying. If your hardware efficiently implements them, user-mode IPCs can dramatically reduce CPU use, because processes in user-mode IPCs communicate without using operating system kernels. In other words, user processes do not have to switch from user execution mode to kernel execution mode.

Oracle 10g RAC's Use of Shared Storage

One of the key things a RAC needs to operate is shared storage. This can be as simple as a set of shared SCSI disks. Or it can be as complicated as a multidisk array on a massive SAN. The one thing all of these solutions have in common is that all the nodes in the cluster will need to have access to write to the physical disks at the same time. To make use of the shared storage, Oracle either uses the drives as RAW devices or as a clustered file system on the shared storage. Either way, Oracle must have access to a group of disks in a cluster configuration for Oracle RAC to operate. Two of the more common options for shared storage are SAN storage and NAS storage. Components of a storage area network are shown in Figure 7-4.

A SAN, or storage area network, consists of a group of disks that are shared via a private network and managed by a specialized controller that is accessed by the clients of the SAN. The only items connected to the external network are the clients

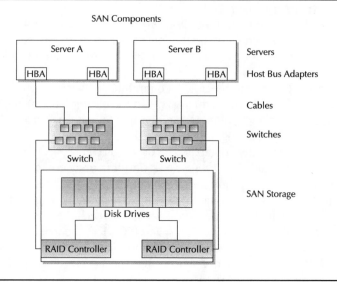

FIGURE 7-4. *Components of a storage area network*

and the SAN controllers. Servers are most commonly connected to the SAN via a Fibre Channel adapter and Fibre Channel cables, since SANs were designed to provide access to storage over a private Fibre Channel network. The components of the SAN may be connected in many different configurations. Some configurations have the components housed as a single unit, while in other configurations the disks themselves are put on separate shelves from the storage processors, which are connected to the servers.

A SAN is very suitable for acting as the shared storage for Oracle RAC. As has been stated earlier, RAC requires shared disk space that can be written to simultaneously by all nodes in the cluster. Oracle itself manages the simultaneous access, but it must have some means for all the nodes to be able to see and write to the disks. This is where a SAN comes in, since SANs were designed with just this type of multiple server access in mind. A SAN is a network whose primary purpose is the transfer of data between storage systems and computer systems.

In addition to providing extremely fast access to data, SANs can be very useful for consolidating your storage, thereby offering many benefits: reduced cost of external storage; increased performance; centralized and improved tape backup (that may be performed on its own private network, thus reducing LAN traffic); elimination of single points of failure; and extremely large storage units, often with many tens of terabytes of storage in a single system.

Fibre Channel, the interconnecting technology used within SANs, provides concurrent communications between servers, storage devices, and other peripherals. It is a Gigabit interconnect technology. Fibre Channel 1 (FC1) offers over 1,000,000,000 bits per second, whereas FC 2 effectively doubles this to over 2,000,000,000 bits per second. In addition, Fibre Channel is a highly reliable interconnect technology. Yet another advantage is that Fibre Channel allows connection of up to 127 devices. This contrasts with SCSI technology, where the limit is 15 devices. The distance limit for Fibre Channel is 10 km of cabling, which compares very favorably with 1–3 m for SCSI. The physical interconnect can be copper or fiber optics and is hot-pluggable. Hot-pluggable devices can be removed or added at will with no ill effects to data communications. Finally, Fibre Channel provides a data link layer above the physical interconnect, analogous to Ethernet, which incorporates sophisticated error detection at the frame level—data is checked and re-sent if necessary.

With a SAN, I/O traffic is limited to the private SAN network, allowing for faster I/O operations. Multiple servers can be connected to a SAN via Fibre Channel switches: you are limited only by the number of ports on the switch. With dual switches and dual HBAs (Host Bus Adapters) in the servers, multiple paths from the servers and the disks are possible, expanding RAC's High-Availability (HA) capabilities even more. A fully redundant SAN configuration can withstand a failure in the Fibre Channel, the HBA, or even a service processor (SP) in the SAN and still not need to fail over to the other node.

Using NAS as Shared Storage

NAS stands for Network Attached Storage. The disks are attached to a generally available network, though often on a segment to which no devices other than the client systems are attached, and the servers access the storage over this public network. This means that there is no need to set up and maintain a separate Fibre Channel network dedicated to shared storage access, as required by a SAN. As in a SAN, however, disks can be attached to the network via a standard copper network or via Fibre Channel, but regardless of the physical nature of the network, Oracle should have exclusive use of the partitions.

It is recommended that you use a dedicated private network between the nodes in the cluster and the NAS appliance. A diagram of a typical NAS design is shown in Figure 7-5.

A dedicated network connection is beneficial for the following reasons:

- In an Oracle 10*g* RAC environment, it is important to eliminate any contentions and latencies.

- Providing a separate network ensures security.

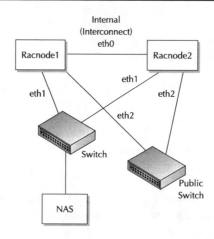

FIGURE 7-5. *A RAC system with NAS*

Summary

For most applications, Oracle RAC both is scalable and provides a highly available clustering solution. Oracle RAC has been thoroughly tested on Linux and performs well and is stable on this platform, especially Oracle 10*g* RAC, which offers significant advantages over Oracle 9*i* RAC in both performance and stability. A high-performance interconnect is required as well as a shared disk subsystem. The RAC cluster allows multiple Oracle instances to access the same database, allowing for both scalability and high availability.

Linux provides a multiuser, multitasking environment that is perfect for Oracle RAC. Oracle RAC (Real Application Clusters) is both a scalable and high-availability clustering solution. The Oracle RAC system has been thoroughly tested on Linux and performs well and is stable on this platform. A high-performance interconnect such as Gigabit is required as a minimum requirement; with newer and faster systems, however, the Gigabit network is fast becoming inadequate for a RAC interconnect. Today a faster interconnect such as InfiniBand is required. Oracle Cluster Ready Services are automatically started at bootup. A system administrator can efficiently maintain a cluster of Oracle 10*g* RAC servers on Linux. If your next assignment is to install Oracle 10*g* RAC on Linux, proceed to the next chapter. It will be worth your time.

CHAPTER
8

Deploying Oracle Real Application Clusters on Linux

n the last chapter, you were introduced to Oracle Real Application Clusters (RAC). Understanding the basic concepts is the first step toward deploying a RAC cluster. In this chapter, you will see how to deploy Cluster Ready Services, install the Oracle Database Server in a RAC environment, and create a RAC cluster.

Here, we will cover the deployment of an Oracle 10g Real Application Cluster (RAC) on Linux. We will cover planning the RAC system, configuring Linux for the RAC installation, and testing the RAC. This chapter will also highlight the differences between Oracle Cluster File System (OCFS), raw devices, and ASM for storage of datafiles and cluster information. We will also provide some tips on the best platform for your particular installation.

Planning the RAC System

The first step to deploying any DBMS system is to create a plan so that you understand your options. First, let's go over the RAC components just in case you skipped the last chapter.

The RAC Components

An Oracle Real Application Cluster (RAC) is made up of several very important components. Between 2 and 32 servers will make up the nodes in your cluster, using a shared storage system of some kind. In the last chapter, we went over the different types of shared storage. See Chapter 7 if you need to review.

Another component that is necessary for the RAC is the Cluster Ready Services (CRS). The CRS must be operational before Oracle can be installed and a database created. It is made up of binaries that reside on each node in the cluster and configuration files that reside on a quorum disk on the shared storage. The CRS must be installed in its own ORACLE_HOME.

After CRS has been installed, it will start automatically. You can also start it manually. It uses the voting disk and the OCR (Oracle Cluster Registry). Only one set of CRS daemons exists per node in the cluster, no matter how many instances are installed. Three daemons make up the CSR: CRSD, OCSSD, and EVMD. The CRSD performs high-availability recovery and management operations such as maintaining the OCR. It also manages application resources, runs as the root user, and restarts automatically upon failure. OCSSD manages cluster node membership and runs as the oracle user. Failure of this process results in cluster restart. EVMD is the event manager daemon that starts the *racgevt* process to manage callouts. There is a fourth daemon, *oprocd,* which will appear only on platforms that do not use vendor clusterware with the CRS. OPROCD is the process monitor for the cluster.

Another important component of a RAC is the virtual IP address. Each server will require at least three IP addresses. One will be used for public or general access to the database. One will be used for the private high-speed interconnect. The final IP address will be used for a virtual IP, or VIP. The VIP will be used to seamlessly fail over to another node in case of a failure. Multiple virtual IP addresses can exist on the same system (during failover). The VIP and the *public* IP must be on the same subnet, be defined in /etc/hosts, and be defined in DNS (Domain Name Service).

The next step is to understand your application requirements. This section is mainly "Know Thyself." If you do not have a good understanding of your application, you might not make the best choices for the RAC. Here are a few things to keep in mind:

- Are your users going to access the database via a direct connection or via a mid-tier, app server connection?

- How many active user connections to the database will you need?

- Is your application mainly read-only, or does it do more writing than reading?

- Do you have experienced SAN personnel and database administrators? Or will you need to hire/farm out the maintenance of the Oracle RAC?

- Is your system going to grow significantly larger in the next few months to a year?

- How big is your database going to be?

- Do you want to use archive logging? If so, where will the log files be stored?

- Is performance or redundancy the most important issue with your application?

- How will you back up the system?

- Do high-availability requirements dictate that Data Guard be used in conjunction with RAC?

It is best to keep these things in mind while you are planning your RAC implementation. Let's take a quick look at each of these items. First, will you be using a mid-tier application server? You will need more database connections if you do not use a mid-tier app server. If you are using a connection pool, where the app server grabs many database connections and shares them with all users, you might not need as many connections. If you have a web-based application and all users connect directly to the database, you might need to make changes to the Linux system parameters.

How many user database connections will your app require? If you need many connections to the database, you may want to design the connections differently.

Is your application mainly read-only, or does your application write more than it reads? The amount of writing your database will require affects the type of RAID you select for the shared storage. If your application is very write intensive, you may want to stay away from RAID 5 for your data.

What is the experience level of your personnel? This is important because you may not want to use a SAN if you do not have the personnel to support it. Or if you are going to outsource support or hire personnel, it may increase your cost.

Is your system going to grow significantly larger in the next few months to a year? This will directly affect the size of your RAC. You may need only one shelf of drives to support your current business, but your company is thinking about expanding overseas. Your database may increase 100-fold nearly overnight! If you are planning on expanding from a two-node RAC to a three-node RAC, it is important to make sure your hardware, such as Ethernet switches and Fibre switches, can handle the third node.

That brings us to the big kicker. Just how big will your database be? This is one of the most important things in designing your RAC. You want to make sure you take the entire system into account when planning for the size of your shared storage. The total size will need to include the sizes of your tables, indexes, redo logs (for all nodes), archive logs, and quorum information. Keep in mind that best practices dictate at least one redo log partition for each node in the cluster. These should be on separate LUNs to ensure that the access stays sequential. The RAID type you choose will also affect the size of the shared storage. Please see the next section, "Sizing the RAC System," for more details.

Is performance or redundancy the most important issue with your application? This question will weigh heavily on the type of failover to set up. It will also help determine the RAID types for your shared data storage. The answer could even help you decide whether or not to team your network interface cards (NICs).

The next step in planning your RAC system is to determine if you're going to use raw devices, the Oracle Cluster File System (OCFS), or ASM to manage your shared files. With raw devices you will get the most performance, but you sacrifice manageability. Raw devices can be accessed only via Oracle programs. They cannot be modified from a Linux mount point. If you try to modify the files, you may corrupt your data files. ASM (which stands for Automatic Storage Management) is the new Oracle storage method. As with all new products, beware of ASM until it has some mileage under its belt. OCFS has been the best choice for most of my customers. Only the most hardcore performance addicts among them need to use raw devices.

Sizing the RAC System

There is a tendency to treat sizing servers as some form of mystic science. Most people assume that the more statistics, benchmarks, and technical specifications that you can arm yourself with, the better. There is more to sizing a RAC system than just gathering all the information you can.

Here are the steps you should follow for sizing a RAC system, or for that matter, any system:

- **Define customer requirements** This is one of the most important steps. You must have a proper starting place before you proceed. Most customers will not deliver their requirements to you on a silver platter. You must be proactive in obtaining the input you require. You must be prepared to translate from business terms into technical terms.

- **Analyze system data** You should always gather as much technical information as possible from a comparable or current production system. This is true even if the hardware platform will be different than your target system, or even if you expect your new system to have significantly improved performance characteristics. You should make sure you gather statistics for CPU utilization, memory utilization, and I/Os per second (IOPS). If the comparison system is Microsoft Windows–based, you may use Performance Monitor to obtain the required data.

- **System determination** The next step is to design a system that will meet the customer requirements according to the system information you have gathered. You will need to predict total CPU usage, total memory usage, and the total I/O load. You may estimate storage resources required for capacity and performance in terms of the I/O load and the total size estimate of customer data. You will want to pull together all of your sizing guidelines. This includes any relevant "rules of thumb" and benchmarks. Compare your requirements to similar existing implementations if possible. The design should cover all aspects of the customer requirements. You should make sure that all of the requirements have been met in the initial design. It is far more expensive to find out you have missed a requirement after the hardware has been purchased.

- **Implementation** Try to deliver the design in incremental steps. Deliberately stagger the full implementation. This allows you to tune performance as you implement.

Basic Oracle RAC Sizing Requirements

There are a number of sizing items that you must take into account with Oracle 10*g* RAC. Several of these are hard requirements from Oracle, and some of these are trial-and-error requirements from personal experience.

At a minimum, I would recommend looking at the current Oracle minimum requirements for the version of Oracle RAC you are installing. These requirements change from release to release, so always check on the Oracle information sites.

One of the hard-and-fast sizing requirements is the minimum number of partitions on the shared storage. You need to have at least two partitions for Oracle 10*g* RAC on Linux. The first partition should be of at least 1GB. This will be used for the quorum information for Cluster Ready Services (CRS). CRS will place the voting disk and the Oracle Cluster Registry (OCR) on this partition. Ultimately, you will want this partition to be separate from your data files. If they are separate, you can lose your cluster information but not lose your data. The storage size for the OCR should be at least 100MB, and the storage size for the voting disk should be at least 20MB. In addition, Oracle recommends that you use a RAID array for storing the OCR and the voting disk to ensure the continuous availability of the partitions.

The second partition will be used for the Oracle database files. These include the redo logs, the archive logs, and the tablespace and index files. The sizing for this part is the most important.

Most of the best practices on Oracle RAC recommend the following partitions, or RAID array, be created:

- **One partition per node in the cluster for redo logs**   It is actually preferable to have two per node. Some may think this is excessive, but for a true high-performance system, two are required. After a log switch, the older log is archived off and the new log is used to keep track of redo information. If you use one RAID array for both logs, the I/Os are no longer sequential. Therefore, two per node are recommended, but one per node is acceptable.

- **One partition for archive logs**   The act of writing archive logs is synchronous. If you have them on a separate partition, the database performance will not be affected.

- **At least one RAID 1/0 partition for your data files**   Oracle recommends SAME, Stripe and Mirror Everything. The more spindles you have allocated to the RAID 1/0, the better chance you have of hitting a free drive with concurrent data requests.

Configuring Linux

Well, now that you've gotten your background information and planned your Oracle RAC, let's get down to the details of Linux. The first thing you should do is verify that your hardware meets the requirements for 10*g* RAC. Setting up the Linux kernel is another very important step in deploying Oracle RAC. The next important step we will be going over is the Linux System setup.

Based on my experience deploying Oracle RAC on Linux, the most important thing to get right is the networking parameters. If you mess up the networking, you may have to reinstall Oracle. I have seen several days' work go down the drain because of a network setup mistake. So pay attention to the next few sections. They could save you a lot of rework.

Verifying Hardware

The system must meet the following minimum hardware requirements:

- 512MB of physical RAM

- 1GB of swap space (or twice the size of RAM). On systems with 2GB or more of RAM, the swap space can be between one and two times the size of RAM

- 400MB of disk space in the /tmp directory

- Up to 4GB of disk space for the Oracle software, depending on the installation type

- 5GB of shared storage for redo log files and quorum information

To verify the amount of physical RAM the server contains, issue the following command:

```
# grep MemTotal /proc/meminfo
```

To determine the size of the configured swap space, enter the following command:

```
# grep SwapTotal /proc/meminfo
```

To determine the amount of disk space available in the /tmp directory, enter the following command:

```
# df -k /tmp
```

If there is less than 400MB of disk space available in the /tmp directory, complete one of the following steps:

- Delete unnecessary files from the /tmp directory to achieve the required disk space.

- Set the TEMP and TMPDIR environment variables when setting the oracle user's environment.

- Extend the file system that contains the /tmp directory. If necessary, contact your system administrator for information about extending file systems.

To determine the amount of free disk space to load the Oracle binaries, run the following command:

```
# df -m
```

To determine whether the system architecture can run the software, enter this command:

```
# grep "model name" /proc/cpuinfo
```

This command displays the processor type. Verify that the processor architecture matches the Oracle software platform that you want to install.

Verifying Network Requirements

Check that you have the networking hardware and Internet Protocol (IP) addresses required for an Oracle Real Application Clusters installation.

NOTE
For the most up-to-date information about supported network protocols and hardware for Oracle Real Application Cluster (RAC) installations, see the Certification pages on the Oracle MetaLink web site.

Network Hardware Requirements

Each node in the cluster must meet the following requirements:

- Each node must have at least two network adapters: one for the public network interface and one for the private network interface (the interconnect).

- The interface names associated with the network adapters for each network must be the same on all nodes.

- For increased reliability, i.e., failover of NICs, you can configure teaming public and private network adapters for each node.

- For the public network, each network adapter must support TCP/IP.

■   For the private network, the interconnect must support the User Datagram
Protocol (UDP) using high-speed network adapters and switches that
support TCP/IP (Gigabit Ethernet or better recommended).

NOTE
*UDP is the default interconnect protocol for
RAC, and TCP is the interconnect protocol
for Oracle CRS.*

Setting Up the Linux Kernel

The first step in configuring the kernel is deciding on the kernel that will be used.
Please go to Oracle MetaLink to identify the latest certified kernel version.

After you have identified and installed the correct kernel, you will need to
configure it for Oracle 10*g* RAC. The first step is to verify that software requirements
for Oracle 10*g* RAC have been met.

Checking the Software Requirements

You must have one of the following operating system versions:

Oracle10*g* R1

■   Red Hat Enterprise Linux AS/ES 2.1 or 3.0 (x86)

■   UnitedLinux 1.0, service pack 3 or higher (x86)

Oracle10*g* R2

■   Red Hat AS/ES 3.0 or 4.0

■   SuSE Linux Enterprise Server 9.0

The required OS packages are the same for RAC as they are for a stand-alone
Oracle installation. This information was provided in Chapter 5.

Oracle Cluster File System (OCFS) version 1.0.9–12 or later

■   ocfs-support

■   ocfs-tools

■   ocfs-kernel_version

NOTE
OCFS is required only if you want to use a cluster file system for database files. If you want to use Automatic Storage Management or raw devices for database file storage, you do not need to install OCFS.

To ensure that the system meets these requirements, follow these steps:

1. To determine which distribution and version of Red Hat Linux is installed, enter the following command:

   ```
   cat /etc/issue
   ```

   or

   ```
   uname -r
   ```

2. On SLES 8 systems only take the output from the preceding command to determine whether Service Pack 3 is installed. The version must be at least 2.4.21-138-default. This command shows the kernel version and type. If the kernel version is less than 2.4.21-138, contact your SLES vendor for information about upgrading to Service Pack 3.

3. To determine whether the required packages are installed, enter a command similar to the following:

   ```
   rpm -q package_name
   ```

   If a package is not installed, install it from your Linux distribution media.

4. To verify OCFS is installed on your system, enter the following command:

   ```
   rpm -qa | grep ocfs
   ```

   If you want to install the Oracle database files on an OCFS file system and the packages are not installed, download them from the OCFS web site, http://oss.oracle.com/projects/ocfs/.

Checking for Required Patches

Depending on the products that you intend to install, verify that any necessary patches have been installed. Always check the latest Oracle documentation for an updated list of requirements.

NOTE
The Oracle Universal Installer performs checks on your system to verify that it meets the requirements listed. To ensure that these checks pass, verify the requirements before you start the Installer, or run the Installer in preinstall mode with the runInstaller –executeSysPrereqs command and install any missing O/S patches or packages.

Setting Kernel Parameter and Shell Limit Values

Oracle will run fairly well out of the box for Linux. However, we need to make sure that certain kernel parameters are at a minimum level before we install Oracle RAC.

NOTE
The kernel parameter and shell limit values shown in the following sections are recommended values only. For production database systems, Oracle recommends that you tune these values to optimize the performance of the system. You must set the kernel parameters and shell limits on all cluster nodes.

Changing the Kernel Parameters

One of the most important items to a RAC deployment on Linux are the kernel parameter changes.

Using any text editor, create or edit the /etc/sysctl.conf file and add or edit lines similar to the following:

```
kernel.shmall = 2097152
kernel.shmmax = 2147483648
kernel.shmmni = 4096
kernel.sem = 250 32000 100 142
fs.file-max = 131072
net.ipv4.ip_local_port_range = 1024 65000
```

Once you've specified the values in the /etc/sysctl.conf file, they persist when you reboot the system.

Enter the following command to change the current values of the kernel parameters:

```
sysctl -p
```

Review the output from this command to verify that the values are correct. If the values are incorrect, edit the /etc/sysctl.conf file and then enter this command again. On SLES only, enter the following command to cause the system to read the /etc/ sysctl.conf file when it reboots:

```
/sbin/chkconfig boot.sysctl on
```

Repeat this procedure on all other cluster nodes.

Setting Shell Limits for the Oracle User

To improve the performance of the software, you must increase the shell limits for the oracle user. This is covered in Chapter 5 and is no different for RAC than it is for a stand-alone Oracle system; therefore, it will not be repeated here.

Setting Up the Linux System

Creation of the Oracle accounts is similar to their creation in the stand-alone Oracle system, but it is very important that the accounts be created identically on all systems in the RAC cluster. It is critical that the group and user IDs be the same on all nodes in the cluster. In addition, it is essential that ssh or rsh be set up correctly.

Account Creation

Depending on whether this is the first time Oracle software is being installed on this system and on the products that you are installing, you may need to create several Linux groups and a Linux user. The following Linux groups and user are required if you are installing an Oracle database.

The OSDBA Group (dba)   You must create this group the first time you install Oracle database software on the system. It identifies Linux users that have database administrative privileges (the SYSDBA privilege). The default name for this group is dba. If you want to specify a group name other than the default dba group, you must choose the Custom installation type to install the software or start the Installer as a user that is not a member of this group. In this case, the Installer prompts you to specify the name of this group.

The OSOPER Group (oper)   This is an optional group. Create this group if you want a separate group of Linux users to have a limited set of database administrative privileges (the SYSOPER privilege). By default, members of the OSDBA group also have the SYSOPER privilege. If you want to specify a separate OSOPER group, other than the default dba group, you must choose the Custom installation type to install the software or start the Installer as a user that is not a member of the dba group. In this case, the Installer prompts you to specify the name of this group. The usual name chosen for this group is oper.

The following Linux group and user are required for all installations.

The Oracle Inventory Group (`oinstall`)   You must create this group the first time you install Oracle software on the system. The usual name chosen for this group is oinstall. This group owns the Oracle inventory, which is a catalog of all Oracle software installed on the system.

NOTE
If Oracle software is already installed on the system, the existing Oracle Inventory group must be the primary group for the Linux user that you use to install new Oracle software. The following sections describe how to identify an existing Oracle Inventory group.

The Oracle Software Owner User (`oracle`)   You must create this user the first time you install Oracle software on the system. This user owns all of the software installed during the installation. The usual name chosen for this user is oracle. This user must have the Oracle Inventory group as its primary group. It must also have the OSDBA and OSOPER groups as secondary groups.

A single Oracle Inventory group is required for all installations of Oracle software on the system. After the first installation of Oracle software, you must use the same Oracle Inventory group for all subsequent Oracle software installations on that system. However, you can choose to create different Oracle software owner users, OSDBA groups, and OSOPER groups (other than oracle, dba, and oper) for separate installations. By using different groups for different installations, you assure that members of these different groups have DBA privileges only on the associated databases rather than on all databases on the system.

When you install Oracle software on the system for the first time, the Installer creates the oraInst.loc file. This file identifies the name of the Oracle Inventory group and the path of the Oracle Inventory directory. To determine whether an Oracle software owner user named oracle exists, enter the following command:

```
id oracle
```

If the oracle user exists, the output from this command is similar to the following:

```
uid=440(oracle) gid=200(oinstall) groups=201(dba),202(oper)
```

If the user exists, determine whether you want to use the existing user or create a new user. If you want to use the existing user, ensure that the user's primary group is the Oracle Inventory group and that it is a member of the appropriate OSDBA and OSOPER groups.

The Oracle software owner user and the Oracle Inventory, OSDBA, and OSOPER groups must exist and be identical on all cluster nodes. To create these identical users and groups, you must identify the user ID and group IDs assigned them on the node where you created them, and then create the user and groups with the same name and ID on the other cluster nodes.

Identifying the User and Group IDs

To determine the user ID (UID) of the Oracle software owner user and the group IDs (GIDs) of the Oracle Inventory, OSDBA, and OSOPER groups, first enter the following command:

```
id oracle
```

The output from this command is similar to the following:

```
uid=440(oracle) gid=200(oinstall) groups=201(dba),202(osoper)
```

From the output, identify the UID for the oracle user and the GIDs for the groups to which it belongs.

Configuring Linux Modules/Programs

Before you install an Oracle Real Application Cluster, you must configure the secure shell (SSH) for the oracle user on all nodes in the cluster. The Oracle Installer uses the ssh and scp commands to run remote commands on and copy files to the other cluster nodes during the installation. You must configure SSH so that these commands do not prompt for a password.

Oracle Directories

There are a number of directories that must be identified or created for the Oracle software. These are as follows:

- Oracle Inventory directory
- Oracle base directory
- CRS home directory
- Oracle home directory

NOTE
CSR must have a separate home from ORACLE_HOME.

The following section describes the requirements for the directories.

Oracle Inventory Directory

The Oracle Inventory directory stores an inventory of all Oracle software that is installed on the system. This is a required directory and is shared by all Oracle software installations on a single system. The Installer prompts you for the specific path to this directory the first time you install Oracle software on a system. Oracle recommends you choose the following path:

 `$ORACLE_BASE/oraInventory`

You will not need to create this directory. The Installer takes the path you specify; creates the directory; and sets the correct owner, group, and permissions on it. Please back this directory up regularly. Do not delete it unless you are removing all Oracle software from your system. You may want to maintain separate oraInventory directories for other types of Oracle products. The different versions of the OUI are notorious for not playing well together. You can maintain separate versions of the oraInst.loc file for the different types of Oracle installations, such as Database, Application Server, or Enterprise Manager Grid Control. Just remember to set oraInst.loc to a new directory for each new type of installation.

Oracle Base Directory

The Oracle base directory is a top-level directory for Oracle software installations. I generally use /opt/oracle. The Oracle user should be the owner of the Oracle base directory.

Regardless of whether you create a new Oracle base directory or decide to use an existing one, you must set the ORACLE_BASE environment variable to the full path to this directory.

NOTE
The Oracle base directory should be located on a local file system. Do not create it on an OCFS version 1 file system. Future versions of OCFS may support Oracle base on an OCFS file system, but OCFS version 1 does not.

Setting Environment Variables

After you have created the directories, you will need to set the following environment variables:

- ORACLE_HOME
- ORACLE_BASE
- CRS_HOME
- PATH

If this is the first Oracle installation on the node, you also need to run orainstRoot.sh under /opt/oracle/oraInventory as prompted by the OUI.

Networking

The next step in deploying Oracle 10*g* RAC on Linux is to set up your networking. This step is very important to complete before you attempt to install 10*g* or CRS. Some of the IP addresses/hostnames are embedded in Oracle. You may need to reinstall parts of 10*g* RAC if you had a typo in the networking configuration files before you installed CRS and 10*g*. The first things you will need are the IP addresses and the hostnames.

IP Address Requirements and Hostnames

Before starting any part of the Oracle installation, you must identify or obtain the following IP addresses for each node in the cluster:

- One IP address and an associated hostname registered in the domain name service (DNS) for each public network interface. If you have two public network interfaces on each node in the cluster, you will need two IP addresses and hostnames set up in DNS for each server.

- One unused virtual IP (VIP) address and an associated virtual hostname registered in DNS. The VIP configuration assistant (VIPCA) will configure the VIP for the primary public network interface. The virtual IP address must be in the same subnet as the associated public interface. After installation, you can configure clients to use the virtual hostname or the IP address. If a node fails, its virtual IP address fails over to another node.

- A private IP address and optional hostname for each private interface. Oracle recommends that you use private network IP addresses for these interfaces, for example, 10.*.*.* or 192.168.*.*. You can use the /etc/hosts file on each node to associate private hostnames with private IP addresses.

For example, if each node has two public and two private interfaces, you might have the following hostnames and IP addresses on one of the nodes (rac1) and similar hostnames and IP addresses on the other nodes:

Hostname	Type	IP Address	Registered In
db01.domain.com	Public	172.20.43.100	DNS
db02.domain.com	Public	172.20.43.102	DNS
db01-vip.domain.com	Virtual	172.20.43.104	DNS
db02-vip.domain.com	Virtual	172.20.43.106	DNS
racnode1	Private	192.168.0.1	/etc/hosts
racnode2	Private	192.168.0.2	/etc/hosts

NOTE
I normally put all the IP address and hostnames in the /etc/hosts file. Make sure you have the loopback placed last in the /etc/hosts files.

Checking the Network Requirements
To verify that each node meets the requirements, follow these steps:

1. If necessary, install the network adapters for the public and private networks and configure them with either public or private IP addresses.

2. Register the hostnames and IP addresses for the public network interfaces in DNS.

3. For each node, register one virtual hostname and IP address in DNS.

4. For each private interface on every node, add a line similar to the following to the /etc/hosts file on each node, specifying the private IP address and associated private hostname:

    ```
    192.168.0.1 racnode1
    ```

5. To identify the interface name and associated IP address for every network adapter, enter the following command:

    ```
    /sbin/ifconfig -a
    ```

From the output, identify the interface name and IP address for all network adapters that you want to specify as public or private network interfaces.

Bonding (Teaming) the Public Interface and the Interconnect

You wanted a fault-tolerant system, so you purchased and are setting up an Oracle 10*g* system. Now is not the time to skimp on the little things that help the system be truly fault tolerant. *Bonding* is the Linux term for teaming two or more network interfaces together. This allows the IP traffic to run over either or both network interfaces. If one of the network interfaces goes down, you still have the other as a backup. The teamed set of network interfaces will have only one IP address to the outside world.

Make sure to set up the teaming correctly. Teaming can be done after the Oracle RAC has been configured. It is not necessary to set up bonding before installing RAC.

Setting up VIP

We mentioned that a virtual IP (VIP) address with an associated hostname in DNS is a requirement. This VIP will be used by Oracle for failover. The VIP is set up after CRS has been installed.

The VIP is used by Oracle networking as the key to the nodes in the cluster. Oracle networking, in the tnsnames.ora file, specifies the hostname or IP address of the Oracle server containing the listener.

If you use VIP, the VIP hostname or IP is placed in the tnsnames.ora file in place of the real hostname or IP. When the server fails, the VIP value is transferred to a remaining host in the cluster. All clients that are trying to access the Oracle instance via VIP are redirected to the host that now has the VIP value. This is a key feature of 10*g* RAC.

Testing the Networking

Always test and retest the networking before you install Oracle.

To test the networking, you should be able to SSH to each of the nodes in the cluster from a root account. You should test all IP address and hostnames.

It is a good idea to be able to SCP from and to all hosts as well. Oracle will use this to copy the binaries to the remote hosts during installation.

NOTE
If you do not have networking successfully set up,
the Oracle installation will fail.

Verifying That the Shared Storage Is Accessible

The final item you need to check off before beginning your 10*g* installation is the shared storage. If not all the nodes in your cluster can access the shared storage, you cannot begin the 10*g* configuration. Here are the steps:

1. Verify the correct driver for the adapters.

   - HBA

   - SCSI

   - RAID

2. Install storage software.

3. Verify storage is set up.

   - RAID groups created

   - Disks partitioned

4. Verify each node sees the RAID groups/LUNs.

   ```
   cat /proc/partitions
   ```

Configuring RAC

In this section, we will go over some of the issues involved in configuring Oracle 10*g* for a RAC deployment. Oracle 10*g* Real Application Clusters (RAC) is made up of several pieces that need to be configured separately. We will cover setting up the Cluster Ready Services (CRS); configuring the interconnect; and configuring the shared disk using OCFS, raw devices, or ASM.

Here are a few things to remember when you deploy your applications on RAC:

- Storage for RAC datafiles must be some kind of shared storage—I recommend that, when you install RAC, you use a Cluster File System for datafile storage.

- Use a hardware cache when possible—as long as it is fault tolerant so that you do not lose data changes.

- Do not create the database when you install the software. Choose software only.

- Create a seed database using the Database Configuration Assistant (DBCA). Clustering functionality has been integrated into DBCA. DBCA is RAC aware.

- Use DBCA to define services for your environment and administer them with the Server Control (SRVCTL) Utility and Oracle Enterprise Manager (OEM).

- Use a server parameter file (SPFILE) and make sure it is located on the shared storage. It can reside on OCFS or a raw device.

- Use Automatic Segment-Space Management.

- Use Automatic Undo Management.

- Adding nodes to a RAC cluster will not automatically give better performance. If there is no load on existing Oracle instances in a cluster, adding another node to the cluster will not increase performance.

Configuring the Cluster Ready Services (CRS)

Cluster Read Services (CRS) are a group of services that allow several nodes in a cluster to communicate with each other. This is the basis for RAC. Before we get started with the CRS configuration, here are some key facts to remember:

- CRS is required to be installed and running prior to the 10g RAC installation.

- CRS can be run without vendor clusterware. Oracle 10g RAC also supports running CRS on top of vendor clusterware, such as Veritas Cluster.

- The Oracle binaries and CRS binaries must be installed in different locations; that is, ORACLE_HOME and CRS_HOME must point to different locations.

- Shared devices for the voting file and the OCR (Oracle Cluster Registry) file must be available prior to installing CRS. The voting file should be at least 20MB in size, and the OCR file should be at least 100MB. The voting file and the OCR must be placed on raw devices. OCFS is not available for these.

- RAC requires that the public and private interfaces be configured prior to the CRS installation.

- Use a RAID array for storing the OCR and the voting disk to ensure the continuous availability of the partitions.

You may want to stage the CRS CD to a local drive on the first node in the cluster. Before you launch the Installer, make sure you have the following information on hand:

- The locations of ORACLE_HOME and CRS_HOME

- Shared devices for the voting disk and OCR

To configure CRS, execute the runInstaller command on the CRS CD from an X Window session on the first node in the cluster. (This is a separate CD in the Oracle 10g CD set.) This will launch the Oracle Installer. The CRS runs as root, and the 10g RAC parts will run under the Oracle account.

The public IP and VIP addresses that you use for all of the nodes in the current installation process must be from the same subnet.

During the installation, the OUI first copies software to the local node and then copies the software to the remote nodes. After the CRS installation has completed, you will want to verify your CRS installation by executing the olsnodes command from the CRS_HOME/bin directory. The olsnodes command syntax is

```
olsnodes [-n] [-l] [-v] [-g]
```

where

- The -n option displays the member number with the member name.

- The -l option displays the local node name.

- The -v option activates verbose mode.

- The -g option activates logging.

Here is an example:

```
olsnodes -n
```

The output from this command should be a listing of the nodes on which CRS was installed.

```
Node1   1
Node2   2
```

Configuring the Interconnect

One of the most important parts of an Oracle RAC deployment is the interconnect. Oracle states that a 100MB interconnect is the minimum requirement. However, I have found that Gigabit Ethernet is mandatory. Several issues arise from having a small pipe for the interconnect. I have seen database errors when the activity level is high and the interconnect was slow.

The interconnect is really a private network and should be segregated from the rest of the network. It should be set up in separate switch from the rest of the networking. At a minimum, you should create a virtual LAN (VLAN) on the switch for the interconnect.

Here is one last hint on setting up the interconnect: for improved performance, set UDP send and receive packet sizes to 256K.

Configuring the Shared Disk

You have several configuration choices for the shared disks. The most common choice is to use the Oracle Cluster File System (OCFS), but raw devices and ASM are also potentially viable choices.

Configuring the Shared Disk Using OCFS

The Oracle Cluster File System (OCFS) is a shared filesystem used within an Oracle RAC cluster. It looks like a filesystem, but it can hold only Oracle data and archive logs. OCFS is similar to a logical volume manager (LVM). OCFS has two components: a drive and a service. The drive, OCFS, is used for operating system filesystem support. The service, cfs, coordinates communication between nodes on the cluster. The service keeps inodes and files in sync. OCFS needs a high-speed interconnect to function properly.

Configuring the Shared Disk Using Raw Devices

On most platforms, Real Application Clusters requires that each instance be able to access a set of unformatted devices on a shared disk subsystem. These shared disks are also referred to as *raw devices*. Oracle instances in Real Application Clusters use raw devices to update control files, server parameter files, datafiles, and online redo logs. All instances in the cluster share these files. Raw devices must be pre-created using OS-specific commands before the database can be created.

A raw *device* is a disk drive that does not yet have a file system set up. Raw devices are used for Real Application Clusters because they enable the sharing of disks.

A raw *partition* is a portion of a physical disk that is accessed at the lowest possible level. A raw partition is created when an extended partition is created and logical partitions are assigned to it without any formatting. Once formatting is complete, it is called a *cooked* partition.

There are several reasons you might want to use raw devices rather than OCFS. OCFS is a file system, and file systems have overhead, do caching, are difficult to cluster, and are difficult to maintain from multiple systems. With raw devices, there is no OS level synchronization. In addition, Oracle uses raw devices to maintain the data and do the locking. With OCFS, the OCFS processes incur some overhead in providing synchronization functions. Raw devices are 3–7 percent faster. However, OCFS offers

- Simpler management

- Use of Oracle Managed Files with RAC

- Single Oracle software installation

- Autoextend enabled on Oracle datafiles

- Uniform accessibility to archive logs in case of physical node failure

Oracle has been heavily developing OCFS, but raw devices have seen no innovation for some time. Raw devices are recommended only if you really need that last bit of performance.

Configuring the Shared Disk Using ASM

The third way to configure the shared disks is using Automatic Storage Management (ASM). ASM is a new feature in Oracle Database 10*g* that frees the DBA from a series of mundane tasks. Here's how it works.

With ASM, you will no longer need to manage files and drives individually. Instead, disk groups can be created consisting of disks and their assigned files. Essentially, the combination of OMF and ASM eliminates the need for a DBA to specify the filenames and locations for the physical database files when creating a new database, as well as in other database operations—you simply identify the destination disk group, and Oracle takes care of the rest. ASM can also be extended to support other administrative procedures, including backup/recovery and disk management.

The physical files must be located using the data provided by the control file before the database can be opened. But the control file itself is part of a disk group, so ASM needs to have its own separate instance available before the actual database instance is started.

As part of the ASM instance startup procedure, the various disk groups and their files are identified. The ASM instance mounts the disks and then creates an extent map, which is passed to the database instance. The database instance itself is responsible for any actual input/output operations. The ASM instance is involved only during the creation or deletion of files and when disk configurations change.

When these types of changes happen, the ASM instance will rebalance the disks and provide the necessary information to refresh the extent map in the SGA of the database instance. This then requires the database instance and the ASM instance to be run concurrently. The ASM instance should be shut down only after the database has been closed.

The impact of the ASM instance on performance of the database instance is minimal. The former does not process transactions affecting the individual database objects; therefore, the average SGA allocation needed by the database instance for ASM is no more than 64MB. Unless the server's memory is already at the maximum recommended operating system/DBMS allocation, 64MB should have no impact on the memory available for the database instance.

Because ASM will manage the disk groups and the database files internally, you simply need to identify the appropriate disks, desired failure groups, and the level of redundancy for the disk group. Because ASM internally balances the workload across all the disks in the disk group, disk contention is reduced and performance increases. An added benefit of ASM is that it automatically and dynamically rebalances the files if you need to change a size of a disk group (adding or dropping a disk). This task can be accomplished without shutting down the database.

With ASM, you have the option to specify a disk group when you create a new data file. For example, to create a new tablespace with 500MB of allocated space, issue the following command:

```
CREATE TABLESPACE tablespace1 DATAFILE '+datagroup1' SIZE 500MB;
```

ASM manages the naming, placement, and distribution of the datafile. You will need to assign only the disk group that would store the datafile. This approach will eliminate the time you spend tuning I/O operations and correcting fragmentation problems later.

NOTE
ASM, like OCFS, is not a general-purpose file system. It is not intended to replace the operating system's file system. ASM should not be used to manage background or user trace files.

The greatest benefits you will gain from ASM include the ability to dynamically change storage resources, the elimination of manual I/O tuning, and automatic rebalancing. When you have thousands of files to manage, you can spend 30–40 percent of your time performing the same operations that ASM handles automatically. Using it, you will free up valuable time to address other aspects of your job.

Testing and Managing the RAC

The most important things to do once you have completed the installation are to test and to manage the RAC. This section will cover why and how to test your Oracle RAC implementation. Part of the testing will be to bring up and stop the instances, so let's go over managing the RAC first.

Most of the management functions can be accomplished with one tool, srvctl. Srvctl is a command-line interface to the RAC, its instances, and its services.

Let's assume you have created a two-node RAC database called seed. It will have two instances, seed1 and seed2. Seed1 is running on rac1, and seed2 is running on rac2. To see the status of database seed, run the following command:

```
srvctl status database -d seed
```

This will give you the following output:

```
Instance seed1 running on node rac1
Instance seed2 running on node rac2
```

The srvctl command may be run from either node in the cluster.

Here is the syntax for the command. You may get the status for a service, the nodeapps, a database, or just an instance.

```
srvctl status database -d <database-name> [-f] [-v] [-S <level>]
srvctl status instance -d <database-name> -i <instance-name> [,<instance-name-
list>]
      [-f] [-v] [-S <level>]
srvctl status service -d <database-name> -s <service-name> [,<service-name-list>]
      [-f] [-v] [-S <level>]
srvctl status nodeapps [-n <node-name>]
srvctl status asm -n <node_name>
```

Here are more examples:

- Status of the database, all instances, and all services

  ```
  srvctl status database -d seed -v
  ```

- Status of named instances with their current services

  ```
  srvctl status instance -d seed -i seed1, seed2 -v
  ```

- Status of a named service

  ```
  srvctl status service -d seed -s CRM  -v
  ```

- Status of all nodes supporting database applications

  ```
  srvctl status node
  ```

The srvctl command can also be used to start and stop the database and its
instances. Here is the syntax for starting a database and an instance. Note that when
you start the database, all enabled instances associated with the database are started.

```
srvctl start database -d <database-name> [-o < start-options>]
      [-c <connect-string> | -q]
srvctl start instance -d <database-name> -i <instance-name>
      [,<instance-name-list>] [-o <start-options>] [-c <connect-string> | -q]
```

Services configured for the cluster, node applications, and ASM can also be
started using srvctl.

```
srvctl start service -d <database-name> [-s <service-name>[,<service-name-list>]]
      [-i <instance-name>]  [-o <start-options>] [-c <connect-string> | -q]
srvctl start nodeapps -n <node-name>
srvctl start asm -n <node_name> [-i <asm_inst_name>] [-o <start_options>]
```

You can also use srvctl to stop CRS resources. Here is the syntax for that:

```
srvctl stop database -d <database-name> [-o <stop-options>]
      [-c <connect-string> | -q]
srvctl stop instance -d <database-name> -i <instance-name> [,<instance-name-list>]
      [-o <stop-options>][-c <connect-string> | -q]
srvctl stop service -d <database-name> [-s <service-name>[,<service-name-list>]]
      [-i <instance-name>][-c <connect-string> | -q] [-f]
srvctl stop nodeapps -n <node-name>
srvctl stop asm -n <node_name> [-i <asm_inst_name>] [-o <start_options>]
```

Here are some examples:

- Stop the database, all instances, and all services.

  ```
  srvctl stop database -d seed
  ```

- Stop named instances.

  ```
  srvctl stop instance -d seed -i seed1,seed2
  ```

- Stop the service.

  ```
  srvctl stop service -d seed -s CRM
  ```

- Stop the service at the named instances.

  ```
  srvctl stop service -d seed -s CRM -i seed2
  ```

- Stop node applications.

  ```
  srvctl stop nodeapps -n rac1
  ```

NOTE
*Instances and services also stop when the nodeapps
are stopped.*

Next, I'll show how to modify the CRS. Here is the syntax:

```
srvctl modify database -d <name> [-n <db_name>] [-o <ohome>] [-m <domain>]
      [-p <spfile>]  [-r {PRIMARY | PHYSICAL_STANDBY | LOGICAL_STANDBY}]
      [-s <start_options>]
srvctl modify instance -d <database-name> -i <instance-name> -n <node-name>
srvctl modify instance -d <name> -i <inst_name> {-s <asm_inst_name> | -r}
srvctl modify service -d <database-name> -s <service_name> -i <instance-name>
      -t <instance-name> [-f]
srvctl modify service -d <database-name> -s <service_name> -i <instance-name>
      -r  [-f]
srvctl modify nodeapps -n <node-name> [-A <address-description> ] [-x]
```

Here are the options for the preceding commands:

- -i <instance-name> -t <instance-name> (The instance name [-i] is replaced by the instance name [-t].)

- -i <instance-name> -r (The named instance is modified to be a preferred instance.)

- -A address-list (For a VIP application, at node level.)

- -s <asm_inst_name> (To add or remove an ASM dependency.)

Here are some examples for using srvctl to modify the CRS:

- Modify an instance to execute on another node.

  ```
  srvctl modify instance -d seed -n rac2
  ```

- Modify a service to execute on another node.

  ```
  srvctl modify service -d seed -s Hot_Backup -i rac2 -t rac3
  ```

- Modify an instance to be a preferred instance for a service.

  ```
  srvctl modify service -d seed -s Hot_Backup -i rac2
  ```

The following commands are used to enable CRS resources. Instances must be enabled in order to be started. The resource may be up or down to use this function.

```
srvctl enable database -d <database-name>
srvctl enable instance -d <database-name> -i <instance-name> [,<instance-name-list>]
srvctl enable service -d <database-name> -s <service-name>] [, <service-name-list>]
-i <instance-name>]
```

Here are some examples for enabling CRS resources:

- Enable the database.

  ```
  srvctl enable database -d seed
  ```

- Enable the named instances.

  ```
  srvctl enable instance -d seed -i seed1, seed2
  ```

- Enable services.

  ```
  srvctl enable service -d seed -s CRM, ERP
  ```

- Enable the service at the named instance.

  ```
  srvctl enable service -d seed -s ERP -i rac3
  ```

The following commands are used to disable CRS resources. The resource you are disabling must be down to use this function:

```
srvctl disable database -d <database-name>
srvctl disable instance -d <database-name> -i <instance-name> [,<instance-name-
list>]
srvctl disable service -d <database-name> -s <service-name>] [,<service-name-list>]
[-i <instance-name>]
```

Here are examples:

- Disable the database globally.

  ```
  srvctl disable database -d seed
  ```

- Disable the named instances.

  ```
  srvctl disable instance -d seed -i rac1, rac2
  ```

- Disable the service globally.

```
srvctl disable service -d seed -s ERP
```

- Disable the service at the named instance.

```
srvctl disable service -d seed -s CRM -i rac3,rac2
```

Now back to testing. When I deploy Oracle 10*g* RAC, I like to thoroughly test it. I will normally perform the tests described next.

Srvctl Tests

You should always test that you can get the status of the database from all nodes in the cluster. You should also be able to test starting and stopping the database from all nodes. I normally test starting the individual instances from all nodes, too. If you are using services, you should test starting and stopping the services from all nodes.

Failover Tests

The amount of failover testing really depends on the kind of failover you will be using. If you are going to set up Transparent Application Failover (TAF), you will want to do extensive testing of transactional failovers.

The basic tests I perform include using sqlplus to connect to the global instance from all nodes; connecting to a specific instance, such as seed1, from each of the nodes; and connecting from outside the cluster.

One of the simplest tests but one that gives you an immediate indication that you have configured the tnsnames.ora correctly for failover is to connect to an instance using sqlplus, for example, with the command sqlplus system/password@seed. Run the following query to see which instance you are connected to:

```
Select instance_number, instance_name, host_name from v$instance;
```

This will return the following lines:

```
INSTANCE_NUMBER   INSTANCE_NAME   HOST_NAME
            1         seed1           rac1
```

You can then shut down the instance returned from the query. After the instance has been shut down, rerun the query. It should show that you are now connected to another node in the cluster:

```
INSTANCE_NUMBER   INSTANCE_NAME   HOST_NAME
            2         seed2           rac2
```

If the sqlplus connection fails over without giving an error, you have probably set up the tnsnames.ora correctly.

Other tests you can perform include a hard reboot while connected to a node and a shutdown immediate, transactional, or abort while connected to an instance. These types of shutdowns will give differing results depending on the type of SQL you are running and the failover options you select in the connect string. The important thing to remember is always to test your 10*g* RAC before putting it into production!

Oracle 10*g* RAC Help

So now you know enough to get you in trouble. This chapter was not designed to be a step-by-step installation guide. It is a deployment guide that should guide you while you are deploying Oracle 10*g* RAC.

If you run into trouble, and you probably will, you should begin with MetaLink. Oracle normally has a step-by-step guide for each platform available. You can also search on Linux and the version of 10*g* you are installing. This should return some hits. Most of the time, someone has already ran into the same issue and solved it.

Here are a few items to keep in mind before you actually start your 10*g* RAC installation.

- Always check with your hardware vendor to make sure you have the certified/tested versions of drives and software before you begin.

- Make sure you have the Linux networking configured before you begin any RAC installation. If you do not have the networking configured correctly, you will have a lot of problems.

- If you can get Cluster Ready Services (CRS) installed and operating on all nodes, you have won half the battle. Do not proceed until CRS is functioning properly!

- Make sure you size your shared storage properly. Most of the poorly performing Oracle RAC implementations I've seen did not have enough physical disk drives or used the wrong RAID type. Remember RAID 1+0 is the preferred RAID type for Oracle data files.

- Remember to have fun. Whenever I get stressed out about a project, I usually end up making mistakes. I've learned to have fun and the job will normally take care of itself.

Summary

The last chapter provided you with an overview of what RAC is and how it's used. In this chapter, you were provided with a much more detailed view of how RAC is installed and configured. Oracle RAC is a very complex product that depends much more on system hardware than a stand-alone Oracle installation. When deploying RAC clusters, I usually warn the client that deploying RAC is about 40 percent deployment and 60 percent debugging. If you look at the deployment that way, you won't be as stressed when things don't go quite right. Just keep on trying and remember to pay attention to the details.

CHAPTER
9

Administering Oracle
and RAC on Linux

n the previous chapters, you have learned how to install and configure Oracle on Linux. This chapter builds on that knowledge and provides information on how to administer the Oracle system on Linux, once the initial configuration steps have been completed and it is running in a production environment. This chapter includes cautions and issues to be aware of when making Linux changes in an Oracle environment, as well as "best practices" for administering your Linux system.

Configuring the Linux Kernel

As mentioned earlier in this book, and in the previous chapters on configuring and installing the Oracle RAC system on Linux, it is necessary to configure the Linux kernel in order for Oracle to allocate sufficient resources to function properly. Those recommendations in previous chapters provided the standard configuration parameters for the Oracle installation and for general Oracle functionality. However, in the event that your configuration needs to be tuned for a larger SGA or for more semaphores, you might have to tune the Linux parameters as well.

Configuring Shared Memory

The Linux shared memory parameters need to be large enough to allow Oracle to allocate enough shared memory for the SGA to fit into.

The maximum size of the SGA is dictated by the shared memory parameters that are found in the /proc/sys/kernel/shmall, /proc/sys/kernel/shmmax, and /proc/sys/kernel/shmmni files; they are described here:

Parameter	Value	Description
shmall	297152	Maximum number of shared memory pages system-wide
shmmax	½ the size of memory (minimum 1610612736)	Maximum size of a shared memory segment
shmmni	4096	Maximum number of shared memory segments system-wide

In order to create an SGA up to 2GB in size, we normally set the value of SHMMAX to be 2147483648. In the event that a larger SGA is needed, SHMMAX should be increased.

Configuring Semaphores and Other Kernel Parameters

When processes connect into the Oracle instance, semaphores are used. As the number of users increases, the number of semaphores might need to be increased as well. The number of semaphores is defined by the following Linux configuration parameters:

Parameter	Value	Description
semmsl	250	Max number of semaphores per ID
semmns	32000	Max number of semaphores in the system (must be equal to or greater than semmni * semmsl)
semopm	100	Max number of operations per semaphore call
semmni	128	Max number of semaphore identifiers
file-max	65536	The maximum number of file handles
ip_local_port_range	1024 65000	Range of port numbers available to a program

Whether or not you need to increase the number of semaphores depends on your configuration. For a normal-sized system, these parameters are a good start.

Monitoring and Changing Linux Configuration Parameters

In order to monitor the usage of shared memory and semaphores, use the Linux command ipcs. With ipcs, you can see how much shared memory has been allocated and how many semaphores are in use, as shown here:

```
[root@ptc6 root]# ipcs

------ Shared Memory Segments --------
key         shmid      owner     perms     bytes        nattch     status
0x00005643 0           root      666       1024         1
0x00005654 32769       root      666       1024         1
0x00000000 262146      root      600       393216       2          dest
0x00000000 294915      root      600       393216       2          dest
0x00000000 327684      root      600       393216       2          dest
0x00000000 360453      root      600       393216       2          dest
0x00000000 393222      root      600       393216       2          dest
0x00000000 425991      root      600       393216       2          dest
0x00000000 458760      root      600       393216       2          dest
0x00000000 491529      root      600       393216       2          dest
0x00000000 524298      root      600       393216       2          dest
0x54250c38 557067      oracle    640       192937984    28
```

```
------ Semaphore Arrays --------
key          semid      owner        perms       nsems
0x00005653 0            root         666         1
0x460de1a4 196609       oracle       640         127
0x460de1a5 229378       oracle       640         127
0x460de1a6 262147       oracle       640         127

------ Message Queues --------
key          msqid      owner        perms       used-bytes   messages
```

The best way to change Linux configuration parameters is to modify the values in the /etc/sysctl.conf file. In this way, the parameters are automatically set each time the system restarts.

NOTE
Remember that if you are using SUSE Linux, you must enable the use of the /etc/sysctl.conf file by running the following command:

```
/sbin/chkconfig boot.sysctl on
```

Configuring the Network

Configuring the network involves the initial setup and configuration of network interface configuration files. These files vary slightly, depending on whether you are using Red Hat Linux or SUSE Linux, but the idea is the same. In the /etc/sysconfig/ network-scripts directory on Red Hat or the /etc/sysconfig/network directory on SUSE Linux, you will find a number of files of the format ifcfg-*device*. The *device* keyword is the name of the device itself, such as eth0 or eth1—if you are using bonding or teaming, it might take some other form, such as bond0.

Whether you are using Red Hat Linux or SUSE Linux, the format of the ifcfg-*device* file is similar and contains parameters that set the value for the IP address, the netmask, the broadcast address, the boot protocol, and whether the device starts at system bootup. These parameters might vary according to your particular version of Linux, and you should consult your Linux documentation for specifics.

Monitoring Linux

Depending on your role, you might work partially as the Linux system administrator as well as hold the role of DBA. In any case, as the Oracle DBA you are responsible for the performance of the Oracle instance. In order to manage Oracle performance, you will be called upon to monitor the system as well as to monitor Oracle. This can be done via third-party tools, of which there are many; Oracle tools such as

Statspack and Oracle Enterprise Manager (also known as Grid Control); as well as
OS tools such as sar, vmstat, and iostat.

sar

The System Activity Reporter (sar) is useful for monitoring the performance of the
system in general. With sar, you can monitor CPU utilization, memory, and network
interfaces. The one thing that sar is not particularly good at is monitoring the I/O
subsystem. There are many different options available to sar, depending on what
you want to monitor on the system, and how.

Running sar with no parameters displays the CPU utilization for the last 24
hours, as shown here:

```
Linux 2.4.21-15.EL (ptc6)          09/28/2004

12:00:00 AM     CPU      %user     %nice    %system     %idle
12:10:00 AM     all       1.13      0.00       0.13     98.74

11:40:00 AM     all       4.01      0.00       3.80     92.18
Average:        all       3.67      0.01       4.58     91.74
```

This information is kept automatically via a crontab process. Running sar with
the –A parameter displays much more information about the system for the last 24
hours. Because of the pure volume of data, this will not be shown here. In addition,
the network interfaces can be monitored with the sar –n DEV command.

```
[root@ptc6 root]# sar -n DEV
Linux 2.4.21-15.EL (ptc6)          09/28/2004

12:00:00 AM    IFACE   rxpck/s   txpck/s   rxbyt/s   txbyt/s   rxcmp/s   txcmp/s
rxmcst/s
12:10:00 AM      lo      3.56      3.56    286.63    286.63      0.00      0.00
0.00
12:10:00 AM    eth0      0.00      0.00      0.00      0.00      0.00      0.00
0.00


11:40:00 AM      lo      3.63      3.63    295.64    295.64      0.00      0.00
0.00
11:40:00 AM    eth0      0.00      0.00      0.00      0.00      0.00      0.00
0.00
Average:         lo      4.08      4.08    330.71    330.71      0.00      0.00
0.00
Average:       eth0      0.00      0.00      0.00      0.00      0.00      0.00
0.00
```

In addition, there are many other sar parameters that can be useful, depending
on what you are debugging.

vmstat

The vmstat command provides information about processes, memory, paging, etc. This command is a good place to go in order to determine if there is free memory and how much, along with information on processes and paging, as shown here:

```
[root@ptc6 root]# vmstat
procs                 memory        swap        io      system        cpu
 r  b   swpd   free   buff  cache   si   so   bi   bo   in    cs us sy id wa
 0  0 133008   9248 122396 274436    0    2    8  128  208   282  2  3 85 10
```

top

The top tool is used for getting an overall view of the activity of the system. Top continually displays the top running processes as well as an overall view of the system, as shown here:

```
11:59:07  up 19:14,   5 users,  load average: 0.26, 0.21, 0.18
121 processes: 120 sleeping, 1 running, 0 zombie, 0 stopped
CPU states:  cpu    user    nice  system    irq  softirq iowait    idle
             total   6.7%    0.0%    3.8%   0.9%    0.0%    6.7%    81.5%
Mem:    512480k av,  504412k used,    8068k free,      0k shrd,  122416k buff
                     354344k actv,   86452k in_d,   9504k in_c
Swap: 5632192k av,  133008k used, 5499184k free                 276000k cached

  PID USER      PRI  NI  SIZE  RSS  SHARE STAT %CPU %MEM   TIME CPU COMMAND
 4991 root       15   0 79560 3032  1868 S     3.8  0.5   1:20   0 /usr/X11R6/bin/X
:0 -auth /var/gdm/:0.Xa
 8358 root       20   0  1176 1176   892 R     2.9  0.2   0:00   0 top c
 5292 oracle     15   0 26272  12M  9132 S     1.9  2.4  21:21   0 ora_arc1_orcl
 8061 oracle     15   0  1196 1196   904 S     1.9  0.2   0:30   0 top
 5290 oracle     15   0 26232  10M  9100 S     0.9  2.0  21:35   0 ora_arc0_orcl
    1 root       15   0   508  480   448 S     0.0  0.0   0:04   0 init
    2 root       15   0     0    0     0 SW    0.0  0.0   0:00   0 keventd
    3 root       15   0     0    0     0 SW    0.0  0.0   0:00   0 kapmd
    4 root       34  19     0    0     0 SWN   0.0  0.0   0:00   0 ksoftirqd/0
    7 root       25   0     0    0     0 SW    0.0  0.0   0:00   0 bdflush
    5 root       15   0     0    0     0 SW    0.0  0.0   0:01   0 kswapd
    6 root       15   0     0    0     0 SW    0.0  0.0   0:00   0 kscand
    8 root       15   0     0    0     0 SW    0.0  0.0   0:00   0 kupdated
    9 root       25   0     0    0     0 SW    0.0  0.0   0:00   0 mdrecoveryd
   15 root       15   0     0    0     0 SW    0.0  0.0   0:00   0 ahc_dv_0
   16 root       25   0     0    0     0 SW    0.0  0.0   0:00   0 scsi_eh_0
   19 root       15   0     0    0     0 SW    0.0  0.0   0:00   0 kjournald
   90 root       25   0     0    0     0 SW    0.0  0.0   0:00   0 khubd
 3668 root       15   0     0    0     0 SW    0.0  0.0   0:00   0 kjournald
 4052 root       15   0   620  580   536 S     0.0  0.1   0:00   0 syslogd -m 0
 4056 root       15   0   452  396   392 S     0.0  0.0   0:00   0 klogd -x
 4084 rpc        15   0   556  484   480 S     0.0  0.0   0:00   0 portmap
 4104 rpcuser    25   0   696  616   612 S     0.0  0.1   0:00   0 rpc.statd
 4118 root       RT   0   556  448   420 S     0.0  0.0   0:00   0 /sbin/auditd
```

```
 4173 root      24   0   508  460   456 S      0.0  0.0   0:00    0 /usr/sbin/apmd -p
10 -w 5 -W -P /etc/sys
 4257 root      15   0  1252 1140  1000 S      0.0  0.2   0:00    0 /usr/sbin/sshd
 4273 root      17   0   856  812   732 S      0.0  0.1   0:00    0 xinetd -stayalive
-pidfile /var/run/xine
 4602 root      15   0  1720  856   812 S      0.0  0.1   0:00    0 vmd
 4607 root      15   0  2944 1260   888 S      0.0  0.2   0:00    0
/usr/openv/netbackup/bin/bprd
 4639 root      15   0  2468 1036   824 S      0.0  0.2   0:00    0
/usr/openv/netbackup/bin/bpdbm
```

I always invoke top with the –c parameter, which displays the command line rather than just the command that is being run. This provides greater detail when monitoring the system.

iostat

Probably one of the most important tools available to you when monitoring the system is iostat, which displays information about the I/O subsystem, such as reads and writes per second, blocks written per second, wait time, and response time. You can invoke iostat with the –x qualifier in order to get detailed I/O information, as shown here:

```
[root@ptc6 root]# iostat -x
Linux 2.4.21-15.EL (ptc6)          09/28/2004

avg-cpu:  %user   %nice    %sys   %idle
           2.49    0.01    2.73   94.76

Device:    rrqm/s wrqm/s   r/s   w/s rsec/s  wsec/s    rkB/s    wkB/s avgrq-sz
avgqu-sz  await  svctm  %util
/dev/hda     1.35 272.29  1.01 111.25  18.75 3068.59     9.38  1534.30    27.50
6.17   1.95   3.80  42.67
/dev/hda1    0.01   0.00  0.00  0.00   0.02    0.00     0.01     0.00    14.26
0.00  33.38  26.62   0.00
/dev/hda2    0.00   0.53  0.11  0.07   0.88    4.77     0.44     2.38    31.86
0.16  91.85  34.08   0.60
/dev/hda3    1.34 271.76  0.90 111.18  17.85 3063.83     8.93  1531.91    27.50
2.03   1.81   1.07  12.02
/dev/hdb     0.00   0.00  0.00  0.00   0.01    0.00     0.01     0.00    11.49
5.44   7.64 483147.76  42.67
/dev/hdb1    0.00   0.00  0.00  0.00   0.00    0.00     0.00     0.00    13.05
0.00   3.16   3.16   0.00
/dev/hdb2    0.00   0.00  0.00  0.00   0.00    0.00     0.00     0.00    13.05
0.00   8.95   8.95   0.00
```

The iostat command is one of the most common tools that I use when monitoring a system, since I/O is usually a problem. This tool and others are discussed in Chapter 15, where we look at performance tuning of the system hardware.

Upgrading the Linux Operating System

Upgrading the Linux Operating System is something that should be done with great care. I do not recommend using up2date (Red Hat) or YAST (SUSE) to automatically update the system because of the potential for problems. The Oracle system has a certain set of requirements that you have seen in previous chapters. The Oracle system depends on specific versions of gcc, libstdc, openmotif, make, binutils, and the Java Runtime Environment. When you automatically update your system, many of these components could be updated as well. This might or might not cause issues with the Oracle system. So, if you update your system automatically, you are doing this at your own risk.

Let's look at some of the Oracle tasks that you are expected to do as an Oracle DBA.

Starting Up the Instance

One of the most basic database administrative tasks is starting up and shutting down the instance. That in itself sounds simple enough, but there are multiple ways to fully start or open an Oracle database, depending on the situation. If we want to start up and open the database, then all that needs to be done is simply to authenticate to the database via sqlplus with a user with sysdba or sysoper system privileges, and issue the startup command.

```
sqlplus
SQL*Plus: Release 10.1.0.2.0 - Production on Mon Jun 21 18:55:06 2004

Copyright (c) 1982, 2004, Oracle. All rights reserved.

Enter user-name: sys as sysdba
Enter password:
Connected to an idle instance.

SQL> startup
ORACLE instance started.

Total System Global Area  188743680 bytes
Fixed Size                     778036 bytes
Variable Size               162537676 bytes
Database Buffers             25165824 bytes
Redo Buffers                   262144 bytes
Database mounted.
Database opened.

SQL>
```

NOTE
When starting up the instance using the startup command with no parameters, it is started up using the default server parameter file (spfile). If you wish to start the instance using a parameter file (pfile), use the following command:

```
startup pfile='?/dbs/init<ORACLE_SID>.ora'
```

With the advent of web-based tools and sophisticated scripting for managing databases, it is possible for someone to start up and shut down a database without ever seeing this banner and startup sequence. With that in mind, let us take a little time to examine the steps involved in starting a database.

Database Startup

Database startup is initiated with the creation of an instance. In terms of an Oracle server, an instance is defined as the memory structures and background processes relating to a database. When the instance is started, the SPFILE or init.ora file is read, and the initialization parameters are set. In addition, sizes of the various defined memory structures are declared when the instance is started.

At this stage of instance-only startup, the database is considered "unmounted." Once again, there are only memory structures and background processes running at this point, the control files have not been read, and the datafiles are not being accessed.

This state can be reached by issuing the following command from the idle state:

```
startup nomount;
```

This is generally done as one of the first steps in database recovery after a database crash, or when a system is a standby database and is Oracle 9*i* or earlier, in which case you would follow this command with ALTER DATABASE MOUNT STANDBY DATABASE. In Oracle 10*g* Data Guard, issuing startup on the physical standby instance opens the database in a READ ONLY mode. No files or dynamic performance views can be accessed in this state.

```
SQL> select name from v$controlfile;

no rows selected
```

Database Mounted

The database mounted state defines when the control files are being accessed and relevant log and datafiles are identified. This state can also be attained from the unmounted state by issuing the following command:

```
SQL> alter database mount;
Or from the idle state by issuing
SQL> startup mount;
```

One of the scenarios where the database needs to be opened in the mounted state is when the database is converted to archivelog mode. In addition, it is in the mounted state that the dynamic performance views can be accessed.

```
SQL> select name from v$controlfile;

NAME
--------------------------------------------------------------------------------
/u01/oradata/lintstb/lintstb/control01.ctl
/u01/oradata/lintstb/lintstb/control02.ctl
/u01/oradata/lintstb/lintstb/control03.ctl
```

However, regular heap tables cannot be accessed in the mounted state.

```
SQL> select count(username) from dba_users;
select count(username) from dba_users
                            *
ERROR at line 1:
ORA-01219: database not open: queries allowed on fixed tables/views only
```

Database Opened

This stage defines when the database (control files and datafiles) is accessible to the background processes, and transactions may start. Barring physical disaster, never having to close an open database is a very attainable goal with careful planning and use of Oracle high-availability features. The database can also be opened from the mounted state by issuing the following command:

```
SQL> alter database open;

SQL> select count(username) from dba_users;

COUNT(USERNAME)
---------------
             62
```

An additional method for opening a database includes opening in read-only mode (such as a standby database, or when you want to prevent database updates).

```
SQL> alter database open read only
```

When it is necessary to shut down the instance to accommodate a planned downtime, the instance may be shut down by issuing the shutdown immediate command. This particular shutdown option will gracefully disconnect any users, and it does not require crash recovery once the instance has restarted.

```
Connected to:
Oracle Database 10g Enterprise Edition Release 10.1.0.2.0 - Production
With the Partitioning, OLAP and Data Mining options

SQL> shutdown immediate;
Database closed.
Database dismounted.
ORACLE instance shut down.
```

As you can see, the sequence displayed is in the opposite order of what is presented when the database is opened normally.

If for any reason the database needs to be shut down rapidly, the shutdown abort command may be issued:

```
SQL> shutdown abort
ORACLE instance shut down.
```

Sometimes this is required when a shutdown immediate hangs. If you open another sqlplus session, this will terminate the shutdown immediate. However, automatic instance crash recovery will be necessary upon startup.

Starting Up from the Enterprise Manager Database Control

In addition to starting the instance via SQL*Plus as shown previously, or via the srvctl commands shown in the preceding chapter with RAC, you can also use the Enterprise Manager Database Control (as opposed to EM Grid Control). The Enterprise Manager Database Control should have been automatically installed via the database server installation process; it uses a web server to listen on port 5500 on your Oracle system.

Accessing Database Control

Database Control is accessed via a web browser. The string used to access the console is

```
http://sysname:5500/em
```

This string should invoke the Enterprise Manager Database Control interface, where you can start up and shut down the instance via your web browser.

Managing the Enterprise Manager Database Control Service

If you cannot access Enterprise Manager, you can check its status via the emctl command, as shown here:

```
[oracle@ptc6 oracle]$ emctl status dbconsole
TZ set to US/Central
Oracle Enterprise Manager 10g Database Control Release 10.1.0.2.0
Copyright (c) 1996, 2004 Oracle Corporation. All rights reserved.
http://ptc6:5500/em/console/aboutApplication
Oracle Enterprise Manager 10g is running.
-----------------------------------------------------------------
Logs are generated in directory
/opt/oracle/product/10.1.0/db_1/ptc6_orcl/sysman/log
```

Starting the Enterprise Manager
If Enterprise Manager Database Control is not running, it can be started with the emctl command. Enterprise Manager can be started with the emctl start dbconsole command, as shown here:

```
[oracle@ptc6 oracle]$ emctl start dbconsole
TZ set to US/Central
Oracle Enterprise Manager 10g Database Control Release 10.1.0.2.0
Copyright (c) 1996, 2004 Oracle Corporation. All rights reserved.
http://ptc6:5500/em/console/aboutApplication
Starting Oracle Enterprise Manager 10g Database Control .............. started.
-----------------------------------------------------------------
Logs are generated in directory
/opt/oracle/product/10.1.0/db_1/ptc6_orcl/sysman/log
```

Stopping the Enterprise Manager
If you wish to stop the Enterprise Manager, it can be stopped with the emctl command. The Enterprise Manager is stopped via the emctl stop dbconsole command, as shown here:

```
[oracle@ptc6 oracle]$ emctl stop dbconsole
TZ set to US/Central
Oracle Enterprise Manager 10g Database Control Release 10.1.0.2.0
Copyright (c) 1996, 2004 Oracle Corporation. All rights reserved.
http://ptc6:5500/em/console/aboutApplication
Stopping Oracle Enterprise Manager 10g Database Control ...
  ... Stopped.
```

Oracle Database 10g and CSSD

In an Oracle RAC environment, the Oracle instance is started automatically via the Oracle Cluster Ready Services. In a stand-alone system, the CSS Daemon (cssd) will automatically start up the Oracle instance. The CSSD (Cluster Services Synchronization Daemon) is automatically installed even in a stand-alone system. This daemon will automatically start up the Oracle instance whenever the system boots. In order to change this behavior, the file /etc/init.d/init.cssd can be modified by hand.

User Authentication

Like managing the status of the instance, another common but critical administration task is user account management. The Oracle server works with several authentication methods. These include database authentication, operating system authentication, network authentication, remote authentication, mid-tier authentication, and SSL authentication.

Database Authentication

This is the "standard" method of authentication to Oracle. The only requirements are an active user account, the associated password, and proper system privileges. Passwords are stored in an encrypted format in the data dictionary. Locking and unlocking of user accounts can further manage authentication. This controls data access without having to drop the user. Passwords can also be set to expire after a set amount of time, and password complexity can be enforced.

Operating System Authentication

The Oracle database can be set up to accept operating system authentication. This is demonstrated with OPS$ accounts, or when a dba can log into the database as "/ as sysdba" or "/ as sysoper." In these cases, it is assumed that the user has passed the username/password challenge from the operation system and is therefore a credible user. The oracle user is made a member of the operating system groups OSDBA and OSOPER created as part of the database installation process.

Network Authentication

Oracle can have authentication predicated on network authorization. This implies the use of a third-party network authentication service (Kerberos, SESAME). In this same grouping, certificate-based PKI (public-key infrastructure) authentication is supported. This is a very sophisticated and secure method with several components, including:

- Session management with SSL
- Supporting OCI and PL/SQL procedures that sign and verify data against a certificate

- The use of "wallets," or defined, transportable collections of security credentials, including a public key, a user certificate, and a set of users trust points

- An X.509v3 certificate from a third-party certificate authority, such as VeriSign or Thawte

Oracle Internet Directory is used to manage user attributes and user privileges.

Remote Authentication

Remote authentication can be used via RADIUS (the Remote Authentication Dial-in User Service) to authenticate.

Mid-Tier Authentication

In multitier environments, such as OracleAS 10g, Oracle controls the integrity of middle-tier applications by preserving identities and limiting privileges. This type of scheme also benefits from connection pooling, which allows multiple users to share access to Oracle. To use connection pooling, it is suggested that the Oracle Call Interface (OCI) be used to create lightweight sessions allowing database password authentication. This preserves the identity of the real user through the middle tier while consolidating database connections. These lightweight sessions can be created with or without passwords.

Authentication by SSL

Depending on the configuration of the database initialization parameter file, the Oracle database can authenticate a session via SSL. This method can be set up to circumvent the Oracle Internet Directory. However, this does not allow for enterprise-class certificate authentication. In addition, Oracle 10g R2 allows the use of the secure HTTP protocol (HTTPS).

SSL is an industry-standard security protocol developed by Netscape in order to provide secure network connections. SSL connections send encrypted data using an RSA public cryptography and symmetric key cryptography. This provides for authentication, encryption, and data integrity.

In order to enable SSL, you must install Oracle Advanced Security on both the client and the server. During the install process, the SSL libraries as well as the Oracle Wallet Manager are installed and configured. In addition, the following entries need to be added to the listener.ora and sqlnet.ora files:

```
wallet_location =
  (SOURCE=
   (METHOD=File)
   (METHOD_DATA=
    (DIRECTORY=wallet_location)))
```

Also, several steps are needed in order to configure SSL on the server system. These include optionally selecting the cypher suite, configuring the tnsnames.ora file to include the Distinguished Name (DN), and specifying the wallet location. Configuring SSL is covered in detail in the *Oracle Advanced Security Administrator's Guide.*

User Authorization

Once the authentication method is established, it is necessary to manage user account system- and object-level privileges. Oracle further extends this by allowing administrators to provision user session duration and resource consumption. The confluence of privileges, session duration, and resource consumption is collectively known as *user authorization.*

User Profiles

One of the sets of adjustable user parameters relating to authorization is known as a profile. A *profile* is a collection of *resource parameters* and *password parameters.* These parameters allow the administrator to put limits on system resources and enforce password policy, thus preventing one user from bogging down the system or another user from hacking a password. Resource parameters set resource limits to provision one aspect of a system's resources, such as CPU or memory. Table 9-1 lists such resource parameters, and Table 9-2 lists the password parameters to control user authorization.

Parameter	Description
SESSION_PER_USER	Limits the number of concurrent sessions per user.
CPU_PER_SESSION	Limits CPU access per session, measured in hundredths of a second.
CPU_PER_CALL	Similar to CPU_PER_SESSION, but is refined to the call level (parse, execute, fetch). It is also measured in hundredths of a second.
CONNECT_TIME	Limits the time, in minutes, that a user can connect to the database.
IDLE_TIME	Limits the time, in minutes, an idle session can stay connected to the database.
LOGIAL_READS_PER_SESSION	Limits the number of memory and disk blocks read in a session.
LOGICAL_READS_PER_CALL	Limits the number of memory and disk blocks read to satisfy a SQL statement.
PRIVATE_SGA	Limits a user's private space, in bytes, in the system global area (SGA).

TABLE 9-1. *Resource Parameters for a User Profile*

Parameter	Description
COMPOSITE_LIMIT	Limits a user's session according to weighted sum, measured in service units. A service unit is a composite value of CPU_PER_SESSION, CONNECT_TIME, LOGICAL_READS_PER_SESSION, and PRIVATE_SGA.

TABLE 9-1.   *Resource Parameters for a User Profile* (continued)

Parameter	Description
FAILED_LOGIN_ATTEMPTS	Sets the number of login attempts allowed before an account is locked.
PASSWORD_LIFE_TIME	Sets the number of days that a password may be used.
PASSWORD_REUSE_TIME / PASSWORD_REUSE_MAX	These two password parameters must be used in conjunction with each other. PASSWORD_REUSE_TIME determines the number of days for which a password cannot be reused. PASSWORD_REUSE_MAX determines the number of times that a password must be changed before the original password can be reissued. If you set either PASSWORD_REUSE_TIME or PASSWORD_REUSE_MAX to unlimited, the password can *never* be reused.
PASSWORD_LOCK_TIME	Determines how long an account will remain locked after the value for FAILED_LOGIN_ATTEMPTS has been reached.
PASSWORD_GRACE_TIME	The number of days a user has to change a password after PASSWORD_LIFE_TIME has been reached.
PASSWORD_VERIFY_FUNCTION	Allows a script to be passed to Oracle to enforce password complexity through PL/SQL.

TABLE 9-2.   *Password Parameters to Control User Authorization*

These password and resource parameters are combined to create a particular profile, which in turn is applied to a user or role. Here is an example of creating a profile:

```
CREATE PROFILE limited_user LIMIT
SESSIONS_PER_USER UNLIMITED
CPU_PER_SESSION UNLIMITED
CPU_PER_CALL 3000
CONNECT_TIME 60
LOGICAL_READS_PER_SESSION DEFAULT
LOGICAL_READS_PER_CALL 1000
PRIVATE_SGA 50K
COMPOSITE_LIMIT 10000000;
```

Privileges

Anther aspect of a user's authorization sets privileges for system and user objects and executes certain classes of SQL.

System Privileges

System privileges allow for execution of SQL commands that generally apply to system-related information. A few common examples follow:

- **CREATE SESSION**   Basic privilege to connect to a database
- **CREATE TABLE**   Allows users to create tables in their own schema
- **CREATE PROCEDEURE**   Allows creation of encapsulated programmatic steps
- **SYSOPER**   Allows for several powerful system functions, including:
  - Starting up and shutting down the database
  - Altering the database state (OPEN, MOUNT, BACKUP)
  - Using the ALTER DATABASE ARCHIVELOG command
  - Using the ALTER DATABASE RECOVER command
  - Using the CREATE SPFILE command
  - Accessing the database while in restricted mode
- **SYSDBA**   Similar to SYSOPER, with the following additional privileges:
  - Altering the database state (CHANGE CHARACTER SET)
  - Using the CREATE DATABASE command

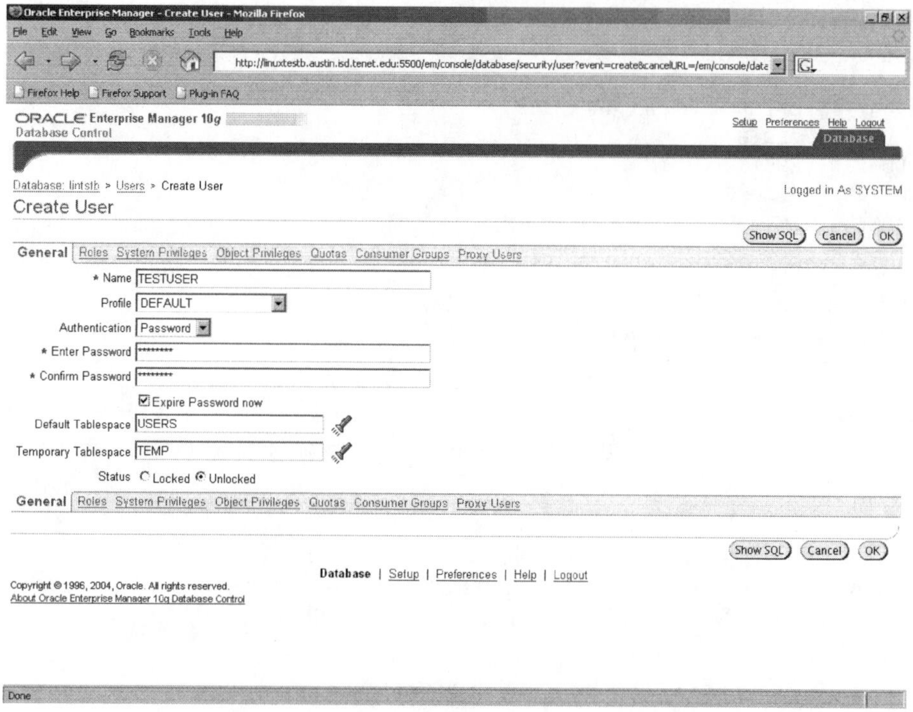

FIGURE 9-1. *Adding a user with Oracle Enterprise Manager*

Object Privileges

Object-level privileges, on the other hand, are granted to a user to access or manipulate objects in a schema. These privileges are generally granted from the object owner to the user wanting access. A list of these type of commands include:

- **ALTER**   Allows a user to change the definition of an object

- **DELETE**   Allows a grantee the capacity to remove rows

- **EXECUTE**   Allows a user to execute code, such as a procedure or function

- **INSERT**   Allows a user to add rows to a table

- **SELECT**   Allows a user to examine data from a table

- **UPDATE**   Allows a user to change existing data

In addition, a user can hand off these object privileges if the original object owner is granted these privileges with the GRANT option.

Adding a User Account

Once the authentication and authorization method of a particular user has been established, the user account itself can be used. Figure 9-1 shows an example of using the Oracle Enterprise Manager Database Control to add a user account.

As seen in Figure 9-1, the initial information required includes a username and password, a profile, an authentication method, and default and temporary tablespaces. The profile, as well as the type of authentication, is selected from a pull-down menu. The default tablespace is the logical location for the user objects, and the temporary tablespace is the location where query sorts are handled. In addition, the account can be created either locked or unlocked, as shown in Figure 9-2.

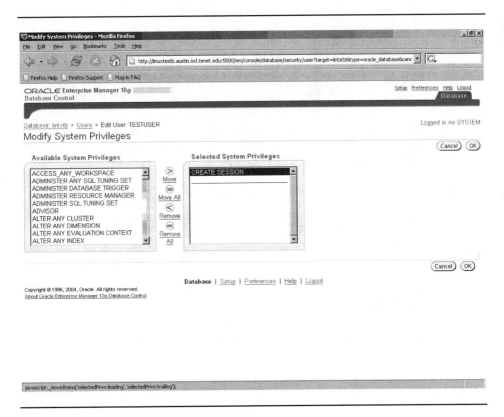

FIGURE 9-2. *Granting system privileges in Oracle Enterprise Manager*

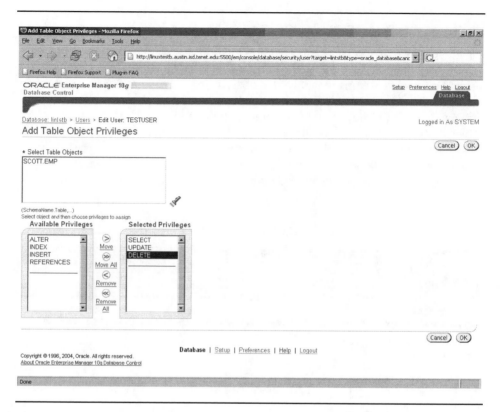

FIGURE 9-3. *Granting object privileges in Oracle Enterprise Manager*

The next step is to grant system-level privileges to the new user, as demonstrated by Figure 9-3. At a minimum, the user should be granted the create session system privilege.

Once the system-level privileges have been established, object-level permissions can then be set. Figure 9-3, using the sample SCOTT schema, illustrates granting general DML permissions on the EMP table. Now that the account TESTUSER has been created and given the proper permissions, this user can now log in and perform functional tasks.

Summary

This chapter has introduced you to both Linux and Oracle tasks that are part of the day-to-day administration of the Oracle system. Many times the jobs of the DBA and the Systems Administrator are separate, but there is a great deal of overlap. By understanding both tasks, you can better work together for a more stable and better-performing system.

CHAPTER
10

Tuning Oracle and
RAC on Linux

uning Oracle is as much an art as a science. Tuning involves scientific investigation, good note taking, intuition, and experience in order to determine if there is a performance problem, what that performance problem is, and how to solve it. Performance tuning is made easier by developing and sticking to a disciplined methodology. By having a methodology that you stick to, you can experience more predicable and reproducible results. In this chapter, I will introduce you to the methodology that I use, but this is something that you should change in order to suit your own needs.

Performance tuning involves taking a system that is performing poorly and making it perform better. This sounds simple enough, but when there are numerous components involved and many layers of applications, hardware, and databases, it can be a very complicated task. It usually involves monitoring and tuning at several layers, including:

- Application tuning

- Instance and database tuning

- Hardware tuning

In addition, architectural design changes might need to be made as well. In this chapter, you will be introduced to all layers of tuning. To begin with, let me explain my personal tuning methodology.

Performance Tuning Methodology

This tuning methodology involves a number of individual steps that lead to a final result. This result might be information, or it might be a recommendation for a change in the way the system performs. The individual steps for the performance tuning methodology are

- Initial assessment

- System monitoring

- Results analysis

- Hypothesis creation

- Solution proposal

- Implementation

- Testing and monitoring

- Go to step 3 (results analysis)

This methodology might not work for everyone, but it is a good starting point. A number of tips and techniques that assure the effectiveness of this methodology are given in the sections that follow. Let's look at the methodology in a little more detail.

Step 1: Initial Assessment

The goal of step 1 is to understand the environment that you are evaluating. If you are tuning your own system, this step might be something that you are quite familiar with. If you have been brought in to tune someone else's system, this might involve a little more work. In either case, it is useful to document your assessment of the system. These are some of the steps involved in the initial assessment:

- **Learn about the application**   It is important that you have a basic understanding of the system and the application and how they work.

- **Ask about how it works and what it does**   You should be able to find someone who can provide information about how the system operates, what the various components are, and how they interact.

- **Determine what the reported problem is**   If a problem has been reported, determine exactly what the reported problem is. Often the reported problem is "everything is slow." Getting more details could help the process.

- **Document database size, tuning parameters, etc.**   Before you start tuning the system, you should document the size of the database, Oracle and Linux parameters, etc.

- **Validate parameters**   Now and then, tuning problems are solved in the first few minutes of the engagement by finding an improperly set parameter. This is rare, but it does happen.

This is a very important stage of the tuning exercise, but the least glamorous. By getting your documentation and information lined up in the beginning, you might have already set in motion a successful project.

Step 2: Monitor the System

The goal of this phase is to monitor the system and gather data. This data can then be used to develop a theory of what might be causing the performance problems that you are experiencing. As with step 1, it is important to document your results so that they can be properly analyzed and repeated as necessary. Some of the tasks involved include the following:

- **Monitor the system**   To do this, use

  - **OS tools: sar, vmstat, iostat**   These tools can give you valuable information on how the system itself is performing at the OS level. High-level problems might be detected with these tools, such as CPU utilization at 100 percent an overloaded I/O subsystem.

  - **Oracle tools: AWR, Statspack, dbastudio, v$views**   These tools can provide information on the performance of the Oracle instance and wait events, and on problems within the Oracle instance and application.

  - **Third-party tools**   Third-party tools such as Veritas InDepth can provide information on how the application and SQL statements are performing.

- **Analyze OS and Oracle configuration parameters**   Analysis of OS and Oracle configuration parameters might highlight a fundamental problem that can be easily solved.

Performance monitoring is much more exciting and interesting than documenting the system configuration; however, documentation is equally important here. If you are saving performance data on the system, be sure to make notations on when that monitoring occurred and what was happening on the system at the time.

Step 3: Analyze Results

The goal of the analysis phase is to take the performance monitoring results in conjunction with the initial assessment and use this data to formulate a hypothesis in the next step. Here are some of the tasks involved:

- **Analyze data**   The data that you have collected during the monitoring phase should be carefully analyzed. You might be surprised at what you find, or it might confirm some suspicion that you might have.

- **Review error logs**   This is one task that is often overlooked. The error logs can be a valuable source of information in the event of some type of configuration error or hardware failure. Remember, there are more logs than just the Oracle alert log. There are the Linux system log, /var/log/messages, and the kernel ring buffer (accessed with dmesg). There are also other log files such as the cluster manager log.

■ **Look for performance data from customer sources** This is where the user and/or the tester have their opportunity to give you feedback on how the tests went. This might also be where the application testers can offer helpful information.

Once you have completed the analysis phase, you are ready to start forming a hypothesis on what the problem might be and how to solve that problem.

Step 4: Create a Hypothesis

The goal of this phase is to develop a theory or hypothesis on what is causing the performance problem. Creating a hypothesis could be very simple or quite complex. In the case of multiple problems, you might just be creating a hypothesis for one or two problems. Remember, you don't have to solve all of the problems in one shot; in fact, you are better off changing only a few, or one thing at a time. The tasks involved include the following:

■ **Determine if there actually is a problem** Sometimes you come to the conclusion that the system is running as designed, and there really isn't a problem. This could be the hypothesis that you come up with.

■ **Formulate a theory** Formulating a theory is the most important part of the tuning art. Here, you have to take in all of the data that you have gotten and try to determine why you are having the problem, if there actually is a problem. The types of problems that you might theorize include I/O problems, locking problems, poorly formulated SQL statements, etc.

■ **Back that theory up with data** A theory with no supporting data isn't worth very much. Even if the data isn't conclusive, there should be some indications from the data to support your theory.

The hypothesis is essential for proposing solutions. If you can't determine what you think the problem is from the data that you have gathered, you need to go back and gather data that is more useful.

Step 5: Propose a Solution

The goal of this phase is to come up with a proposed solution or a test in order to determine what the actual solution should be. In some cases, the solution might be to purchase more hardware, such as disk drives or memory. In other cases, the solution might be to tune some SQL statements or add an index. This phase is where you get to actually propose the tuning solution, which needs to consist of these tasks:

■ **Develop a solution** This solution could involve adding indexes, changing SQL statements, changing the hardware layout, or adding more hardware.

- **Develop a validation plan** The validation plan should include some procedures that can validate that the change has been made correctly.

- **Document expected results** It is easier to run a test when you have some expectations of what the results should be. This allows you to determine if the test might be flawed in some way. If you don't get the expected results, either the test is flawed or the solution is flawed.

When proposing a solution, you should always have the result of that solution in mind. If you don't know what the proposed solution is going to do, then why do it?

Step 6: Implementation of Solution

This step is the really fun part. The goal of this phase is to actually fix the performance problem. Here is where you get to make the changes that you have proposed and get ready to test the solution in order to validate your hypothesis. Implementing the solution could be as easy as adding an index, or as difficult as changing out the entire storage subsystem. In any case, this is where the action takes place and can involve some of the following tasks:

- **Make the hardware change** This might involve upgrading hardware, changing the I/O subsystem, or replacing the entire system and migrating to a new system.

- **Make the configuration parameter change** This is usually pretty easy and doesn't involve too much risk.

- **Add an index** Adding indexes can be quite time-consuming on large tables. The time it takes depends on the data and the complexity of the index.

It is important when making changes to follow a few simple rules. These rules will make your job easier and give you better results in the end:

- **Document your changes** By documenting your changes, you will be better able to reproduce them and be able to determine which changes helped.

- **Only change one thing at a time** Multiple changes at a time lead to unpredictable results.

- **Document your changes** This is in the list twice because it is so important.

By being methodical and careful, you can achieve great results.

Step 7: Test and Monitor

This phase involves running validation and performance tests against the changed system. The goal of this step is to validate the solution that you have executed in the previous step. This validation involves confirming that the change made an improvement, that the change made things worse, or in some cases, that the test is flawed.

- **If possible, test the change in a nonproduction environment.** This requirement is sometimes impossible, but it should be a goal of all tuning. In any case, the risk of the change should be evaluated and a determination of how to test and implement the change should be made. For example; adding or changing an index could affect performance, but not the resulting data returned by a query. A change to a query itself could return incorrect results.

- **QA the change before deploying.** Any code change should have quality assurance tests performed on it before it is deployed.

- **If possible, run load tests.** Load tests can help you to measure and document the performance gain from the change. The better the test, the better the results. A third-party I/O stress tool can be used, such as Loadrunner, iozone, postmark, or ORION.

- **Monitor the changes using the monitoring tools described in step 2**. If you use the same tools and monitor in a similar fashion, you can compare the results with those collected in step 2.

- **Document the changes.** If you don't document what you did, it might be very difficult to reproduce the change and to determine how it affected performance.

It is important that changes be made carefully and methodically. Too many changes at one time can lead to unpredictable results.

Further Analysis and Testing

You should now pick up with step 3 and repeat until you are satisfied with the results of your tuning, or you are out of time or budget. Unfortunately, tuning is like cutting grass; it always grows back. The end point of tuning is when one of several events occur:

- **The performance goals have been met** This could be a certain average response time, batch jobs running within a specific time window, etc.

■ **The time has expired** Sometimes you only have test equipment for a limited time frame and you must end testing when that time frame has been met.

■ **The budget has been used up** Many performance tuning exercises have a specific budget, and once those funds have been used up, tuning must stop.

These and many other reasons could dictate the end of the tuning engagement. Hopefully, once you are done, the results are better performance or a recommendation on how to improve performance.

But how do you actually tune the system? That is the subject of the remainder of the chapter. This will start with monitoring and tuning the Oracle instance.

Tuning Oracle on Linux

Tuning Oracle on Linux, or on any platform for that matter, can be broken down into three major areas: application tuning, instance/database tuning, and hardware tuning. These different tuning areas can be attacked in any order, but typically application tuning is tackled first, then instance and database tuning, and then hardware tuning. However, a general survey of the entire system should be performed first, and then a determination made of which area deserves the most immediate attention. Each of these areas of focus can be quite involved but might lead to the solution to the root cause of your performance problems.

■ **Application tuning** This involves modification of application code, SQL statements, and processes that might be inefficient or a bottleneck. Application tuning also includes stored procedures and modification of the database schema, including index tuning.

■ **Instance/database tuning** Instance tuning involves the modification of Oracle initialization parameters to change the configuration of the Oracle instance. Instance tuning might also involve the need to modify Linux parameters.

■ **Hardware tuning** Hardware tuning involves the modification, reconfiguration, and addition of hardware in order to improve Oracle performance.

Tuning only one of these areas will not provide a complete performance evaluation and improvement. Tuning the Oracle instance when the application code is a problem will not be effective. Similarly, tuning the application and Oracle instance when you have an I/O problem can also be ineffective. A complete performance evaluation and tuning exercise needs application, instance, database, and hardware tuning.

Application Tuning

Application tuning involves the tuning of SQL statements and indexes in order to achieve different execution plans and data access patterns. In addition, application tuning can involve taking advantage of Oracle features such as partitioning and parallel query.

Chapter 16 focuses on tuning SQL statements in order to improve their performance. SQL statements can be tuned by analyzing the execution plan and changing that execution plan either by changing the text of the SQL statement or by providing a hint to the Oracle optimizer. Either method can be quite effective.

Chapter 17 focuses on indexes, partitioning, and other Oracle features. Partitioning can be a powerful method of reducing the amount of data accessed during certain operations. Indexes are the best way to reduce the number of I/Os necessary to find a specific piece of data.

Since application tuning is covered later in this book, it will not be covered here. Those pieces are covered later, since the early part of this book is dedicated to the Oracle instance and configuration, rather than the application.

Instance Tuning Basics

Instance tuning involves tuning the Oracle instance. As a reminder, the Oracle instance is made up of the memory and processes used to access the Oracle database. The instance is tuned by adjusting the parameters in the Oracle initialization file. The Oracle initialization file could be either a pfile (parameter file) that is a client-side configuration file or an spfile (server parameter file). Regardless of which one is used, the parameter file is used to configure the Oracle initialization parameters that are used to adjust the characteristics of the Oracle instance.

Parameters set in the initialization file are read by the Oracle instance during instance startup. However, there are a number of parameters that can be changed dynamically. Changing both dynamic parameters and parameters stored in an spfile is done via the ALTER SYSTEM or ALTER SESSION command. The spfile is the recommended method of tuning the Oracle instance, since the spfile is resident on the database server itself. However, in some cases it is preferred or even recommended that a pfile be used.

Using a PFILE

The pfile is an ASCII file that can be edited via vi (or any other text editor). The pfile contains a list of parameter names and values. Simply add or modify the value that you want to change. When starting up the Oracle instance, specify the pfile to be used, and the Oracle database server will start using those parameters. If there is an error in the pfile, you will receive an error and the Oracle instance will fail to start.

Using an SPFILE

The spfile, or server parameter file, exists on the database server. When starting the Oracle instance, the Oracle database server will start up using the file $ORACLE_HOME/dbs/init*SID*.ora. In an Oracle RAC configuration, the spfile is usually stored on a shared disk, and the $ORACLE_HOME/dbs/init*SID*.ora file consists of one line,

```
SPFILE='/u03/oradata/test/spfiletest.ora'
```

This specification simply points the Oracle instance to the shared spfile.

NOTE
All nodes in a RAC cluster can share the same spfile. Since there are instance specific parameters in the spfile, they should be set on a per instance basis.

When using the spfile, it is unnecessary to specify the parameter file in the Oracle startup command. The spfile will automatically be used to start up the Oracle instance. In order to determine what spfile is being used, you can use the Oracle command

```
SQL> SHOW PARAMETER SPFILE;
```

This will display the name of the current spfile that is being used. It is recommended that the spfile be used, however, there are some cases where a pfile is convenient.

Creating an SPFILE

The spfile can be created from the Oracle database configuration assistant (DBCA), or it can be created at any time by using the CREATE SPFILE command, as follows:

```
SQL> CREATE SPFILE='/u03/oradata/test/spfiletest.ora' FROM
PFILE='/opt/oracle/admin/test/inittest.ora';
```

Conversely, you can create a pfile from the spfile by using the CREATE PFILE command, as shown here:

```
SQL> CREATE PFILE='/opt/oracle/admin/test/inittest.ora' FROM
SPFILE='/u03/oradata/test/spfiletest.ora';
```

It is always a good idea to create a pfile from the spfile as a backup. Since the pfile can be modified by a text editor, you can modify it before starting the Oracle instance. The spfile can only be modified from within the Oracle instance and requires Oracle to be running.

Setting SPFILE Parameters

Once you are running with the spfile, parameters are modified by using either the ALTER SYSTEM or ALTER SESSION command. ALTER SYSTEM will modify the parameter on a system-wide basis, whereas ALTER SESSION will only modify the parameter for the duration of the session. When setting a parameter with the ALTER SYSTEM command, there are a number of optional qualifiers you can use, as shown in Table 10-1.

The initialization parameters are used to set the instance characteristics for one or more instances. These parameters take effect either immediately or whenever the instance is restarted, depending on the parameter and what it does. Let's look at a few examples.

In order to set the size of the buffer cache on both nodes in a RAC cluster, use the following syntax:

```
SQL> ALTER SYSTEM SET db_cache_size=24M COMMENT='6/2/2004 Increased buffer cache to
800M' SCOPE=BOTH SID='*';
```

Option	Description
COMMENT	The COMMENT clause allows you to insert a comment into the parameter file. This comment is only for the last occurrence of the change and is not to be used for a history.
SCOPE	The SCOPE clause allows you to specify whether the change is to affect MEMORY (the current instance), SPFILE (the spfile only), or BOTH (instance and spfile). Note: If you specify MEMORY, the change will not survive a restart.
SID	The SID clause allows you to specify which instance the parameter is to be set for. The potential values are 'SID' or '*'. Setting the SID to '*' specifies all instances in the cluster.
DEFERRED	The DEFERRED clause specifies that future sessions will be started with the new parameter value. All current sessions will retain their current settings.

TABLE 10-1.   *Qualifiers to the ALTER SYSTEM Command*

In order to set the shared pool size on one node in the RAC cluster, use the following syntax:

```
SQL> ALTER SYSTEM SET shared_pool_size=150M COMMENT='6/2/2004
Set shared pool size
to 150M' SCOPE=BOTH SID='RAC1';
```

The ALTER SESSION command can be used to set session variables, not initialization parameters. In the case of the ALTER SYSTEM command with the parameters shown in the preceding table, the order of the parameters is important in some cases.

When to Use a PFILE

Even though the spfile is the recommended method of tuning the Oracle instance, the use of a pfile is sometimes a convenient way of setting parameters. Some reasons that a pfile might be more convenient include the following:

- Several parameters need to be set. When you are setting a number of parameters, you can change them in the pfile, start up the instance, and then create the spfile file from the pfile.

- The instance can't start. If memory has been removed from the system, you might have trouble starting the instance. By using a pfile, you can restart the instance with new parameters.

Regardless of whether you use a pfile or an spfile, the result is the same. The characteristics of the instance are changed.

Monitoring the Oracle Instance

So, how do you actually know what to tune? There are a number of different Oracle parameters that can be set (over 200 in Oracle 10g). Which ones you need to set and how to set them can fill up an entire book, and often does. In this book, you will not learn all of the Oracle initialization parameters that can be set, or how to set them. Rather, you will learn how to monitor and interpret some performance data in Oracle and Linux, and how to set some of the most common parameters.

Monitoring the Instance with v$ and gv$ Views

There are many different ways to monitor the Oracle instance, including a number of excellent third-party tools. Most of these tools get their data from the same place: the v$ views. Oracle maintains a set of views that are a window into the performance of the Oracle instance. These views are known as the *v$* views or the *dynamic performance* views. These views appear to be normal table data but in fact are dynamic values that keep track of the performance of the Oracle instance since the last time it was started.

If you are running in an Oracle RAC cluster, there are also a set of dynamic performance views for the entire cluster. These are the global dynamic performance views and are known as the gv$ views. The gv$ views are similar in nature to the v$ views but contain an additional column, the instance name.

The view v$session contains information about sessions running in the current instance. The view gv$session includes information about all of the sessions running in the RAC cluster. The gv$ views can be very useful, as are the v$ views.

The contents of the dynamic performance views report on various instance metrics. For example, the v$session view contains a row for every session that is running in the instance and will change in size according to the number of sessions. The view v$sysstat contains system information, and the number of rows in the view never changes. Many of the views are essentially counters and are always increasing in value, whereas other views contain data that goes up and down dynamically.

An example of using the v$ views is to determine the buffer cache hit ratio. The statistics about the buffer cache are found in the dynamic performance view v$sysstat (system statistics). The columns physical_reads represent a cache miss, and the columns consistent_gets and db_block_gets represent cache hits. In order to determine the buffer cache hit ratio, use the following formula:

```
1 - (physical_reads / (db_block_gets + consistent gets))
```

These values are found in v$sysstat and can be gathered using the following query:

```
SQL> SELECT name, value FROM v$systat
WHERE NAME IN ('db block gets from cache', 'consistent gets from cache',
'physical reads cache');
NAME                                                             VALUE
---------------------------------------------------------------- ----------
db block gets from cache                                         206884
consistent gets from cache                                       137869
physical reads cache                                             12065
```

From this point, it is just a matter of mathematics, as follows:

```
Cache Hit Ratio = 1 - (12065 / (206884 + 137869)) = 1 - .035 = .965 = 96.5%
```

This query represents the overall buffer cache hit ratio. However, remember that there are multiple buffer caches now. In addition to the DEFAULT cache, there are the KEEP and RECYCLE caches for the standard block size. There are also the nonstandard cache sizes. The following query provides cache hit ratios for all of these caches:

```
SQL> SELECT name, 1 - (physical_reads / (db_block_gets + consistent_gets)) AS
"Cache Hit Ratio"
  FROM v$buffer_pool_statistics;
NAME                    Cache Hit Ratio
--------------------    ---------------
DEFAULT                    .965642687
```

The v$ views provide a great deal of excellent information, however, retrieving this information by hand using queries can be quite time-consuming and tedious. In order to help with this task, Oracle provided some SQL scripts that help to calculate a number of different metrics for you. These scripts were utlbstat.sql and utlestat.sql. In Oracle 9*i*, these scripts were pretty much made obsolete by Statspack. Statspack is an Oracle-provided package that saves snapshots of v$ and gv$ data and compares these snapshots to subsequent snapshots in order to provide not only dynamic data like cache hit ratios but rates as well. In the next section, you will learn how to configure and use Statspack on Linux.

Using AWR

The Automatic Workload Repository (AWR) is a new feature in Oracle10*g*. AWR is an automated method of gathering performance data. By default, AWR statistics are gathered every hour and are retained for one week. The AWR statistics-gathering settings can be viewed and set via the DBMS_WORKLOAD PL/SQL package.

AWR reports are created by running the SQL script awrrpt.sql, which is found in $ORACLE_HOME/rdbms/admin. When awrrpt.sql is run, you must select beginning and ending points. These snapshots are used to create difference reports depending on these beginning and ending points. The AWR is very similar to Statspack reports, so use the next section to assist with interpreting AWR data.

In addition, there are several procedures that can be used to tune both the interval between AWR data collections and the amount of time the AWR statistics are retained. These settings can be set by using the MODIFY_SNAPSHOT_SETTINGS procedure in the DBMS_WORKLOAD_REPOSITORY package. To change the settings, use the following SQL statement.

```
SQL> DBMS_WORKLOAD_REPOSITORY.MODIFY_SNAPSHOT_SETTINGS( retention => minutes,
interval => minutes, topnsql => number, dbid => number or NULL);
```

By setting the snapshot settings, you can tune AWR to better suit your needs. The longer the retention period and shorter the interval, the more space you will use.

Using Statspack

All of the values stored in the v$ and gv$ views represent that value at a single point of time. Many of these values are fairly useless at a single point in time, such as a count of how many I/Os have occurred on each Oracle datafile. A more reasonable representation of this data would be made by taking this measurement at two points, subtracting the earlier value from the later value, and dividing by the time between the two measurements. This would provide a rate of I/Os per time period. I/O performance makes much more sense when you can find out how many I/Os per second are being done.

Statspack helps with this by taking snapshots of dynamic performance data and storing that information in a table. At a later time, another snapshot can be taken. Statspack also includes a utility to take the difference between two snapshots and calculate rates and statistics for you. In a few pages, you will see how this is done and what kind of data is provided.

Configuring Statspack   Statspack requires several Oracle tables to be created, thus you must provide Statspack space for this data to be stored. So, the first step in setting up Statspack is to create a tablespace. Next, connect into Oracle and install the Statspack package. These steps are shown here:

1. Create a sufficiently large tablespace for statistics (mainly for number of extents).

2. Install Statspack using SQLPLUS.

   a. Start SQLPLUS.

   b. At the SQL> prompt, enter **@?/rdbms/admin/spcreate**.

   c. When prompted, specify the tablespace where the stats are to be stored.

   d. Supply a password for the perfstat user.

   e. When prompted, specify the temporary tablespace.

Once the Statspack tables and the perfstat user are configured, you are ready to begin using Statspack. How to do this is shown in the next section.

Using Statspack   Using Statspack involves connecting into the Oracle instance as the perfstat user and running snapshots. Whenever you have two or more snapshots that you want to compare, run the spreport procedure to create a Statspack report. These steps are shown here, with command sequences shown as substeps:

1. Connect into SQLPLUS as perfstat.

   a. `sqlplus /nolog`

   b. `SQL> CONNECT perfstat/perfstat`

   c. `SQL> EXECUTE statspack.snap;`

2. Continue and snap whenever you need to.

Statspack reports are run on two different snapshots. To find what snapshots are available, use the following query:

- Connect into SQLPLUS as perfstat.

    - `sqlplus /nolog`

    - `SQL> CONNECT perfstat/perfstat`

    - `SQL> Variable snap number;`

    - `SQL> Begin :snap := statspack.snap; end;`

    - `SQL> /`

    - `SQL> print snap;`

This will provide a list of Statspack IDs that can be used to create Statspack reports.

Creating Statspack reports is done by using the spreport procedure. The spreport function is also run from within sqlplus as the perfstat user. Spreport will ask for beginning and ending snapshots, and it will create a report from the differences in those snapshots. Running spreport is shown here:

- Connect into SQLPLUS as perfstat.

    - `Sqlplus /nolog`

    - `SQL> CONNECT perfstat/perfstat`

    - `SQL> @?/rdbms/admin/spreport`

You are prompted for beginning and ending snapshots. The report is saved for you, as shown here:

```
SQL> @?/rdbms/admin/spreport

Current Instance
~~~~~~~~~~~~~~~~

   DB Id    DB Name      Inst Num Instance
----------- ------------ -------- ------------
 1053994617 ORCL                1 orcl

Instances in this Statspack schema
~~~~~~~~~~~~~~~~~~~~~~~~~~~~~~~~~~~~

   DB Id    Inst Num DB Name      Instance     Host
----------- -------- ------------ ------------ ------------
 1053994617        1 ORCL         orcl         ptc6.perftuning.com

Using 1053994617 for database Id
```

```
Using           1 for instance number

Specify the number of days of snapshots to choose from
~~~~~~~~~~~~~~~~~~~~~~~~~~~~~~~~~~~~~~~~~~~~~~~~~~~~~~~~~~~~
Entering the number of days (n) will result in the most recent
(n) days of snapshots being listed. Pressing <return> without
specifying a number lists all completed snapshots.

Listing all Completed Snapshots

                                                    Snap
Instance     DB Name      Snap Id  Snap Started     Level Comment
------------ ------------ --------- ---------------- ----- --------------------
orcl         ORCL               1 05 Jun 2004 22:41     5
                                 2 06 Jun 2004 12:42     5

Specify the Begin and End Snapshot Ids
~~~~~~~~~~~~~~~~~~~~~~~~~~~~~~~~~~~~~~~~~
Enter value for begin_snap: 1
Begin Snapshot Id specified: 1

Enter value for end_snap: 2
End   Snapshot Id specified: 2

Specify the Report Name
~~~~~~~~~~~~~~~~~~~~~~~~~
The default report file name is sp_1_2. To use this name,
press <return> to continue, otherwise enter an alternative. Enter
value for report_name:
uneReport.txt
Using the report name JuneReport.txt
STATSPACK report for
```

This is followed by the Statspack report itself. In addition, the Statspack report is written out to the file that was specified by your response to the questions that were asked in the spreport.sql script.

Once you have a Statspack report, you are then ready to begin analysis into what is going on in the Oracle instance, as well as some of the sessions.

Interpreting Statspack Data   Statspack data is found in the report file that is created by spreport.sql. This report has many Oracle statistics already calculated for you. This information is very useful for both instance tuning and application tuning. A few samples follow of what Statspack has to offer.

The Statspack report begins with information about the collection of data and the Statspack report, as shown here:

```
STATSPACK report for

DB Name      DB Id       Instance     Inst Num Release     RAC Host
------------ ----------- ------------ -------- ----------- --- ----------------
ORCL         1053994617 orcl               1 10.1.0.2.0  NO  ptc6.perftuning.
                                                              com
```

```
                   Snap Id    Snap Time      Sessions Curs/Sess Comment
                 --------- ------------------ -------- --------- ------------------

Begin Snap:       1 05-Jun-04 22:41:49          14       5.4
  End Snap:       2 06-Jun-04 12:42:35          14       5.0
   Elapsed:           840.77 (mins)
```

This is followed by information about the memory configuration and the load
that the system has experienced during the measurement interval. This is shown here:

```
Cache Sizes (end)
~~~~~~~~~~~~~~~~~
                    Buffer Cache:      24M      Std Block Size:       8K
                Shared Pool Size:      96M         Log Buffer:     256K

Load Profile
~~~~~~~~~~~~                        Per Second        Per Transaction
                                    ---------------   ---------------
                     Redo size:          647.77           7,103.81
                 Logical reads:           18.84             206.57
                 Block changes:            3.97              43.51
                Physical reads:            0.58               6.37
               Physical writes:            0.23               2.48
                    User calls:            0.06               0.68
                        Parses:            0.70               7.70
                   Hard parses:            0.01               0.07
                         Sorts:            0.48               5.25
                        Logons:            0.02               0.22
                      Executes:            1.65              18.08
                  Transactions:            0.09

  % Blocks changed per Read:   21.06    Recursive Call %:    99.26
  Rollback per transaction %:   2.57    Rows per Sort:       10.07
```

Once the housekeeping has been taken care of and you have the background
information, you can start looking at the actual tuning information. The first information
that appears is cache information on the buffer cache and shared pool, as shown here:

```
Instance Efficiency Percentages (Target 100%)
~~~~~~~~~~~~~~~~~~~~~~~~~~~~~~~~~~~~~~~~~~~~~~~
                Buffer Nowait %:   100.00       Redo NoWait %:    99.99
                Buffer  Hit   %:    96.92    In-memory Sort %:   100.00
                Library Hit   %:    99.35       Soft Parse %:     99.06
             Execute to Parse %:    57.43       Latch Hit %:     100.00
  Parse CPU to Parse Elapsd %:      93.74     % Non-Parse CPU:    69.69

  Shared Pool Statistics           Begin    End
                                   ------   ------
                 Memory Usage %:   70.36    83.46
          % SQL with executions>1: 68.63    73.23
        % Memory for SQL w/exec>1: 54.27    53.24
```

In addition to the cache statistics, numerous wait events and information on the SQL statements consuming the most resources and running for the longest time are listed and sorted by various resources. This can be very useful for finding the SQL that is consuming the most resources, and these statements are good candidates for tuning.

One thing that Statspack provides that is very useful is a list of the nondefault Oracle initialization parameters. This can be very helpful in determining if something obvious has been poorly tuned or not configured at all. This is usually my starting point for tuning a system: look for the obvious.

Tuning for Wait Events

With the value of the Oracle statistics that are provided, you can often be quite effective by tuning Oracle SQL statements by using the wait events and session wait events. This information can often provide valuable information on what individual sessions are waiting on. Some common wait events are for buffers or latches. Because there are so many wait events, they will not be covered here in their entirety.

Several third-party tools available on the market, such as Indepth from Veritas, actually monitor the system by monitoring the wait events. If you know what events your system is waiting on, you can often tune it more effectively. Wait stats are a great way to tune the system because you are going right to the heart of the performance problem; the things that are taking the most time. Wait-based tuning can be quite effective but should be used in conjunction with other tuning methods, such as instance tuning and I/O tuning.

Hardware Tuning

The third type of tuning is *hardware* tuning. Hardware tuning involves reconfiguring or adding new hardware to your system in order to improve performance. Hardware tuning is often necessary when you have exceeded the hardware resources of your system. This is most often the case with both the I/O subsystem and system RAM. When system resources have been consumed, and when efforts to tune the application and Oracle instance to reduce resource use have not improved performance enough, you really don't have much choice but to add more hardware.

Hardware tuning is similar in nature to sizing and capacity planning, which were covered earlier in this book.

Hardware usually should be the last resort; however, it is often the first resort. This is due to the fact that it is easier to add new hardware than to spend the time and effort to find out what the real problem is. This can sometimes work for a while, but eventually you get to the point where adding more hardware is either impossible or becomes prohibitively expensive. This is not to say that hardware tuning isn't necessary; it just shouldn't be the first step in tuning the system.

Monitoring the Linux System

In addition to monitoring the Oracle system via Statspack, it is also important to monitor the Linux system. There are not very many parameters that you can tune in the Linux system, however, a poorly tuned system can experience severe performance problems because of that. Some of the parameters involve resources that must be allocated for Oracle, including shared memory and semaphores. As shown earlier in this book, these parameters can be set in the /etc/sysctl.conf parameter file. Let's look at a few of these parameters.

Shown here are the parameters set in /etc/sysctl.conf for shared memory and semaphores:

```
kernel.shmall = 2097152
kernel.shmmax = 2147483648
kernel.shmmni = 4096
kernel.sem = 250 32000 100 128
```

These parameters configure how large the shared memory segment can be. With this setting, you could have an SGA that is up to 2GB in size (assuming no other programs are using shared memory). In order to view the shared memory and semaphores that are currently in use, use the Linux ipcs command, as shown here:

```
[root@ptc6 root]# ipcs

------ Shared Memory Segments --------
key          shmid      owner    perms    bytes        nattch     status
0x00005643 0            root     666      1024         1
0x00005654 32769        root     666      1024         1
0x00000000 262146       gdm      777      196608       2          dest
0x00000000 327683       gdm      777      196608       2          dest
0x54250c38 360452       oracle   640      188747776    15

------ Semaphore Arrays --------
key          semid      owner    perms    nsems        status
0x00005653 0            root     666      1
0x460de1a4 196609       oracle   640      127
0x460de1a5 229378       oracle   640      127
0x460de1a6 262147       oracle   640      127

------ Message Queues --------
key          msqid      owner    perms    used-bytes   messages
```

Additional tuning parameters that are needed to install Oracle include the following:

```
fs.file-max = 65536
net.ipv4.ip_local_port_range = 1024 65000
```

These parameters set the maximum number of open files that can be open in the system, as well as the IP ports that are available for use.

If you are running in an Oracle RAC cluster, the following UDP and IP parameters should be set as well:

```
net.core.rmem_default = 262144
net.core.rmem_max = 262144
net.core.wmem_default = 262144
net.core.wmem_max = 262144
net.ipv4.tcp_keepalive_time = 3000
net.ipv4.tcp_keepalive_intvl = 30
net.ipv4.tcp_retries2 = 3
net.ipv4.tcp_syn_retries = 2
```

These parameters are used to improve UDP performance on the RAC interconnect, and the IP parameters improve failover time. There might be other Linux parameters that need tuning, but these are the basics. To monitor what is going on with your system, you have a number of tools available.

Monitoring Linux with ps

Linux draws its history from UNIX. The philosophy of the original UNIX developers was to make the names of the commands as short as possible in order to avoid typing any more than necessary. This is why many of the Linux commands are two characters in length. The ps command provides process statistics. Here you can see information on processes that are currently running. The ps command allows for a number of additional parameters that provide more detailed information on the currently running processes. Here is an example of ps:

```
ptc6:/var/log # ps -elf
F S UID        PID  PPID  C PRI  NI ADDR SZ WCHAN  STIME TTY        TIME CMD
0 S root         1     0  0  75   0 -   113 schedu Jun19 ?     00:00:03 init
0 S root         2     1  0  75   0 -     0 contex Jun19 ?     00:00:00
[keventd]
0 S root         3     1  0  94  19 -     0 ksofti Jun19 ?     00:00:00
[ksoftirqd_CPU0]
 .



 .



 .
0 S oracle    8906     1  0  75   0 - 65517 schedu Jun20 ?     00:00:00
ora_pmon_orcl
0 S oracle    8908     1  0  75   0 - 65355 schedu Jun20 ?     00:00:00
ora_mman_orcl
0 S oracle    8910     1  0  75   0 - 65876 schedu Jun20 ?     00:00:10
ora_dbw0_orcl
0 S oracle    8912     1  0  75   0 - 68972 schedu Jun20 ?     00:00:04
ora_lgwr_orcl
0 S oracle    8914     1  0  75   0 - 65615 schedu Jun20 ?     00:01:30
ora_ckpt_orcl
0 S oracle    8916     1  0  76   0 - 65625 schedu Jun20 ?     00:00:26
```

```
ora_smon_orcl
0 S oracle    8918     1  0  75   0 -  65363 schedu Jun20 ?       00:00:00
ora_reco_orcl
0 S oracle    8920     1  0  75   0 -  65378 schedu Jun20 ?       00:00:02
ora_cjq0_orcl
0 S oracle    8922     1  0  75   0 -  65634 schedu Jun20 ?       00:00:00
ora_d000_orcl
0 S oracle    8924     1  0  75   0 -  65499 schedu Jun20 ?       00:00:00
ora_s000_orcl
0 S oracle    8930     1  0  75   0 -  69120 schedu Jun20 ?       00:00:00
ora_arc0_orcl
0 S oracle    8932     1  0  75   0 -  69121 schedu Jun20 ?       00:00:04
ora_arc1_orcl
0 S oracle    8934     1  0  75   0 -  65355 schedu Jun20 ?       00:00:00
ora_qmnc_orcl
0 S oracle    8936     1  0  75   0 -  65633 schedu Jun20 ?       00:00:59
ora_mmon_orcl
0 S oracle    8938     1  0  75   0 -  65363 schedu Jun20 ?       00:00:00
ora_mmnl_orcl
0 S oracle   10903     1  0  75   0 -  65361 schedu Jun20 ?       00:00:00
ora_q001_orcl
0 S root     15857   733  0  75   0 -   1184 schedu 04:33 ?       00:00:00
/usr/sbin/sshd
0 S root     15858 15857  0  75   0 -    688 schedu 04:33 pts/0   00:00:00 -bash
0 S postfix  17157   816  0  75   0 -   1096 schedu 14:29 ?       00:00:00 pickup -
l -t fifo -u
0 S root     17252   733  0  76   0 -   1184 schedu 15:07 ?       00:00:00
/usr/sbin/sshd
0 S root     17253 17252  0  75   0 -    688 wait4  15:07 pts/4   00:00:00 -bash
0 R root     17488 17253  0  78   0 -    887 -      16:02 pts/4   00:00:00
ps -elf
```

The ps command is valuable for finding which processes are consuming resources, have been running for a long time, or need to be killed, since they are no longer performing useful work. One of the most useful things to notice with ps is the process state code (column 2). The possible process states are

- R, runnable (on run queue)
- S, sleeping
- D, uninterruptible sleep (usually I/O)
- T, traced or stopped
- W, paging
- X, dead
- Z, a defunct ("zombie") process

A runnable process is currently running on a CPU, a sleeping process is waiting for something to happen, and an uninterruptible sleep (D) usually indicates that the process is waiting on I/O.

Monitoring Linux Using vmstat

The vmstat command provides information related to the virtual memory subsystem. This is where you find out if there is memory available, what swapping is happening, and how much data is cached. If you see the free memory get too low (less than 1000), you are experiencing some problems. Output of vmstat is shown here:

```
[root@ptc6 root]# vmstat 10 10
procs                    memory      swap        io    system       cpu
 r  b   swpd   free   buff  cache   si   so   bi   bo   in   cs us sy id wa
 0  0      0 110160  13408 242292    0    0  176  248  135  180 10  3 82  5
 0  0      0 110160  13424 242292    0    0    0   12  111  170  0  0 100  0
 1  0      0 105760  13456 242480    0    0    2   46  174  673 52 12 36  0
 0  0      0 105776  13472 242496    0    0    0    9  110  188  4  0 96  0
 0  0      0 105776  13488 242496    0    0    0   18  112  182  0  0 99  0
 0  0      0 105776  13504 242496    0    0    0   12  111  183  0  0 99  0
 0  0      0 105776  13520 242496    0    0    0    6  109  181  0  0 100  0
```

As with many of these commands, the vmstat command can be run in a loop. The two numbers provided to vmstat specify the interval and the duration. Running vmstat 10 100 specifies that vmstat is run every 10 seconds for 100 times.

Monitoring Linux Using iostat

The iostat command provides information about the I/O subsystem. This command is useful for determining if latencies are too high and if the subsystem is being overdriven. Both the average wait time (await) and the service time (svctm) are important data points. The number of reads per second (r/s) and writes per second (w/s) are also very important.

```
[root@ptc6 root]# iostat -x 10 100
Linux 2.4.21-4.EL (ptc6)          06/06/2004

avg-cpu:  %user   %nice    %sys   %idle
          10.01    0.08    2.54   87.37

Device:    rrqm/s wrqm/s   r/s   w/s rsec/s wsec/s    rkB/s    wkB/s avgrq-sz avgqu-sz
await  svctm  %util
/dev/hda   10.91   0.06  1.59  0.09  97.75   1.22    48.87     0.61    58.92
327.49   6.61 621.04 104.31
/dev/hda1   0.05   0.00  0.03  0.00   0.16   0.00     0.08     0.00     5.14
0.00   13.93   7.14   0.02
/dev/hda2  10.73   0.06  1.47  0.09  97.07   1.22    48.54     0.61    63.01
0.09    5.70   3.81   0.59
/dev/hda3   0.03   0.00  0.03  0.00   0.18   0.00     0.09     0.00     7.30
0.00   10.43   5.65   0.01
/dev/hdb   18.67  51.28 10.33  6.85 230.03 465.22   115.02   232.61    40.46
372.19 199.32  60.40 103.81
/dev/hdb1   0.07   0.00  0.04  0.01   0.23   0.02     0.12     0.01     4.79
0.00    5.62   3.96   0.02
/dev/hdb2  18.44  51.28 10.22  6.85 229.28 465.20   114.64   232.60    40.70
34.24 200.67   3.30   5.63
/dev/hdb3   0.04   0.00  0.02  0.00   0.18   0.00     0.09     0.00     7.64
0.00    4.09   2.27   0.01

avg-cpu:  %user   %nice    %sys   %idle
```

```
         0.10    0.00    0.50   99.40

Device:      rrqm/s wrqm/s   r/s   w/s rsec/s  wsec/s   rkB/s   wkB/s avgrq-sz
avgqu-sz  await svctm  %util
/dev/hda      0.00    0.00  0.00  0.00   0.00    0.00    0.00    0.00    0.00
4294827.30    0.00    0.00 100.00
/dev/hda1     0.00    0.00  0.00  0.00   0.00    0.00    0.00    0.00    0.00
0.00    0.00    0.00    0.00
/dev/hda2     0.00    0.00  0.00  0.00   0.00    0.00    0.00    0.00    0.00
0.00    0.00    0.00    0.00
/dev/hda3     0.00    0.00  0.00  0.00   0.00    0.00    0.00    0.00    0.00
0.00    0.00    0.00    0.00
/dev/hdb      0.00    1.40  0.00  1.40   0.00   22.40    0.00   11.20   16.00
4294837.30    0.00 714.29 100.00
/dev/hdb1     0.00    0.00  0.00  0.00   0.00    0.00    0.00    0.00    0.00
0.00    0.00    0.00    0.00
/dev/hdb2     0.00    1.40  0.00  1.40   0.00   22.40    0.00   11.20   16.00
0.00    0.00    0.00    0.00
/dev/hdb3     0.00    0.00  0.00  0.00   0.00    0.00    0.00    0.00    0.00
0.00    0.00    0.00    0.00
```

As with vmstat, this is a repeating program. Since this data is displayed as rates, it takes at least two samples in order to provide the data.

Monitoring Linux Using sar

The sar program is the system activity reporter and provides information in a number of different areas. By default, sar reports CPU information, as shown here:

```
[root@ptc6 root]# sar 10 100
Linux 2.4.21-4.EL (ptc6)   06/06/2004

05:34:09 PM  CPU   %user  %nice %system  %idle
05:34:19 PM  all   68.34 0.50   31.16 0.00
05:34:29 PM  all   71.60 0.24   28.16 0.00
05:34:39 PM  all   68.09 0.99   30.92 0.00
05:34:49 PM  all   63.94 0.29   35.78 0.00
05:34:59 PM  all   59.18 0.21   40.62 0.00
05:35:09 PM  all   69.49 0.42   30.10 0.00
05:35:19 PM  all   62.35 0.60   37.05 0.00
```

Running sar with the –n qualifier displays network statistics. This is shown here:

```
[root@ptc6 root]# sar -n DEV 10 100
Linux 2.4.21-4.EL (ptc6)        06/06/2004

05:30:51 PM    IFACE   rxpck/s  txpck/s  rxbyt/s  txbyt/s  rxcmp/s  txcmp/s
rxmcst/s
05:31:01 PM       lo     2.20     2.20   234.80   234.80     0.00     0.00
0.00
05:31:01 PM     eth0     0.50     0.10    39.60    13.40     0.00     0.00
0.00

05:31:01 PM    IFACE   rxpck/s  txpck/s  rxbyt/s  txbyt/s  rxcmp/s  txcmp/s
rxmcst/s
05:31:11 PM       lo     2.20     2.20   234.80   234.80     0.00     0.00
0.00
```

```
05:31:11 PM     eth0      0.70     0.10    70.00    37.40     0.00     0.00
0.00

05:31:11 PM    IFACE   rxpck/s  txpck/s  rxbyt/s  txbyt/s  rxcmp/s  txcmp/s
rxmcst/s
05:31:21 PM       lo      2.20     2.20   235.04   235.04     0.00     0.00
0.00
05:31:21 PM     eth0      0.50     0.10    39.64    37.44     0.00     0.00
0.00

05:31:21 PM    IFACE   rxpck/s  txpck/s  rxbyt/s  txbyt/s  rxcmp/s  txcmp/s
rxmcst/s
05:31:31 PM       lo      2.20     2.20   234.80   234.80     0.00     0.00
0.00
05:31:31 PM     eth0      0.50     0.10    39.60    37.40     0.00     0.00
0.00
```

The sar command is yet another repeating program that will run with whatever interval and duration you specify.

Monitoring Linux Using Top

Top is a great tool for graphically viewing the system statistics. It is not visible in this snapshot, but the top program dynamically updates the various data that are displayed. This sample is run with top –c, which shows the complete command name, including parameters.

```
17:37:04  up 26 min,  4 users,  load average: 3.04, 1.72, 0.77
72 processes: 71 sleeping, 1 running, 0 zombie, 0 stopped
CPU states:   cpu    user    nice   system     irq  softirq  iowait    idle
            total    0.9%    0.0%     5.6%    2.8%     0.0%   90.5%    0.0%
Mem:   512464k av,   505880k used,     6584k free,       0k shrd,   31376k buff
                     254816k actv,   104788k in_d,     7232k in_c
Swap: 1572464k av,        0k used, 1572464k free                  323812k cached

  PID USER      PRI  NI  SIZE  RSS SHARE STAT %CPU %MEM   TIME CPU COMMAND
   13 root       15   0     0    0     0 DW    3.7  0.0   0:02   0 kjournald
 2227 root       15   0  5768 5768  4836 S     1.8  1.1   0:04   0 magicdev --sm-
client-id default4
 2503 root       19   0  1116 1116   900 R     0.9  0.2   0:00   0 top c
    1 root       15   0   504  504   448 S     0.0  0.0   0:04   0 init
    2 root       15   0     0    0     0 SW    0.0  0.0   0:00   0 keventd
    3 root       15   0     0    0     0 SW    0.0  0.0   0:00   0 kapmd
    4 root       34  19     0    0     0 SWN   0.0  0.0   0:00   0 ksoftirqd/0
    7 root       25   0     0    0     0 SW    0.0  0.0   0:00   0 bdflush
    5 root       15   0     0    0     0 SW    0.0  0.0   0:01   0 kswapd
    6 root       15   0     0    0     0 SW    0.0  0.0   0:00   0 kscand
    8 root       15   0     0    0     0 SW    0.0  0.0   0:00   0 kupdated
    9 root       25   0     0    0     0 SW    0.0  0.0   0:00   0 mdrecoveryd
   75 root       25   0     0    0     0 SW    0.0  0.0   0:00   0 khubd
 1258 root       23   0     0    0     0 SW    0.0  0.0   0:00   0 kjournald
 1589 root       15   0   608  608   528 S     0.0  0.1   0:00   0 syslogd -m 0
 1593 root       15   0   456  456   400 S     0.0  0.0   0:00   0 klogd -x
 1619 rpc        15   0   580  580   508 S     0.0  0.1   0:00   0 portmap
 1638 rpcuser    25   0   732  732   652 S     0.0  0.1   0:00   0 rpc.statd
 1707 root       24   0   520  520   464 S     0.0  0.1   0:00   0 /usr/sbin/apmd -p
```

```
10 -w 5 -W -P /etc/sys
 1746 root      15    0  1968 1968  1448 S      0.0  0.3   0:00    0 cupsd
 1786 root      15    0  1512 1512  1276 S      0.0  0.2   0:00    0 /usr/sbin/sshd
 1800 root      16    0   900  900   784 S      0.0  0.1   0:00    0 xinetd -stayalive
-pidfile /var/run/xine
 1819 root      25    0  1160 1160  1028 S      0.0  0.2   0:00    0 /bin/sh
/usr/bin/safe_mysqld --defaults-
 1854 mysql     25    0  4244 4244  1616 S      0.0  0.8   0:00    0
/usr/libexec/mysqld --defaults-file=/etc
 1862 root      15    0  2600 2600  1940 S      0.0  0.5   0:00    0 sendmail:
accepting connections
 1872 smmsp     25    0  2320 2312  1768 S ·    0.0  0.4   0:00    0 sendmail: Queue
runner@01:00:00 for /var
 1882 root      15    0   464  464   412 S      0.0  0.0   0:00    0 gpm -t imps2 -m
/dev/mouse
 1892 root      15    0  8912 8912  6352 S      0.0  1.7   0:00    0 /usr/sbin/httpd
 1901 root      15    0   616  616   544 S      0.0  0.1   0:00    0 crond
 1933 xfs       15    0  3452 3452   876 S      0.0  0.6   0:00    0 xfs -droppriv -
daemon
```

As with any tool, you must interpret the results and determine what those results mean. A tool is only as good as the person that is using it.

Using Large Memory Models

By default, the Oracle database server can have an SGA configured of up to 1.7GB in size without any additional changes. With some minor changes, you can create an SGA that uses up to 2.7GB of RAM. For sizes over 4GB, there are other changes that must be made.

NOTE
When using the hugemem kernel, these limits are 2.7GB and 3.7GB. However, due to extra overhead with the hugemem kernel, it should only be used in systems with 16GB of RAM or more.

Configuring Linux for > 1.7GB (and <= 2.7GB) of SGA

In order to create an SGA that is greater than 1.7GB, but less than 2.8GB, you must lower the base address where Oracle loads. This is known as the *mapped* base. In order to lower the mapped base, the following steps should be taken:

1. Change (cd) to the $ORACLE_HOME/rdbms/lib directory.

2. Create a assembler file using the genksms program, as shown here:

   ```
   genksms -s 0x15000000 > ksms.s
   ```

3. Create the object file.

```
make -f ins_rdbms.mk ksms.o
```

4. Create the Oracle executable file.

```
make -f ins_rdbms.mk ioracle
```

Now all that is necessary is to increase the shared memory parameter SHMMAX to between 1.7GB and 2.7GB, and to start up the Oracle server with the newly built binary.

Configuring Oracle for >2.7GB SGA

In order to configure the Oracle database server to use more than 2.7GB of SGA, a two-step process must be used. First, a RAM disk must be created. Once the RAM disk is created, Oracle is configured to use indirect data buffers. The indirect data buffers are essentially a RAM disk file that Oracle uses for database block buffers. By using a RAM disk, you avoid all of the 32-bit limitations.

The RAM disk can be created by mounting a filesystem of type ramfs. In versions of Red Hat Linux prior to Red Hat ES 3.0, this was created with the shmfs, but with 3.0, ramfs is used. The following syntax is used to mount the RAM disk:

```
umount /dev/shm
mount -t ramfs ramfs /dev/shm
chown oracle:dba /dev/shm
```

It is then necessary to add the following to /etc/security/limits.conf.

```
oracle soft memlock 3145728
oracle hard memlock 3145728
```

If you use ssh to log in to your system, you must also add the following to /etc/init.d/ssh as a work-around for an ssh bug.

```
ulimit -l 3145728
```

Also include " UseLogin yes" in the file /etc/ssh/sshd_config. The final step is to add "use_indirect_data_buffers=true" to the Oracle initialization parameters.

The next step is to set the Linux shared memory sufficiently high that the large memory can be used. To set the max shared memory size to 8GB, do the following:

```
echo 8589934592 >/proc/sys/kernel/shmmax
```

or put the following into /etc/sysctl.conf:

```
sys.kernel.shmmax = 8589934592
```

This will allow you to create a much larger SGA. The last step is to set use_ indirect_data_buffers in the Oracle initialization file. You can now create a much larger SGA.

NOTE
Indirect data buffers can only be used for Oracle block buffers. Lower memory must still be used for other shared memory items such as the shared poolor the log buffer.

Using Load Testing for Performance Validation

If at all possible, it is a great idea to perform load testing on any new Oracle system prior to putting this system into production. Load testing can be used to validate several aspects of the application that functional testing cannot validate. These attributes of the application cannot be validated during functional testing:

- **Locking**   Unless several or many concurrent processes are accessing the same tables, you will not discover locking issues.

- **Memory**   Although an individual process might achieve an extremely high cache hit ratio, many together might have contention if the buffer cache or shared pool is overtaxed. In addition, each dedicated server process utilizes memory as well.

- **Processor**   One or two processes might run at < 50 percent CPU utilization, whereas many processes together might run the CPUs at 100 percent.

- **I/O**   As you have learned earlier in this book, the I/O subsystem has finite performance characteristics. Many processes running together might overload the I/O subsystem.

Whenever a new application or database is going to be introduced into a production environment, load testing should be performed. The type and extent of load testing are determined by the type of application that is being introduced and the performance requirements. Here are some things to keep in mind:

- **Why is the system being tested?**   The reason for performing load tests will determine the type of test and how valuable the results of the test are.

- **Batch systems**   Since batch systems usually are automated and are not initiated by users, the actual batch jobs can be run in a test environment.

- **Loading** Loading data into the database can be simulated in a test environment using the production data.

- **OLTP** Here is where it gets interesting. It is desirable to simulate the entire application environment (i.e., web servers, application tier, database layer) if at all possible, with as many simulated users as you can.

Let's look at the first question and then some of these environments in a little more detail.

Why Is the System Being Tested?

There are a few basic goals in load testing. These goals vary, depending on what is changing. Load testing can be used to validate the performance impact of new changes to an application, to validate new or upgraded hardware with an existing application, or to baseline the performance of a brand-new application on a brand-new hardware platform. The results of the load test are analyzed and interpreted in accordance with the change being tested.

New Application

A new application does not allow you to compare the results of the load test with your current production environment. However, you can establish baseline performance metrics, analyze execution plans and data access patterns, collect instance data, collect OS and hardware performance data, and possibly even begin tuning. It is very difficult to compare functions such as accounts payable on one application to accounts payable on another application, since the application, the database schema, and the basic operational tasks are so different. However, this is a great starting point for collecting baseline data and beginning the tuning process.

New Version of an Existing Application

A new version of an existing application provides more flexibility to compare the results of the load test with performance in your current production environment. With the new version, the basic results of functional tasks such as accounts payable should be comparable. In addition, the database schema should be similar. Here you should be able to make some comparisons. However, keep in mind that the new version might be providing greater functionality and more features. Thus, you might expect performance to be slightly slower than on the existing application.

New Hardware with an Existing Application

Load testing works best in this type of environment, since you are replacing existing hardware with newer and, hopefully, faster hardware. You should expect performance to be better and response times to be faster. These expectations are based on assumptions that the newer hardware is faster than the existing hardware. This assumption may or may not be correct. Remember that two disk drives perform better than one disk drive. One of the most common performance problems that I run into is when the customer replaces four 18GB disk drives with one 72GB disk drive (or something similar). I would automatically expect this system to perform more slowly than the original.

Load-testing the same application on two different hardware platforms provides an excellent comparison. Keep in mind that this test will provide useful data only if the application is not the problem. You must keep this in mind because you might actually be experiencing a performance improvement that you don't realize, because that improvement is masked by other factors. The result of any performance test always has three possible outcomes:

- **Performance has improved**   This is pretty easy to measure and determine.

- **Performance has gotten worse**   This is also fairly easy to measure and determine.

- **The test is flawed or there are outside factors affecting the test**   For example, if you believe you have an I/O problem and you add I/O performance capacity and see no improvement, it might be that you really don't have an I/O problem at all, or that the load test itself is not driving enough load to show the improvement. This is why proper metrics are important.

With this type of comparison, you can often collect a lot of excellent data. It is important that it be analyzed and interpreted correctly.

New Hardware and a New Application

This is probably the most difficult type of data to interpret. With a new application and new hardware, you can still collect baseline performance data, analyze execution plans and data access patterns, and develop metrics that you will use in the future. With this type of test, it is still important to perform load testing and, if possible, compare the results against service-level agreement (SLA) metrics. This is your opportunity to determine if the new application and hardware will meet your needs before introducing them to the user community.

Load-Testing Batch Jobs

Load-testing batch jobs is fairly easy relative to load-testing OLTP applications. This is due to the fact that batch jobs are not run interactively and the queuing and execution of batch jobs is usually controlled by the application or by the DBA staff. Because of this, it is a relatively straightforward task to run the batch jobs, monitor performance of Oracle and the OS while these jobs are running, and document batch performance.

Most batch processing systems log the performance of each batch job run, including information such as

- Start time

- End time

- Duration

- Job parameters

- User information

Because you have this information, you can run the same batch job on the test system and compare the run time on the current system with that on the test system. Keep in mind that unless you are moving to a new hardware platform, this data will provide baseline performance data only.

Load-Testing Loading

As with batch jobs, load-testing database loading is fairly easy relative to load-testing OLTP applications. Loading data into the database is done in an offline fashion, usually when there is not a lot of other activity on the system, and it is almost always timed. When setting up performance metrics on loading, try to collect at least the following data:

- Start time

- End time

- Duration

- Job parameters

- Number of rows being loaded

- Amount of data (size) being loaded

If this information is stored in a database table, you can easily track trends and potential issues before they become problems. From this data, of particular interest is the amount of data being loaded vs. the duration. Any significant slowdowns should alert the DBA staff.

Load-Testing OLTP Applications

Load testing of OLTP applications is the most difficult, since OLTP systems are characterized by

- Many online users

- Multiple applications performing different functions

- Random data access patterns
- Continuous activity
- Peak and low utilization periods

In order to properly load-test OLTP applications, you must simulate many users simultaneously accessing the system. This simulation can take several forms and can work in several different ways. The following list represents different types of load tests that can be done with different levels of cost and quality of data.

- Full end-to-end testing with 100%+ users
- Full end-to-end testing with partial users
- Database testing only with full application emulation
- Database testing only with partial application emulation

The value of the load testing diminishes as you go down the list, but then so does the cost. Although the load-testing software available today is very good, it is also very expensive. It is priced beyond the reach of many budgets. Minimal load testing is still much better than no load testing at all.

Full End-to-End Testing with 100%+ Users
In this type of test, load-testing software emulates the user load against the full application environment. This means that HTML is emulated and is requesting data from the application, which in turn requests this data from the database. If possible, the number of users that you expect to support should be emulated, and then ramped up until the system cannot support any more load. This point will be your maximum capacity. In full end-to-end load testing, components such as keyboard time and think time are factored into the test.

The TPC-C benchmark is a perfect example of where a full end-to-end test is done. This type of test actually simulates all of the users that might be connected to this type of system, and runs a complete application. The system being tested includes web servers, the application, and the database itself.

Full End-to-End Testing with Partial Users
This type of test can also be effective. With a partial user test, you would most likely remove the think time and key time from the simulation, and blast the system with requests as quickly as possible. The data is useful, since it can point out flaws in the application or database. However, the user count information is not as valuable.

The reason to perform partial user testing is to reduce the amount of hardware and software necessary in order to create the user load. Many of the commercial load-testing software packages, such as Loadrunner and Silk Performer, are licensed according to the number of simulated users that you will be emulating. By reducing the number of users, you reduce the software cost. In addition, you might be able to reduce the number of load-driving systems that are necessary in order to produce the required load.

Database Testing Only with Full Application Emulation

You can test the database layer through the application by modifying the application layer to simulate database requests. This involves some modification of the application in order to create this load. With this type of testing, you can simulate the user load on the database system and capture response times without having to incur the cost of load-generating systems. This type of testing works only if you have built this type of feature into your application.

The data collected will allow you to determine database response times and information about the database calls such as execution plans, data access patterns, and instance performance information, but doesn't tell you much about additional latencies introduced at the application server layer. However, if the database layer is the problem, this type of testing can be useful.

Database Testing Only with No Application Emulation

With this type of testing, the application is taken out of the picture. SQL statements can be captured from users running against the application, and a load test can be developed that simulates these types of SQL statements without running any application code. This is not the best type of test, since the application layer is completely removed, but it is better than no load testing at all.

This type of test can sometimes be developed in a few weeks in C code, Perl, or shell scripts, and it can be deployed quickly. This type of test cannot provide sizing information, but it is great for putting a system under load in order to validate new hardware components and system settings. It is also a great way to stress the database instance.

This is by far the most economical load test, since it can often be developed in-house. As the testing evolves, so can the test itself. I often use this type of test in my performance tuning classes in order to simulate some load on the system quickly and easily.

Performance Metrics

When doing any kind of load testing, it is important to determine the performance metrics before the testing begins. Don't focus on one single metric, but use many metrics. There are a number of great metrics that you can use. Here is a list of some of them:

- OS Metrics

    - **CPU** CPU utilization is one of the best metrics, since you can only use 100 percent of the CPU time. This should be broken down into system CPU time, user time, and kernel time.

- **I/O** As with CPU, this is a finite thing. Your system can do only so many I/Os per second. You should collect I/Os per second, reads/sec, writes/sec, read latency, write latency, and queue depth, at a minimum.

- **Number of processes** You should always keep track of how many processes are running as a comparison.

- **Paging** This should be monitored to determine if external factors are affecting the system performance.

- Application Metrics

  - **Number of connections** You should monitor how many users are simultaneously connected to the web server.

  - **Pages/sec** The number of web pages per second is useful information.

  - **Requests/sec** The number of application requests per second can give you an indication on how the application layer is working.

  - **Response time** If you can collect and analyze the response times from application requests, you can determine when and if problems are occurring.

- Database Metrics

  - **Cache hit ratio** The buffer cache hit ratio is one of the most important metrics because it tells you how efficient the buffer cache is.

  - **Shared pool hit ratio** This is similar, but on the shared pool.

  - **Wait statistics** Many Oracle database tuning experts rely on the wait statistics in order to indicate where performance bottlenecks are.

By collecting the right metrics, you can often determine where problems are, and possibly get hints on how to fix them. It is important to collect the right data in order to get the right results.

Load Testing Tips

Here are a few tips that can be helpful when performing load testing. These are simply a random collection of dos and don'ts when performing load testing.

- Restart the database between tests. Hit ratios and other metrics can be skewed by data left in the cache from the previous test.

- Rotate the logfiles between tests in order to make sure that the tests are starting at the same point in the logfile. This can be done with an ALTER SYSTEM SWITCH LOGFILE command.

- Reboot web servers between tests. The web server cache is very efficient and can skew application test results.

- Measure all layers of the system. The database is only one layer of the total system. Often, performance problems can occur in the application or web server layer, or even in the browser.

- Occasionally evaluate the test. A flawed test can cause flawed results. The test should be reevaluated by more than one person.

- Be skeptical. Don't always believe the results if they don't make sense. Sometimes you need to reevaluate and change the test.

- Don't change too many things at once. This is the most common problem. Different changes can cancel each other out.

Load testing can be a powerful tool and can actually save you money in the long run. However, budgets often overlook this type of testing. With the World Wide Web and applications that affect thousands of customers, you can't afford not to test your application before deploying it.

Summary

This chapter has covered a number of different topics related to tuning Oracle and Oracle RAC on Linux. As we have discussed, there is a methodology that you should follow in order to achieve effective results. By sticking to a methodology, you will be able to reproduce your results and be able to logically come to conclusions. This chapter has covered various aspects of tuning applications, the Oracle instance, and the hardware. In addition, you have learned why load testing is important, and gotten some ideas of how to do that testing.

I would like to stress again how important documentation is. When tuning your system, it is critical to document all of the changes you are making. You might later need to go back and determine if your changes were effective or not, and good documentation will help.

PART
IV

Administering and Tuning Oracle Database 10g on Linux

CHAPTER
11

Backup and Recovery

robably the most important task for the DBA is to back up the database. This is because the DBA's highest responsibility is to ensure the stability and security of the database. In the event of a catastrophic system failure, the DBA must be able to quickly and effectively restore the database to a point in time as close to the time of failure as possible. Although this task is one of the most important tasks for the DBA, it is also one of the least glamorous and least visible. It is up to you to make sure that everyone understands its criticality.

Backup Overview

The Oracle DBA is responsible for the maintenance and proper operation of the Oracle database server. In the event of a system failure, the Oracle DBA must be able to get the system back up and running as quickly as possible. To be able to do this, several tasks must be accomplished:

- The database must be backed up regularly in a timely manner. The longer the time between backups, the longer the time to restore the database.

- The database must be backed up in a manner that affects the performance of the production system as little as possible.

- The DBA must be ready to restore the database as quickly as possible in the event of a catastrophic system failure.

- The database restore must be done properly, as quickly as possible, and with as little disruption to the users as possible.

- The DBA must have a methodology to restore individual tables and users' data as necessary to correct user error.

- The DBA must be able to accomplish all of this while at the same time being able to calmly deal with excited management and an excited, frustrated, and impatient user community.

- The restore and recovery procedures must be documented so that they can be executed correctly even if the lead DBA is not available. Remember, things might happen when you are on vacation.

- The backups must be protected. Backups that have been done to disk should immediately (or as soon as feasible) be copied on to tape.

As you can see, there are many considerations that must be taken into account. In this chapter, you will learn the fundamentals and procedures for performing database backups. You will also learn the difference between recovery and restoring the database, and how to properly restore the database. You will also learn different methods for restoring individual tables, tablespaces, data files, and complete databases.

The integrity and security of the data is the most important responsibility of the DBA. By learning proper techniques, documentation, and methods, you will quickly become adept at backup and recovery.

One might ask, why are backups even necessary with the prevalence of RAID controllers and error-correcting memory? RAID controllers and fault-tolerant disk subsystems are not an excuse for not doing a backup. User error is one of the most important reasons for doing backups, and one of the most common reasons for recovery. If a user were to drop a table by accident, the table would instantly be lost, regardless of whether the disk volume is fault tolerant or not. In addition, occasionally software problems occur that cause the loss of data. The only way to get back to normal is by restoring the database to the last known good state.

Backup and Recovery Concepts

Before you learn about how backups work, let's review how Oracle works. We will not cover all of the Oracle functions and processes, just those that are pertinent to the integrity of the data in the database.

If none of the data in the database ever changed, there would never be a need to back up that data. In this scenario, any past backup could be used to restore the data to a useful state. Well, this is not the case in most systems, although by using some read-only tablespaces, this can be partially achieved.

Since most real systems' data is changing, the database is a constantly changing system. It is of the highest importance that this data be protected. If a system failure should occur, it is unreasonable to think that all changes in progress could be recovered, but a reasonable expectation is that all committed transactions be recovered.

In fact, if you have a good backup and recovery plan, no committed transactions should ever be lost. In recovering the database from a failure, two different types of failures and recovery mechanisms must be used. The two types of recovery are *instance recovery* and *data recovery.*

Instance Recovery

An instance failure can occur due to a system failure, such as a power outage or a hardware failure, or even a software problem. When an instance failure occurs, the Oracle recovery background process (RECO) can completely recover the database upon instance startup. All committed transactions will be recovered, or *rolled forward,* and all noncommitted transactions will be undone, or *rolled back.*

As you will see later in this chapter and in the next chapter, instance recovery can and should be tuned to provide for the shortest possible recovery time.

Instance Recovery

Instance recovery can be quite time-consuming. The amount of time that instance recovery takes depends on the number of dirty buffers in the SGA. The number of dirty buffers depends on the amount of time since the last checkpoint. The time it takes for instance recovery also depends on the recovery parallelism.

By tuning the checkpoint interval and recovery parallelism, the recovery time can be shortened. However, even with careful configuration, extremely long transactions can take a long time to roll back.

Data Recovery or Media Recovery

Media recovery is necessary when media failure has occurred. For example, when a data file is damaged due to a disk failure or a software failure, or even some types of human error, you must first restore the damaged file from backup before you can recover it. The Oracle recovery process will then apply archive log files and redo log files to restore the damaged data file to its state just prior to the failure. All of the archive log files created since the last backup until the failure will be required to recover the restored data file. This process can be quite time-consuming.

NOTE
By scheduling frequent backups, the restoration and recovery time can be shortened. The recovery time is proportional to the time between the last full backup and the time of failure, as well as to the amount of data that has changed since that backup. By shortening the time between backups, the volume of data change since that backup can be minimized.

As you will see in this chapter, the goal is to have the shortest possible downtime in the event of a catastrophic system failure.

Online and Archived Redo Log File Recovery

You cannot recover from the loss of an archived log file if a datafile also needs to be recovered. The sections that follow describe the steps to recover from the loss of an online or archived redo log file when the data files are intact. It is always recommended that redo and archived log volumes be created on fault-tolerant disk volumes, and that the redo log files be multiplexed within Oracle.

Current Online Redo Log Recovery

Loss of one member of a current online redo log group will not cause the database to cease operations as long as another Oracle-multiplexed member of that group is not affected. Error information is written to the alert log and operation continues.

If all members of a redo log group are lost, you must do a point-in-time restore to the latest archived redo log extended through any redo logs not already overwritten. You can specify both these archived and valid online redo logs during recovery. Recovery from loss of all members of a current online multiplexed redo log group is done by executing a point-in-time recovery.

Mirroring the members of a redo log group to separate disks/controllers is optional, but Oracle strongly recommends operating with each member of a redo log group on separate disks, away from Oracle data files (three members in each group on separate disks under separate controllers, if feasible) to prevent a single point of failure.

Inactive Online Redo Log Recovery

Loss of one member of an inactive online redo log file group will not cause the database to cease operations as long as another multiplexed member of that group is not affected.

You can recover from loss of a single member of an inactive online redo log group as follows:

1. If the instance is running, query the v$recovery_file view to find the file needing recovery; otherwise, do a startup, bring the instance to the MOUNT stage, and perform the query.

2. Shut down the instance normally.

3. Copy the archived log containing the sequence number of the missing/bad redo log to the location of the original redo log.

4. Issue the startup command.

You can recover from loss of an entire inactive online redo log group as follows:

1. If the instance is running, perform a normal shutdown.

2. Start the instance and bring it to the MOUNT stage.

3. Query the V$LOG view to ensure the log file has been archived.

4. Issue the command ALTER DATABASE CLEAR LOGFILE <file_name> for the bad redo log files. (Use the UNARCHIVED flag if the log file has not been archived.)

5. Delete the physical files at the OS level if necessary.

6. Issue the ALTER DATABASE DROP LOGFILE GROUP command.

7. Issue the ALTER DATABASE ADD LOGFILE GROUP command with the desired naming and storage for the initial log member in the group.

8. Add other redo log file members to the group as necessary.

9. Issue the ALTER DATABASE OPEN command.

Archived Redo Log Recovery

Loss of an archived redo log file does not affect the current operation of the database, but it can impact the ability to do either full or incomplete (i.e., point-in-time) recovery.

If there is little or no likelihood of needing to perform point-in-time or incomplete recovery, the simplest method of resolving this situation is to perform an immediate full backup. This eliminates the need for the archived redo log files that were created prior to the full backup. This will also allow for full recovery to a time beyond the lost archived redo log from the full backup datafiles.

If there is a possible need to do point-in-time or incomplete recovery, and if a backup of the archived redo log exists on other media (e.g., as a tape backup), restore the lost archived redo log from tape to the archive destination. If no backup copy of the lost archived redo log exists, recovery will only be possible to the point in time of the last complete archived redo log prior to the one lost.

Oracle strongly recommends making a backup copy of the archived redo logs in order to prevent a single point of failure for recovery.

How Transactions Work

Remember, the term transaction is used to describe a logical group of work. This group of work can consist of one or many SQL statements and must end with a commit or a rollback. Because this example assumes a client/server application, SQL*Net is necessary. The following steps are executed to complete the transaction:

- The application processes the user input and creates a connection to the server via SQL*Net.

- The server picks up the connection request and creates a server process on behalf of the user.

- The user executes a SQL statement and commits the transaction. In this example, the user changes the value of a row in a table.

- The server process takes this SQL statement and checks the shared pool to see whether there is a shared SQL area that has this identical SQL statement (assuming CURSOR_SHARING=EXACT). If it finds an identical shared SQL area, the server process checks to see whether the user has access privileges to the data. If the user has access privileges, the server process uses the shared SQL area to process the request. If a shared SQL area is not found, a new shared SQL area is allocated, and the statement is parsed and then executed.

■ The server process retrieves the data from the SGA (if present) or retrieves it from the data file into the SGA.

■ The server process modifies the data in the SGA. Remember that the server processes can only read from the data files. Because the transaction has been committed, the LGWR process immediately records the transaction in the redo log file. At some later time, the DBWR process writes the modified blocks to permanent storage.

■ If the transaction is successful, a completion code is returned across the network to the client process. If a failure has occurred, an error message is returned.

NOTE
A transaction is not considered committed until the write to the redo log file has been completed. This arrangement ensures that in the event of instance failure, a committed transaction can be recovered. If a transaction has been committed, it is guaranteed to be recovered in the event of instance failure.

While transactions are occurring, the Oracle background processes are all doing their jobs, keeping the system running smoothly. Keep in mind that while this process is going on, hundreds of other users may be doing similar tasks. It is Oracle's job to keep the system in a consistent state, to manage contention and locking, and to perform at the necessary rate.

It is because of the recoverability requirements that the redo log entries must be written out to disk before the commit operation can complete. If a failure occurs before that entry has been written, the transaction will not be recovered.

RDBMS Functionality

If the Oracle database server is to provide data integrity features such as recovery from failure and error handling, it must provide a certain set of functions and procedures. The following sections list and describe some of these functions.

Checkpoint

Because all modifications done to data blocks are done on the block buffers, there are changes to data in memory that are not necessarily reflected in the blocks on disk. Because caching is done using a least recently used (LRU) algorithm, if a buffer is constantly modified, it is always marked as recently used and is therefore unlikely to be written out by the DBWR for a long time. The time it takes to perform instance recovery in the event of a failure is dependent on how many dirty buffers were in the buffer cache at the time of the failure.

The checkpoint process is used to ensure that these "dirty" buffers are written to disk periodically by forcing all dirty buffers to be written out on a regular basis. This does not mean that all work stops during a checkpoint; the checkpoint process has several methods of operation: the incremental checkpoint, fast-start checkpointing, and normal checkpoints.

The checkpoint itself is the point in the log file that is the starting point for instance recovery. In order to speed recovery, there are several mechanisms that control how checkpoints are done, and thus different recovery intervals.

With Oracle10g, an incremental checkpoint is automatically enabled. This is known as automatic checkpoint tuning. With automatic checkpoint tuning, idle times are used to write data out to disk, thus advancing the checkpoint. This takes advantage of idle times, thus reducing the effect on system performance, but isn't very reliable in terms of recovery time.

For a more predictable recovery time, enable fast-start checkpointing by setting the FAST_START_MTTR_TARGET initialization parameter to a value other than 0. This parameter is used to specify the number of seconds instance recovery should take. The lower the value of this parameter, the more aggressive the checkpoint operation. Fast-start checkpointing tags on additional writes to the DBWR operations. The more aggressive the recovery interval, the more aggressive the additional writes. However, it is always better to enable fast-start checkpointing, even if you specify the maximum value for FAST_START_MTTR_TARGET of 3600 seconds.

Fast-start checkpointing is overridden by setting the LOG_CHECKPOINT_INTERVAL initialization parameter. This parameter specifies how many operating system blocks of data can be written to the redo log since the last incremental checkpoint before a traditional checkpoint is initiated. If this value is reached, all dirty blocks in the buffer cache will be written out to disk. The initialization parameter LOG_CHECKPOINT_TIMEOUT can also be set. This parameter specifies the amount of time in seconds since the last incremental checkpoint that can pass before a checkpoint is issued.

Reducing the time between checkpoints improves instance recovery. Frequent checkpoints reduce the time required to recover in the event of a system failure. In addition to the checkpoints that are triggered by the number of OS blocks or time since the last checkpoint, checkpoints automatically occur at a log switch as well.

Logging and Archiving
The redo log records all changes made to the Oracle database. The purpose of the redo log is to ensure that, in the event of the loss of a data file caused by some sort of system failure, the database can be recovered. By restoring the data files back to

a known good state from backups, the redo log files (including the archive log files) can replay all the transactions to the restored data file, thus recovering the database to the point of failure.

When a redo log file is filled in normal operation, a log switch occurs and the LGWR process starts writing to a different redo log file. When this switch occurs, the ARCH process copies the filled redo log file to an archive log file—this is how Archiving works (if you are running in NOARCHIVELOG mode, these files will be discarded). When this archive is complete, the redo log file is marked as available. It is critical that this archive log file be safely stored because it may be needed for recovery. This is why ARCHIVELOG mode is critical for production systems.

NOTE
Remember that a transaction has not been committed until the redo log file has been written. Slow I/Os to the redo log files can slow down the entire system.

ARCHIVELOG Mode

The Oracle RDBMS is not required to run in ARCHIVELOG mode. In NOARCHIVELOG mode, archiving of redo logs does not occur. If you do not run in ARCHIVELOG mode, it is impossible to recover any transactions that are not in the current redo log files. Normally, a database is created in NOARCHIVELOG mode and then altered to ARCHIVELOG mode after creation. Putting a database in ARCHIVELOG mode starts the ARCH background process.

NOTE
If you do not run in ARCHIVELOG mode, you will most likely lose valuable data in the event of the loss of a data file. It is always recommended that production systems be run in ARCHIVELOG mode. You may run test systems without archiving, unless doing performance benchmarking, in which case you will want to run in ARCHIVELOG mode to factor in the additional overhead.

Enabling Archiving

Archiving is enabled by running ALTER DATABASE command with the parameter ARCHIVELOG in MOUNT mode.

To permanently enable archiving, use

```
ALTER DATABASE ARCHIVELOG;
```

To automatically begin archiving only for the current startup, enter the SQL*Plus command ARCHIVE LOG START in MOUNT or OPEN mode.

Disabling Archiving

To permanently disable archiving, use the following command in MOUNT mode:

```
ALTER DATABASE NOARCHIVELOG;
```

If you are in ARCHIVELOG mode and want to disable it for a particular startup, issue the ARCHIVE LOG STOP command.

Listing Archive Log Status

The following SQL*Plus command shows the range of redo log files to be archived, the current log file group's sequence number, and the current archive destination.

```
SQL> ARCHIVE LOG LIST
```

If you are using both ARCHIVELOG mode and automatic archiving, the display will look something like this:

```
Database log mode      Archive Mode
Automatic archival     Enabled
Archive destination    /opt/oracle/admin/PROD/arch
Oldest online log sequence   221
Next log sequence to archive 222
Current log sequence   222
```

Setting the Archiving Destination

With Enterprise Edition, the Oracle parameter LOG_ARCHIVE_DEST_*n* (where *n* = 1, 2, 3, …, 10) sets up to ten archive log destinations for Oracle archiving. Typically, LOG_ARCHIVE_DEST_1 is used for the local archive destination. The form LOG_ ARCHIVE_DEST (without the numbers) has been deprecated in Oracle 10*g* Enterprise Edition. With standard edition, LOG_ARCHIVE_DEST is still used. Archive log files will be created in the directory with a different filename for each archive log file. This filename is defined by the Oracle parameter LOG_ARCHIVE_FORMAT. Both of these parameters are described in the Oracle documentation.

Comparing ARCHIVELOG mode and NOARCHIVELOG mode

Although NOARCHIVELOG mode might seem to be more economical, it is unwise to run in NOARCHIVELOG mode under most circumstances. The following table describes the differences in the two modes.

Log Mode	Recoverability	Performance	Disk Space	Notes
ARCHIVELOG	Point of failure	Archive log overhead	Significant	Recommended
NOARCHIVELOG	Last backup	No additional overhead	No additional disk space	Benchmarks, development, testing only

Because of the lack of recoverability, NOARCHIVELOG mode is not recommended for any production environments.

Introduction to Backup

There are a variety of options available for backing up the Oracle database. Each option provides a different amount of protection and typically causes a different amount of downtime. These options are as follows:

Backup Type	Description
Archivelog backup	A backup of the archive log files
Controlfile backup	A backup of the control files
Datafile backup	A backup of a single datafile
Full backup	A backup of all datafiles and control files
Tablespace backup	A backup of a single tablespace
Incremental backup	A backup of data that has changed since the last backup

In this section, you will learn how each of these backup types differ, how to perform them, and how they complement each other. In addition, most of these backup types can be completed either by using traditional Oracle backup methods or by using Oracle RMAN (Recovery Manager).

Archivelog Backup

As archive log files are continually being created, these files are periodically backed up to offline storage and purged from both disk and tape in accordance with retention policies dictated by the business' SLA. Since the archive log information can be quite large (logs can range from 10MB each to over 1GB for databases with high volume, and they usually are tuned to switch at least every half hour), it is usually not feasible to keep this data online indefinitely. If possible, you should keep all archive log files required for a complete database recovery online that were created from the start of the latest backup, which ideally is also stored on disk (and also backed up to tape).

Remember, once a datafile is restored from backup, the archive log files that were created since that backup are applied to the newly restored system in order to reapply transactions that occurred after the backup was taken. Archive log files older than the last backup are needed only if the restore operation fails and an older backup needs to be used, or to roll forward to a specific point between past backups, typically for auditing purposes.

NOTE
A good procedure would be to save at least the last set of archive log files created since the last datafile backup until the next datafile backup, and then to back up those archive log files to tape or other archival storage.

While online, these archive log files need to be protected. I recommend keeping your online archive log files on a RAID-protected disk volume and to back up the archive log files to tape (many sites maintain multiple copies on tape) as soon as possible. In the event of a failure, the loss of a single archive log file could mean that you can't completely recover your database.

Another way to protect your archive log files is to use the Oracle archive log duplexing feature. In addition to backing up archive logs to tape, by setting the Oracle parameter LOG_ARCHIVE_DEST_n to two archive destinations, one copy of each archive log file will be created in each directory. In this way, the archive log files are protected against any single point of failure.

NOTE
The LOG_ARCHIVE_DEST_n parameters are valid only for Oracle10g Enterprise Edition. If you are running Standard Edition, LOG_ARCHIVE_DEST is used and you can duplex archive log destinations by using the parameter LOG_ARCHIVE_DUPLEX_ DEST. This should only be used for Standard Edition; if you are running Enterprise Edition, use LOG_ ARCHIVE_DEST_n parameters.

By default, only one archive log destination needs to be written to in order for the redo log file to be released for reuse. The Oracle initialization parameter LOG_

ARCHIVE_MIN_SUCCEED_DEST is used to specify the minimum number of archive log files that must be successfully written to before the redo log file can be reused.

Controlfile Backup

The control files are very important to the operation of the Oracle RDBMS. These control files contain information about the physical construction of the database. If all copies of the control file are lost, it may still be possible to re-create it, but it will be more difficult.

The two options to the ALTER DATABASE *database* BACKUP CONTROLFILE command are as follows:

TO '*filename*'	This will create a new control file with this name. If the file already exists, the optional REUSE qualifier must be used.
TO TRACE	The TO TRACE parameter optionally writes SQL to a trace file that can be used to re-create the control files. The SQL statements are complete enough to start up the database, re-create the control files, and recover and open the database appropriately.

Another option is to simply back up the control file(s) when performing operating system backups. In the event of the loss of a control file, it can be restored from that backup.

In addition, RMAN can easily be configured to back up the control file each time the database is backed up. RMAN will be covered in just a few pages.

The control file(s) need to be backed up any time there is a structural change to the database. If these changes are made, the control file will be altered.

Full Backup

A *full* backup occurs when the entire database and associated control files are backed up. A full backup can occur in one of two ways, as either an offline backup or an online backup. The best type of backup to perform is the offline full backup, since you get a consistent view of the entire database, but for many systems this is not an option because little or no downtime is allotted for backups.

Full Offline Backup

The *full offline* backup, sometimes called a consistent whole database backup, is taken when the database instance has been shut down cleanly. With the database shutdown, the datafiles and control files are backed up using OS or third-party backup software and hardware.

NOTE
Even though you have backed up the datafiles and the control files, you should restore the control files only if necessary. Never overwrite a newer control file with an older one unless there is no other alternative.

In the past, I would say that a full offline backup offered the most complete and reliable backup. However, RMAN backups and other options such as hardware snapshots have changed my position on this issue. I believe that there is no significant difference between online and offline backups. If the system is shut down nightly or weekly, it can't hurt to do an offline backup, but it is not required.

Full Online Backup

In many cases where systems need to be up and running 7 days a week, 24 hours per day, the offline backup is not an option, and the online backup is your only choice.

A *full online* backup is really just a combination of tablespace backups and archive log and control file backups. With the full online backup, the control files, and in turn the tablespaces, are backed up using the online tablespace backup facility (ALTER TABLESPACE <tablespace_name> [BEGIN | END] BACKUP). All archive logs created during the backup are required in order for the online backup to be used for recovery.

NOTE
Online backups are only possible if you are running in ARCHIVELOG mode. If you are not running in ARCHIVELOG mode, your only choice is an offline backup.

Tablespace and Datafile Backups

The tablespace backup allows you to back up a single tablespace while the database is online and running. By notifying Oracle that you will be performing a backup on that tablespace, you cause special actions to be taken, which are covered in the later section "OS Facilities: Online Backup." Once the tablespace has been marked for backup, one or more of the datafiles that make up the tablespace are backed up using OS or third-party utilities.

NOTE
Regardless of whether you are doing an online or offline backup, if you are backing up data files from an OCFS partition, you should make sure that you use a utility that supports O_DIRECT. OCFS-aware versions of common programs such as cp, mv, and dd are available from www.ocfs.org. At this web site, you will be able to find the proper package for your application and platform.

When you mark the tablespace for backup, the Oracle RDBMS will know that this online backup has occurred, and if recovery is necessary, it will know how to recover the database. In the next section, you will learn the actual mechanics of how to perform this type of backup.

Incremental Backups

Incremental backups are possible only with RMAN or with a third-party backup application, such as Legato, NetBackup, or Veritas; the older, external method of backing up the system allows you to back up only an entire datafile. The contents of the datafile are unknown to the OS; thus, incremental backups don't work. With RMAN, you can back up only data that has changed since a previous backup.

There are two types of incremental backups. The differential incremental backup backs up all of the data that has changed since the last incremental backup. The cumulative incremental backup backs up all of the data that has changed since the last full backup.

Differential Incremental Backup

The *differential* incremental backup takes data that has been changed since the last full backup or the last incremental backup and backs up this data. Only the changed data is backed up, so the amount of data backed up is minimized. However, since only the changed data is backed up, in order to restore the data to the point of failure, the full backup and all differential incremental backups since the full backup must be restored. This can potentially be very time-consuming and requires more work. A differential incremental backup is shown in Figure 11-1. As you can see, each backup only takes the changes that have been made since the last full or incremental backup.

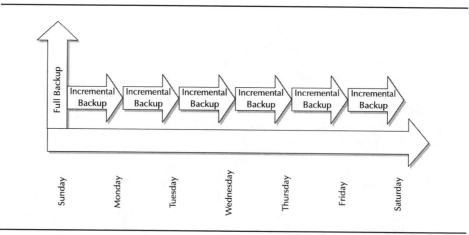

FIGURE 11-1. *The differential incremental backup*

Cumulative Incremental Backup

With a *cumulative* incremental backup, all of the changes since the last full backup are backed up. Each cumulative incremental backup takes more space than a differential incremental backup, but in the event that a restore is required, only the full backup and the last cumulative incremental backup need be applied. This process is shown in Figure 11-2.

How to Back Up the Database

There are several different ways that the Oracle database can be backed up. These various methods consist of

- Recovery Manager (RMAN)
- Automatic disk-based backup and recovery (flash recovery area)
- OS facilities
- Export and Data Pump
- Commercially available backup utilities

Each of these utilities can perform an effective backup. It is usually your own personal preference that can help you decide which one to use.

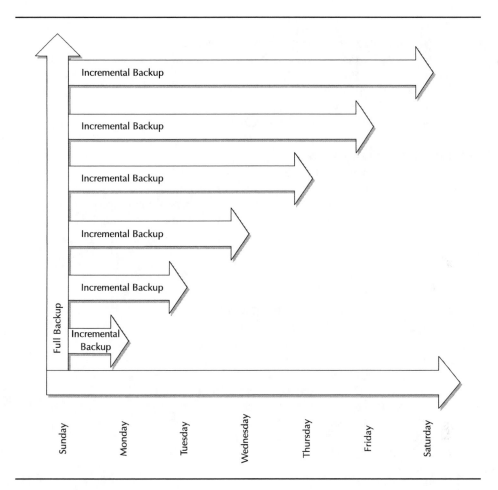

FIGURE 11-2.   *The cumulative incremental backup*

Recovery Manager (RMAN)

Recovery Manager (RMAN) is a tool that Oracle provides for performing backup
and recovery operations and that integrates with many third-party tools for backing
up the Oracle database. RMAN has been around since Oracle 7.3 and has become
one of the most preferred methods of performing Oracle backups. It is part of the
Oracle Server and so does not require a separate license.

TIP
RMAN is run by the executable "rman." In some operating systems such as Linux, there is an additional rman command not related to Oracle. In order to make sure that you are executing the correct rman command, you might want to invoke it by using the command "$ORACLE_HOME/bin/rman."

Setting Up Recovery Manager

Before Recovery Manager can be used, the recovery catalog must be created. The recovery catalog resides in its own tablespace, typically called rcvcat, which, along with a schema and owner for the catalog, must be created before the catalog itself. Use the SQL statements that follow to create the tablespace, schema, owner, and catalog.

1. Connect to the DBMS.

   ```
   SQL> connect / as sysdba
   ```

2. Create the tablespace, schema, and user for the recovery catalog.

   ```
   SQL> SPOOL recovery.log
   SQL> CREATE TABLESPACE rcvcat DATAFILE
   '/opt/oracle/product/10.1.0/oradata/rcvcat01.dbf'
   SIZE 512m AUTOEXTEND ON NEXT 32m MAXSIZE UNLIMITED
   EXTENT MANAGEMENT LOCAL AUTOALLOCATE
   SEGMENT SPACE MANAGEMENT AUTO;
   SQL> CREATE USER rman IDENTIFIED BY rman
   TEMPORARY TABLESPACE temp
   DEFAULT TABLESPACE rcvcat QUOTA unlimited ON rcvcat;
     2    3
   User created.
   ```

3. Grant the RECOVERY_CATALOG_OWNER role to the schema owner. This role provides the user with all privileges required to maintain and query the recovery catalog.

   ```
   SQL> GRANT RECOVERY_CATALOG_OWNER TO rman;
   Grant succeeded.
   SQL> exit;
   Disconnected from Oracle Database 10g Enterprise Edition Release 10.1.0.2.0 -
   Production
   With the Partitioning, OLAP and Data Mining options
   ```

4. After creating the catalog owner, create the catalog tables with the RMAN CREATE CATALOG command. The command creates the catalog in the default tablespace of the catalog owner.

   ```
   [oracle@ptc6 admin]$ $ORACLE_HOME/bin/rman CATALOG rman/rman

   Recovery Manager: Release 10.1.0.2.0 - Production
   ```

```
Copyright (c) 1995, 2004, Oracle. All rights reserved.

connected to recovery catalog database
recovery catalog is not installed

RMAN> CREATE CATALOG
recovery catalog created

RMAN>
```

This will create the recovery catalog. Once the catalog has been created, you can use RMAN to back up the database.

NOTE
The recovery catalog should be created in its own database. If the database that you are backing up is damaged, the recovery catalog will also be damaged.

Using RMAN

Recovery Manager (RMAN) can be used both with and without a recovery catalog or repository. In order to take full advantage of Recovery Manager, however, you should use the recovery catalog. Once the recovery catalog has been created as shown in the preceding section, you can connect using the following commands:

1. If the target database is not mounted, then mount or open it.

```
SQL> STARTUP MOUNT;
[oracle@ptc6 admin]$ $ORACLE_HOME/bin/rman TARGET / CATALOG rman/rman

Recovery Manager: Release 10.1.0.2.0 - Production

Copyright (c) 1995, 2004, Oracle. All rights reserved.

connected to target database: ORCL (DBID=1053597856)
connected to recovery catalog database
RMAN>
```

NOTE
This code assumes ORACLE_SID, ORACLE_HOME, LD_LIBRARY_PATH, and PATH are set in the environment to the target database, referencing the database Oracle Home; if ORACLE_SID is not set, you must use the TNS alias for the database as follows:

```
[oracle@ptc6 admin]$ $ORACLE_HOME/bin/rman TARGET
sys/<passwd>@<target_database> CATALOG rman/rman
```

2. Once you have invoked the RMAN utility, you must register the target database in the recovery catalog so that it can be backed up. This is done via the REGISTER DATABASE command from within RMAN.

```
RMAN> REGISTER DATABASE;

database registered in recovery catalog
starting full resync of recovery catalog
full resync complete
```

3. Once the database has been registered, you can view the database tablespaces via the REPORT SCHEMA command.

```
RMAN> REPORT SCHEMA;

Report of database schema
File K-bytes     Tablespace          RB segs Datafile Name
---- ---------- -------------------- ------- -------------------
1       460800 SYSTEM               YES
/opt/oracle/product/10.1.0/oradata/orcl/system01.dbf
2        30720 UNDOTBS1             YES
/opt/oracle/product/10.1.0/oradata/orcl/undotbs01.dbf
3       245760 SYSAUX               NO
/opt/oracle/product/10.1.0/oradata/orcl/sysaux01.dbf
4         5120 USERS                NO
/opt/oracle/product/10.1.0/oradata/orcl/users01.dbf
5       153600 EXAMPLE              NO
/opt/oracle/product/10.1.0/oradata/orcl/example01.dbf
6        51200 RCVCAT               NO
/opt/oracle/product/10.1.0/oradata/orcl/RCVCAT.dbf

RMAN>
```

4. Once the catalog is created and the database is registered, you are ready to begin backing up this database. Before you begin the backup operation, you can specify the channel, which tells Oracle where you want the backup to go to. In order to set RMAN to back up to a specific directory and increment the filename, use the following command:

```
RMAN> CONFIGURE CHANNEL DEVICE TYPE DISK FORMAT
'/u01/oracle/backup/ora_df%t_s%s_s%p';

new RMAN configuration parameters:
CONFIGURE CHANNEL DEVICE TYPE DISK FORMAT
 '/u01/oracle/backup/ora_df%t_s%s_s%p';
new RMAN configuration parameters are successfully stored

RMAN>
```

NOTE
In addition to configuring the channels, there are other configuration settings such as the backup retention period and the control file autobackup setting. These configuration settings are listed in the Oracle documentation.

5. Once the channel is set up, you can now back up the database, tablespaces, datafiles, etc., using the BACKUP command. For example,

```
RMAN> backup tablespace system;

Starting backup at 13-MAY-04
starting full resync of recovery catalog
full resync complete
allocated channel: ORA_DISK_1
channel ORA_DISK_1: sid=253 devtype=DISK
channel ORA_DISK_1: starting full datafile backupset
channel ORA_DISK_1: specifying datafile(s) in backupset
input datafile fno=00001 name=/opt/oracle/product/10.1.0/oradata/orcl/system01.dbf
channel ORA_DISK_1: starting piece 1 at 13-MAY-04
channel ORA_DISK_1: finished piece 1 at 13-MAY-04
piece handle=/u01/oracle/backup/ora_df526064474_s3_s1 comment=NONE
channel ORA_DISK_1: backup set complete, elapsed time: 00:06:36
channel ORA_DISK_1: starting full datafile backupset
channel ORA_DISK_1: specifying datafile(s) in backupset
including current controlfile in backupset
including current SPFILE in backupset
channel ORA_DISK_1: starting piece 1 at 13-MAY-04
channel ORA_DISK_1: finished piece 1 at 13-MAY-04
piece handle=/u01/oracle/backup/ora_df526064870_s4_s1 comment=NONE
channel ORA_DISK_1: backup set complete, elapsed time: 00:00:09
Finished backup at 13-MAY-04

RMAN>
```

This will back up the SYSTEM tablespace. The BACKUP command can take the parameters BACKUPSET, SPFILE, RECOVERY AREA, RECOVERY FILES, TABLESPACE, DATAFILE, DATABASE, and CURRENT CONTROLFILE. You also have the option to back up full or incremental.

NOTE
With Oracle10g R2, you are now able to use automatic channel allocation among nodes in a RAC cluster. This means that the load generated by performing backups can be spread among those nodes. Remember, however, that since RAC uses a shared disk, the I/O load might be increased by generating RMAN work across a RAC cluster.

Many third-party tools that are used to back up Oracle actually use the RMAN command. In addition to using RMAN, you can also use OS facilities to back up the database.

NOTE
In order to use RMAN for online backups, the database must be in ARCHIVELOG mode.

Automatic Disk-Based Backup and Recovery (Flash Recovery Area)

New with Oracle 10*g* is the concept of automatic disk-based backup and recovery. This method actually uses RMAN for backup and recovery but adds additional features to the Oracle instance that helps to manage those backups. By having backups maintained on disk automatically, you can perform a much quicker restore in the event of a failure; however, the fact that those files are stored locally might be a problem if you are experiencing storage difficulties.

In order to set up automatic disk-based backup and recovery, you must allocate a place on disk that has at least as much space as the database, log files, and control files that it will be backing up. This area, known as the *flash recovery area,* is used for storing automatic disk-based backups that are used both for restoration and for the Oracle Flashback Database feature.

The Oracle Flashback features allow you either to access data as it was in the past or to revert a table or database to a state as it was in the past. Most flashback functions use the UNDO records in the UNDO tablespace. However, the FLASHBACK DATABASE command requires the flash recovery area.

The flash recovery area can be created with the database configuration assistant when your database is created, or by creating it manually at any point. The creation and setup of the flash recovery area consist of several steps, which are outlined here:

1. Set up a directory for flash recovery. Make sure there is sufficient space for the flash recovery database.

2. Set the Oracle initialization parameters DB_RECOVERY_FILE_DEST_SIZE and DB_RECOVERY_FILE_DEST to the appropriate values.

3. Within RMAN, configure the backup retention policy.

4. Configure the flash recovery area for disk-based backups.

5. Run the disk-based backups from within RMAN.

Once everything is set up for disk-based backups using the flash recovery area, you are ready for immediate recovery if necessary. The flashback features are covered in more detail in the next chapter.

OS Facilities: Online Backup

Performing a backup with your OS facilities is a very straightforward process. As with the Recovery Manager, you can perform a full database backup or a tablespace backup. The basic process is different, depending on whether you will be performing an offline backup or an online backup. These will be presented separately.

Offline Backup

The offline backup is perhaps the most straightforward and simplest backup method. The offline database backup is performed by following these steps:

1. Shut down the database normally (or immediate).

2. Back up all of the datafiles, all the control files, and the parameter file using OS or third-party utilities.

3. Restart the database.

This is all there is to performing an offline database backup using OS facilities. The backup of these files can be done using OS facilities or third-party facilities. There are a number of very good third-party backup utilities that include bar coding, catalog management, and other features.

Online Backup

The online backup is not actually a full backup without the archive logs generated during this backup, since each tablespace is backed up separately. You can think of this as a set of online tablespace backups that make up the entire database. In order to perform an online tablespace backup, follow this procedure:

■ Mark the beginning of the tablespace backup using the SQL command ALTER TABLESPACE *tsname* BEGIN BACKUP.

- Back up the datafiles that constitute that tablespace using OS or third-party utilities.

- Mark the end of the tablespace backup using the SQL command ALTER TABLESPACE *tsname* END BACKUP.

By marking the beginning and end of the backup, Oracle synchronizes the data files so that they will be useful for restoration. This is all that is necessary to perform the online tablespace backup.

NOTE
During an online backup (whenever a tablespace has been marked for backup), additional log records are generated. This is because whole blocks, not just deltas, are written for tablespaces in backup mode. The difference between the amount of redo log information generated in backup mode and non-backup mode can be significant. Thus, it is important to complete online backups as quickly as possible.

It is important that tablespaces not be left in backup mode for a long period of time. If you think that a tablespace might be in backup mode, you can use the following query to determine the backup state of each of the tablespaces and datafiles in your database:

```
SET linesize 120;
Set pagesize 200;

ALTER SESSION SET NLS_DATE_FORMAT = 'YYYY-MM-DD HH24:MI:SS';

COL "Status" FORMAT a10;
COL "Change No" FORMAT 9999;
COL "Backup Started" FORMAT a14;
COL "Tablespace Name" FORMAT a20;
COL "Datafile Name" FORMAT a40;

SELECT
ts.name AS "Tablespace Name"
, b.status AS "Status"
, b.change# AS "Change No"
, b.time AS "Backup Started"
, df.name AS "Datafile Name"
FROM v$backup b, v$tablespace ts, v$datafile df
WHERE b.file# = df.file#
AND df.ts# = ts.ts#;
```

When using the online backup method of backing up your database, your goal should be to complete the backup as quickly as possible and reduce the time that each tablespace is in backup mode. Put only the tablespaces into backup mode that you are going to back up. For example, this command sequence represents good practice:

```
alter tablespace ts1 begin backup;
copy ts1 data files
alter tablespace ts1 end backup;
alter tablespace ts2 begin backup;
copy ts2 data files
alter tablespace ts2 end backup;
```

A sequence like this one, on the other hand, spells trouble:

```
alter tablespace ts1 begin backup;
alter tablespace ts2 begin backup;
copy ts1 data files
copy ts2 data files
alter tablespace ts1 end backup;
alter tablespace ts2 end backup;
```

The exception to this rule is a backup that uses snapshot technology. Snapshot technology is available on SAN and NAS storage from most storage vendors. Snapshot technology allows you to very quickly take a time-consistent picture of the storage system, which can then be read from independently. With this technology, you can put all of your tablespaces into backup mode at once, quickly take a snapshot (in a matter of seconds), and quickly take these tablespaces out of backup mode.

Snapshot technology can be very useful, especially in systems where the database is very large. This will allow you to take a backup of a very large system while only incurring a minimum load on the Oracle database. However, most snapshots incur the same amount of load on the I/O subsystem as you would if the backup were accessing the data files directly. Consult your storage vendor on how their particular snapshot technology works.

Export and Data Pump

The EXPORT utility can also be used to perform system backups. Export has an advantage over other backup methods in that the data is reorganized when it is imported. For this reason, you will often hear a backup taken using the Export utility being referred to as a "logical backup." Export is an Oracle-supplied utility that allows you to extract an entire database, a set of schemas, or individual tables from an Oracle database. Export data is stored in an export file that is directly readable only by the import utility.

The Oracle Data Pump is a much-improved version of export and import that is available with Oracle 10*g* only. The Data Pump is much faster than export and import, but it requires a little more setup and maintenance. Export/import and the Data Pump are similar, so they will be covered here together.

Advantages of export/import and the Data Pump are that individual schemas can be saved individually and thus can easily be restored individually. In addition, exports of schema data can easily be imported into other schemas. This allows for a great deal of flexibility. A shell/SQL script can easily be created to individually export all schemas in the database.

The downside of export/import is that it is slower than traditional backup methods. Even the Data Pump is much slower than RMAN, because export and import operate through the SQL layer of Oracle, whereas RMAN uses a more direct path to the data.

A key advantage of export/import is the ability to move data between different versions of Oracle. A set of schemas or tables can easily be transported between systems and versions of Oracle. The Data Pump includes a number of built-in Oracle monitoring features. These features have been enhanced with Oracle 10*g* R2 (such as the extended job status display).

Although I would not recommend export/import as a primary backup method, it can be a good supplement if you can afford the additional storage space and the additional time spent doing these exports.

Export/import or the Data Pump is also recommended as another way to back up the RMAN recovery catalog (see the earlier section "Recovery Manager [RMAN]").

Here is an example of how to set up the Data Pump for the recovery catalog itself:

```
SQL> create directory dpump_dir1 as '/nas1/dump1/RMANP1';
Directory created.

SQL> GRANT READ, WRITE ON DIRECTORY dpump_dir1 TO rman;

Grant succeeded.

oracle@njdbaprdora1:/opt/oracle/admin/RMANP1/scripts> cat RMANP1_expdp.sh
#!/bin/ksh
. ~/.local_env_db_RMANP1
rm -f dpump_dir1:exp_rman.dmp
expdp rman/gmen10x DUMPFILE=dpump_dir1:exp_rman.dmp LOGFILE=dpump_dir1:exp_rman.log
JOB_NAME=exp_rman


oracle@njdbaprdora1:/opt/oracle/admin/RMANP1/scripts> ./RMANP1_expdp.sh

Export: Release 10.1.0.4.0 - Production on Wednesday, 13 July, 2005 17:11

Copyright (c) 2003, Oracle. All rights reserved.

Connected to: Oracle Database 10g Enterprise Edition Release 10.1.0.4.0 -
Production
With the Partitioning, OLAP and Data Mining options
FLASHBACK automatically enabled to preserve database integrity.
Starting "RMAN"."EXP_RMAN":  rman/******** DUMPFILE=dpump_dir1:exp_rman.dmp
```

```
LOGFILE=dpump_dir1:exp_rman.log JOB_NAME=exp_rman
Estimate in progress using BLOCKS method...
Processing object type SCHEMA_EXPORT/TABLE/TABLE_DATA
Total estimation using BLOCKS method: 5 MB
Processing object type SCHEMA_EXPORT/SE_PRE_SCHEMA_PROCOBJACT/PROCACT_SCHEMA
Processing object type SCHEMA_EXPORT/TYPE/TYPE_SPEC
Processing object type SCHEMA_EXPORT/SEQUENCE/SEQUENCE
Processing object type SCHEMA_EXPORT/TABLE/TABLE
Processing object type SCHEMA_EXPORT/TABLE/INDEX/INDEX
Processing object type SCHEMA_EXPORT/TABLE/CONSTRAINT/CONSTRAINT
Processing object type SCHEMA_EXPORT/TABLE/INDEX/STATISTICS/INDEX_STATISTICS
Processing object type SCHEMA_EXPORT/TABLE/STATISTICS/TABLE_STATISTICS
Processing object type SCHEMA_EXPORT/TABLE/COMMENT
Processing object type SCHEMA_EXPORT/PACKAGE/PACKAGE_SPEC
Processing object type SCHEMA_EXPORT/FUNCTION/FUNCTION
Processing object type
SCHEMA_EXPORT/PACKAGE/COMPILE_PACKAGE/PACKAGE_SPEC/ALTER_PACKAGE_SPEC
Processing object type SCHEMA_EXPORT/FUNCTION/ALTER_FUNCTION
Processing object type SCHEMA_EXPORT/VIEW/VIEW
Processing object type SCHEMA_EXPORT/PACKAGE/PACKAGE_BODY
Processing object type SCHEMA_EXPORT/TABLE/CONSTRAINT/REF_CONSTRAINT
. . exported "RMAN"."AL"                         374.4 KB     1823 rows
. . exported "RMAN"."RLH"                        100.1 KB     1824 rows
. . exported "RMAN"."BCF"                        9.125 KB        3 rows
. . exported "RMAN"."BDF"                        11.04 KB        7 rows
. . exported "RMAN"."BP"                         12.21 KB        4 rows
. . exported "RMAN"."BS"                         9.789 KB        4 rows
. . exported "RMAN"."BSF"                        6.851 KB        3 rows
. . exported "RMAN"."CCF"                        10.59 KB        1 rows
. . exported "RMAN"."CDF"                        14.00 KB        7 rows
. . exported "RMAN"."CKP"                        7.960 KB        5 rows
. . exported "RMAN"."CONF"                       6.695 KB        4 rows
. . exported "RMAN"."CONFIG"                     5.242 KB        1 rows
. . exported "RMAN"."DB"                         6.476 KB        1 rows
. . exported "RMAN"."DBINC"                      13.72 KB        1 rows
. . exported "RMAN"."DF"                         9.195 KB        7 rows
. . exported "RMAN"."DFATT"                      7.398 KB       11 rows
. . exported "RMAN"."FB"                         5.890 KB        1 rows
. . exported "RMAN"."NODE"                       5.875 KB        1 rows
. . exported "RMAN"."ORL"                        6.171 KB        8 rows
. . exported "RMAN"."RCVER"                      4.929 KB        1 rows
. . exported "RMAN"."RSR"                        20.82 KB      125 rows
. . exported "RMAN"."RT"                         7.078 KB        1 rows
. . exported "RMAN"."TS"                         7.656 KB        7 rows
. . exported "RMAN"."TSATT"                      6.578 KB        7 rows
. . exported "RMAN"."BCB"                            0 KB        0 rows
. . exported "RMAN"."BRL"                            0 KB        0 rows
. . exported "RMAN"."CCB"                            0 KB        0 rows
. . exported "RMAN"."OFFR"                           0 KB        0 rows
. . exported "RMAN"."RR"                             0 KB        0 rows
. . exported "RMAN"."SCR"                            0 KB        0 rows
. . exported "RMAN"."SCRL"                           0 KB        0 rows
. . exported "RMAN"."XAL"                            0 KB        0 rows
. . exported "RMAN"."XCF"                            0 KB        0 rows
. . exported "RMAN"."XDF"                            0 KB        0 rows
Master table "RMAN"."EXP_RMAN" successfully loaded/unloaded
******************************************************************************
Dump file set for RMAN.EXP_RMAN is:
  /nas1/dump1/RMANP1/exp_rman.dmp
Job "RMAN"."EXP_RMAN" successfully completed at 17:12
```

Commercially Available Backup Utilities

There are several commercially available backup utilities available on the market today. These have several advantages over manual operations using system utilities, export/import, and even RMAN. Most of these commercially available backup utilities actually use RMAN to get its data out of the database but have enhanced features necessary for an enterprise backup solution. Here are some of these features:

- **Tape library support**   Most large installations must use sophisticated tape libraries in order to support the amount of data that must be backed up.

- **Automatic scheduling**   This allows you to schedule regular backups.

- **Disk staging**   Several commercially available backup solutions allow for disk staging as well as tape backup.

- **Bar code support**   In large tape libraries, bar coding the tapes is a must.

- **Sophisticated cataloging**   This allows for backup information to be quickly and effectively found.

Although it is not necessary to use a commercially available backup solution, many of these products, such as Veritas NetBackup, are very sophisticated, stable, and proven utilities that often form part of an enterprise-wide information management policy.

So far in this chapter, you have seen how to back up your system. Equally as important is determining what to back up and how to schedule those backups. In the next section, you will learn how to develop a backup strategy and how to implement it.

Backup Strategies

Knowing how to back up a system is only one part of the process. Putting together a backup and recovery plan or strategy is also very important. Many times you are limited in the time allotted for backups and must be very creative. Remember that your highest priority is to protect the data in your database.

In developing a backup and recovery strategy, you must first look at the parameters of your system. There are many variables that affect the backup strategy and the backup process. These variables may include:

- Time allotted for the backup
- Amount of data to be backed up
- Speed of the backup device(s)
- System downtime allotted for backups (if any)

- Off-hours (if no downtime allotted)

- Performance degradation allowed

These factors and others will affect the backup strategy and must then be measured against the main goals of the backup process, including:

- Protect the database by having a current backup.

- Reduce the time necessary for recovery.

- Affect the performance of the system as little as possible.

By putting together all of these factors, you should be able to come up with a backup strategy that meets as many of these requirements as possible.

NOTE
It is unlikely that you will be able to meet all of the goals of a backup strategy. Do your best to come up with the best compromises that you can.

When and What to Back Up

Scheduling backups is usually not a very easy task. Backups should be taken often enough to protect the system's data from loss, yet they should not interfere with the normal business operations.

Depending on the size of the data that needs to be backed up and the operational schedule of your business, you may choose from various different options. The options vary, depending on which type of operation your business runs.

5x8 Operation	This term designates a business where the corporate data must be available 5 days a week, 8 hours a day.
7x24 Operation	This term designates a business where the corporate data must be available 7 days a week, 24 hours a day. No downtime is allowed.

Each of these types of operations has different backup needs, depending on the type of data and the frequency of modifications to that data. Let's look at those cases.

Scheduling Backups in a 5x8 Shop

The 5x8 shop is a little easier to schedule a backup for, since there is plenty of time that the system need not be available to the users and can be backed up without disturbing them.

The frequency of the backups in this type of operation can depend in some part on the activity in the database. Here are some guidelines that may help you determine your backup schedule.

Small database	If the database is small, perform a full offline backup every night. This will offer the most protection possible for your data.
Large database	If the database is very large but infrequently modified, perform a full offline backup every weekend and incremental backups during the week.
Active tablespaces	If certain tablespaces are very active, target them for frequent tablespace backups.
Structural changes	Anytime a structural change is made to the database, you should perform a full offline backup.
Unrecoverable operations	Anytime unrecoverable operations are performed on the database, a full offline backup should be done.
Resetlogs	Anytime that you have to reset the redo logs with the resetlogs command, you should perform a full offline backup.
Recover until	Anytime you have recovered with the recovery UNTIL option, you should perform a full offline backup.
Archive log files	Every night, back up the archive log files. The frequency depends on the number of archive log files created every day.

These are a few guidelines that may help you to determine an effective backup strategy for your system.

Scheduling Backups in a 7x24 Shop

The 7x24 shop is much more difficult to plan a backup strategy for, since there is never a time when the system is not in use. Whenever you perform the backups, there will be one or more people that may be inconvenienced by a performance drop. Backups do tend to degrade performance.

The frequency and type of backups will be influenced by the activity of the system. Here are some guidelines that may help you determine your backup schedule.

Small database	If the database is small, perform a full online backup every night. This will offer the most protection possible for your data.
Large database	If the database is very large but infrequently modified, perform a full online backup every weekend and incremental online backups during the week.
Very large database	It is frequently necessary to rotate the backup schedule such that a tablespace or set of tablespaces gets backed up every night. It may take several days to get a complete backup set. This can shorten the time each night that the backup is active.
Active tablespaces	If certain tablespaces are very active, target them for frequent tablespace backups.
Unrecoverable operations	Anytime unrecoverable operations are performed on the database, a full offline backup should be done. If this is not acceptable, avoid unrecoverable operations.
Resetlogs	Anytime that you have to reset the redo logs with the resetlogs command, you should perform a full offline backup. If this is not acceptable, avoid the resetlogs operation.
Recover until	Anytime you have recovered with the recovery UNTIL option, you should perform a full offline backup.
Archive log files	In a 7x24 shop, it is a good idea to back up the archive log files as soon as they are created. Keep at least as many as are needed to recover from the oldest tablespace backup that is online and available.

I hope that these guidelines will help you in developing your own backup strategy.

Examples of Backup Strategies

This section provides a few examples for setting up a backup strategy. I hope that these examples may help you in setting up your backup strategy. Your backup strategy may be more complicated.

Example 1

The scenario: A small business that is only open during the day. There is fairly good activity on the database, and the data is very important.

Example backup strategy: Perhaps in this case, the database is small enough that a complete offline backup can be run every night to tape. The previous night's tape is archived to storage every day. After a month, the tapes can be reused, keeping a tape from each month permanently. If a problem occurs and a restore must be performed, the backup tape is available. If the computer room and backup tape are destroyed, previous backup tapes are available in offsite storage.

Example 2

The scenario: A large business that is open 24 hours a day, 7 days a week. There is high database activity, and no downtime is allowed. The data is extremely critical to the operation of the company.

Example backup strategy: In this example, I would recommend some sort of standby system, such as Data Guard (as described in Chapter 13). For backups, I would suggest that to minimize the impact on the users, a partial online backup of the standby database (to offload the primary) be done every night on a rotational basis such that all of the tablespaces are backed up in three or four days. To reduce user impact, these backups should be done to disk, perhaps across a network. These backup files on disk should in turn be backed up every night and archived offsite. The backup files should remain online for at least two backup cycles before being removed. The archive log files should also be backed up to disk locally on a networked system and backed up to tape and sent offsite. This will offer a good level of protection and provide for quick restoration, if necessary. A fault-tolerant system should be part of this solution also.

Summary

This chapter has covered quite a bit of material on both backup and restore utilities and techniques. There is a great deal of information in this chapter that will help you develop a backup strategy. It is important that you regularly back up your system and test your backup media occasionally in order to make sure that your backups are being done effectively.

In addition to a good backup, it is important to use fault-tolerant technology such as RAID I/O subsystems and UPS power. In addition, if appropriate, RAC provides a high level of fault tolerance for the entire database system. Finally, for disaster recovery, Oracle provides Data Guard. All of these technologies work well on Linux.

Restoring and recovering the database is as important as backing it up. It is important to understand the techniques and to practice recovery occasionally. Also make sure that you have a recovery plan documented. This process is covered in detail in the next chapter.

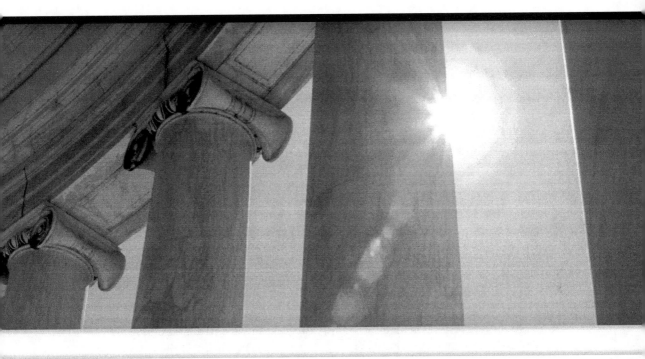

CHAPTER
12

Restore

robably the most important task that the DBA has is to back up the database. This is because the DBA's greatest responsibility is to ensure the database's stability and security. In the event of a catastrophic system failure, the DBA must be able to quickly and effectively restore the database to a point in time immediately prior to the failure. Although this task is paramount, it is also the least glamorous and visible of the DBA's duties. Nevertheless, it's up to you, the DBA, to make sure everyone understands its criticality.

Recovering the Database

In the previous chapter, you learned how to back up your database. In this chapter, you'll find out how to recover your database in the event of an emergency. Several types of failures will require a recovery.

An instance failure, for example, will need an instance recovery. As long as no permanent hardware failures have occurred, the instance recovery will be automatic and complete. By enabling parallel recovery, the performance will be improved.

If a hardware failure has occurred causing the loss of a datafile, you must perform a media recovery. This involves both recovering the lost data and performing an instance recovery (if necessary). This process is explained in the "Instance Recovery" section later in this chapter.

If a user error has occurred causing data to be lost, a point-in-time recovery may be necessary. A point-in-time recovery allows you to recover up to a certain point just before the failure has occurred. This can be very useful, but also very problematic. The point-in-time recovery is also detailed later in this chapter in the "Point-in-Time Recovery" section.

Whatever type of recovery is called for, you should keep in mind that the recovery operation is a very important task and should be performed as quickly as possible. Typically, in the event of a failure that requires recovery, there will be many users with nothing to do until the recovery is complete.

Even though the recovery operation is critical and must be completed quickly, you should not rush through it. Any mistakes during the recovery will only delay the resumption of normal operations, and some errors may render recovery impossible.

Recovery vs. Restoration

In this chapter, you will be learning about both recovery operations and restoration operations. These two concepts may sometimes be thought of as the same, but actually they have quite different meanings. In this chapter, you will learn about both of them.

Recovery   Recovery is the process whereby Oracle rolls forward committed transactions and rolls back noncommitted transactions. It is the act of returning the database to where it was an instant before the failure.

Restoration Restoration is the act of replacing a datafile with a backup copy. If
you are running in ARCHIVELOG mode, you can restore up to the
point of failure. If you are not running in ARCHIVELOG mode, you
can only restore back to your last backup.

Typically, recovery is automatic, with the recovery process prompting you to apply
archived log files if necessary. The act of restoring is a manual operation where operator
intervention is required either by hand or with the graphical administration tools.

In this chapter, you will learn both how recovery works and how to restore
damaged datafiles.

How to Recover Your Database

As reliable as hardware has become today, there are still occasions when the system
may fail. This may be due to a hardware component failure, or an external event such
as a power failure. If the failure does not cause any data to be lost, Oracle can recover
itself. This is referred to as an instance recovery. If data has been lost, it must be
restored from a previous backup and recovered—a process known as media recovery.
If some event has occurred, such as an accidental dropping of a table, a point-in-time
recovery must be done in order to not recover the DROP TABLE statement and
repeat the mistake.

In this section, you will learn how to perform each of these recoveries and how
they work.

Instance Recovery

When an instance failure occurs, the Oracle recovery process can completely recover
the database upon instance startup. All transactions committed at the time of the
failure will be recovered or *rolled forward* and all transactions that were in process
(also known as *in-flight transactions*) will be *rolled back*.

NOTE
*Instance recovery can be quite time-consuming. The
amount of time it takes depends on the number of
dirty buffers in the SGA, and the number of dirty
buffers depends on the amount of time since the last
checkpoint and the amount of data modifications.*

The instance recovery process is automatic. When the instance is started up, it
examines the datafiles and redo log files and determines whether the instance was
shut down properly. At this point, the redo log will be read and the affected transactions
will be rolled forward or rolled back. If the checkpoint launched by the last log switch
had completed only the transactions in one log file, it alone will need to be recovered.

TIP
By tuning the checkpoint interval and recovery parallelism, recovery time can be shortened.

Once the instance recovery has finished, the database will be opened and users will again be allowed to access it. During the recovery process, users cannot access the database. It is for this reason that the recovery time should be as short as possible.

The parallel recovery feature of the Parallel Query Option can help reduce the time it takes for instance recovery to complete. This is done by setting the Oracle initialization parameter RECOVERY_PARALLELISM. By tuning the number of recovery processes to run best with your system, the recovery interval can be optimized.

Media Recovery

Data recovery is necessary when media failure has occurred. For instance, when a datafile is damaged. In this case, you must first restore the damaged file with a good copy from a backup before recovery can occur. The Oracle recovery process will then apply archive log files and redo log files to restore the good copy of the damaged datafile to its state just prior to the failure. This may require all of the archive log files created since the backup in order to recover the restored datafile, which can be quite time-consuming.

TIP
By scheduling frequent backups, the restoration and recovery time can be shortened. The restore time is dependent on the time since the last backup and the amount of data modified since that backup.

By having the latest backup files online as well as the archive log files that had been created since the last backup, you can shorten the time it takes to start the recovery process. By having a plan, and having everything ready to go, things will also run more smoothly.

There are several different ways that the Oracle database can be recovered. These various methods consist of:

- Recovery Manager
- OS Facilities
- Import
- Commercially Available Backup Utilities that work with RMAN

Each of these utilities can perform an effective backup. Which of them you use is your own personal preference. However, the preferred method of *restore* in virtually all cases is via the Recovery Manager.

The Recovery Manager

As with the database backup procedure, you can perform a recovery through the Recovery Manager (RMAN) utility.

As you have seen, it is not difficult to back up and restore a database using the Recovery Manager. Nevertheless, it's still important to test the recovery process periodically to make sure it's working correctly.

In order to restore a database using RMAN invoke the rman utility and use the RESTORE command in order to restore databases, tablespaces, and datafiles.

OS Facilities

Restoring a datafile using OS facilities is just a simple as the method used to create the backup using OS facilities. With the tablespace offline, copy the datafile from the backup to the original datafile. Once the tablespace is brought back online by either the ALTER TABLESPACE command or by restarting the Oracle instance, Oracle will realize that the datafile has been replaced and prompt you to apply the archived log files.

Tablespace and datafile recovery can only be done if the RDBMS is running in ARCHIVELOG mode. If you are not running in ARCHIVELOG mode, you must restore the entire database from the last full offline backup. No rollforward or rollback is done.

Import

The IMPORT utility can also be used to restore the database if, and only if, EXPORT was used to create the backup. The exp and imp utilities can be quite useful for moving data from one system to another and for reorganizing data in a database; however, the exp and imp utilities are not really an effective method of backup and restore operations.

Commercially Available Backup Utilities

There are several excellent commercially available backup utilities on the market today. These range from low-end, single-system utilities to high-end packages. Most of these backup utilities actually use RMAN to communicate with the database to get the backup data. How you use these utilities for recovery really depends on how the backup was done, and how the utility works.

Log File Recovery

You cannot recover from the loss of a log file. If a log file is damaged and the system is still functional, you can drop the log file, re-create it, and immediately perform a full backup. The backup is necessary since you will no longer be able to use the archived log files and redo log files for any recovery on this database. This is why I always recommend that redo log files reside on fault-tolerant disk volumes, and that log file groups comprised of multiple members are used.

TIP
The loss of a log file may result in the need to recover a lot of work. Therefore, I recommend using RAID mirroring on the redo log files to protect them in the event of a disk failure.

Point-in-Time Recovery

The point-in-time recovery is a somewhat complex operation and should only be performed when absolutely necessary due to its potential side effects. It allows you to recover a database back to a specified point in time, which permits you to recover from user errors or software problems that caused the failure to occur in the first place. The point-in-time recovery can be performed as a database point-in-time recovery, as demonstrated here. The point-in-time recovery can also be performed as a tablespace point-in-time recovery. The processes and outcome are similar; however, in some cases a tablespace point-in-time recovery is more suitable for your needs.

The point-in-time recovery can be done both by using the Recovery Manager or by using the RECOVER administrative SQL command. In either case, the syntax for performing the point-in-time recovery is done through the command-line interface. There is no GUI option for the point-in-time recovery.

CAUTION
The point-in-time recovery can be dangerous to use, since you are restoring to an older point in time. Always perform a full backup of your current database before attempting the point-in-time recovery.

The method for restoring your data depends partly on the type of error that propmpted recovery. If a media failure occurred, you must restore the datafile, and then perform the media recovery with the point-in-time recovery option. If a user error caused the problem, you should follow these steps:

1. Create a temporary copy of the database.

2. Restore that database from a previous backup.

3. Perform the point-in-time recovery to a period just before the failure.

4. Export the table that has been damaged.

5. Import that table to the real database.

This task can be quite time-consuming and dangerous. If you mix up the temporary copy of the database and the real copy of the database, you may destroy valuable data.

Point-in-Time Recovery Using the Recovery Manager

The Recovery Manager can be used to perform a point-in-time recovery by using its command-line syntax. Because of the complexity of the command-line interface to the Recovery Manager and the rarity of its use, I will not go into detail on how to use it. Oracle manuals contain complete documentation on this subject.

When using the command-line interface with the Recovery Manager, you must specify the additional parameter:

```
SET UNTIL
```

This parameter takes one of the following qualifiers:

```
TIME date
LOG SEQ number THREAD number
SCN scn
```

With this syntax, you can specify the exact time where you want the recovery to stop by either listing the time, the log sequence, or the system change number. Using the SET UNTIL parameter when performing a recovery using the Recovery Manager will restore until the specified time.

Point-in-Time Recovery Using the RECOVER Command

When performing a recovery with the RECOVER command, you can restore to any point in time by using the RECOVER UNTIL syntax. The RECOVER command has a number of options but those that are important for point-in-time recovery are

```
RECOVER UNTIL CANCEL
RECOVER UNTIL TIME date
RECOVER UNTIL CHANGE scn
```

This command can be used to recover a database, a tablespace, or a datafile, just like the Recovery Manager, and can include a parallel clause. By increasing the degree of parallelism, you may see a performance benefit.

As with the Recovery Manager, I mentioned the point-in-time recovery so you would be aware it existed. If you plan on using the point-in-time recovery, you should study the Oracle documentation and carefully plan a restore before attempting it.

Using the Flashback Features of Oracle 10g

New in Oracle 10g is the flashback technology that allows you to view (or manipulate) data as it was in the past. The flashback technology is made up of several different tools, including:

■ Flashback Query

■ Flashback Version Query

- Flashback Transaction Query
- Flashback Table
- Flashback Drop
- Flashback Database

This can be a very powerful tool when used correctly, and can save you hours of restoration and recovery time.

Flashback Query

The flashback query feature allows you to query the database regarding how it looked at some point in the past. It's run by using the AS OF clause. The AS OF clause can take either a timestamp or an SCN, as shown next:

```
SELECT * FROM scott.emp AS OF TIMESTAMP
    TO_TIMESTAMP('2004-05-16 08:00:00', 'YYYY-MM-DD HH:MI:SS')
    WHERE ename = 'SCOTT';
```

You can actually reset the data in question to its past value by using the flashback query within an insert statement. Keep in mind, however, that if this record still exists in the database, you may be unable to insert the data due to a unique constraint.

```
INSERT INTO scott.emp
    (SELECT * FROM scott.emp AS OF TIMESTAMP
    TO_TIMESTAMP('2004-05-16 08:00:00', 'YYYY-MM-DD HH:MI:SS')
    WHERE ename = 'SCOTT');
```

The flashback query feature can help you avoid the situation where you have to restore a table to a secondary system in order to restore data that a user has inadvertently changed or dropped. This feature lets you restore a table, a set of tables, or a particular row in a table that has been mistakenly changed or deleted, and allows you to do this without having to go through a full media restore (assuming the data is still available in the UNDO tablespace).

The Flashback Version Query

By selecting flashback data as part of your query and using the VERSIONS BETWEEN clause, you are able to view changes that have occurred to a particular record or set of records in the database. In the following example, I have selected a timeframe where I have changed the salary for employee Miller in the scott.emp table. The following SQL script called fbversion.sql is used to display this data.

```
set linesize 256
set pagesize 100
```

```
SELECT SUBSTR(versions_startscn,1,10) AS "StartSCN",
       SUBSTR(versions_endscn,1,10) AS "EndSCN",
       SUBSTR(versions_starttime,1,25) AS "StartTime",
       SUBSTR(versions_endtime,1,25) AS "EndTime",
       SUBSTR(versions_xid,1,20) AS "XID",
       SUBSTR(versions_operation,1,20) AS "Operation",
       ename, sal
  FROM scott.emp
VERSIONS BETWEEN TIMESTAMP
      TO_TIMESTAMP('2004-05-16 11:00:00', 'YYYY-MM-DD HH24:MI:SS')
AND TO_TIMESTAMP('2004-05-16 11:20:00', 'YYYY-MM-DD HH24:MI:SS')
WHERE ename='MILLER';
```

During this timeframe, I changed the value for Miller's salary several times. This example shows that you can retrieve those changes quite easily.

```
SQL> @fbversion;

StartS EndSCN StartTime               EndTime                 XID                  O ENAME  SAL
------ ------ --------------------    ----------------------  ----------------     - ------ ----
462855        16-MAY-04 11.18.03 AM                           0300260084060000     U MILLER 1500
462680 462855 16-MAY-04 11.13.55 AM   16-MAY-04 11.18.03 AM   010022006A020000     U MILLER 1400
       462680                         16-MAY-04 11.13.55 AM                           MILLER 1300
```

This can be a very powerful and useful tool in tracking changes to particular objects, but remember, it only works within the UNDO_RETENTION period. Once the UNDO information has been removed, you can no longer track changes in this manner.

The Flashback Transaction Query
The flashback transaction query is similar to the flashback version query except that it shows transactional changes rather than data changes. The flashback transaction query can be used in conjunction with the flashback version query to give you a picture of who has made changes to the data at a particular time. The following script can be used to help you track transactional changes:

```
set linesize 256
set pagesize 100;

SELECT xid,
       SUBSTR(logon_user,1,20) AS "User",
       SUBSTR(operation,1,8) AS "Oper",
       SUBSTR(undo_sql,1,40) AS "UNDO SQL"
FROM flashback_transaction_query
    WHERE xid IN
(SELECT versions_xid
  FROM scott.emp
```

```
VERSIONS BETWEEN TIMESTAMP
        TO_TIMESTAMP('2004-05-16 11:00:00', 'YYYY-MM-DD HH24:MI:SS')
AND TO_TIMESTAMP('2004-05-16 11:55:00', 'YYYY-MM-DD HH24:MI:SS')
WHERE ename='MILLER');
```

As you can see here, the data that this query provides can be very useful:

```
SQL> @fbtransaction;

XID                User      Oper    UNDO SQL
----------------   --------- ------- ----------------------------------------
010022006A020000   SYSTEM    UPDATE  update "SCOTT"."EMP" set "SAL" = '1300'
010022006A020000   SYSTEM    BEGIN
0300260084060000   SYSTEM    UPDATE  update "SCOTT"."EMP" set "SAL" = '1400'
0300260084060000   SYSTEM    BEGIN
0B002C0018000000   SYSTEM    UPDATE  update "SCOTT"."EMP" set "SAL" = '1500'
0B002C0018000000   SYSTEM    BEGIN

6 rows selected.
```

As with the flashback version query, the flashback transaction query can be a very powerful and useful tool in tracking changes to particular objects, but remember, as with flashback version, it only works within the UNDO_RETENTION period. Once the UNDO information has been removed, you can no longer track changes in this manner.

Flashback Table

Flashback table allows you to restore a table to a previous point in time. The flashback table feature can be accessed either through the Oracle Enterprise Manager or with the FLASHBACK TABLE command. In either case, the result is the same. As with the previous flashback features, the flashback table feature also uses the UNDO information, thus you can only flash back for a certain period of time.

In addition, there are several prerequisites that are necessary in order to perform a flashback table. These prerequisites are

- You must have the FLASHBACK ANY TABLE system privilege or the FLASHBACK object privilege on the table you want to flash back to.

- You must have SELECT, UPDATE, INSERT, and DELETE privileges on the table in question.

- Row movement must be enabled on the table. This can be done with the command: ALTER TABLE *tname* ENABLE ROW MOVEMENT. Row movement allows a row to be moved to another partition if it is updated.

Once these prerequisites are in place, the table can be reverted to an earlier stage
by performing the FLASHBACK TABLE command, as shown next:

```
SQL> FLASHBACK TABLE scott.emp TO TIMESHARE
     TO_TIMESTAMP('2004-05-16 11:00:00', 'YYYY-MM-DD HH24:MI:SS');
2
Flashback complete.
```

CAUTION
The FLASHBACK TABLE command is dangerous
because the entire table is reverted. Unlike flashback
query where you can revert a single record, or revert
changes for a particular user, this command reverts
everything.

As with the other flashback features, the flashback transaction query can be
very powerful and useful, but remember, as with the others, it only works within the
UNDO_RETENTION period. Once the UNDO information has been removed, you
can no longer track changes in this manner.

This tool can be both constructive or destructive depending on how you use it.
Since flashback table reverts the entire table, it should only be used with careful
planning and knowledge of the changes that have been done to the table.

Flashback Drop

Flashback Drop is Oracle's way of undoing a DROP TABLE statement. The flashback
drop feature works by retaining dropped tables for a period of time so that they can
be recovered if necessary. A dropped table is renamed and moved to a recycle bin.
This recycle bin can be used to undo the drop table operation. The tables that currently
exist in the recycle bin can be viewed by querying the recyclebin table, as shown
in Figure 12-1.

In order to restore the dropped table, you can use the FLASHBACK TABLE command
with the BEFORE DROP qualifier. This command is shown next:

```
SQL> FLASHBACK TABLE emp TO BEFORE DROP;

Flashback complete.
SQL> SELECT COUNT(*) FROM emp;

COUNT(*)
----------
14
```

```
SQL> DROP TABLE emp;

Table dropped.

SQL> SELECT COUNT(*) FROM emp;
SELECT COUNT(*) FROM emp
                     *
ERROR at line 1:
ORA-00942: table or view does not exist

SQL> SELECT * FROM recyclebin;

OBJECT_NAME                      ORIGINAL_NAME OPERATION TYPE  TS_NAME CREATETIME          DROPTIME            DROPSCN PARTITION_NAME CAN CAN RELATED BASE_OBJECT PURGE_OBJECT SPACE
-------------------------------- ------------- --------- ----- ------- ------------------- ------------------- ------- -------------- --- --- ------- ----------- ------------ -----
BINS2o6Wz0jqU4ngMKjABgF52A==$0   PK_EMP        DROP      INDEX USERS   2004-02-05:13:44:43 2004-05-16:13:08:00 475426                 NO  YES   49059       49059        49060     8
BINS2o6Wz0jrU4ngMKjABgF52A==$0   EMP           DROP      TABLE USERS   2004-02-05:13:44:43 2004-05-16:13:08:00 475428                 YES YES   49059       49059        49059     8
```

FIGURE 12-1. *The Contents of the Recycle Bin*

As with other flashback features, the flashback drop query is a great feature. Since the flashback drop feature stores data in the recycle bin, you are not really freeing up space in your database when you drop a table.

In order to permanently remove the space from your database, you must follow up the DROP TABLE statement with a PURGE command. The PURGE command is used to permanently remove a dropped object from the database. The PURGE command can be used in several different ways, depending on what you want to accomplish.

Purge Command	Effect
PURGE TABLE *table*	Purges the listed table from the recycle area.
PURGE TABLESPACE *tablespace_name*	Purges all of the dropped tables for the listed tablespace.
PURGE TABLESPACE *tablespace_name* USER *user*	This will purge all of the dropped tables for a particular user in a tablespace.
PURGE RECYCLEBIN	Purges the recycle bin for the current user.
PURGE DBA_RECYCLEBIN	A user with SYSDBA privileges can purge all of the recycle bins for all of the users.

As with the other flashback features, this feature can save you a great deal of time and effort if used properly.

NOTE
The flashback drop feature is only for tables. Tablespaces, users, and other objects are dropped immediately and cannot be recovered via the flashback drop feature.

Flashback Database

The flashback database feature combines both flashback features and RMAN to automatically flash back a database to a point in time. The flashback database feature requires the automatic disk-based backup and a flash recovery area. With flashback database, the backup files and archive logs stored in the flash recovery area are used to restore the database to a specific point in time.

The flashback database command is similar in nature to a point-in-time recovery, except that much of it is done automatically. Flashback database is set up with a default flashback retention period and has its database configured to flashback mode. Once this is accomplished, the database can be restored to a point in time by using the FLASHBACK DATABASE command within RMAN. There are several methods of specifying the flashback point, as shown in the following table:

FLASHBACK DATABASE TO SCN *scn#*	Flash back to a specific SCN.
FLASHBACK DATABASE TO SEQUENCE *sequence#*	Flash back to a specific log sequence.
FLASHBACK DATABASE TO TIME (SYSDATE-1/24);	Flash back to a specific point in the past.
FLASHBACK DATABASE TO TIME timestamp('2004-05-16 14:00:00');	Flash back to a specific point in time.

As with the other flashback features, this can be very powerful, or very dangerous. The flashback database feature will revert your database to a previous point in time, thus overwriting any changes that have been made since then. This can be very useful, or it can cause more problems.

Developing a Recovery Strategy

It is very important that you plan your recovery process and recovery strategy so you're prepared should a system failure occur. Several scenarios must be planned for, depending on the type of failure. The types of failure that require recovery are

- Instance failure
- Media failure
- Operator error

Each is different and each calls for a different recovery strategy.

Planning for Instance Recovery

Instance failure typically calls for no operator intervention, as described earlier. The main planning that should be done is in the area of the parallel recovery option. By evaluating your system, you should determine the degree of parallelism for the recovery process. This is set as the Oracle initialization parameter RECOVERY_PARALLISM.

The number of disk drives and CPUs typically determines the degree of parallelism in your system. My rule of thumb is one process (thread) per every two disk drives, up to twenty. By setting this too high, you may cause additional overhead.

Try starting with a number like this, and adjust it to suit your particular system. Since every system is different, it is difficult to offer blanket recommendations.

Other than setting the degree of parallelism for recovery, the instance recovery process is automatic and requires no operator intervention.

Planning for Media Recovery

Planning for media recovery involves not only the steps required to recover the damaged media, but the restoration of data as well. Some of the key items necessary for quick media recovery include the following:

Hardware Availability   Most computer system vendors offer hot-swappable disk drives. A failed disk drive need only be removed and replaced with the same type disk in order to start automatic recovery. It is necessary to keep spares available for this reason.

Backup Files   The previous backup files should remain immediately available until such time as the next backup has finished and verified. By having these files available either on the system or on a network drive, you can perform quick media recovery.

Archived Log Files   The archived log files that were created since the last backup should be kept available, either on the system itself or on a network server. Once the next backup has occurred, you may want to archive them to tape, but for quick recovery they should be immediately available.

If downtime is not an option, you should think about using some sort of fault-tolerant disk subsystem. By protecting your disk drives with a RAID disk array, a lot of downtime can be avoided.

NOTE
The system component most likely to fail is your disk drive. In fact, the more disk drives you have in your system, the more likely they are to fail. Media recovery takes time, by protecting your disk drives with either hardware or software RAID you can save yourself a lot of downtime.

As you have learned in this section, you should be prepared for media recovery by planning ahead and having all of the components on hand to recover quickly. The components needed to perform media recovery are

- Backup files
- Archived log files
- Spare hardware components

By having these components on hand, media recovery can start immediately, thus avoiding costly time spent reloading from tape.

Planning for Operator Error Recovery

Recovering from operator error is similar to recovering from media failure. To recover, you need the following components:

- Backup files
- Archived log files
- Large temporary space
- Recycle bin
- Sufficient UNDO space.

The difference between media recovery and error recovery is that with error recovery you may need a large amount of disk space to recover your database temporarily. Fortunately, the users can typically continue working on the permanent database unless their duties require them to access the table(s) that have been deleted or corrupted.

Some of the new flashback features in Oracle 10g have made the recovery from operator and user errors much easier, provided the errors are caught in time. The ability to use the flashback features depend entirely on the configuration of the system. Therefore, the UNDO tablespaces should be configured sufficiently large enough for you to recover in the event of user or operator mistakes.

Summary

These last two chapters have covered quite a bit of material on both backup and restore utilities and techniques. There is a great deal of information in this chapter that can help you develop a backup strategy. It is important you regularly back up your system and occasionally test your backup media in order to make sure your backups are being done effectively.

It is important to understand the techniques and practice them occasionally. Also, make sure you have a restore plan documented. It might not always be the case that the person who developed the backup and restore plan is available when they are needed most. A good, documented plan can be invaluable.

CHAPTER
13

Oracle Data Guard
on Linux

racle Data Guard is a high-availability disaster recovery solution that provides services to maintain, manage, and monitor one or more standby databases. These standby databases utilize the online redo logs or archive log files created by the primary server to keep one or more standby servers up to date. This is done by applying these archive log files to the standby database. There are two types of Oracle Data Guard standby databases: physical and logical. The physical standby database places the standby server into managed recovery mode and continually applies redo information in order to keep the standby database in sync with the primary. With the logical standby database, the archive log files are converted into transactions that are run on the standby database. Both of these methods have the same end goal, to keep the standby database up to date, but they operate differently.

NOTE
Data Guard requires the same Oracle platform on both the primary and standby servers. For example, you can mix 32-bit and 64-bit Linux systems; however, both must be running the 32-bit version of Oracle for Linux.

Data Guard Concepts

A Data Guard system consists of a primary database and one or more standby databases. These standby databases may be located near the production database, or they may be located thousands of miles away. The purpose of the standby database is to take over for the production database in the event of a catastrophic failure or planned downtime of the primary database. In addition to being in a state to take over for the primary server in the event of a failure, the standby database can also be configured to perform read-only (for physical standby) or read/write (for logical standby) reporting functions.

The standby database is part of an overall disaster survival plan and can be indispensable in bringing your business back on line quickly in the event of a failure. However, Data Guard is not a substitution for backups. It is only one part of an overall DR and HA solution. Data Guard and backups serve a different purpose. Backups are used not only to recover from media failure, but also to recover from user error or to recover data that was removed from the database either intentionally or unintentionally. Data Guard is designed to take over in the event of a catastrophic system failure or a planned switchover.

Distance Matters to Data Guard

Data Guard provides one instance where you get to use your college physics knowledge. The time it takes to copy data from the primary database to the standby partially depends on the distance and the speed of light. If you are setting up Data Guard between Boston and Los Angeles, which are 2,595 miles apart, and the speed of light is 186,000 miles per second, it will take at least 13.95 milliseconds for each packet to be sent. If you consider the acknowledgment as well, this brings the time up to 27.9 ms. This is a huge time in computer terms. If you are using a satellite network, the distance is more like 25,000 miles. So, consider the distance from your primary site to the standby site when designing your DR plan, and remember that distance matters.

Data Guard can run in a number of different modes, depending on your requirements. They include:

- **Maximum protection**   In this mode, no data loss will occur, as a transaction is not committed on the primary server until it has been written into the primary server's redo log as well as to at least one standby redo log. This guarantees no loss of transactions, but at a high price. If the standby server is not available or is slow, transaction processing on the primary server will stop due to database shutdown, or at least will suffer. In the event that no standby servers are available, the primary database will shut down.

- **Maximum availability**   This mode is similar to the maximum protection mode; however, transaction processing on the primary server does not stop in the event of a failure. If it cannot continue to write a stream or redo information to the standby redo log files, it will operate in maximum performance mode and will queue its redo data until the failure has been corrected, when it will resume in maximum protection mode.

- **Maximum performance**   This is the default mode and has a minimal effect on the primary server. Rather than requiring a synchronous transfer of data to the standby redo log files, it permits data to be transferred asynchronously. This can result, however, in transactions committed on the standby lagging behind those committed on the primary database.

NOTE
The performance of the network between the primary database server and the standby database servers is very important in a Data Guard environment. A slow network can cause severe problems. The performance of the network between these servers should be part of the planning process. Please refer to the Oracle White Paper, Oracle9i Data Guard: Primary Site and Network Configuration Best Practices, October 2003. It is available on Oracle TechNet.

Data Guard is made up of a number of services that are used to configure, maintain, and monitor a standby copy of your primary database. The Data Guard configuration is made up of one primary database and one or more standby databases that can be distributed geographically. The primary database or the standby database(s) can be made up of either stand-alone databases or Oracle RAC clusters.

Data Guard Services

The Data Guard services are made up of log transport services, log apply services, and role management services. Whether you choose a physical standby database or a logical standby database, the log transport services are the same. However, the log apply services are different, depending on whether you are on a physical or logical standby database. In either case, the end result is similar; the log data is transported from the primary server and applied to the standby server or servers.

Log Transport Services

The log transport services do just what the name suggests. This service is responsible for transmitting redo log data from the primary system to the standby system or systems. It is also responsible for catching up in the event that some past logs were not transmitted, and to automatically detect any problems with the archive or standby log files on the standby systems and replace them as necessary.

The log transport services can work in two modes. In the first mode, the log writer process (LGWR) uses standby redo log files that are kept entirely in sync with the primary redo log files. In the second mode, the archiver process (ARCn) ships archive log files from the primary to the standby system. In the first mode, the redo logs are kept in sync, while in the second mode, the standby is one archive log file behind the primary.

Using the Log Writer for Log Transport   Using the log writer process allows you to keep the standby system completely in sync with the primary system. The log writer will write redo data to both the online redo log files and the standby redo log files. This allows for no loss of data and for immediate failover in the event of a failure. The downside is that this method is not advisable when the interconnect is not completely reliable and fast. Since a transaction will not be considered committed until the redo record has been written to both the primary and standby systems, the commit will wait on the slower of the two; specifically, the standby system.

Using the Archiver for Log Transport   Using the archiver process for log transport services causes less degradation of performance on the primary, since transactions do not wait on log transport. When a log switch occurs, the archiver will archive that log to both the primary archive log location and the standby archive log location. This means that the standby is always one archive log behind the primary. In order to reduce the time that the standby is out of sync with the primary, set the parameter ARCHIVE_LAG_TARGET. This will set the maximum time in seconds between primary log switches, typically recommended to be between 1800 seconds (30 minutes) and 7200 seconds (2 hours).

Log Transport O/S and Network Tuning   The log transport services work automatically to make sure that the correct standby log files are copied to the standby system or systems. The performance of the log transport services depends on the speed and reliability of your network. By having a well-tuned network, you should be able to achieve good Data Guard performance. As with the Oracle RAC system, the network parameters can be tuned for optimal performance. The OS maximum send and receive buffers can be set in the /etc/sysctl.conf file by adding the following lines to increase the default and max receive read and write buffer sizes:

```
net.core.rmem_default=262144
net.core.wmem_default=262144
net.core.rmem_max=8388608
net.core.wmem_max=8388608
```

In addition, the TCP read and write buffer sizes can also be set. These parameters take min, max, and default values and can be set by putting the following lines in the /etc/sysctl.conf file:

```
net.ipv4.tcp_rmem='4096 262144 8388608'
net.ipv4.tcp_wmem='4096 262144 8388608'
```

These parameters tell Linux how much buffer space to reserve for each socket. By increasing the buffer space, you can achieve higher network performance, and thus better Data Guard performance, since it will take less time to transmit and receive the data.

Log Apply Services

The log apply services provide the mechanism that applies the standby redo logs (SRLs) or archive log to the standby database. Log apply services function differently, depending upon whether you are using a physical standby database or a logical standby database. With a physical standby database, the SRLs or archive logs are applied to the standby instance using the built-in Oracle media recovery mechanism. With a logical standby database, the redo log entries are transformed into SQL statements that are then applied to the standby database. The remote file server process (RFS) receives redo data transmitted from the primary database and writes it to either the SRLs or archived redo log files on the standby database. If you use SRLs, you can optionally enable real-time apply, which allows Data Guard to recover redo data from the current SRL as it is being filled up by the RFS process. Not having to wait for the current SRL to be archived results in faster switchover and failover. The managed recovery process (MRP*n*) applies the SRLs or the archived redo logs to the standby database.

An alternative to real-time apply is to specify a time lag between the time redo data is received from the primary and the time it is applied to the standby database. This delay protects against the application of corrupted or erroneous data to the standby database. (A flashback database can also be used for this purpose.) This does not delay transport of the redo logs from the primary, just the application of that data to the standby database. For physical standby databases, this delay is set on the primary database using the DELAY=*minutes* attribute of the LOG_ARCHIVE_DEST_n initialization parameter. You can also set up a time delay on the physical standby database using the command RECOVER MANAGED STANDBY DATABASE DELAY <minutes>. (This delay supercedes any delay set from the primary database.) On logical standby databases, use the command ALTER DATABASE START LOGICAL STANDBY APPLY DELAY <minutes>, or the DBMS_LOGSTDBY.APPLY_SET procedure.

Role Management Services

The role management services are used to maintain and modify the roles of the primary and standby database servers. With role management services, you can change the standby system to become the primary system in the event of a catastrophic failure or for maintenance. This is accomplished either via a switchover (no failure) or a failover operation. There is no data loss during a switchover, and each database continues in its new role within the Data Guard configuration. In a failover, the standby database transitions to the primary role due to a primary database failure. If the primary database was in maximum performance mode, some data loss may occur. After a failover, the primary database is no longer part of the Data Guard configuration and must be recommissioned as the new standby database or rebuilt as the new primary database.

Data Guard Broker

The Data Guard Broker is the set of utilities and services that manage Data Guard. Included in the Data Guard Broker are both a GUI interface using Oracle Enterprise Manager and a command-line interface (CLI). The Data Guard Broker is used to set up Data Guard, to manage the configuration, and to monitor Data Guard. As I have mentioned throughout the book, I prefer to use the CLI so that I can script and document my actions.

Physical Standby Database

The *physical* standby database stays constantly in recovery mode and serves the purpose of preparing for a failover operation. With a physical standby database, the primary and failover systems are identical, and the datafiles contain exactly the same data on a block-by-block basis.

The physical standby database stays synchronized with the primary server by remaining constantly in recovery mode. As new redo information is generated and moved to the standby server via log transport services, it is constantly being applied to the standby server via log apply services. This process keeps the database on the standby server in sync with the primary. The physical standby database is shown in Figure 13-1.

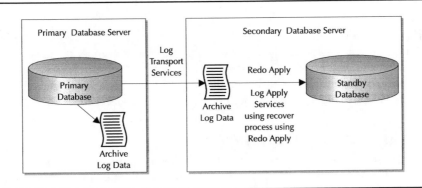

FIGURE 13-1. *Physical standby database*

The physical standby database can be opened in read-only mode so that reports and queries can be run against the database; however, the log apply services are suspended during this operation. This might seem like a problem, but the instance can be changed from redo apply mode to read-only mode and back again without too much of a problem. This allows you certain times of the day when queries can be run and other times when the logs are applied.

There are several benefits to the physical standby database. Among these benefits are performance and fault tolerance.

Performance

Physical standby databases apply redo information in a very efficient manner. Oracle has spent years optimizing the recovery paths within the Oracle database server. Recovery does not involve going through the same code paths as replaying the transactions. The SQL statements do not need to be reparsed, nor does the Oracle server need to perform the SQL operations. The path used by the recover operations is very efficient and fast.

Another performance benefit of a physical standby database is the ability to offload read-only functions such as reporting queries and even RMAN backups (the RMAN recovery catalog is required so that backups taken on one server can be restored on another server). Since the database is kept entirely in sync via Data Guard, backups of the primary database can be performed on the standby database server in either managed recovery or read-only mode, and they can be used to recover the primary or standby database. You can back up just the standby site, provided the primary site can access the backup via the network or via some other means (such as tape) and can do so in a timely manner to meet the SLA. Otherwise, back up both the primary and standby databases. For more information on using Data Guard with RMAN, see *Using Recovery Manager with Oracle Data Guard in Oracle Database 10*g, *An Oracle White Paper, March 2005.*

Fault Tolerance

The standby database can easily be moved into the role of primary database server via either a switchover or failover operation. This can be useful in either a planned or unplanned downtime scenario. In addition, Data Guard can be configured in a variety of modes that can assure no loss of transactional data.

Logical Standby Database

The *logical* standby database takes an entirely different approach than the physical standby database. Rather than applying redo log data to the standby database server, the log apply services converts the redo information into SQL statements that are executed on the standby database. This standby database is constantly replaying INSERT, UPDATE, and DELETE statements that have been run on the primary database server. Although this is not nearly as efficient as the recovery operations used by the physical standby database, there are several advantages, including:

- **Flexible use of the standby database server**   Since the log apply services are simply running SQL statements, other users can be performing operations on this database, including operations that modify data.

- **Offloading of primary operations**   Since the database can be both in standby mode and running queries, reports and other work can be offloaded.

- **Heterogeneous environment support**   The standby database need not be identical to the primary server; it can be placed on a different environment, with different hardware and different OS configuration. This allows you to maintain the standby server on less expensive hardware. However, remember that both the primary and standby systems must run the same version of Oracle. The configurations can be different, but the Oracle software must be the same.

Although the logical standby database seems to have many advantages over the physical standby database, there are some major drawbacks. Since the standby operations from the primary server are replayed as SQL statements, they are not as fast as the recovery operations used in the physical standby database. In fact, if the standby server is used for additional reporting operations, there might be a significant lag in applying redo information, and thus in the event of a failover, your system might be out of date. In addition, since the standby database structure would not be identical to the primary database, the logical standby database is not a good platform for performing RMAN backups for the primary server. The logical standby database is shown in Figure 13-2.

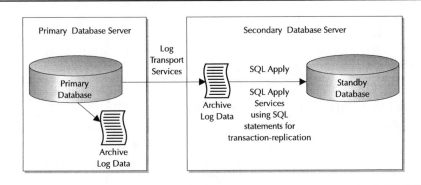

FIGURE 13-2.   *Logical standby database*

There are pros and cons to both the physical and logical standby database servers. You should research both physical and logical before making your decision. If fault tolerance or performance is your primary concern, then a physical standby database might be the better choice; if use of resources is your primary concern, then a logical standby database might be your best option.

NOTE
The logical standby database has several strict requirements. Table rows on the primary database must be uniquely identifiable. In addition, some data types are not allowed. These restrictions are clearly outlined in the Oracle Data Guard Concepts and Administration Guide. Any database can participate in a physical standby database without any restrictions.

Configuring and Managing Oracle Data Guard

There are many similarities between physical and logical standby database configurations, and many differences. In order to offer the clearest explanation on how to configure and implement both of these, the procedures will be split into two sections. Even though there is some overlap, it is easier to understand the complete process by having two sections. In addition, since these steps are well documented in the Oracle documentation, they will not be repeated here in detail. For a more detailed description of configuring and using Data Guard as just one component of the Maximum Availability Architecture (MAA), see the MAA White Papers and documentation available on TechNet at http://www.oracle.com/technology/deploy/availability/htdocs/maa.htm.

An overview will be presented with special notes for Linux-specific issues. We will start out by looking at the procedures for creating a physical standby database, and then for a logical standby database.

Physical Standby Database Configuration

As with the configuration and deployment of the Oracle database server itself as well as RAC, the procedure for setting up a physical standby database can be broken down into three steps: the preparation stage, the deployment stage, and the postconfiguration stage. Each of these stages is very important.

Preparation

In order to prepare the database server to become a primary server in a physical standby database configuration, you must perform the following measures:

- **Archivelog mode** If the database isn't already in archivelog mode, it must be put into that mode. Archivelog mode is required for Data Guard. (In any case, however, it is always wise to run a production database in archivelog mode.)

- **Forced Logging mode** The instance must be set into forced logging mode, thus assuring that direct path inserts and other unrecoverable operations are logged and transported in the redo stream to the standby, even if NOLOGGING is set for a primary database operation.

- **Password file** If a password file isn't already created, you must create one. Each system must have a password file, and this password file must contain the same SYS password for the primary and the standby servers. REMOTE_LOGIN_PASSWORDFILE must be set to EXCLUSIVE.

These actions should all be completed before you can set up the physical standby database server.

Deployment

Deploying the physical standby database is also broken down into several steps. These steps involve creating the database backup and moving it to the standby server, setting up an initialization file on the standby server and setting up the processes to invoke Data Guard, as detailed here.

Create a Backup of the Primary Database You should be able to create either an online or offline backup of the database using the skills you have learned in Chapters 11 and 12. Use Recovery Manager (RMAN) and create a full backup of the primary database. This backup copy will then be restored on the standby database server, thus creating the database that will be turned into a standby database. Temporary tablespace datafiles do not need to be copied—they need to be created on the standby database in read-only mode after it is recovered (see "Post Deployment" later in this chapter). Redo log files can be copied, or can be created on the standby (see "Post Deployment" later in this chapter). These redo logs are created on the standby and cleared in preparation for use in a switchover or failover.

If you do not want to use RMAN, and you are able to shut down the primary database, you can simply copy the datafiles from the primary system to the standby system. You will probably achieve better performance if you use dd, since you can specify a larger block size than with rcp or scp. With Linux, the following command is very efficient for copying data files from one system to another:

```
dd bs=64k if=<data file spec> | ssh standby "( dd bs=64k of=<data file spec>)"
```

If you are using OCFS, make the following modification to the preceding command:

```
dd -O_DIRECT=64k if=<data file spec> | ssh standby "
( dd -O_DIRECT=64k of=<data file spec>)"
```

Using dd can be ten times faster than using scp or rcp.

Create a Control File for the Standby Database   Create the standby control file on the primary database using the ALTER DATABASE CREATE STANDBY CONTROLFILE AS '<filename>'. This standby control file will be copied to the standby database system that is described in this section. This standby control file must be created with the database in MOUNT mode, and after the latest timestamp for the backup datafiles.

Create Standby Initialization Parameters   The parameter set for the standby server will be similar to that used on the primary server; however, a few of the parameters are set differently. The standby database must have a different DB_UNIQUE_NAME from the primary server. In addition, the FAL_CLIENT and FAL_SERVER parameters are reversed on the standby database server. Other parameters specific to Data Guard include LOG_ARCHIVE_DEST_2, LOG_ARCHIVE_DEST_STATE_2, LOG_ARCHIVE_CONFIG, and STANDBY_FILE_MANAGEMENT.

A new feature of Oracle 10*g* is that parameters like LOG_ARCHIVE_DEST_2, formerly requiring that they be changed on role reversal, now have additional attributes to specify what role they apply to. This allows the same initialization parameter file to be used on each site (though it must be different between sites), regardless of database role.

> **TIP**
> *It is often much easier to create a PFILE and use the PFILE for the initial configuration steps. Once the standby server has been set up correctly, an SPFILE can be created.*

Copy Files to the Standby Server   Next, copy the backup files (if you haven't already done this as part of the backup process itself as shown earlier in this chapter), the standby control file (copy to same locations and name as the primary controlfiles), and the initialization parameter file to the standby system. In order to create identical primary and standby sites, you also need to copy initialization scripts for environment setup (such as .profile and other scripts), as well as DBA scripts. These files can be copied via scp or sftp or by using an NFS-mounted volume. As mentioned earlier in this chapter, the /etc/oratab file should be copied as well, and unless you are installing Oracle 10*g* on the standby site from scratch using the OUI, you will also need to copy the ORACLE_HOME directory, the admin directory (including subdirectories bdump, cdump, create, pfile, and udump), and the /etc/hosts file to the standby site (you may need to add new entries to the /etc/ hosts file for any new NICs dedicated to redo traffic). The network parameters can be important when configuring your system for Data Guard.

As mentioned previously, the data files can be copied as part of the backup process itself, as shown here:

```
dd bs=64k if=<data file spec> | ssh standby "( dd bs=64k of=<data file spec>)"
```

If you are using OCFS, make the following modification to the preceding command:

```
dd -O_DIRECT=64k if=<data file spec> | ssh standby "
( dd -O_DIRECT=64k of=<data file spec>)"
```

As was mentioned, using dd can be ten times faster than using scp or rcp.

Finally, synchronize OS clocks. Not doing so can make it very confusing later on when comparing log files (particularly alert logs) containing timestamps, because they will probably not dovetail. If servers are not already synchronized, you may want to ask the Systems Administrator to implement enterprise-wide synchronization software such as NTP to keep all server clocks synchronized all the time.

Set Up the Network Environment   Once all of the needed files are on the standby server, configure an Oracle network service name for listeners configured for the primary and standby databases for log transport services to use. Configuration files include listener.ora, tnsnames.ora, and sqlnet.ora files. On the primary site, either use a second connect string for redo data on the current database listener, specifying a different port, or create a separate listener than that used to connect to the primary database. Do the same on both systems in preparation of a role switch. Also add aliases to the tnsnames.ora files for redo log transfer. You will probably want to use the Oracle Net parameter SDU (session data unit) in the tnsnames.ora file to set the transport size to 32K. For more information, see *Data Guard Concepts and Administration, 10g Release 1, Section A.6.* To enable broken connection detection, set =2 (in minutes) as recommended by Oracle. When configuring the Oracle Net service, the SQLNET.EXPIRE_TIME needs to be set in the sqlnet.ora file.

Additional Steps   At this point, the following optional steps can be done (if desired):

- Create standby redo logs (SRLs). This step is highly recommended for all protection modes, even maximum performance mode. The standby redo log files are created using the ALTER DATABASE command, as shown here:

```
SQL> ALTER DATABASE ADD STANDBY LOGFILE THREAD 10
2> ('<log file spec 1>', '<log file spec 2>') SIZE 100M;
```

- Create/clear the online redo log files on the standby to prepare for role reversal (optional). When the standby becomes the primary, the online redo log files are created for you automatically. This step can be done ahead of time by creating the redo log files on the standby system. This is done very easily via the ALTER DATABASE CLEAR LOGFILE statement. This is done as follows:

```
ALTER DATABASE CLEAR LOGFILE GROUP 1;
ALTER DATABASE CLEAR LOGFILE GROUP 2;
...
ALTER DATABASE CLEAR LOGFILE GROUP n;
```

- Start the DG Broker. Start the Data Guard monitor (DMON) process on each site by setting the initialization parameter DB_BROKER_START to TRUE on both sites. You now need to create and enable the broker configuration.

- Enable Flashback Database (as additional protection).

Start the Standby Database   The database is almost ready to begin functioning as a standby database; however, the standby database requires additional temporary space. All temporary tablespaces and data on the primary site file should be created on the standby site. You can use the CREATE TEMPORARY TABLESPACE command(s) on the standby database from the text controlfile created on the primary from running ALTER DATABASE BACKUP CONTROLFILE TO TRACE. To create a temporary tablespace, the standby database needs to be started in read-only mode using the command STARTUP OPEN READ ONLY. In this mode, additional temp files can be added to the database.

At this point, you are ready to begin standby mode. This is done by starting the Redo Apply by issuing the SQL command ALTER DATABASE RECOVER MANAGED STANDBY DATABASE DISCONNECT [FROM SESSION]. The DISCONNECT statement makes this command run in a background session.

Test the Standby Database   The Data Guard log transport and apply services can be tested by issuing an ALTER DATABASE SWITCH LOGFILE command on the primary server and making sure that the redo data is transmitted and applied to the standby server. In addition, the following steps can be used to validate that Data Guard is working properly:

1. Identify existing archived log files on the standby:

```
SELECT SEQUENCE#, FIRST_TIME, NEXT_TIME FROM
V$ARCHIVED_LOG ORDER BY SEQUENCE#;
```

2. Force a log switch on the primary to archive the current online redo log file:

```
ALTER SYSTEM ARCHIVE LOG CURRENT;
```

3. Verify new redo data was archived on the standby:

```
SELECT SEQUENCE#, FIRST_TIME, NEXT_TIME FROM
V$ARCHIVED_LOG ORDER BY SEQUENCE#;
```

It is important to validate that Data Guard is functioning properly before continuing. Don't assume that everything is working properly.

Post-Deployment

Once the basic physical standby database has been created, there are a few more optional tasks that can be performed. Now, you should create the temporary data files.

Additional temp datafiles should be created; one for each temp datafile that you currently have in the database. This is done as follows:

```
STANDBY> ALTER TABLESPACE TEMP ADD TEMPFILE
'D:\oracle\oradata\stby\temp02.dbf'
SIZE 20M REUSE;
```

The new temp datafiles are used in the event that the standby becomes the primary.

If you wish, you can change the data protection mode. As mentioned earlier, these are data protection modes that can be used:

■ **Maximum protection** In this mode, a transaction is not committed on the primary server until it has been written into the primary server's redo log as well as at least one standby redo log.

■ **Maximum availability** This mode is similar to the maximum protection mode; however, transaction processing on the primary server does not stop in the event of a failure.

■ **Maximum performance** This is the default mode; it transfers data to the standby redo log files in an asynchronous fashion.

In addition to setting the data protection mode, it is also a good idea to test and verify the operation of the standby database.

Logical Standby Database Configuration

As with the configuration of a physical standby database, the logical standby database configuration can be broken down into three steps: the preparation stage, the configuration stage and the postconfiguration stage. The prerequisites for a logical standby database are stricter than for a physical standby database.

Preparation

Before starting logical standby database creation, you should check the prerequisites. In this configuration, some datatypes are not supported. The unsupported datatypes are BFILE, ROWID, UROWID, REFs, varrays, nested tables, XML types, and user-defined data types. If you are using any of these datatypes in your tables, these tables will be skipped by SQL Apply. If you need to, change the datatype on the primary database before you begin configuring the logical standby database. In addition to the skipped data types, there are a number of tables, sequences and views, and DDL statements (including, notably, ALTER DATABASE, ALTER SESSION, and ALTER SYSTEM) that will be skipped as well, including:

- Most schemas that ship with the Oracle database
- Tables with unsupported datatypes
- Tables using table compression

Oracle PL/SQL-supplied packages that modify system metadata typically are not supported by SQL Apply. Examples of such packages include DBMS_JAVA, DBMS_REGISTRY, DBMS_ALERT, DBMS_SPACE_ADMIN, DBMS_REFRESH, DBMS_SCHEDULER, and DBMS_AQ.

To determine if the primary database contains any unsupported objects, query the DBA_LOGSTDBY_UNSUPPORTED view. Unlike the physical standby database, where the ROWIDs of each record in the database are identical, those in the logical standby database might be different. Therefore, you must use a different mechanism to match updated rows on the standby database with rows on the primary database. This could be via either primary keys or unique indexes.

Deployment

The first step in creating a logical standby database is to follow the steps earlier in the chapter in order to create a physical standby database. In addition, you must make sure that supplemental logging is enabled on the primary database. If supplemental logging has not been enabled, it can be enabled via the ALTER DATABASE ADD SUPPLEMENTAL LOG DATA (PRIMARY KEY, UNIQUE INDEX) COLUMNS statement. This creates additional logging data that will be used by the SQL Apply service.

Once these steps have been done, you are ready to activate the logical standby database by performing the following steps:

1. Prepare primary and standby databases for role transition by setting up init params to take effect on role reversal. On primary and standby, set LOG_ARCHIVE_DEST_1,2,3 and LOG_ARCHIVE_DEST_STATE_1, 2, 3, and UNDO_RETENTION=3600 (for the LogMiner dictionary). On standby, set PARALLEL_MAX_SERVERS=9.(minimum). Issue a SHUTDOWN IMMEDIATE on the standby.

2. Create a logical standby control file with ALTER DATABASE CREATE LOGICAL STANDBY CONTROLFILE AS 'filename';

3. On standby, issue STARTUP MOUNT PFILE='<pfile>';

4. Prepare the standby database for SQL Apply by running the SQL statement ALTER DATABASE RECOVER MANAGED STANDBY DATABASE.

5. Activate the logical standby database by running the SQL statement ALTER DATABASE ACTIVATE STANDBY DATABASE.

6. Run the nid (DBNEWID) utility in order to change the name of the database on the standby server (requires SHUTDOWN IMMEDIATE and STARTUP MOUNT).

7. Change the database name DB_NAME in the parameter file to that used in DBNEWID.

8. Create SPFILE for logical standby, and restart the database with ALTER DATABASE OPEN RESETLOGS.

9. Change the standby database global name using the SQL statement ALTER DATABASE RENAME GLOBAL_NAME TO *newname.*

10. Create new temporary files as you did with the physical standby database.

11. Start SQL Apply with the SQL statement ALTER DATABASE START LOGICAL STANDBY APPLY.

Post-Deployment

Once a basic physical standby database has been created, there are a few more optional tasks that can be performed. Of course, this includes testing the standby database. There are a number of ways that the standby database can be monitored. These include the following Oracle tables and dynamic performance views:

- **DBA_LOGSTDBY_LOG**   This table provides information on redo log files that were registered on the standby system.

- **DBA_LOGSTDBY_PROGRESS**   This table provides statistics on the overall progress of SQL Apply.

- **V$LOGSTDBY_STATS**   This view provides information on LogMiner statistics.

- **V$LOGSTDBY**   Provides a snapshot of information about the log Apply process.

As with a physical standby database, you can change the data protection mode. These are the same data protection modes that are used with the physical standby database (described earlier) and are maximum protection, maximum availability, and maximum performance.

In addition to setting the data protection mode, it is always a good idea to test and verify the operation of the standby database.

Summary

In addition to the information provided here, there is much more that can be configured and tuned with Oracle Data Guard. There are many options and many modes of operation that can be configured. How you configure your system depends on your needs and requirements. As with many Oracle features such as Oracle RAC, deploying Data Guard in a Linux environment is all about the details. Careful planning and testing will make your deployment successful.

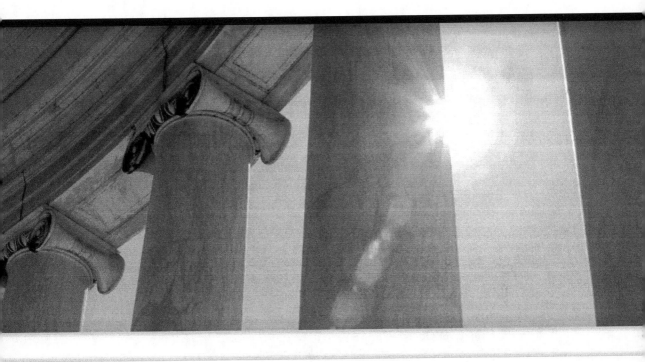

CHAPTER
14

Oracle Advanced
Replication on Linux

eplication is the process of taking a database, table, or subset of those or other Oracle objects and copying them to another system automatically. Replication can be configured to work on an entire database or just a subset of the database. Regardless of how much or how little data there is to replicate, the functions and mechanisms are the same. This chapter will examine the methods that Oracle uses to replicate data from one system to another.

Although the end result might look similar to Oracle Data Guard, replication is actually quite different. Replication is designed to create one or more copies of a database or subset of the database. These copies are designed to be open and available to users. Replication can also be used in a bidirectional manner, where there are multiple masters. Data Guard is designed as a disaster recovery system, whereas replication is not primarily designed for DR. Data Guard works by transfer and applying redo data from the primary to the standby system, whereas replication is API- or trigger-based.

NOTE
Whereas Data Guard requires Oracle Enterprise Edition, replication comes with Standard Edition.

Introduction to Oracle Replication

Oracle Advanced Replication is composed of processes and utilities that work together to configure, deploy, and maintain database objects on different systems throughout your enterprise. Replicated objects can reside in a database on the same computer system as the source database, or they can reside on systems thousands of miles away. The replicated objects can be configured to be read-only or read/write, depending on your needs and preferences. Advanced Replication is Oracle's implementation of replication. In this chapter, the term replication will be used to describe advanced replication.

Oracle Advanced Replication is used for a number of purposes. It can be used to replicate read-only data that must be locally available to remote locations, such as stores. In this manner, you can replicate price data, parts details, documentation, etc., to each store, where that data can be readily available even when network problems might prevent communication to the main data center. This data can be used autonomously at each store, and only sales data needs to be sent back to the main data center. This will allow stores to keep running if the network is down or if there are problems with the main corporate systems.

In addition to availability, in this case replication can also provide for greater performance, since the data is located locally and can be quickly accessed by the local users. This allows the Oracle buffer cache to work effectively for each store or remote database. Other topologies allow you to replicate data from the main OLTP system to other systems that can be used for reporting purposes. These reporting servers can be tuned differently from the OLTP server and can be dedicated to reporting and data mining. This is almost always a distinct advantage, since tuning strategies for OLTP systems and reporting systems are often in conflict with each other. By replicating to reporting servers, you can offload work from the main system and allow each system to perform optimally.

Replication is defined by means of objects, groups, and sites. These terms define what is being replicated, how it is being replicated, and where it is being replicated to. Each of these terms is defined as follows:

- **Replication object**   This is the type of object being replicated and includes tables, indexes, views, packages, etc. Individual objects are defined as part of the replication and can be collected together as a group.

- **Replication group**   A replication group is a set of objects that are replicated together. These replication groups are treated and managed together as a single entity.

- **Replication sites**   These can either be a master site or a materialized view site. The master site is the system where the original data exists, whereas the materialized view site is the system that is being replicated to. *N*-way replication (also called peer-to-peer replication) is done with a multimaster configuration.

There are several different types of replication that can be used, depending on the requirements for data to be replicated. These are multimaster replication, materialized view replication, and hybrid configurations.

Multimaster Replication

Multimaster (or peer-to-peer) replication can use either asynchronous or synchronous replication between systems. Each system is a master system and communicates with other master systems in the replication group, as shown in Figure 14-1.

As just stated, multimaster replication can be asynchronous, synchronous, or procedural. With *asynchronous* replication, the changes to the database are stored and pushed out to the other replication systems at regular intervals. Asynchronous replication is the most common type of replication, and it allows you to control how often replication is done. Synchronous replication keeps systems more up-to-date, but at a price in performance. In addition, there is procedural replication as well.

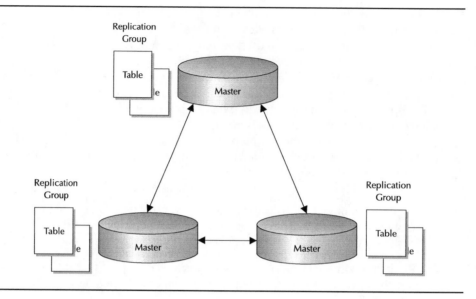

FIGURE 14-1. *Multimaster replication sites*

With synchronous and asynchronous replication, information about a DML change on a table is stored in the deferred transactions queue at the master site where the change occurred. These changes are called *deferred transactions.* The deferred transactions are pushed to the other participating master sites at regular intervals, which you define. It is possible to configure asynchronous replication so that it simulates synchronous replication.

Synchronous replication keeps systems more up-to-date, but at a price in performance. Table updates are immediately replicated at all master sites. If one master site cannot process a transaction for any reason, then the transaction is rolled back at all master sites. Although you avoid the possibility of conflicts with synchronous replication, it requires a very stable environment to operate smoothly. If communication to one master site is not possible because of a network problem, for example, then users can still query replicated tables, but no transactions can be completed until communication is reestablished.

In addition, there is procedural replication as well. *Procedural* replication replicates only the call to a stored procedure that an application uses to update a table. It does not replicate the data modifications themselves. Procedural replication is typically used with batch processing applications that change large amounts of data within a single transaction. In such cases, typical row-level replication might load a network with many data changes. To use procedural replication, you must replicate the packages that modify data in the system to all sites. After replicating a package, you must generate a wrapper for the package at each site. When an application calls a packaged procedure at the local site to modify data, the wrapper ensures that the call is ultimately made to the same packaged procedure at all other replication sites. Procedural replication can occur asynchronously or synchronously.

Materialized View Replication

Materialized view replication creates a copy of a database object being replicated at a particular point in time. This replicated copy of the database object is not kept up-to-date, being simply a snapshot of the data at a particular point in time. Materialized view replication systems can be read-only or updatable. An update to an updatable materialized view causes the data on the master also to be updated. Materialized view replication systems are usually refreshed at regular intervals, bringing the data in the target in sync with the master as of the time of the refresh.

Hybrid Replication

Hybrid materialized view replication systems consist of combinations of multimaster and materialized view replication systems. These hybrids can include systems that are members of one or more different replication groups. This can be useful when several objects need multimaster replication and other objects can work with materialized view replication. These hybrid systems can be configured in a number of different ways.

One important difference between multimaster and materialized view replication is that with multimaster replication, any table being replicated must be replicated in its entirety, whereas with materialized view replication, it is possible to replicate only a subset of that table.

Oracle Replication on Linux

Oracle Advanced Replication on Linux is similar to Oracle replication on other UNIX-based platforms. Tuning replication for optimal performance on Linux is usually focused on the configuration of the hardware, the OS tuning parameters, and the database layout itself. The Oracle configuration parameters for a replicated system should be tuned for the type of application that the master and materialized view systems will be servicing. There are several configuration issues that should be considered when setting up a system for replication:

- **I/O performance**   I/O performance can be critical during times when materialized views are being refreshed. You must make sure that you have sufficient I/O performance capacity to handle the peak loads.

- **Database layout**   The disk layout of datafiles, redo logs, and archive logs needs to be distributed to provide fault tolerance and optimal performance.

- **Network performance**   Network performance can have extreme peak activity. Make sure that the network is sufficient to handle the load.

You need to plan and implement replication with these considerations in mind. Configuration planning should include the following items that will be described next.

I/O Capacity

I/O capacity should be sufficient to handle the bursts in I/O operations that can be generated by a replicating system. Chapter 4 gave you some insight into how to plan and size an I/O subsystem for performance. The I/O subsystem should be monitored with iostat to make sure that it is performing optimally. The output of iostat includes avwait and svctm: avwait is the average time that an I/O operation spends queued up, and svctm, or service time, is the time that it takes for the I/O to be processed. Both of these numbers are in milliseconds, and neither should exceed 20ms on a regular basis. Of course there will be peaks, but if the latencies are too high for too long, you will experience performance problems.

Database Layout

To configure I/O for better performance and fault tolerance, be sure to separate the redo log files, the datafiles, and the archive log files across different disk volumes. This will provide a greater level of protection in the event of a disk failure, as well as provide a higher-performing I/O solution. In this regard, the replication system is no different from any other Oracle system.

Sufficient Network Capacity

It is also necessary to make sure that you have sufficient network capacity to perform replication from a primary server to a remote replication site. It is not uncommon to underestimate the amount of network capacity needed for database operations. Network bandwidth is not usually predictable unless you have a dedicated network, as you are often contending with other network traffic, and thus you cannot always count on being able to transmit data at the nominal speed of the network. Several tasks are required to ensure you have sufficient network capacity to use Oracle Advanced Replication successfully:

- Select a sufficiently high-bandwidth, low-latency network.
- Calculate network throughput and latency.
- Test the network.

Network Bandwidth Selection

There are many different networks available for your replication configuration. In addition to the local area network (LAN) choices, such as Ethernet 10baseT, 100baseT, and Gigabit, there are many selections for broadband networks (WANs), such as T1 or T3. The Internet is usually much slower than your LAN, a fact that should be taken into consideration when architecting your configuration.

In addition to the bandwidth selections, you will also need to determine if your network will be dedicated to replication or will be shared with other systems. Several years ago, I had a consulting assignment where we determined a replication problem to be caused by a single network segment that then branched out to other network segments. Replication was performing properly; however, it could replicate only as fast as the network would allow.

Network Throughput Calculation

To determine how fast you can replicate data, you should translate network bandwidth into units appropriate for planning data replication. Network speeds are typically quoted in megabits per second (Mbps), whereas in planning replication strategies, you will often be interested in how many gigabytes can be transferred per hour. Table 14-1 provides network bandwidths in terms of megabits/sec, megabyes/sec and gigabytes/hr. In addition to the network bandwidth rating, you must also take into account the fact that there are other factors affecting the performance—it is unrealistic to expect to actually achieve full network bandwidth. A realistic approximation for network overhead is 30 percent.

If you know the bandwidth of the network that you are using, you should then be able to calculate approximately how long it will take to copy a specific amount of data. Table 14-2 gives you an approximate idea of how many hours it takes to transfer different amounts of data (in seconds) at different bandwidths. Time is shown in hours and includes 30 percent network overhead.

Network	Local Area Network (LAN)			Wide Area Network (WAN)	
	10baseT	100baseT	Gigabit	T1	T3
Megabits/sec	10	100	1000	1.5	44.74
Megabytes/sec	1.25	12.5	125	0.19	5.59
Gigabytes/hr	4.39	43.94	439.45	0.66	19.66

TABLE 14-1. *Network Bandwidths and Other Performance Factors*

Data (in GigaBytes)	Local Area Network (LAN)			Wide Area Network (WAN)	
	10baseT	100baseT	Gigabit	T1	T3
1	0.30	0.03	0.00	1.97	0.07
10	2.96	0.30	0.03	19.72	0.66
50	14.79	1.48	0.15	98.61	3.31
100	29.58	2.96	0.30	197.21	6.61
240	71.00	7.10	0.71	473.32	15.87
500	147.91	14.79	1.48	986.07	33.06

TABLE 14-2. *The Amount of Time It Takes to Transfer Data at Different Bandwidths*

As you can see, it can take longer to transmit data than you might have thought. It is important to understand that each of these devices has limitations. In addition, if processes are using the same network, your performance will be further reduced.

Network Testing
In addition to calculating the network throughput, you should test it to make sure you are not experiencing network problems. There is a great tool for testing your network called TTCP. TTCP is available on the Internet and is used to test network bandwidth. Since this tool tests just the network, it does not consider other performance factors, such as the time it takes to copy data to disk. To run TTCP, you start it up in receive mode on one system and run it in transmit mode on the other. TTCP will transmit data as quickly as possible and report the bandwidth it was able to achieve.

CAUTION
Do not run TTCP on a live network unless you are prepared to consume the entire bandwidth of that network. Please check with your network administrator first.

Once these tasks have been completed, you will know if your network is sufficient for performing the necessary tasks for using Oracle Advanced Replication. If you do not have sufficient network performance, you should rethink your architecture and make the necessary changes.

Summary

Replication is no different on Linux than on other platforms that Oracle supports. In order to make replication work optimally, you should configure your system with sufficient resources. These resources should be properly sized to handle the amount of data transmitted and I/O generated by replication, in addition to the resources used in normal operations. If the database is tuned properly and sufficient resources are allocated, a system employing Oracle Advanced Replication should perform well.

CHAPTER
15

Configuring the
Hardware for Linux
and Oracle

uning the hardware is as important as tuning the operating system and tuning the Oracle instance. But what is hardware tuning? Hardware tuning involves proper installation and configuration of the server hardware and storage. Purchasing sufficient storage capacity and configuring it properly is also crucial to the proper performance and, in some cases, such as with Oracle RAC, the functionality of your Oracle system.

Hardware Tuning Fundamentals

Hardware tuning picks up from where hardware sizing, which you learned about in Chapter 4, leaves off. Where hardware sizing is the act of determining how much and what kind of hardware to purchase, hardware tuning is the act of properly configuring (or reconfiguring) that hardware for optimal performance. Material in this chapter overlaps a bit with that in Chapter 4, as some hardware topics are extremely important to both tuning and sizing.

As hardware components become more and more sophisticated, the amount of tuning that can be done has also increased. Both SAN storage and SCSI RAID controllers have numerous tuning parameters, and the system BIOS and even the processors now offer optional settings. In fact, at the publication of this book, both Intel and AMD have CPUs that can operate in 32-bit or 64-bit modes, depending on what operating system you install. In this chapter, you will learn how to configure and tune the hardware components for optimal performance.

In addition to tuning the individual hardware components, the "system" might consist of several or many different tiers of web, application, and database servers. With multiple layers and sophisticated interactions between the different layers, infrastructure tuning is also important, but it is beyond the scope of this book.

Choosing the Right Hardware

The computer system is made up of many individual components all working together. Each of these components has its own job to perform, and each has its own performance characteristics.

The core of the system is the central processing unit (CPU), which actually processes all the calculations and instructions that run on the computer. It is better to be bound by the performance of the CPUs than by that of other subsystems. Built-in Linux operating system CPU utilities such as ps, top, and vmstat make it easy to tell when the CPUs are at full capacity. For example, CPU is saturated if the vmstsat run queue is more than four times the number of CPUs. Or you may run across a single process consuming an entire CPU. The job of the hardware tuner is to configure the system to use CPU resources efficiently.

The base computer system utilizes three main resources (and many peripheral layers): CPU, memory, and the I/O subsystem. This section describes these components and what makes them tick.

CPU

The CPU and its cache(s) are the fastest components of the system. The cache(s) are one or more pieces of very high-speed memory, usually located on the same chip as the CPU, that are used to store recently used data and instructions so that they can provide quick access if this data is used again in a short time. Most modern CPU hardware designs actually take advantage of a cache built into the CPU core. This internal cache is known as a Level 1 (or L1) cache. Typically, an L1 cache is very small, on the order of 8 to 16 kilobytes in size, and is accessible in a few nanoseconds.

When a certain piece of data is wanted, the hardware first looks in the L1 cache. If the data is there, the hardware processes that data immediately. If the data is not available in the L1 cache, the hardware looks in the L2 cache, which is external to the CPU core but resides on the same chip in order to maximize performance. The L2 cache is connected to the CPU chip(s) on the same side of the memory bus as the CPU. To get to main memory, you need to use the memory bus, thereby reducing the speed of the memory access. Although the L2 cache is typically much slower than the L1 cache, it is usually much larger. Its larger size provides a better chance of getting a "cache hit." Typical L2 caches range from 128K to 4M in size and are accessible in hundreds of nanoseconds.

Slower yet is the speed of the main memory. It is characteristically much slower than the L2 cache, on the order of 2–10 microseconds (roughly 1000 times slower than the L1 cache). The size of system memory can vary widely: 32-bit CPUs are limited to 4GB of directly addressed memory (they can address more through a multiphase operation), while 64-bit CPUs can directly address terabytes of memory directly. A comparison of component speeds is shown in Figure 15-1.

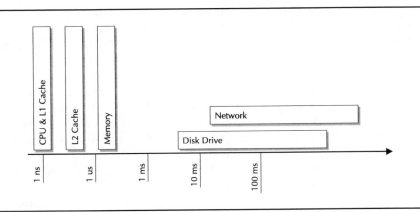

FIGURE 15-1. *Component speed comparison*

As you can see from the comparison of CPU speeds, the advantage in speed is enormous when you can retrieve data from the L1 cache rather than from disk. This is why we spend so much time trying to take advantage of the SGA in memory. This is also why hardware vendors expend such effort to improve CPU cache and memory bus speeds. However, other hardware vendor considerations also affect performance, as described in the following sections.

CPU Design   The CPU works in synchronization with the system clock and executes instructions based on clock signals. The clock rate and CPU type determine how fast these instructions are executed. Virtually all modern CPUs are one of two types of processors: complex instruction set computer (CISC) or reduced instruction set computer (RISC), as described next.

CISC processors (such as those built by Intel and AMD) are by far the most common processors sold today. CISC processors are more common (in terms of volume of processors shipped) and offer a larger instruction set to the program developer than do RISC processors. Some of these instructions can be quite complicated, requiring several clock cycles to complete.

CISC processors are very complex and difficult to build. Because these CPU chips contain millions of internal components, the components are extremely close together. The physical scale causes problems because there is no room for error. Each year, technology allows more complex and faster chips to be built, but chip designers are starting to run into fundamental limits imposed by physics (at least the physics we know today).

These complex processors carry out a wide range of tasks and can sometimes perform two or more instructions at a time in parallel. CISC processors perform most tasks very efficiently, including those involved in RDBMS processing.

By contrast, RISC processors are based on the theory that if you can reduce the complexity and number of distinct instructions the CPU processes, the CPU can be simpler to build and can run faster. In addition, by putting fewer internal components inside the chip, its speed can be increased. One of the most popular RISC chips on the market today is the PA RISC chip from HP.

The system compiler determines what instructions are executed by the CPU. When the number of types of instructions was reduced, compilers were written to take advantage of this fact and to compensate for the missing instructions.

By reducing the instruction set, RISC manufacturers have been able to increase the clock speed to many times that of CISC chips. Although this faster clock speed is beneficial in some cases, it offers little improvement in others. One effect of a faster CPU is that the surrounding components such as L2 cache and memory must also run faster, at an increase in hardware cost.

Another goal of some RISC manufacturers is to design the chip so that the majority of instructions complete within one clock cycle. Some RISC chips today can already do this. However, because some operations that can be performed by a single instruction on a CISC chip may require many instructions for a RISC chip, speed-to-speed comparisons cannot be made.

Multiprocessors   Multiprocessor systems can provide significant performance with very good value. With many multiprocessor systems, you can start out with one or two processors and add additional processors as your business needs grow. However, planning is required, since not all systems are upgradeable. For example, you can purchase a four-CPU system with one CPU and upgrade it, but not past four CPUs. Multiprocessors fall into several categories; the two main types are symmetric multiprocessor (SMP) systems and massively parallel processing (MPP) systems.

Oracle typically scales very well with additional CPUs. By adding additional CPUs, you can see significant performance improvement with very little additional cost. Some factors that determine how much improvement you will get by adding more processors are the CPU cache and memory bus bandwidth. Systems that support large numbers of users performing small independent operations, such as OLTP systems, tend to scale very well with multiple CPUs. Other systems such as data warehouses might not benefit from large numbers of CPUs.

Symmetric multiprocessor (SMP) systems usually consist of a standard computer architecture with two or more CPUs that share the system memory, I/O bus, and disks. The CPUs are called symmetric because each processor is identical to any other processor in terms of function. Because the processors share system memory, each processor looks at the same data and the same operating system. In fact, the SMP architecture is sometimes called a tightly coupled architecture because the CPUs can even share the operating system.

In a typical SMP system, only one copy of the operating system runs. Each processor works independently of the others by taking the next available process that is ready to run. Because the Oracle architecture is based on many processes, each working independently, you can see great improvement by adding additional processors.

The SMP system has several advantages: it is cost effective, high performing, and easily upgradeable. The biggest advantage of SMP systems is that they are the most common and (because of economies of scale) the most cost effective. A typical SMP system supports from four to eight CPUs. A disadvantage of an SMP system is that all CPUs typically share the system bus and memory, so adding more processors increases the likelihood that the bandwidth of the bus will become saturated.

Massively parallel processor (MPP) architecture systems are based on many independent units. Each processor in an MPP system typically has its own resources such as its own local memory and I/O system. Each processor in an MPP system runs an independent copy of the operating system and its own independent copy of Oracle. An MPP system is sometimes referred to as a loosely coupled architecture.

You can think of an MPP system as large clusters of independent units that communicate through a high-speed interconnect. As with SMP systems, as you add processors, you will eventually hit the bandwidth limitations of the interconnect. However, the number of processors with which you hit this limit is typically much larger than with SMP systems.

If you can divide the application among the nodes in the cluster, MPP systems can achieve quite high scalability. Although MPP systems can achieve much higher performance than SMP systems, they generally cost more.

Regardless of whether you use a single-processor system, an SMP system, or an MPP system, the basic architecture of the CPUs is similar. In fact, you can find the same Intel processors in both SMP and MPP systems. It is the way those processors handle memory and how CPUs are clustered together that differs between SMP and MPP systems. Included in MPP systems are computers that utilize the NUMA (Non-Uniform Memory Architecture) design. NUMA systems do not share main memory like SMP systems; instead, each processor or set of processors uses its own memory. In some ways, a NUMA system is almost like a cluster of individual systems; in other ways, it is like a big multiprocessor.

CPU and CPU Cache   As you learned earlier in this chapter, the system cache is very important to overall system performance. The job of the cache is to allow quick access to recently used instructions or data. In addition, the cache is used to perform read-aheads, much in the same way that DB_FILE_MULTIBLOCK_READ_COUNT allows Oracle to perform read-ahead operations in the database. A cache is always used to store and retrieve data faster than the next level of storage (the L1 cache is faster than the L2 cache, and the L2 cache is faster than main memory).

By caching frequently used instructions and data, you increase the likelihood of a cache hit, which can save precious clock cycles that otherwise would have been spent retrieving data from memory or disk.

A large CPU cache allows more data and executable code to be stored on the local processor than in memory, thereby reducing the number of times the CPU must access main memory. Whenever the CPU accesses memory, system performance suffers while the CPU waits for that data or code to be retrieved; if the memory bus is busy at that time, the CPU must wait for the bus to become free, lengthening the delay even more.

Random Access Memory (RAM)

The main system memory is a set of memory chips, either protected or not protected from faults, that stores data and instructions used by the system. System memory can be protected by parity or a more sophisticated, advanced ECC correction method. The system memory can theoretically range in size from 4MB on a small PC to 4GB (or more using the Intel PAE architecture) on a large 32-bit server, and up to 16TB on a 64-bit processor; however, today even the smallest PCs come with at least 256MB of RAM.

Given our discussion earlier in this chapter on how the system hardware operates, it is obvious that any operation that has to access slower components, such as a disk or a network, will slow down processing operations. Thus, it is very important to have a sufficient amount of memory in your system. This system memory is allocated to the Oracle System Global Area (SGA), and the user memory (the Program Global Area). Tune the shared pool first, as an insufficient shared pool can hurt Oracle performance more than problems with any other SGA component. Once the Shared Pool has enough memory resources, the more database buffers you can allocate to the DBMS, the better. Be careful, though, to not starve out the PGA memory that is needed by your processes, and at all costs, avoid paging. You can never have too much memory in your system. Anything that can be cached will reduce system I/O, thus improving performance.

System memory is accessed by the CPUs through a high-speed bus that allows large amounts of data and instructions to be moved from the CPU to the L2 cache very quickly. Typically, data and instructions are read from memory in large chunks and put into the cache, anticipating that the next instruction or data in that chunk is likely to be accessed next. This process is known as prefetching.

Depending on the specific implementation of an SMP system, the memory bus may be shared by all system processors. Alternatively, each processor may have a private bus to memory.

The amount of memory available to processes is limited by the physical memory in the system, or extended if you are using a virtual memory system.

Linux Memory Tuning for Oracle   Linux does not require much memory tuning for Oracle, but the little that is needed is critical. The Linux parameters that need to be set are as follows:

/proc/sys/kernel/shmall 2097152

/proc/sys/kernel/shmmni 4096

/proc/sys/kernel/shmmax <slightly larger than the SGA size>

The parameter shmmax is typically set to 2147483648 (2GB), by default.

If you need to create an SGA greater than 2GB, you must increase the value of shmmax. This parameter represents the maximum size of a single shared memory segment.

Virtual Memory System   In a virtual memory system, special memory management functions allow programs to address more memory than is physically installed in the system. This memory, known as *virtual memory,* appears to programs as a large amount of memory that can be mapped to physical memory. Data that is stored in virtual memory must be paged into physical memory for the CPU to use it, and then copied out to disk to make room in physical memory for another process. The process of paging in or paging out can be quite time-consuming and uses a lot of system resources. It bears repeating that access to disk is approximately 1,000 times slower than an access to memory. Paging should be avoided at all costs, even if it means reducing the size of the Oracle SGA.

32-bit vs. 64-bit Processors

The more powerful 64-bit processors have been available for well over a decade but have not become mainstream, because each 64-bit processor architecture was proprietary and was not supported by more than one operating system. Nonetheless, 64-bit processors offer several advantages over 32-bit processors, including the ability to address more memory and to process more information in a single clock cycle. Unfortunately, these 64-bit processors have not achieved the popularity of 32-bit processors. However, the new hybrid 64-bit / 32-bit processors are gaining popularity quickly. These processors are described in a few paragraphs.

32-bit Addressing   Various 32-bit architectures have been around for many years and are the most common architecture in production. Almost every PC uses a 32-bit processor from either Intel or AMD. The disadvantage of the 32-bit processor is that 32 bits can directly address a maximum of 4GB of RAM. In the past few years, there have been some workarounds by allowing more memory to be addressed via the Physical Address Extension (PAE).

PAE allows physical memory to be accessed above 4GB, but it does not increase the amount of virtual memory available to a process. Although it does allow for more

Linux Paging and Swapping

Linux does not require as much swap space as most Unix operating systems. In fact it is not uncommon to find Linux systems with 4GB or more memory with 1GB or less swap space. Since swap space is used only when you run out of physical memory, theoretically the more memory that you have, the less chance that you will use the swap space.

physical memory to be accessed, it is somewhat inefficient and does not provide all of the benefits of a 64-bit system. Oracle can access this memory using indirect data buffers. With indirect data buffers, a RAM disk is created that Oracle uses as an intermediate storage area. Although much faster than disk access, it is significantly slower than accessing memory directly.

64-bit Addressing   With 64-bit systems, you can access up to 16 terabytes of RAM. This can be a great advantage for larger databases. Although it is unlikely that systems will be built with 16 terabytes of RAM in the near future, systems with hundreds of gigabytes of RAM are becoming commonplace.

The 64-bit bus is twice as large as the 32-bit bus, thus allowing twice as much data to be transferred from one subsystem to another at a time. This is very useful, especially when performing 64-bit mathematical calculations.

Hybrid X86-64 Systems   Some of the newer processors such as the Opteron and Athlon-64 from AMD and the EM64T from Intel are hybrid systems, essentially 32-bit processors that are fully compatible with both x86 operating systems and 64-bit memory addressing. These systems are fast becoming very popular and are now supported by both Linux and Windows operating systems. Oracle 10*g* for both Linux and Windows is available for the x86-64 architecture in 64-bit mode.

These systems have the advantage of running either a 64-bit or 32-bit operating system. If you are running a 64-bit operating system, you have the option of running either a 64-bit or 32-bit version of Oracle. Of course, if you are running 64-bit, you can access more memory with higher performance.

Since these processors are currently shipping in large quantities from vendors such as Dell, HP, and IBM, you might actually be running a 64-bit-capable CPU and not even know it. Check with your hardware vendor. You might consider upgrading your system from 32-bit processing to 64-bit processing by just changing the operating system.

Tuning Hardware for Linux

In addition to choosing the right hardware, it is very important to properly configure and tune this hardware. Probably the most important areas of hardware tuning are in both the hardware and the filesystem.

I/O Tuning

I/O tuning is key to the performance of the Oracle database server, since the main task of Oracle is to serve up data, and moving and delivering data means I/Os. The I/O subsystem was covered in some detail in Chapter 4. Tuning the I/O subsystem is not much different from sizing it. Care should be taken to configure and tune the I/O subsystem to optimize I/O performance. The iostat command is one of the most useful for monitoring the I/O subsystem in Linux. Running this command with the –x flag shows a great deal of information about the performance of the I/O subsystem, as shown here:

```
ptc6:~ # iostat -x 10 100
Linux 2.4.21-138-default (ptc6)          06/19/04

avg-cpu:   %user    %nice    %sys    %idle
            1.77     0.00     0.68    97.55

Device:    rrqm/s wrqm/s    r/s    w/s rsec/s  wsec/s    rkB/s    wkB/s avgrq-sz
avgqu-sz   await  svctm   %util
/dev/hda      8.64   2.14   4.23   1.16  100.30   26.42    50.15    13.21    23.49
2.92  541.04  48.52    2.62
/dev/hda1     0.36   0.00   0.02   0.00    0.75    0.00     0.38     0.00    44.33
0.00   56.67  40.00    0.01
/dev/hda2     0.00   0.00   0.00   0.00    0.01    0.00     0.00     0.00     8.00
0.00   50.00  50.00    0.00
/dev/hda3     8.27   2.14   4.21   1.16   99.51   26.42    49.76    13.21    23.44
2.92  542.98  48.49    2.61
/dev/hdb      0.05   1.84   4.11   0.57   33.09   19.30    16.55     9.65    11.17
1.10  234.95  91.98    4.31
/dev/hdb1     0.00   0.00   0.00   0.00    0.00    0.00     0.00     0.00     8.00
0.00  100.00 100.00    0.00
/dev/hdb2     0.03   1.84   4.11   0.57   33.05   19.30    16.52     9.65    11.18
1.10  235.12  91.99    4.31

avg-cpu:   %user    %nice    %sys    %idle
            0.40     0.00     1.60    98.00

Device:    rrqm/s wrqm/s    r/s    w/s rsec/s  wsec/s    rkB/s    wkB/s avgrq-sz
avgqu-sz   await  svctm   %util
/dev/hda      0.00  24.40   0.00  34.50    0.00  491.20     0.00   245.60    14.24
314.54 8297.97 53.91   18.60
/dev/hda1     0.00   0.00   0.00   0.00    0.00    0.00     0.00     0.00     0.00
0.00    0.00   0.00    0.00
/dev/hda2     0.00   0.00   0.00   0.00    0.00    0.00     0.00     0.00     0.00
0.00    0.00   0.00    0.00
/dev/hda3     0.00  24.40   0.00  34.50    0.00  491.20     0.00   245.60    14.24
314.54 8297.97 53.91   18.60
/dev/hdb      0.10  63.00  77.70  22.80  623.20  686.40   311.60   343.20    13.03
38.24  380.40 94.73   95.20
/dev/hdb1     0.00   0.00   0.00   0.00    0.00    0.00     0.00     0.00     0.00
0.00    0.00   0.00    0.00
/dev/hdb2     0.10  63.00  77.70  22.80  623.20  686.40   311.60   343.20    13.03
38.24  380.40 94.73   95.20
```

By default, the iostat command outputs one line of I/O information for all devices. The command **iostat –x 10 100** outputs data 100 times at ten-second intervals, and if you are interested in only one device, you can specify the device name, as shown here:

```
ptc6:~ # iostat -x /dev/hdb 10 100
Linux 2.4.21-138-default (ptc6)          06/19/04

avg-cpu:  %user   %nice    %sys   %idle
           1.68    0.00    0.78   97.54

Device:    rrqm/s wrqm/s   r/s   w/s rsec/s  wsec/s    rkB/s    wkB/s avgrq-sz
avgqu-sz   await  svctm  %util
/dev/hdb     0.04   9.18  6.80  4.27  54.55  109.85    27.27    54.92    14.86
50.06 4221.90  80.42    8.90

avg-cpu:  %user   %nice    %sys   %idle
           3.10    0.00    3.30   93.60

Device:    rrqm/s wrqm/s   r/s   w/s rsec/s  wsec/s    rkB/s    wkB/s avgrq-sz
avgqu-sz   await  svctm  %util
/dev/hdb     0.00 235.50  0.00 68.50   0.00 2044.80     0.00  1022.40    29.85
765.52 20539.27  51.53  35.30
```

The iostat command is very useful in determining if you are experiencing an
I/O bottleneck. I/O problems are related to capacity and sizing, misconfiguration,
or tuning.

I/O and Oracle Datafile Placement   Recently, Oracle started recommending that
all data, index, and redo log files be placed across one or more large hardware LUNs
extending over many disk drives. This approach is referred to as SAME (stripe and
mirror everything or storage administration made easy, depending on which paper
you read).

Although some believe that using large hardware volumes is preferable, I still
prefer to store redo log files and data files on different physical volumes. Although
this is somewhat contrary to the Oracle-recommended method, there are several
reasons that I recommend this approach.

■ Redo log files use sequential I/O. By separating the redo log files, you can
achieve better performance on those volumes with fewer drives, as discussed
in Chapter 4. However, a logical drive (LUN) might not consist of a dedicated
disk drive.

■ In the event of a single disk failure, you would not lose both the data files and
the online redo log files if they were separated onto separate sets of drives.

■ Even though most I/O subsystems are protected against a single point of
failure such as a single disk failure, you could lose an entire RAID set due
to human error. By separating the redo log files and data files, you gain an
additional level of protection.

I feel that, for both performance and data protection, the redo logs, the undo
tablespace(s), and the data files should be separated.

Miscellaneous I/O Tuning   There are a number of tunable parameters in the I/O subsystem and the filesystem. The filesystem can be tuned via the tune2fs command and can be viewed with the dumpe2fs command, as shown here:

```
ptc6:~ # dumpe2fs /dev/hdb2 | less
dumpe2fs 1.28 (31-Aug-2002)
Filesystem volume name:    /1
Last mounted on:           <not available>
Filesystem UUID:           aa00942b-4b36-4248-bb9f-962dce0b5bab
Filesystem magic number:   0xEF53
Filesystem revision #:     1 (dynamic)
Filesystem features:       has_journal filetype needs_recovery sparse_super
Filesystem state:          clean
Errors behavior:           Continue
Filesystem OS type:        Linux
Inode count:               7225344
Block count:               14430150
Reserved block count:      721507
Free blocks:               12709195
Free inodes:               7079490
First block:               0
Block size:                4096
Fragment size:             4096
Blocks per group:          32768
Fragments per group:       32768
Inodes per group:          16384
Inode blocks per group:    512
Last mount time:           Sat Jun 19 08:38:59 2004
Last write time:           Sat Jun 19 08:38:59 2004
Mount count:               27
Maximum mount count:       -1
Last checked:              Sun Nov  2 10:13:11 2003
Check interval:            0 (<none>)
Reserved blocks uid:       0 (user root)
Reserved blocks gid:       0 (group root)
First inode:               11
Inode size:                128
Journal UUID:              <none>
Journal inode:             8
Journal device:            0x0000
First orphan inode:        0
```

Although it is interesting to see how the filesystem is configured, there is not really much to tune after it has been created. The most important filesystem tuning is done at creation time. One of the most important parameters is the block size. Since the typical Oracle database uses an 8K block size, a smaller OS block size means that the OS must perform multiple I/Os for each Oracle request. This does not mean that I/Os occur in OS block size units, only that it can perform an I/O operation up to that size. You should make the OS block size as close to the Oracle block size as possible, or larger. Unfortunately, ext2 and ext3 filesystems have a maximum of 4K block sizes. The Oracle Cluster Filesystem (OCFS) can create a 1M block size. I usually prefer a 128K block size in OCFS. When creating an ext filesystem, use 4K as the block size.

This does not mean OCFS writes only 128K at a time. The actual size of the write will be the size of the I/O that has been issued to the filesystem. This is merely a function of how space is allocated on the system, and how efficiently OCFS responds to small files as opposed to large files. IOs to OCFS are a minimum of 4K in size but can be much larger if necessary.

In addition to the filesystem parameters, the command elvtune can be used to tune the elevator sorting algorithm in Linux. Elevator sorting is used to sort I/Os such that the heads pick up requests in physical sequence, rather than bouncing back and forth. When an elevator is moving up, it will stop at floor 3 and then 4, even if 4 was pushed before 3. Running **elvtune *device*** will show you the current settings, as shown here:

```
ptc6:~ # elvtune /dev/hdb2

/dev/hdb2 elevator ID          2
        read_latency:         128
        write_latency:        512
        max_bomb_segments:    8192
```

These parameters specify an artificial latency that is designed to allow multiple I/Os to queue up in order to allow for elevator sorting. Although this is a good thing for a single disk drive, it is bad for a RAID controller or a SAN. This is because it essentially delays I/Os so that the device driver can sort them. But with a RAID controller or SAN, the hardware, not the device driver, does elevator sorting.

Tuning RAID Controllers   Sometimes it is possible to tune your RAID controller or SAN in order to achieve better performance. What can be tuned and how depend upon the type and brand of RAID controller. Typically, you can tune the following components:

- **Cache page size**   The cache page size should be at least as large as the Oracle page size. This reduces extra overhead that might be incurred by having to allocate multiple cache pages for one Oracle I/O.

- **Read and write cache sizes**   Typically, the read and write caches can be specified independently. Depending on what your application does, you might want more read cache or you might want more write cache.

- **Read and write cache usage** Most RAID and SAN systems allow you to allocate read and write caches on a per-LUN basis. Some LUNs might benefit from a read cache, others from a write cache, and some from both. Random I/Os (OLTP) don't benefit from a read cache. Heavy writes (redo, archive, etc.) benefit from a write cache.

- **Read-ahead or prefetch** In some cases, the prefetch might help Oracle performance when an application requires a significant number of table scans, such as in data warehouse environments. In an OLTP environment, when I/Os are mostly random in nature, prefetching probably won't help.

There are a number of ways that you can tune the I/O subsystem's hardware, depending on what brand and type of hardware you have. How to tune it depends on the type of application, I/O access patterns, and the number of I/Os that are occurring.

OCFS Tuning

The Oracle Cluster Filesystem (OCFS) was introduced to provide a convenient, high-performance filesystem that is clusterable. By being clusterable, OCFS allows multiple systems in a RAC cluster to access the same data files, which is key to RAC. Accessing OCFS is done via a mechanism called O_DIRECT. O_DIRECT allows direct mode access to the filesystem, bypassing the Linux I/O cache.

Because of characteristics of OCFS, you should access OCFS files only with O_DIRECT. Oracle provides a set of utilities known as the coreutils. The coreutils from Oracle replaces standard Linux utilities such as cp, dd, and mv with utilities of the same name with the addition of the O_DIRECT option. By using the O_DIRECT option (–o) with a block size option (*direct*), performance can be dramatically improved. In a recent test that I performed, dd performance

RAC I/O Access

Oracle Real Application Clusters (RAC) require shared storage that can be seen by all nodes in the cluster. Various options for this shared storage are raw partitions, ASM (Automatic Storage Management), and OCFS (Oracle Cluster Filesystem). Each has its own characteristics and is a viable option. The option you choose will depend on your needs.

was increased from 1.5 MBps to nearly 50 MBps using a 256K block size, as shown in the following table.

O_DIRECT size	Time	MB/sec	GB/hr
0	815.00	1.26	4.42
64K	24.03	42.62	149.84
128K	21.28	48.13	169.20
256K	20.58	49.75	174.91
512K	43.78	23.39	82.23
1M	44.10	23.22	81.64

These tests were performed by copying a 1GB file from disk to /dev/null, as follows:

```
time dd if=filetest | dd of=/dev/null
time dd -o_direct=256K if=filetest | dd of=/dev/null
```

This test used an EMC SAN configured using RAID 10. As you can see in the table, the performance difference is dramatic. This test was performed multiple times and is reproducible.

Tuning OCFS using the O_DIRECT flag can dramatically improve backup and restore operations as well as other file operations that are necessary as part of regular DBA duties. Don't be afraid to experiment and take advantage of O_DIRECT features.

Network Tuning on Linux

The network is very important to overall system performance. This is especially true of an Oracle RAC cluster. The performance of the interconnect can be very important to the performance of the cluster because of the amount of interconnect traffic and global buffer caching. There are a few things that can be done to improve the performance of the network.

Coreutils
The Oracle coreutils for OCFS are available at www.ocfs.org.

Choosing the Right Network

The first step in configuring your system for optimal network performance is to configure the network properly. It is important to make sure that the network is performing as specified. When configuring a network to run at gigabit speeds, it is usually necessary to configure the adapter for autonegotiation (depending on the controller). If your network switches are configured incorrectly, it is possible that the adapter will not run at the proper speed.

The Linux utility ethtool will show you how your adapter is configured. Run the command **ethtool *adapter*** in order to view the adapter settings, as shown here:

```
ptc6:~ # ethtool eth0
Settings for eth0:
    Supported ports: [ TP ]
    Supported link modes:   10baseT/Half 10baseT/Full
                            100baseT/Half 100baseT/Full
                            1000baseT/Full
    Supports auto-negotiation: Yes
    Advertised link modes:  10baseT/Half 10baseT/Full
                            100baseT/Half 100baseT/Full
                            1000baseT/Full
    Advertised auto-negotiation: Yes
    Speed: 1000Mb/s
    Duplex: Full
    Port: Twisted Pair
    PHYAD: 0
    Transceiver: internal
    Auto-negotiation: on
    Supports Wake-on: umbg
    Wake-on: g
    Link detected: yes
```

If the adapter is not running at the correct speed and duplex setting, you must determine the source of the problem and correct it in order for the adapter to run correctly.

Tuning Linux for Network Performance

It is often advantageous to tune the UDP send and receive buffers in order to achieve higher UDP performance. This is especially important if you are running in an Oracle RAC cluster. These parameters are as follows:

Parameter	Explanation
/proc/sys/net/core/rmem_default	Default receive window
/proc/sys/net/core/rmem_max	Maximum receive window
/proc/sys/net/core/wmem_default	Default send window
/proc/sys/net/core/wmem_max	Maximum send window
/proc/sys/net/ipv4/tcp_rmem	Memory reserved for TCP rcv buffers
/proc/sys/net/ipv4/tcp_wmem	Memory reserved for TCP snd buffers

In order to set these parameters, you can echo to the preceding filenames, as shown here:

```
echo 262144 > /proc/sys/net/core/rmem_default
echo 262144 > /proc/sys/net/core/rmem_max
echo 262144 > /proc/sys/net/core/wmem_default
echo 262144 > /proc/sys/net/core/wmem_max
echo "4096 65536 4194304" > /proc/sys/net/ipv4/tcp_rmem
echo "4096 65536 4194304" > /proc/sys/net/ipv4/tcp_wmem
```

Alternatively, you can set them in the /etc/sysctl.conf file, as shown here:

```
net.core.rmem_default = 262144
net.core.rmem_max = 262144
net.core.wmem_default = 262144
net.core.wmem_max = 262144
net.ipv4.tcp_rmem = 4096 65536 4194304
net.ipv4.tcp_wmem = 4096 65536 4194304
```

In addition, the following /etc/sysctl.conf network parameters can help improve the failover performance in a RAC cluster:

```
net.ipv4.tcp_keepalive_time = 3000
net.ipv4.tcp_keepalive_intvl = 30
net.ipv4.tcp_retries2 = 3
net.ipv4.tcp_syn_retries = 2
```

Configuring the network properly can improve the performance of the system greatly. As mentioned earlier, the interconnect performance is critical to the performance of an Oracle RAC cluster.

Summary

In this chapter, you have seen many different ways that the system hardware itself can be tuned via the modification of driver parameters and firmware configurations. The configuration parameters to be changed depend on the type of hardware and the way your system and application operate. What might work well for an OLTP system might not work well for a batch or decision support system. The difference between hardware tuning and sizing is that sizing is the act of choosing the right hardware for your needs, whereas hardware tuning is the act of modifying that hardware to perform optimally in your configuration.

CHAPTER
16

Tuning SQL

his chapter focuses on tuning actual SQL statements. The next section will introduce you to the Oracle explain plan, the method of visualizing the path that Oracle will take to process the data requested by the SQL statement. There are a number of ways to identify poorly performing SQL and these methods are discussed later in this chapter, starting with the section "Finding Poorly Performing SQL." This chapter will then conclude with an introduction to several useful tools supplied by Oracle to capture poorly performing SQL.

Examining the Execution Plan

The execution plan is the path that Oracle will use to process the data being requested by the SQL statement. Oracle supplies a Plan_Table that is used to store the execution plan. This plan table is used by many Oracle tools, such as TKProf, as well as the ad-hoc character-mode tool SQL*Plus.

Plan Table Review

Oracle populates the Plan_Table with the execution plan information when requested to do so. The plan table holds one explain plan per SQL statement. Listing 16-1 illustrates the Oracle version 10 release 1 plan table. The utlxplan.sql script is used to create the plan table in your schema. This script is always found in your ORACLE_HOME/rdbms/admin directory.

Listing 16-1: An Oracle 10.1 plan table

```
create table PLAN_TABLE (
        statement_id       varchar2(30),
        plan_id            number,
        timestamp          date,
        remarks            varchar2(4000),
        operation          varchar2(30),
        options            varchar2(255),
        object_node        varchar2(128),
        object_owner       varchar2(30),
        object_name        varchar2(30),
        object_alias       varchar2(65),
        object_instance    numeric,
        object_type        varchar2(30),
        optimizer          varchar2(255),
        search_columns     number,
        id                 numeric,
        parent_id          numeric,
        depth              numeric,
        position           numeric,
        cost               numeric,
        cardinality        numeric,
```

```
        bytes                numeric,
        other_tag            varchar2(255),
        partition_start      varchar2(255),
        partition_stop       varchar2(255),
        partition_id         numeric,
        other                long,
        distribution         varchar2(30),
        cpu_cost             numeric,
        io_cost              numeric,
        temp_space           numeric,
        access_predicates    varchar2(4000),
        filter_predicates    varchar2(4000),
        projection           varchar2(4000),
        time                 numeric,
        qblock_name          varchar2(30)
);
```

TIP
Make sure to use the plan table associated with your particular Oracle database. It will always have the latest supported features for that particular Oracle release level. Prior versions of the plan table will work, but you will simply miss out on the latest features.

The plan table will be populated by Oracle when directed to do so. The contents of this table will refer to one and only one SQL statement unless the STATEMENT_ID is set. Oracle 10g further separates multiple users utilizing the same plan table with the PLAN_ID column. There are some new columns in this object with Oracle 10g. Table 16-1 documents the new columns. For those readers new to the tuning environment, Table 16-2 documents all of the plan table columns.

Column	Description
plan_id	Oracle Assigned plan identifier
object_alias	Table alias that was used in the FROM clause of the SQL statement
Depth	Replaces the need to use CONNECT by PRIOR syntax...maintains the row relationship
projection	Syntax generated internally by the operation (that is, the query rewrite might have produced an additional selection predicate)
Time	Time in seconds for this step
qblock_name	Name of the query block used with DML and subqueries

TABLE 16-1.   *New PLAN_TABLE Columns in Oracle 10g*

Column	Description
statement_id	Unique identifier recognized using SQL*Plus (Figure 16-2)
plan_id	Oracle-assigned plan identifier
timestamp	Date and time of this operation
remarks	Comment field
operation	In the first row, this describes the type of operation being performed: SELECT STATEMENT, INSERT STATEMENT, UPDATE STATEMENT, DELETE STATEMENT.
Options	Internal representation of the preceding operation
object_node	Database link if object is remote, or if a parallel query (denotes order of processing)
object_owner	Schema owner for this particular object
object_name	Name of the Object involved (table or Index)
object_alias	Alias from the FROM clause of the SQL statement
object_instance	Position of the object in the original SQL statement
object_type	Useful information about the object (such as index type)
optimizer	Optimizer Mode setting
search_columns	Not currently implemented
Id	Unique ID for this explain plan row
parent_id	Contains the ID of the parent id (in other words, the explain plan step that this result set will be passed to)
Depth	Used to denote the relationships of the ID/Parent Ids
position	For the first row in the plan table, this denotes the total cost of the SQL. For the remaining rows, this works in conjunction with DEPTH.
Cost	A weighted value determined by the Cost-Based optimizer. This is discussed in detail later in this chapter.
cardinality	Estimated number of rows returned by this explain plan step
Bytes	Estimated number of bytes returned by this explain plan step
other_tag	Description of the OTHER column

TABLE 16-2. *All PLAN_TABLE Columns in Oracle 10g*

Column	Description
partition_start	Used with partitioned objects—the starting range of partitions for search
partition_stop	Used with partitioned objects—the ending range of partitions for search
partition_id	step ID that initiated the partition_start/Partition_stop
Other	Additional information about this execution step
distribution	Contains information about consumer and producer servers
cpu_cost	Estimated CPU cost factor for this execution step
io_cost	Estimated IO cost factor for this execution step
temp_space	Temp space used for this execution step
access_predicates	Contains the WHERE clause predicates used to access rows
filter_predicates	Contains the WHERE clause predicates used to limit the return of rows
projection	Syntax generated internally by the operation (in other words, the query rewrite might have produced an additional selection predicate)
Time	Time in seconds for this explain plan step
qblock_name	Name of the query block used with DML and subqueries

TABLE 16-2.   *All PLAN_TABLE Columns in Oracle 10g (continued)*

TIP
*The author recommends running the UTLXPLAN.sql
script for each user doing SQL tuning.*

The PROJECTION clause will definitely enhance the visibility of the actual selection criteria for this explain plan step. Oracle has already included the ACCESS_PREDICATES used to select rows from a result set and FILTER_PREDICATES used to limit the rows returned. A result set is an intermediate workspace that is used by each step in an explain plan. Data is returned, put into this result set, and then passed to the next level up in the explain plan. The final result set is then returned to the application's cursor area. The TIME column will be of great assistance by showing which step/steps are consuming the most time.

NOTE
The execution plan is the path that Oracle uses to process the SQL statement. The explain plan is the external representation of this execution plan. For our purposes in this chapter, the terms can be used interchangeably.

Viewing the Execution Plan

There are many ways to view the SQL execution plan. This section will cover a few of these methods using SQL*Plus. There are many third-party tools available, such as RapidSQL from Embarcadero Technologies, TOAD from Quest Software, and SQL Station from Computer Associates, that also aid in the tuning of SQL statements.

NOTE
I wrote an interface that produces the explain plans using the extra predicates discussed in the previous section. This tool I call JSTuner and is downloadable from www.DanHotka.com. I will use this tool in many of the illustrations in this chapter.

Using the autotrace feature of SQL*Plus is probably the easiest way to get an explain plan for a given SQL statement. Figure 16-1 shows the autotrace feature and the resulting execution plan.

Sometimes you are trying to tune a long-running SQL statement and all you want is to see the execution plan. This method, again using SQL*Plus, populates the PLAN_TABLE, and then you can use SQL to see your execution plan steps. There are many SQL scripts available to view the contents of the PLAN_TABLE; one such script is included in Figure 16-2. This method uses the STATEMENT_ID. You will also have to delete the rows from the PLAN_TABLE after viewing the execution plan. autotrace performed this cleanup for you but this is a more manual method.

Notice the very first line in Figure 16-2. This line causes the PLAN_TABLE to be populated with the execution plan for the SQL that follows it. The SHOW_PLAN.sql script takes the STATEMENT_ID as input and formats the execution plan. Listing 16-2 illustrates the SHOW_PLAN.sql script.

TIP
This script and the explain plan syntax could easily be incorporated into the same script for ease of use. The SHOW_PLAN.sql script can be downloaded from www.DanHotka.com.

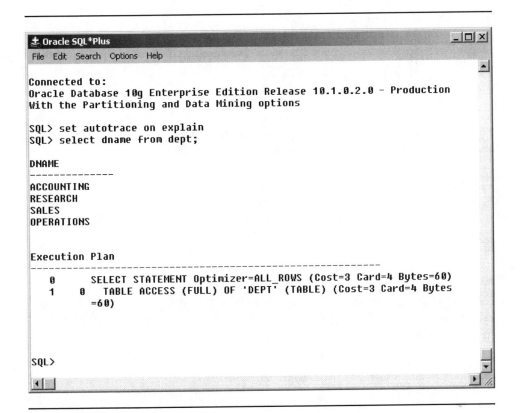

FIGURE 16-1.   *SQL*Plus using autotrace*

Listing 16-2: The show_plan.sql SQL script used to format the contents of the PLAN_TABLE

```
1:  set pagesize 20
2:  set linesize 80
3:  column id format 999 heading 'ID'
4:  column parent_id format 999 heading 'P_ID'
5:  column cost format 999 heading 'Cost'
6:  column rows format 9,999,999 heading 'Rows'
7:  column access_plan format a30 heading 'Access|Plan'
8:  column access_path format a15 heading 'Access|Path'
9:  column object_name format a15 heading 'Object|Name'
10: select cost, time, cardinality rows, time, id, parent_id,
lpad (' ', 2 * level) || operation Access_Plan,
options Access_Path, object_name
```

```
11: from plan_table
12: where statement_id = '&1'
13: connect by prior id = parent_id
14: start with id = 0;
15: delete from plan_table where statement_id = '&1';
```

Listing 16-2 uses standard SQL*Plus formatting commands (lines 1 through 9) to make the appearance of the output more attractive. The actual SQL is at lines 10 through 14, which accesses the rows in the PLAN_TABLE. Line 15 cleans up the PLAN_TABLE in preparation for its next use.

TIP
A SPOOL <file name> command could easily be inserted after line 9, and a SPOOL OFF after line 14, to capture this formatted execution plan in a text file.

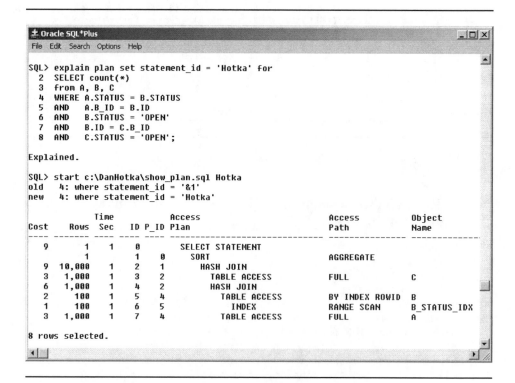

FIGURE 16-2. *The execution plan without running the SQL statement*

Understanding the Explain Plan

Review one of the explain plans shown (Figures 16-2 or 16-3). Oracle processes the most-indented items first. Each step of the explain plan illustrates how Oracle will process the rows or functions (such as a sort) on behalf of the SQL code, and each step of the explain plan has a result set that gets passed to the ID that relates to the Parent_ID of the particular step. The show_plan.sql table in Listing 16-2 allows the user to see the relationships from one step to another. If there is more than one table in the FROM clause, then there will be join conditions that will be processed first. Oracle will process two tables at a time, creating a result set and then bringing in each additional table from the FROM clause (creating new result sets that are passed to the next step) until all the tables have been processed.

The explain plan in Figure 16-3 has eight lines in it (ID 0 through 7). Notice the first line indicates the type of SQL statement being processed. Notice the indentation

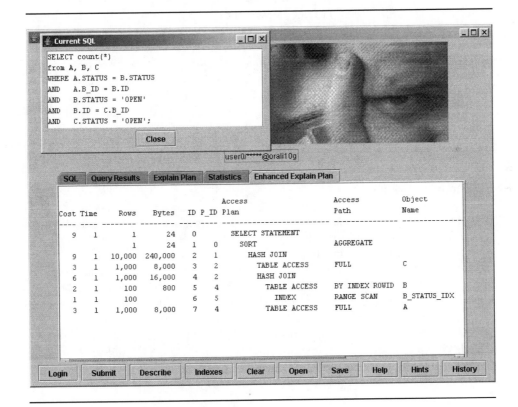

FIGURE 16-3. *The freeware Explain Plan tool*

and the relationship between the ID and the Parent ID columns. Step 4 is a hash-join. Both steps 5 and 7 pass their results to step 4. Step 5 works with an index (step 6). The hash-join will create an intermediate output that will be passed to step 2. Notice that step 3 also sends its output to step 2. This table (table C) will be joined with the intermediate result set from step 4 and then passed to step 1 where Oracle will complete the request of the SQL. In this case, it is the aggregate function count. Other aggregate functions include min, max, avg, and so forth.

NOTE
Oracle 10g still supports the Rule-Based Optimizer,
but just for backward compatibility.

The explain plan contains verbiage that indicates how the SQL is being processed. The first line is always the type of SQL that is being processed: SELECT Statement, INSERT Statement, UPDATE Statement, or DELETE Statement. Oracle 10g uses the Cost-Based Optimizer (CBO) to decide which explain plan step to even consider. The CBO considers thousands of explain plans and selects the one with the total lowest cost. Event dump 10053 will show all of the explain plans considered. These dumps are discussed later in this chapter under the TKProf tool topic. The cost column on the first line of the explain plan is the total cost. This cost figure constitutes an estimation of the amount of Disk IO/CPU time/computer load and arrives at this "cost" figure for each line of the explain plan. Some of these cost figures come from statistics collected on the various database objects using DBMS_STATS or by letting Oracle 10g derive its own object statistics using dynamic sampling.

If the explain plan is lengthy, sometimes just using the indentation is not enough. The show_plan.sql script (Listing 16-2) and JSTuner (see Figure 16-3) shows the ID and Parent_ID columns.

If there is more than one table in the FROM clause, you will see terms like Nested Loop, Merge Join, and Hash Join as the tables are being processed. Table 16-3 contains the basic description of these terms. Nested Loop processes the second table (inner table), once for each row returned in the first table (outer table). Merge Join sorts both tables involved and merges the rows based on the lookup criteria. Hash Join creates a work area in the user's program global area (controlled by HASH_SIZE) and creates a key for lookup based on an arithmetic function. This allows Oracle to "read" the table once and then look up its values based on this arithmetic function.

When there are two or more tables in the FROM clause, Oracle creates a result set, which is an internal temporary table (if this result set gets over 64K in size, it is written out/worked with from the assigned temporary tablespace). Each inner step of an explain plan creates a result set that is passed to the parent ID explain plan step.

HASH JOIN	Tables are processed (possibly with filter conditions) and put into a memory structure accessed by a key produced by a mathematical calculation (known as a HASH key).
MERGE JOIN	Oracle sorts the two result sets (possibly with filter conditions) being joined over the join columns and then merges the results via the join columns.
NESTED LOOPS	One row is retrieved from the outer or driving table (table listed first in the explain plan) and then joined to all matching rows in the inner or looping table referenced second in the NESTED LOOP.

TABLE 16-3.   *Explain Plan Join Conditions*

Oracle will tend to use nested loops when the optimization mode is set to FIRST_ROWS, during an equality condition, and when the optimizer senses that the driving table is not necessarily very large. Merge-join conditions are considered when there is an inequality condition present (<, <=, >, or >=) and the source rows are already sorted. The CBO will tend to use hash joins when it sees tables that are small in size. Hash joins can also only be used in equality conditions.

TIP
When using nested loops or merge joins, make sure the data types being equated are of the same type.

Table 16-4 lists some of the commoner items found in the explain plan. Table Access Full is a full table scan. A Table Access by ROWID is always followed by an indented line indicating the index being used to provide the ROWIDs. An index access not associated with a table occurs when the index contains all the information being requested by the SQL, and Oracle recognizes that it doesn't have to access the table at all.

NOTE
This is by no means a complete list of explain plan features. Consult the Oracle Performance Tuning Guide *for all of the explain plan options/ descriptions.*

FILTER	FILTERs indicate that rows are checked against a condition to see if they should be included in the result set.
TABLE ACCESS FULL	Table being accessed from beginning to end, not using an Index
TABLE ACCESS BY INDEX ROWID	Table is working with an index; this index will be on the next indented line.
HAVING	SQL statement contains a HAVING statement.
INDEX (UNIQUE)	SQL statement utilized a unique index to search for a specific value.
INDEX (RANGE SCAN)	SQL statement contains a nonequality or BETWEEN condition.
INLIST ITERATOR	SQL statement contains an IN clause.
BITMAP INDEX	Single value lookup
BITMAP RANGE SCAN	Scans the index based on a range of values
BITMAP FULL SCAN	Processes all leaf blocks in the index
COUNT	Operation that counts the rows in the result set
SORT AGGREGATE	Sort operation associated with a GROUP BY function
SORT JOIN	Sort operation associated with a MERGE-JOIN condition
SORT ORDER BY	Sort operation initiated by a ORDER BY clause

TABLE 16-4. *Explain Plan Descriptions*

Understanding the Optimizer Decision Process

The CBO makes its decisions based on collected object statistics and machine load. These object statistics include histograms, block count, row counts, fragmentation, and so on. Statistics on indexes include the clustering factor (the relationship of how many different data blocks each leaf block points to), the granularity of the key, type of index, and so on. If no statistics exist, then Oracle 10g will do dynamic sampling to get an educated guess on each of the involved objects. If dynamic sampling is disabled, then Oracle 10*g* reverts back to the assumptions it used in prior versions of Oracle.

The first thing the CBO looks for is how many tables are in the FROM clause. If there is more than one table, then the CBO starts looking to see the best way to join these tables together. It first looks to see if one or more of the involved tables' result set would contain only one row. The CBO can easily tell this if the selection criteria involves a unique or primary-key index. The CBO will then start with this table (called the driving table) and work on processing all the other tables from there. The ORDERED hint overrides this selection process by telling the CBO to process the tables in the order they appear in the from clause.

In the event of any tie condition (in the preceding example: two tables have primary key selection), the CBO uses the object with the newer object_id.

If the SQL contains an outer join (using the + syntax) or contains a subquery, then this table is not considered for the driving table.

The CBO then generates a series of execution plans using the different join methods and access paths previously discussed. The CBO, based on statistics, estimates the IO cost of each plan step. The CBO then factors into the cost various other collected statistics such as machine load, buffer cache hit ratio, disk IO load, sort area size, multiblock read-ahead, and so on. Then the CBO simply chooses the one with the lowest overall cost. All of these considered execution plans can be visualized using the Oracle trace 10053. Running these traces is discussed in the "Using the Oracle Trace Facility" section later in this chapter. The cost of both the hash join and merge joins is calculated from the amount of IO required to read the objects into memory. The merge join also considers the amount of sorting (if any) that will be required. Oracle 10*g* will return the rows to the execution plan based on an index that is in the correct order. Nested loop costs are based on reading the individual rows from the outer table times the number of expected IOs from the inner table.

A full table scan retrieves all the rows and checks them for the selection criteria. The tables blocks are read up to the block marked as the high-water mark (the last block to receive inserts).

Index scans show up as full scan or fast full scan and the index is named as the object. Oracle processes just the leaf level of the index in this instance. The full scan proceeds one leaf block at a time, while the fastfull scan reads the leaf blocks using multiblock read-ahead (controlled by startup parameter DB_FILE_MULTIBLOCK_READ_COUNT).

Index scans are always related to a table access unless the index key columns satisfy the SQL request for data.

Full table scans can be selected based on a number of criteria. The simple solution is the lack of an index on any of the table's selection criteria. If the CBO determines, based on the selection criteria, that most of the rows need to be examined, then the CBO will cost out an execution plan for consideration using a full table scan. Other criteria include if the table is small in that it has less total blocks than the multiblock read-ahead value, and thus the index has a poor clustering factor (the clustering factor is closer to the number of rows in the table than the number of blocks in the table). The FULL(<table name>) hint will also initiate a full table scan.

Index scans are considered if the index columns match up with selection criteria, sort criteria, and group by criteria. Fast full scans are used on sort and group by criteria. You might see full scans when the selection criteria includes an indexed column with a > , >= , or between syntax.

A Working Example

Tuning SQL statements is more of an art than rocket science. The first thing to look for is the number of rows being returned by each step of the explain plan. The more rows that can be eliminated earlier in the execution plan process, the less rows that will be written/stored/processed by the intermediate result sets that are passed up the ID chain of processing. The CBO exposes the rows, along with the bytes, and next includes the time in seconds taken by each step of the explain plan. It is now easier to see where Oracle is spending its time or efforts when processing a particular SQL statement.

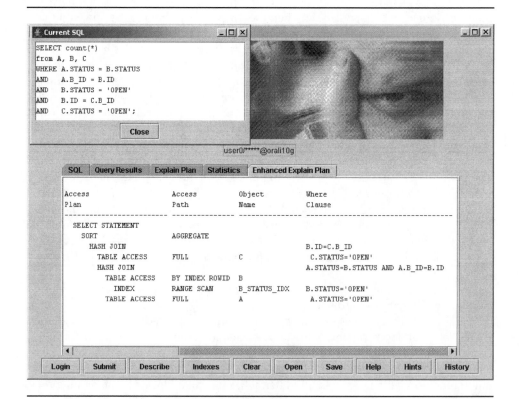

FIGURE 16-4. *JSTuner displaying WHERE clause predicates*

Reviewing the SQL in Figure 16-2, notice ID steps 5 and 6 are working with 100 rows and the hash join at step 4 brings in 1000 rows from step 7. After processing table C at step 3, this SQL has arrived at 10,000 rows at step 2! Normally, this would indicate a SQL statement that sorely needed some attention in that it started with a low number of rows and brought in a larger number of them later in the processing. Desirable explain plans have larger numbers of rows in the earlier steps, and as rows are eliminated, smaller result sets are passed up the execution plan.

Figure 16-4 illustrates the significance of seeing the WHERE clause statements as they relate to the explain plan steps. It is important to see the selection criteria when reviewing an explain plan like this one so the user can see exactly what is causing so many rows to be selected and make either coding adjustments, adding/changing indexing structures, or even adding hints. The real problem with this particular SQL statement is that all of the selection columns contain the same data. This is why the CBO chose to do full table scans even when there were indexes available.

Figure 16-5 shows the CBO making decisions based on more realistic data, while Figure 16-6 displays the WHERE clause predicates that go with each explain plan

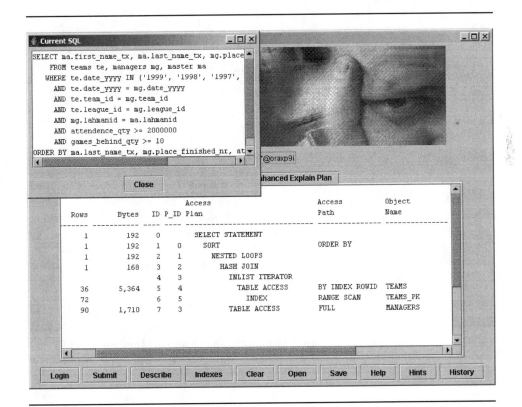

FIGURE 16-5. *A larger database example*

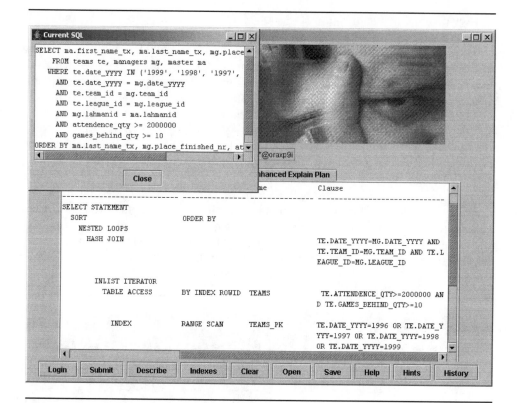

FIGURE 16-6. *A larger database example with WHERE clause predicates*

step. There are several interesting Access Paths in this explain plan. Notice the CBO starts with the IN-List. Reviewing Figure 16-6, you can see that this comes from the Index access at ID step 6 where the CBO has picked the first line of the WHERE clause. Notice in ID step 5 that the rows being returned to the table are then processed using the attendance_qty and games_behind_qty (these columns don't have an index). The CBO picked the Teams table to drive off of because it felt, based on statistics, that it could eliminate most of the rows that will need to be processed with this selection criteria. Notice that the INLIST at step 4 returns its result set to step 3 (a hash join), as does step 7. After this step, the explain plan is quickly down to 160 rows. If there were room in the display to show everything, the Time column would also support the IO effort seen here in that most of the time was spent on processing the INLIST at step 4.

Controlling the Optimizer Decisions

Hints are syntax that can be added to SELECT, UPDATE, and DELETE statements to direct the CBO to make different decisions. A hint is a directive, and in most cases the CBO will arrive at explain plans using the hint(s). More than one hint can be applied. If two or more hints conflict with one another (for instance, one hint says to use one index on a table and the next hint says to use a different index on the same object, then one would conflict with the other), Oracle will take the last hint in the conflict and ignore the others. (Oracle still parses backwards, so the first hint it comes to is the last one in the list.) The CBO also ignores any hint with a syntax error. Oracle does not complain, but the explain plan will simply not reflect the desired hint.

NOTE
If you still have applications using PL/SQL v1 (Forms 3.0, Forms 4.5, Reports 2.5), hints will be ignored.

Table 16-5 illustrates some of the commoner hints. Hints fall into a number of categories. Optimization goal hints can change the optimizer behavior. Choose the Oracle8 and Oracle9 default optimization behavior. This tells Oracle that if there are any statistics on any of the objects, use the Cost-Based Optimizer; otherwise, use the Rule-Based Optimizer. First-rows optimization tends to look for primary/unique key situations where it can try to pick explain plans that will process the SQL in the least amount of time.

Hints	Description
Optimization Goal Hints	
/*+ ALL_ROWS */	Instructs CBO to search for overall best response time
/*+ FIRST_ROWS(<number>) */	Instructs CBO to search for best initial row response time
/*+RULE */	Instructs Oracle to use the Rule-Based Optimizer
/*+ CHOOSE */	Instructs Oracle to pick an optimizer based on the existence of object statistics

TABLE 16-5. *Short Summary of Oracle 10g SQL Hints*

Hints	Description
Join Hints	
/*+ USE_HASH(<table name>) */	Instructs CBO to use a hash join
/*+ USE_MERGE(<table name>) */	Instructs CBO to use a merge join
/*+ USE_NL(<table name>) */	Instructs CBO to use a nested loop join
Access Path Hints	
/*+ FULL(<table name>) */	Full table scan
/*+ HASH(<table name>) */	Instructs CBO to make a hash table in memory
/*+ INDEX(<table name> <index name>) */	Instructs CBO to use a particular index
/*+ INDEX_ASC(<table name> <index name>) */	Instructs CBO to use a particular index for an ascending search, perhaps a sort or group by
/*+ INDEX_COMBINE(<table name> <index name>) */	Instructs CBO to combine two or more indexes; very useful with bitmap indexes
/*+ INDEX_FFS(<table name> <index name>) */	Instructs CBO to do a fastfull scan on an index
/*+ INDEX_JOIN(<table name> <index name>) */	Same as INDEX_COMBINE
/*+ LEADING(<table name>) */	Instructs CBO to start join considerations with this table and allows CBO to pick the other tables based on statistics
/*+ ORDERED */	Instructs CBO to join the tables in the FROM clause based on this order and not based on statistics.
/*+AND_EQUAL(emp index1, index2, …)*/	Oracle will only use up to five indexes per table in an explain plan. This hint allows the user to determine which indexes to consider
Misc Hints	
/*+ CACHE(<table name>) */	Instructs CBO to read the whole table into the buffer cache
/*+ NOCACHE(<table name>) */	Instructs CBO to NOT read the whole table into the buffer cache

TABLE 16-5. *Short Summary of Oracle 10g SQL Hints* (continued)

All-rows tries to optimize the SQL (usually long-running SQL) for the best overall performance. Oracle 10g's default optimization mode is First-rows.

Other categories include join orders (forcing the CBO to use a nested loop, merge join, or hash join), access goals (most of the index hints fall into this category), and some specialty goals such as query rewrite, parallel, and so on.

NOTE
See the SQL Reference Guide for a complete list of all Hints.

Figure 16-7 illustrates using hints. Notice the '/*+FULL(B) */' syntax in the smaller window. This hint was added to the example that created Figure 16-5. Notice in this explain plan that the hint was indeed used and that the cost figure of that explain plan line increased as did the overall cost of the execution plan (9 to 10). The CBO really does make pretty good decisions.

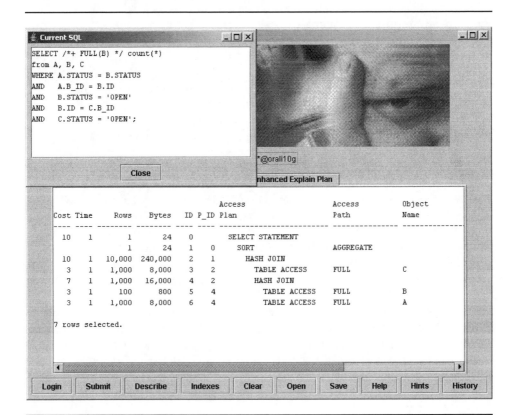

FIGURE 16-7. *Hint example*

TIP
I have found the ORDERED and the INDEX_JOIN /INDEX_COMBINE hints to be the most useful. Usually when the CBO did not choose to use an index, it was for a particular reason (such as the clustering factor, and so on).

TIP
If the FROM clause is using table aliases, make sure to use the table alias in the HINT instead of the table name.

SQL Tuning Tips

There are some things from a coding point-of-view that can be done to help the CBO make better decisions or to use an index where it otherwise might not work. Other things would be to code in such a way as to make for a shorter execution plan and therefore fewer trips to the database.

Oracle will not use an index on a column if that column has a function of any kind on it. For example, …WHERE SUBSTR(ename,1,5) = 'SMITH' would not use an available index on the ename column, but a coding style like this would: …WHERE ename LIKE 'SMITH%'. This coding style works well when the leading columns are being searched. The LIKE function will use the index if it starts off with a string and not one of its global characters. Oracle8*i* introduced function-based indexes, which allow for index usage for these situations when there is no easy workaround and performance is an issue on columns with functions.

Make sure both sides of the WHERE clause have the same data type. Oracle will only compare items with like data types. When parsing the SQL statement, if Oracle notices that two columns being compared do not have the same data type, it will add a TO_CHAR or TO_NUMBER function to one side of the other. This internal addition will not be visible but will be a function on an indexed column (in this example, assume the columns are indexed), and Oracle simply will not use the available index on the column where the function was added. If you must compare unlike data types, control where Oracle does the conversion by adding the proper function yourself to the WHERE clause.

Calculations in the WHERE clause will also cause Oracle to not use an available index. Where-clause code such as …WHERE SAL * 1.1 > 1000 should be written as WHERE SAL > 1000/1.1, moving the calculation away from the indexed column.

Do not concatenate indexed columns together in the WHERE clause for comparison to a string such as WHERE deptno || manager = '201346'. Always have each indexed column on its own line in the WHERE clause like: WHERE deptno = 20 AND manager = 1346.

Try to avoid using NOT when referencing indexed columns. For example, 'NOT <' is the same as '>=', 'NOT <=' is the same as '>', 'NOT >' is the same as '<=', and 'NOT >=' is the same as '<'.

Using the IN clause is more efficient than multiple WHERE statements interrogating the same column for multiple values. Use EXISTS in the WHERE clause versus DISTINCT in the SELECT clause (DISTINCT is applied after all rows are returned; WHERE clause predicates limit the number of rows returned).

When using the GROUP BY clause, limit the rows with a WHERE clause line versus using a HAVING clause. The WHERE clause will limit the rows coming back, while the HAVING clause will be applied after all rows are returned.

Finding Poorly Performing SQL

There are several methods for finding poorly performing SQL. Oracle supplies several tools that are useful, such as Enterprise Manager's TOP (which lists the top SQL that matches the selected criteria, such as IO, time, and so on), the Oracle Trace Facility (a.k.a., trace files and TKProf/Trace Analyzer), and Statspack (statistic and SQL text collections). There are many scripts written by numerous experts/DBAs/IT staff to drill into Oracle's dynamic performance views (a.k.a., the V$ tables) to identify specific performance issues.

Using Scripts

The SQL that Oracle runs is easily accessed from a couple of locations. Listing 16-3 illustrates the V_$SQLAREA view. This view shows the SQL and a significant amount of information about the particular SQL statement. SQL can easily be written to view SQL statements that match a variety of conditions. Information from this view can also be combined with other V$ information to find specific SQL causing specific issues.

Listing 16-3: Listing of V_$SQLAREA

```
dhotkaun:ORALI10g:SYSTEM>desc v_$sqlarea
 Name                                      Null?    Type
 ----------------------------------------- -------- --------------
 SQL_TEXT                                           VARCHAR2(1000)
 SQL_ID                                             VARCHAR2(13)
 SHARABLE_MEM                                       NUMBER
 PERSISTENT_MEM                                     NUMBER
 RUNTIME_MEM                                        NUMBER
 SORTS                                              NUMBER
 VERSION_COUNT                                      NUMBER
 LOADED_VERSIONS                                    NUMBER
 OPEN_VERSIONS                                      NUMBER
 USERS_OPENING                                      NUMBER
 FETCHES                                            NUMBER
```

EXECUTIONS	NUMBER
END_OF_FETCH_COUNT	NUMBER
USERS_EXECUTING	NUMBER
LOADS	NUMBER
FIRST_LOAD_TIME	VARCHAR2(19)
INVALIDATIONS	NUMBER
PARSE_CALLS	NUMBER
DISK_READS	NUMBER
DIRECT_WRITES	NUMBER
BUFFER_GETS	NUMBER
APPLICATION_WAIT_TIME	NUMBER
CONCURRENCY_WAIT_TIME	NUMBER
CLUSTER_WAIT_TIME	NUMBER
USER_IO_WAIT_TIME	NUMBER
PLSQL_EXEC_TIME	NUMBER
JAVA_EXEC_TIME	NUMBER
ROWS_PROCESSED	NUMBER
COMMAND_TYPE	NUMBER
OPTIMIZER_MODE	VARCHAR2(25)
PARSING_USER_ID	NUMBER
PARSING_SCHEMA_ID	NUMBER
KEPT_VERSIONS	NUMBER
ADDRESS	RAW(4)
HASH_VALUE	NUMBER
OLD_HASH_VALUE	NUMBER
MODULE	VARCHAR2(64)
MODULE_HASH	NUMBER
ACTION	VARCHAR2(64)
ACTION_HASH	NUMBER
SERIALIZABLE_ABORTS	NUMBER
CPU_TIME	NUMBER
ELAPSED_TIME	NUMBER
IS_OBSOLETE	VARCHAR2(1)
CHILD_LATCH	NUMBER
PROGRAM_ID	NUMBER

The key columns to look up the SQL text of any SQL statement are ADDRESS and HASH_VALUE. Use both of these fields to uniquely identify the exact SQL required.

Scripts in Listings 16-6 and 16-7 return both the ADDRESS and HASH_VALUE for SQL causing the particular issues being identified. These scripts can easily be modified to include the actual SQL text. Listings 16-4 and 16-5 are two additional V$ tables that display the SQL text. Listing 16-4 shows the columns available in V_$SQLTEXT and Figure 16-8 shows the columns available in V_$SQLTEXT_WITH_NEWLINES. This V$ table formats the SQL much nicer for display on character-mode displays or in reports. Both V_$SQLAREA and V_$SQLTEXT have the SQL statement in one contiguous string.

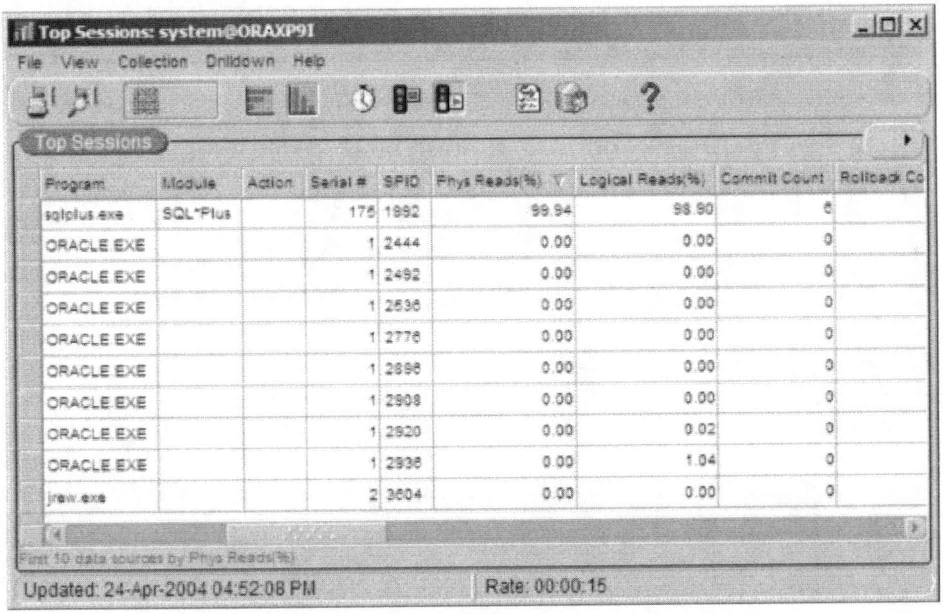

FIGURE 16-8. *Oracle Enterprise Manager's Top Sessions window*

Review the V_$SQLAREA columns and notice the variety of types of SQL that can be accessed when looking for problem SQL.

Listing 16-4: Listing of V_$SQLTEXT

```
dhotkaun:ORALI10g:SYSTEM>desc v_$sqltext
 Name                                      Null?    Type
 ----------------------------------------- -------- ------------
 ADDRESS                                             RAW(4)
 HASH_VALUE                                          NUMBER
 SQL_ID                                              VARCHAR2(13)
 COMMAND_TYPE                                        NUMBER
 PIECE                                               NUMBER
 SQL_TEXT                                            VARCHAR2(64)
```

Listing 16-5: Listing of V_$SQLTEXT_WITH_NEWLINES

```
dhotkaun:ORALI10g:SYSTEM>desc v_$sqltext_with_newlines
 Name                                      Null?    Type
 ----------------------------------------- -------- ------------
 ADDRESS                                             RAW(4)
 HASH_VALUE                                          NUMBER
```

```
SQL_ID                                      VARCHAR2(13)
COMMAND_TYPE                                 NUMBER
PIECE                                        NUMBER
SQL_TEXT
```

Listing 16-6: Script to find long-running SQL statements

```
/**********************************************************************
 * File:      Long_Running_SQL.sql
 * Type:      SQL*Plus script
 * Author:    Dan Hotka (www.DanHotka.com)
 * Date:      July 9, 2003
 *
 * Description:
 *     This script lists the SQL statements associated with IO Activity
 *
 *
 * Modifications:
 **********************************************************************/
select a.event, a.sid, d.name, b.segment_name, c.sql_address,
c.sql_hash_value from v$session_wait a, dba_extents b, v$session c,
v$datafile d
where a.event in ('buffer busy waits','db file sequential read','db file
scattered read')
and b.file_id = a.p1
and a.p2 between b.block_id and b.block_id + b.blocks + 1
and a.sid = c.sid
and a.p1 = d.file#;
```

The script in Listing 16-6 is useful to find long-running SQL. It primarily drives off of the V$SESSION_WAIT view and looks both for events that are waiting for the buffer cache to load (indicative of SQL accessing lots of data blocks) and sequential reads (full table scans). This script identifies the tables being accessed via available information. The SQL statement can then be easily looked up using the HASH_VALUE and ADDRESS available from this script.

Listing 16-7: Script to find problem SQL

```
/**********************************************************************
 * File:      waiting.sql
 * Type:      SQL*Plus script
 * Author:    Dan Hotka (www.DanHotka.com)
 * Date:      Feb 21, 2003
 *
 * Description:
 *     This script lists top wait events
 *
 *
 * Modifications:
```

```
*******************************************************************/
select w.event, w.p1 "File", w.p2 "Blocks", w.p3 "Total Blocks", wait_time,
e.segment_name, s.sql_address, s.sql_hash_value
from v$session_wait w, dba_extents e, v$session s
where w.event in ('db file sequential read','db file scattered read','buffer
busy waits','write complete waits')
and e.file_id = w.p1
and w.p2 between e.block_id and e.block_id + e.blocks -1
and w.sid = s.sid;
```

The script in Listing 16-7 is useful to identify SQL, causing important wait events such as full table scans, which frequently fills the buffer cache and causes lots of writes. This type of SQL prompts a lot of IO activity and might be a good place to start when looking for SQL that's causing overall performance issues.

Listing 16-8: Script to find hot tablespaces

```
/*****************************************************************
 * File:      tablespace_file_IO.sql
 * Type:      SQL*Plus script
 * Author:    Dan Hotka (www.DanHotka.com)
 * Date:      Feb 21, 2003
 *
 * Description:
 *     This script lists the hot database files and their associated
tablespaces.
 *
 *
 * Modifications:
 *****************************************************************/
select t.name, d.name,PHYRDS, PHYWRTS, PHYBLKRD, PHYBLKWRT
from v$tablespace t,v$datafile d, v$filestat s
where d.file# = s.file#
and t.ts# = d.ts#
order by 1,2;
```

Sometimes the problem is not the SQL statements, but maybe some contention on Oracle resources. The script in Listing 16-8 displays the Oracle tablespaces and their files that have the most IO activity. This kind of problem is caused because too many tables or indexes that are being accessed frequently are on the same particular datafile or tablespace.

Using Top Sessions

Oracle Enterprise Manager includes Top Sessions, which is found on the diagnostic pack. Top Sessions is useful in easily unearthing problem SQL found in the V_$SQL_AREA. Figure 16-8 shows the processes and the IO, timings, and other information associated with these sessions. Click the heading and Top Sessions will reorder the data based on the column that was clicked. This tool makes it very easy to find problem SQL currently running.

Figure 16-9 shows the actual SQL causing the activity illustrated in Figure 16-8. This information is easily accessed by clicking the Drilldowns button on the menu bar. Other options are available but the one illustrated here is Current SQL.

Using Statspack

Sometimes it is difficult to capture the problem SQL while the application is running, or perhaps the problem SQL only shows up occasionally and might be hard to visualize using either the previously discussed scripts or Enterprise Manager Top Sessions. The last two tools will identify a variety of issues as well as the problem SQL. Statspack is useful in collecting statistics that help determine when problems are occurring. Sometimes this facility can even capture the problem SQL. The Oracle Trace Facility collects all of the SQL for a session, process, or does so globally across the database.

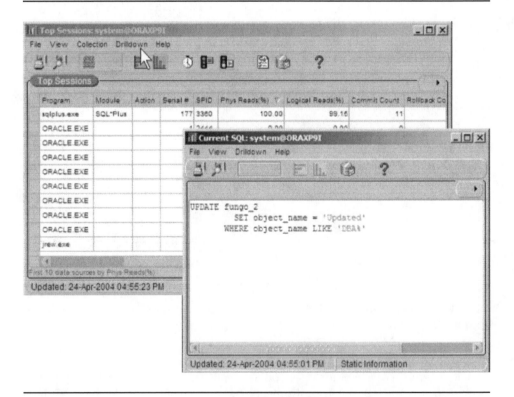

FIGURE 16-9. *Oracle Enterprise Manager's Current SQL Drilldown*

Statspack is easy to set up and utilize. Consult the Oracle documentation for installation procedures.

Statspack collects periodic statistics (called snapshots) and can compare these snapshots and report on the differences. Listing 16-9 shows a sample report from Statspack. The variety of information available will help uncover when a problem is occurring.

Listing 16-9: Statspack report example (partial listing)

```
Snap Id         Snap Time       Sessions
                               ------- ------------------ --------
      Begin Snap:               45   29-Apr-04  10:01:47      8
        End Snap:               46   29-Jul-03  11:01:35      8
        Elapsed:                     60.00 (mins)


     Cache Sizes
     ~~~~~~~~~~~
     db_block_buffers:      2400        log_buffer:   1024
     db_block_size:         8192   shared_pool_size:  10000000


     Load Profile
     ~~~~~~~~~~~~
                               Per Second      Per Transaction
                               --------------   ---------------
                 Redo size:       220.85              835.11
             Logical reads:       447.82             1487.67
             Block changes:        14.24                7.76
            Physical reads:     1,677.88              885.45
           Physical writes:       362.00               18.00
                User calls:        18.00               23.51
                    Parses:           19                  19
               Hard parses:         7.28                7.28
                     Sorts:        1,025              223.33
                    Logons:          002                 002
                  Executes:          223                 223
              Transactions:            1                   1

Instance Efficiency Percentages (Target 100%)
     ~~~~~~~~~~~~~~~~~~~~~~~~~~~~~~~~~~~~~~~~~~~~~~~
                 Buffer Nowait %:   99.99        Redo NoWait %: 99.97
                 Buffer  Hit   %:   99.99     In-memory Sort %: 100.00


     Top 5 Wait Events
     Wait                                   Total
     Event                                  Waits  Time (cs)  Wt  Time
     ------------------------------------   ------------ ------------ -------
     buffer busy waits                      27,845     3,454    60.70
     db file sequential read                 1,753     4,225    24.00
     db file scattered read                  1,145     1,890    16.00
     SQL*Net                                   459       976     2.59
     Enqueue                                     3         9     2.21
```

Statspack can be run as frequently as required. Most shops using Statspack collect the statistics once an hour, while problematic systems might collect statistics every minute or every five minutes. Statspack includes utilities to purge old/stale/obsolete collections. The STATSPACK.SNAP procedure is executed from the command line or from a schedule to perform the periodic collections. Statspack has three levels of collections: Level 0 is general performance, Level 5 is Level 0 with the associated SQL statements, and Level 10 is both Levels 0 and 5 with additional child-level statistics. The default collection type is Level 5. RPT_LAST.sql is used to produce the output report. By default, this script will compare the last two collections. It can be used to compare any two collections.

Using the Oracle Trace Facility

Oracle has had the ability to collect SQL via a trace function for quite a while. This ability enables the user to capture all the SQL associated with a session/application/ or multiple applications. The trace can be set according to when the problem is occurring, just prior to when the problem is being re-created, or before a test. Collecting SQL statements gives the user/developer the ability to capture all the SQL in the order that it was processed by Oracle.

There are many kinds of traces. This section will focus on the 10046 (pronounced ten-forty-six) trace. For example, the 10053 trace will show all of the Cost-Based Optimizer's execution plans considered. Other traces allow the user to capture all SQL performing sorts, and so on.

The 10046 trace is an application SQL capturing trace. It is easy to set to on, and there are a few ways to trip this trace on and off.

Method 1 uses the syntax: ALTER SYSTEM SET SQL_TRACE = TRUE to create a 10046 trace to capture ALL SQL being processed by Oracle. This makes an extremely large trace file, so the SQL you are looking for will be difficult to find. The ALTER SESSION SET SQL_TRACE = TRUE will capture all of the SQL for this particular session. When the application is done processing, issue the ALTER SESSION SET SQL_TRACE = FALSE to stop tracing and close the trace file.

NOTE
If your system is limited on disk space, you might want to use this syntax to limit the size of the resulting trace file: ALTER SESSION SET MAX_ DUMP_FILE_SIZE=<size in bytes>.

Method 2 allows you to trace another session. The information required for this trace can be found by querying the V$SESSION view. Trip this trace on with the DBMS_SYSTEM.set_sql_trace_in_session(<sid>, <serial#>, true) statement and off with the DBMS_SUPPORT.stop_trace_in_session(<sid>, <serial#>) statement.

Method 3 gives you a bit more control over the content of the trace file. The syntax in Listing 16-10 trips the trace on. Notice the Level syntax. These levels allow you to collect additional information with each SQL statement in the trace file. Table 16-6 describes the various level meanings.

Listing 16-10: Method 3 setting Oracle trace to on/off

```
Alter session set timed_statistics=true;
Alter session set max_dump_file_size = unlimited;
Alter session set tracefile_identifier='Hotka';
Alter session set events '10046 trace name context forever, level 12';
Select 'Hello World!' from dual;
Alter session set events '10046 trace name context off'
```

TIP
I like to set the tracefile_identifier syntax since it makes your trace file easier to find in the Oracle Dump Dest location. The tracefile_identifier syntax works with any of the preceding methods for turning trace on. This identifier can be up to 60 characters long.

NOTE
The location of these trace files is the user dump destination. This location is easily found using this query: SELECT value FROM v$parameter WHERE name = 'user_dump_dest'.

TKProf is a character-mode application used to interpret the trace file into a readable format. Figure 16-10 shows all of the options available with TKProf. The

Level	Description
0	no statistics
1	Trace file with parse, execute, and fetch statistics
4	Trace file with option 1 with the SQL bind variable contents
8	Trace file with option 1 with the Oracle Wait Event information
12	Trace file with options 1, 4, and 8

TABLE 16-6.   *Trace Level Descriptions*

```
 user0@dhotkaun:/home/oracle/product/10.1.0/rdbms/log         _ □ x
[user0@dhotkaun log]$ tkprof
Usage: tkprof tracefile outputfile [explain= ] [table= ]
                [print= ] [insert= ] [sys= ] [sort= ]
  table=schema.tablename   Use 'schema.tablename' with 'explain=' option.
  explain=user/password    Connect to ORACLE and issue EXPLAIN PLAN.
  print=integer     List only the first 'integer' SQL statements.
  aggregate=yes|no
  insert=filename   List SQL statements and data inside INSERT statements.
  sys=no            TKPROF does not list SQL statements run as user SYS.
  record=filename   Record non-recursive statements found in the trace file.
  waits=yes|no      Record summary for any wait events found in the trace file.
  sort=option       Set of zero or more of the following sort options:
    prscnt  number of times parse was called
    prscpu  cpu time parsing
    prsela  elapsed time parsing
    prsdsk  number of disk reads during parse
    prsqry  number of buffers for consistent read during parse
    prscu   number of buffers for current read during parse
    prsmis  number of misses in library cache during parse
    execnt  number of execute was called
    execpu  cpu time spent executing
    exeela  elapsed time executing
    exedsk  number of disk reads during execute
    exeqry  number of buffers for consistent read during execute
```

FIGURE 16-10.   *TKProf command-line options*

important feature is the 'sort=' option. This will sort the output into the order you desire. The sequence of the output can be sorted by about any of the output numbers (see Listing 16-11 for an example of the output). The 'print=' option will limit the output to many SQL statements. SYS=no designates that the system-generated SQL should not be displayed.

Listing 16-11: TKProf trace file output

```
TKPROF: Release 10.1.0.2.0 - Production on Sun Apr 25 11:37:14 2004

Copyright (c) 1982, 2004, Oracle.  All rights reserved.

Trace file: orali10g_ora_20655_Hotka.trc
Sort options: fchela
********************************************************************************
count   = number of times OCI procedure was executed
cpu     = cpu time in seconds executing
elapsed = elapsed time in seconds executing
```

```
disk    = number of physical reads of buffers from disk
query   = number of buffers gotten for consistent read
current = number of buffers gotten in current mode (usually for update)
rows    = number of rows processed by the fetch or execute call
**************************************************************************
```

```
SELECT count(*)
from B, C, A
WHERE A.STATUS = B.STATUS
AND   A.B_ID = B.ID
AND   B.STATUS = 'OPEN'
AND   B.ID = C.B_ID
AND   C.STATUS = 'OPEN'
```

call	count	cpu	elapsed	disk	query	current	rows
Parse	1	0.07	0.09	2	148	0	0
Execute	1	0.00	0.00	0	0	0	0
Fetch	2	0.03	0.14	14	16	0	1
total	4	0.10	0.23	16	164	0	1

```
Misses in library cache during parse: 1
Optimizer mode: ALL_ROWS
Parsing user id: 58
```

```
Rows      Row Source Operation
-------   ----------------------------------------------------
      1   SORT AGGREGATE (cr=16 pr=14 pw=0 time=142823 us)
  10000    HASH JOIN  (cr=16 pr=14 pw=0 time=173224 us)
   1000     TABLE ACCESS FULL A (cr=7 pr=6 pw=0 time=67065 us)
   1000     HASH JOIN  (cr=9 pr=8 pw=0 time=64218 us)
    100      TABLE ACCESS BY INDEX ROWID B (cr=2 pr=2 pw=0 time=49407 us)

    100       INDEX RANGE SCAN B_STATUS_IDX (cr=1 pr=1 pw=0 time=32783 us)
              (object id 49477)
   1000      TABLE ACCESS FULL C (cr=7 pr=6 pw=0 time=5299 us)
```

```
Elapsed times include waiting on following events:
```

Event waited on	Times Waited	Max. Wait	Total Waited
SQL*Net message to client	2	0.00	0.00
db file sequential read	4	0.03	0.06
db file scattered read	2	0.00	0.00
SQL*Net message from client	2	17.32	17.32

```
.
. (other SQL removed for space purposes
.
```

```
*************************************************************************
Trace file: orali10g_ora_20655_Hotka.trc
Trace file compatibility: 10.01.00
Sort options: fchela
      1  session in tracefile.
      8  user  SQL statements in trace file.
     47  internal SQL statements in trace file.
     55  SQL statements in trace file.
     22  unique SQL statements in trace file.
   1161  lines in trace file.
elapsed seconds in trace file.
```

Figure 16-11 shows TKProf in action. Notice that the 'pwd' command shows the dump destination on this Oracle 10g instance. Also note the trace file name. The TRACEFILE_IDENTIFIER was set to 'Hotka', which makes this trace file easier to identify.

The trace file output (output from TKProf) displays all of the options at the top of the file. Listing 16-11 illustrates part of the trace file output. At the beginning is all of the information about the instance of Oracle, the name of the trace file, and any

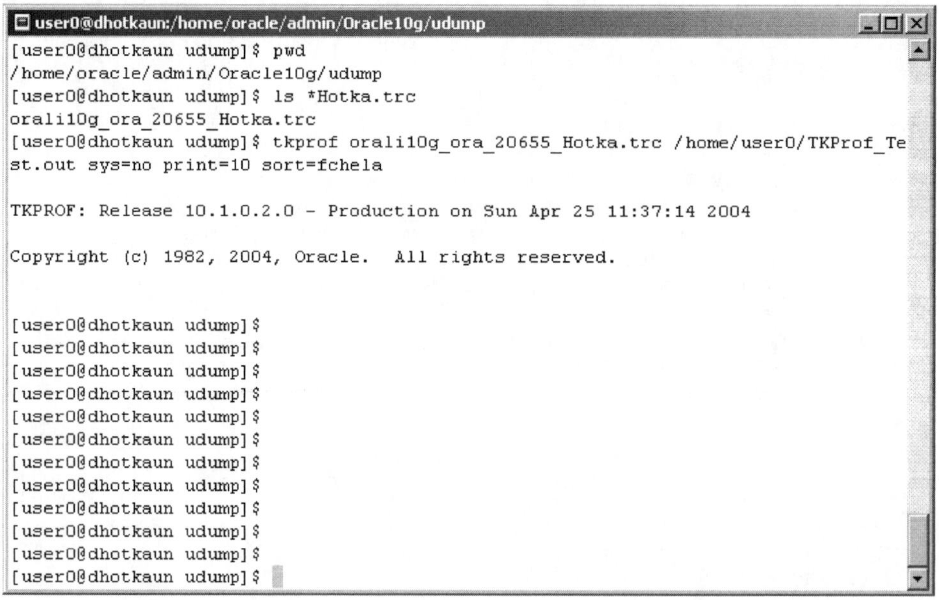

FIGURE 16-11.   *TKProf in action*

options used to process the trace file. Notice the first SQL statement. The block of numbers after the SQL statement are the items that TKProf can sort by. Some additional information is displayed (optimizer mode and so on) and then the execution plan. Notice that the time appears with each step of the explain plan down to a hundredth of a second. Since this trace was a Level-12 trace, the Oracle wait information appears. If this SQL statement had bind variables, these too would have appeared here.

Listing 16-11 is condensed for space purposes. At the end of the trace output file is extra information about the trace, like its name and the information within the trace file that was interpreted.

Summary

This chapter introduced the reader to SQL statement tuning. Execution plans or explain plans are used to visualize exactly how Oracle 10g interpreted the SQL and how it will retrieve the data for the SQL. This chapter also discussed how to interpret these plans, and how to control them using both hints and coding techniques. The chapter then concluded with several different methods for finding problem SQL.

CHAPTER
17

Indexes and
Partitioning

his chapter focuses on a couple of important tuning topics: indexing and partitioning. Indexes store key values and row IDs (physical row addresses); in most cases, they can greatly decrease the response time of SQL. Partitioning is a way of subdividing larger objects into smaller pieces. Applications can use partitioning to easily delete data and load it while not affecting other users. These smaller pieces are easier to manage (backup and recovery) and, when used with the proper knowledge, can have considerable performance benefits.

Introduction to Oracle 10g Indexing Options

Oracle 10g supports both B*Tree index structures and bitmap index structures. The table object has a pseudo-column called ROWID. A *pseudo-column* is a column you can specifically select but that is not physically part of the structure. ROWID is one such column in that this is the location of this physical row in the database. ROWNUM is another such column. ROWNUM is the number of the row in the output cursor. An index stores this ROWID and associates it with one or more columns from the table object. These columns are referred to as *key fields* in the index. Multiple-column index keys are called *composite* keys. Indexes allow for greatly increased access time, particularly for tables that occupy more than just a few database blocks. In fact, tables can have multiple indexes.

Oracle uses B*Tree, or balanced tree, structures to store the index information. Even bitmap indexes use the B*Tree structure. This structure resembles an upside-down tree in that there are multiple branch levels (blocks with partial keys that point to either the next branch block or the leaf block), and at the bottom or last level are the leaf blocks. These leaf blocks actually contain the index key values and their associated ROWIDs. Indexes are maintained in key value sequence always. If a leaf block fills, it splits and half of the leaf rows are moved to a new block; the new row is then inserted into the proper sequence location. Pointers are adjusted so that the new leaf block will be accessed in the key value sequence.

Figure 17-1 shows what an index might look like on EMPNO in the EMP table. In most cases, Oracle processes the index from the top down. The top branch has a partial key value and indicates where to find the next branch block that is associated with this key. The next branch block will also have a partial key (but with more of the value) and will either point again to another branch block or to a leaf block. Leaf blocks actually store the entire key value and the ROWID of the table data that also has the key value.

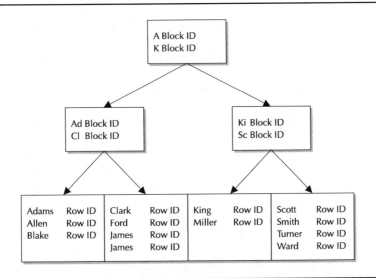

FIGURE 17-1. *A simple b-tree index structure*

TIP
Oracle 10g supports multiple block sizes at the tablespace level. The larger the block size, the more key values/ROWIDs you can store per physical read. This means faster index processing for larger objects.

NOTE
ROWID is made up of four parts that uniquely identify a row and its location within Oracle. The four parts are object ID, file number, block number, and row number. This number is stored in base64 character format. The DBMS_ROWID package is useful to interpret parts of this ROWID field back to meaningful numbers.

When Oracle uses an index for a single-row lookup (an equal condition), it will start at the top branch and navigate through the branch blocks to the leaf block with that key value. In the case of repeating key values, the branch block always points to the left-most leaf block where the key value is found, since Oracle always reads the leaf blocks from left to right. When Oracle is doing a range scan (initiated by a >, between, or group by clause), it traverses down through the branch levels until it reaches the left-most, or low-end, key value of the range; then it reads leaf block to leaf block until the condition is satisfied. Oracle can do this because each leaf block always points to the next leaf block in the proper sequence.

Oracle can also do a full scan of just the index. It will always use just the index when the index key values satisfy the SQL requirements. A full scan of the index reads just at the leaf level and traverses the whole index. Oracle sometimes does this instead of doing a sort. A fast full scan of the index does the same thing as the full scan, except it utilizes the multiblock read-ahead features of Oracle. The INDEX_FFS hint also tells Oracle to consider doing a fast full scan.

NOTE
Fast full scans require one of the key fields in the index to have the NOT NULL constraint.

Oracle 10*g* Index Options

There are four major index types in Oracle 10*g*: nonunique b-tree, unique b-tree, bitmap, and function-based indexes. Some options exist with each of these types of indexes, such as reverse-key storage, key compression, index-organized tables, and partitioned indexes (discussed in the section "Oracle 10*g* Partitioning" later in this chapter).

Nonunique indexes allow for multiple occurrences of the key value. Such an index can also have multiple keys, or concatenated keys, per index. An example of nonunique index syntax is shown next:

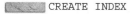
```
CREATE INDEX    SCOTT.EMPIDX_Deptno ON SCOTT.EMP(DEPTNO)
```

This type of index stores the first unique value of the key value and the ROWID, so that each subsequent leaf row does not need to store the key value. This allows for more leaf rows per block, which aids range scans because Oracle doesn't have to do as many I/O operations to satisfy the needs of the range.

Unique indexes store the key value and ROWID for each leaf row. This aids Oracle in single-row lookups. An example unique-key index is shown next:

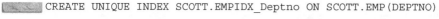
```
CREATE UNIQUE INDEX SCOTT.EMPIDX_Deptno ON SCOTT.EMP(DEPTNO)
```

When the primary-key constraint is used, Oracle will create one of these types of indexes.

NOTE
Don't create a unique index on any primary key constraints, since Oracle will create one for you.

The reverse option on indexes is useful for primary key indexes or indexes where only single-row lookups will be performed. Reverse-key indexes allow Oracle to maintain a better-balanced index structure and also eliminate the contention of inserts into single-leaf blocks. Reverse key says to take a key that looks like 1345, 1346, 1347, or the like, and store the key as 5431, 6431, and 7431. In the case of the b-tree structure, each of these keys would probably be assigned to a different leaf block. Because the key values are no longer back-to-back in the index structure, Oracle will not, and cannot, range-scan on an index with this clause defined. For example, applications that use a sequence generator for the primary key value will have all the users doing inserts into the same leaf block, and Oracle will only allow one insert at a time. Notice Figure 17-2. This example shows an example primary-key index structure with all inserts going into the right-most block. Figure 17-3 illustrates the reverse-key concept, showing that the keys are now evenly divided across the leaf-level structure. This kind of index is much more friendly to multiple users using the application and also creates a better-balanced index structure.

Function-based indexes are useful for those instances where you simply cannot get around a function in the WHERE clause and an index would definitely improve query performance. The SQL statement SELECT * FROM EMP WHERE SUM(SAL) = (sub query...); would definitely benefit from an index created with a syntax like this: CREATE INDEX SCOTT.EMPIDX_Deptno ON SCOTT.EMP (deptno, sum(sal)).

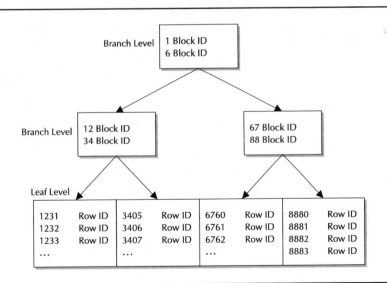

FIGURE 17-2. *A primary-key index*

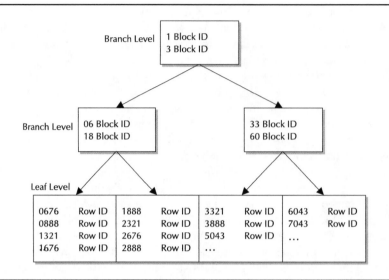

FIGURE 17-3. *A primary-key index showing a reverse clause*

Bitmap indexes are useful for low-cardinality-type column data. This index type stores the key value, the beginning ROWID, and the ending ROWID as part of the key value. The bitmap is stored in the location where the ROWID would appear in the leaf level of the nonunique index structure. The bitmap is a string of 1's and 0's that indicate the presence of the indexed value that is positional with a range of beginning and ending ROWIDs stored as part of the key. A string like '0010001000...' says that the first and second ROWIDs do not contain the value, whereas the third ROWID in the string of ROWIDs does.

Bitmap indexes are very efficient due to their compact nature. Too many values in the indexed column, however, will make this type of index inefficient. Likewise, Oracle 10g will not be able to use its row-level locking mechanism when performing updates. Instead, it will try to look at the block level (depending on the values of the ROWIDs themselves) and will typically request an exclusive lock on the table when performing updates on a column with a bitmap index. Updates also cause the bitmap index to grow exponentially, leading to fragmentation of the bitmap index. When this happens, the bitmap index is a candidate for rebuilding.

TIP
Drop bitmap indexes when performing large batch inserts or large batch updates. Bitmap indexes can be created quickly, so it is more efficient to simply drop them and re-create them.

NOTE
Bitmap indexes are useful for read-only type applications where there are just a few different column values across a larger structure.

Bitmap join indexes help with common join conditions found in the application SQL. This index type tracks the common columns in the table being indexed to those in the join condition. The syntax is

```
CREATE BITMAP INDEX EMP_HIREDATE_BJI on EMP (HIREDATE) FROM EMP E,
DEPT D WHERE E.DEPTNO = D.DEPTNO
```

This illustrates how this feature is implemented. In this syntax example, the index is on the EMP table and tracks the join condition in the DEPT table based on the DEPTNO column and will be used when the HIREDATE column and the DEPTNO column are referenced in the SQL WHERE clause. For example, the SQL in Listing 17-1 would use this bitmap join index.

Listing 17-1: Example SQL that would use bitmap index illustrated

```
SELECT SUM(INV_SALE_AMT)
FROM ST_INV I, ST_VENDOR V
WHERE I.INV_PURCHASE_VENDOR_ID = V.VENDOR_ID
AND V.VENDOR_STATE = 'IA';
```

NOTE
The join conditions using bitmap join indexes must have the unique or primary key constraints. If using a bitmap join composite key, all values must be in the SQL join condition.

Multiple-key indexes can benefit from key compression if there are a lot of repeating values in the concatenated index key. The COMPRESS option stores the unique index values once per leaf block. The COMPRESS option only compresses the total number of key columns minus one. Oracle will not compress all of the columns, as it needs some key data to associate with the ROWID. The COMPRESS option has an optional number that will tell Oracle how many key columns to compress on. Just specifying COMPRESS tells Oracle to compress all but the last key column in the index. This syntax example,

```
CREATE INDEX empidx ON emp (deptno,job,sal) COMPRESS 2;
```

compresses the deptno and job key values per leaf block.

NOTE
A multiple-key index is also known as a composite index. Its multiple keys are, as a unit, known as the composite key.

TIP
The commoner the first key values are, the better the compression on the whole key you will get. The more compression, the more index/ROWID pointers there will be per leaf block. The more index/ROWID pointers in a leaf block, the faster Oracle can process the index on a range scan, full scan, or fast full scan.

Multiple-key indexes can also benefit from skip scanning. *Skip* scanning is the ability for Oracle to use a multiple-key index when the leading column of the index is not referenced in the SQL. The second or third key column might be referenced in a WHERE clause. How this works is that Oracle can tell at the branch level if there is a possibility that the key value appears in any of the leaf blocks. This technique allows Oracle to make use of a multiple-key index so that it doesn't have to have another index structure on that desired field. After all, fewer indexes improve performance in DML operations.

TIP
Order the keys just the opposite as you would to maximize compression. The more selective column should appear first in the multiple-key index, and the column desired for skip scanning should be second or even third in order in a multiple-key index.

Index-organized tables (IOTs) are also a b-tree structure, but such an index is both the table and the index, since there is no underlying table. This structure stores all of the table's columns in the index leaf blocks. Listing 17-2 illustrates the basic syntax for an IOT. Notice that the syntax is very similar to that of a table except for the keywords ORGANIZATION INDEX. The PCTTHRESHOLD ... USING clause indicates which fields to leave in the index structure and which will go to the overflow tablespace. The PCTTHRESHOLD says if the row is this percentage of the block, put most of it in the overflow tablespace. The USING clause tells Oracle which columns, up to and including this column, to leave in the leaf block. The overflow tablespace is accessed via OBJECT_ID.

Listing 17-2: An IOT example syntax

```
CREATE TABLE emp_iot
  (empno      number,
   ename      varchar2(20),
   salary     number(9,2) Not Null,
   comm       number,
   CONSTRAINT pk_emp_iot_index PRIMARY KEY (empno))
   ORGANIZATION INDEX
TABLESPACE users
OVERFLOW TABLESPACE users_overflow
PCTHRESHOLD 20 INCLUDING ename;
```

NOTE
There is a distinct performance advantage when Oracle does not need to access the table, because all of the needed data items are in the index. IOTs came to be because all the required data items had to be stored in the b-tree index structure. Under such circumstances, why even have a table to maintain?

The advantage of an IOT is not having to store the data items twice if the table object doesn't need to ever be referenced. Remember that Oracle will not go to the underlying table if the index satisfies the SQL statement's request for data.

The objective with an IOT is to get as many rows into the index structure as possible. The more rows in the leaf blocks, the faster Oracle will be able to process the IOT structure on range scans.

IOTs are completely transparent to the application and are useful for reference tables or tables with a low number of columns. They can also be partitioned.

TIP
I have used IOTs to reference long or blob columns, putting the key values in the index and letting the long datatype column go to the overflow tablespace.

The overflow tablespace holds the less-frequently-accessed columns or, perhaps, holds a long column that the index key values make reference to. The USING clause in the IOT syntax is useful to tell Oracle which columns will be frequently accessed or used for access, and which columns are only needed when requested. For example, put the WHERE clause columns in the leaf block and put the SELECT columns in the overflow tablespace. The exception to this rule is an amount field that might have a sum function applied. This would fall into the frequently required field and should be in the leaf block as well.

IOTs can have b-tree indexes on their non–primary key columns. An index does not have a ROWID, since rows can be relocated/moved within the index structure (indexes maintain sequence). Oracle uses a universal ROWID that is a logical ROWID. This UROWID is based on the primary key of the IOT and will not change unless the primary key value changes. The UROWID is visualized using the ROWID pseudo-column. This UROWID allows for indexes on other columns in the IOT. These additional indexes are called secondary indexes.

> **NOTE**
> *IOTs do not support bitmap indexes as secondary indexes.*

Index Monitoring

Oracle 10g can easily monitor to see whether an index is being used or not. There are a lot of reasons why Oracle will not use an index, even if it appears obvious that it should. Indexes that are never used simply slow the insert/update/delete processes on the table.

The syntax to initiate monitoring is

```
ALTER INDEX <index name> MONITORING USAGE
```

The following illustration shows the V$OBJECT_USAGE view, where you can see the results of the monitoring. Use this syntax to stop the monitoring:

```
ALTER INDEX <index name> NOMONITORING USAGE
```

```
SQD> desc V$OBJECT_USAGE

Name                                 Null?     Type

----------------------------------- -------- -------------

INDEX_NAME                           NOT NULL VARCHAR2(30)

CABLE_NAME                           NOT NULL VARCHAR2(30)

MONITORING                                    VARCHAR2(3)

USED                                          VARCHAR2(3)

START_MONITORING                              VARCHAR2(19)

END_MONITORING                                VARCHAR2(19)
```

NOTE
Do remember that every object associated with a table is subject to Oracle's recovery mechanism. Redo information is recorded for each index as well as the table when performing inserts/updates/deletes whether the index is ever used or not. The fewer indexes, the faster the DML occurs.

Index Space Utilization

Oracle uses the PCTFREE storage clause parameter to leave room behind in the index for growth. Oracle ignores the PCTUSED storage clause parameter, since it has no meaning to an index. PCTFREE tells Oracle how much to fill the data blocks on inserts before continuing to the next block. The idea is to have the index leaf blocks as full as possible without having an additional update/insert cause the index leaf block to split into two half-full blocks. This split would cause additional I/O operations when Oracle uses the index for range-scan operations.

NOTE
An update operation to an index is a delete and an insert. Remember that the index always maintains the proper sequence for the key values.

TIP
You can see how full the leaf blocks are, the average keys per block, and the rows per block by analyzing the table and viewing the columns in USER_INDEXES, DBA_INDEXES, or ALL_INDEXES.

Setting the PCTFREE parameter depends on how the index is being loaded. For example, using a sequence generator for a primary-key field with little chance of doing any additional inserts other than using the sequence generator, set PCTFREE very high so that the blocks fill, since there is little chance that any additional inserts will occur (an application issue) and cause leaf-block splits. If these splits occur, it is not probable that these blocks will ever fill. If the index is using the REVERSE clause, set the PCTFREE at, say, 40, depending on how the key values relate to one another.

Indexing Tips

ALTER INDEX REBUILD <parallel> UNRECOVERABLE is much faster than CREATE INDEX because the index rebuild command uses multiblock read-ahead and allows for parallel and unrecoverable features to be utilized. CREATE INDEX uses a full table scan when creating the index.

This technique also works for primary-key constraints. Use CREATE UNIQUE INDEX ... UNUSEABLE, then Alter INDEX REBUILD <parallel> UNRECOVERABLE, and then ALTER TABLE ADD CONSTRAINT ... PRIMARY KEY (key column) USING INDEX. Not only does this method build the index very quickly, but it also allows you to name the primary key index.

NOTE
UNRECOVERABLE turns off the Oracle redo journaling that would normally occur. Not incurring this overhead greatly speeds up the index creation process.

Unique indexes perform better on single-row lookups, since they store a key value and the ROWID together.

Nonunique indexes perform better on range scans, as ROWIDs are stored with each common key value. The commoner the keys, the more ROWIDs that are stored in each leaf block, and the better the range scans perform (for instance, less I/O).

Reverse-key indexes perform better on inserts, especially when the key value is always ascending (for example, when used with a sequence generator), since the locking contention is spread out evenly across the leaf-level structure. These indexes can be used only for single-row lookups, though.

Function-based indexes are useful when it is necessary to include a function in the WHERE clause and where an index would definitely improve performance.

Bitmap indexes are useful when indexing just a few column values in a table with a large number of rows. Use INDEX_COMBINE or INDEX_JOIN hints when the SQL will access two or more bitmap indexes.

Index columns frequently appear in WHERE clauses (which are part of a join between tables) and in foreign keys accessed by primary keys in other tables.

Avoid indexing columns that are frequently updated and only have a few values across a larger table.

Multiple-key (composite) indexes can increase performance, especially if the composite key satisfies the requesting SQL's need for data. Oracle will not read the table if it doesn't have to.

Composite key selection should be based on the frequency that the key columns appear in WHERE clauses. If one of the key values appears more frequently in WHERE clauses than others, then consider making it the leading key field. If the data in a column in the table is in a particular order, and if this column is also frequently used in WHERE clauses, consider putting this column as the leading key in the composite key (see the following section).

Composite key selection, meanwhile, should be on WHERE clauses using the AND operator.

If it is more advantageous to do a full table scan than to access the index, use the FULL or NO_INDEX hints.

The Index Clustering Factor

The index clustering factor is the relationship between the rows in each index leaf-level block and how many different table data blocks they make reference to. The cost-based optimizer (CBO) makes decisions on execution plans based on this relationship. If the clustering factor is high, the CBO will probably choose to do a full scan on the table rather than incur the additional I/O of using the index.

If the table is in a particular order in a column and there is an index on that same column, then the clustering factor would be low, since there would be many key values in the index pointing to the same table data block. Conversely, if the table was in sequence by a primary key value and there was an index on birthdate, for example, this index would probably have quite a poor clustering factor, since each birth-date key value would point to a row in a different data block. If Oracle were to range-scan across the index looking for all the employees with a particular birth date, Oracle might have to read each block in the underlying table several times, versus just doing a full scan on the table to begin with.

NOTE
A good clustering factor is when the clustering factor is close to the number of data blocks in the table. A poor clustering factor is when the clustering factor is close to the number of rows in the table.

TIP
The best range-scan performance is to have the table sorted and loaded in the sequence of a major query used by the application and have an index or multikey index but with the leading key column being the column that the table is in sequence by. Data design plays a key role in application performance.

If the clustering factor is not good, Oracle will only use the index for single-row lookups. If the application or SQL accessing the table by this index only does range scans, then Oracle will never use the index. Listing 17-3 shows the Index_Info.sql script that highlights key index information, including the clustering factor. Listing 17-4 shows some sample output from this script. Notice that both tables have 6000 rows and 101 blocks. Both also have the same key values and data values. The first difference to note is the number of key values per leaf block. TABLE1 has 1 key value per leaf block, while TABLE2 has 11 key values per leaf block. The real indicator here is that TABLE1's clustering factor is very close to the number of blocks in the table, compared to TABLE2's clustering factor, which is closer to the number of rows in the block. See the preceding Tip for more information on this, but the likelihood of Oracle 10g using the index on TABLE2 is remote at best. Oracle 10g would incur significant amounts of I/O to use this index versus just doing a full table scan.

Listing 17-3: The Index_Info.sql script

```
/**********************************************************************

 * File:     Index_Info.sql

 * Type:     SQL*Plus script

 * Author:   Jonathan Lewis (www.jlcomp.demon.co.uk)
 *               Enhanced by Dan Hotka

 * Date:     May 9, 2003

 *

 * Description:

 *     This script lists statistics about indexes.

 *

 *

 * Modifications: 10-22-03 Added Table Block and Row info
 *

 **********************************************************************/
column table_name format a15 heading 'Table'
column index_name format a15 heading 'Index'
column num_rows format 999,999 heading 'Rows'
column num_blocks format 999,999 heading 'Data Blocks'
column avg_data_blocks_per_key format 999,999 heading 'Data Blks per Key'
column avg_leaf_blocks_per_key format 999,999 heading 'Leaf Blks per Key'
column clustering_factor format 999,999 heading 'Clust Factor'

SELECT i.table_name, i.index_name, t.num_rows, t.blocks,
i.avg_data_blocks_per_key,
i.avg_leaf_blocks_per_key,i.clustering_factor,
to_char(o.created,'MM/DD/YYYY HH24:MI:SSSSS') Created
from user_indexes i, user_objects o, user_tables t
where i.index_name = o.object_name
  and i.table_name = t.table_name
order by 1;
/
```

Listing 17-4: Output from the Index_Info.sql script

Table	Index	Rows	BLOCKS	Data Blks/Key	Leaf Blks/Key	Clust Factor
TABLE1	TABLE1_IDX	6,000	101	1	1	132
TABLE2	TABLE2_IDX	6,000	101	11	1	2,222

Oracle 10*g* Partitioning

Partitioning is a way of dividing large amounts of data across multiple disk devices by a key value. The cost-based optimizer recognizes a partitioned object (tables and/or indexes) and can select the required data from just the correct partitions (known as *partition pruning*) rather than searching the entire object. There are a couple of reasons for doing this: SQL performance and ease of maintenance.

Partitions can greatly aid in the maintenance of larger objects. Partitioning subdivides data across tablespaces. These tablespaces are the regular Oracle 10*g* type of tablespaces in that they can be backed up while available, restored without affecting the other partitions, loaded without affecting the other partitions, dropped, added, and so on.

SQL performance can be enhanced by considering how the data is partitioned and whether the SQL is specifically asking for a subset of the data that follows the partitioning boundaries.

The particular criteria used to partition data can have a dramatic effect on the performance of SQL used to query the data. Well-designed partitioning schemes can improve the performance of queries against subsets of the data many times over.

This section will cover the syntax and performance implications of Oracle 10*g* partitioning.

Oracle 10*g* Partitioning Features

Oracle 10*g* offers four major kinds of partitioning. Each option has particular features and some limitations, and each type utilizes a key value known as the *partition key*. Indexes can be partitioned on the value of the partition key, or on a different value in the table, and can use the same partitioning parameters or different partitioning parameters.

There are two main reasons to consider partitioning: performance and maintenance. Performance can be enhanced by splitting the data and index structures across multiple physical devices. This allows for multiple processes to be using different parts of the objects without any contention with other processes. Smaller objects scan more quickly, and partitioning also allows for objects to be nicely split across hardware devices according to a key value. This is a way of "striping" or putting different parts of the object on various devices. Performance is enhanced only if the applications and partitioning structures are planned carefully. Oracle's optimizers can see what a SQL statement is going to request, and can also see the way that partitioning has been implemented. The application has no control over how a hardware device would do its striping. Other methods of data striping include using smaller database files assigned to a tablespace. Again, the application has little control over which datafile will contain the desired data.

Maintenance times can also be improved using partitioning. It is very easy to add and drop partitions, as well as back up and recover single partitions. Data that can be periodically purged can easily be both removed or re-added using partitioning if the need arises. Backup and recovery can happen more quickly because the objects themselves are smaller when partitioned (that is, each partition is like its own object, where the object itself becomes a logical entity, while the partition level is the actual object itself).

Range partitioning is where each partition is loaded with data that meets a certain range of numeric or date values. Hash partitioning evenly distributes the numeric or date partition key values across the available partitions on the basis of a hash value computed on the partition key. Composite partitioning is a combination of range and hash partitioning: the data are partitioned based on a range of values and are then assigned to subpartitions on the basis of a hash value. This feature gives Oracle the ability to store and access only parts of the data by the partitioning key, but the data can subsequently be evenly distributed across a series of subpartitions. List partitioning allows for the partitioning of character data.

NOTE
Oracle 10g supports the use of multiple block sizes for different tablespaces. The tablespaces of a partitioned object (table or index) must all have the same block size per object. However, the table and index can use different block sizes.

Range Partitioning

Range partitioning distributes rows across the assigned tablespaces according to one or more columns in the table that become the partition key. Listing 17-5 shows an example of range partitioning syntax. Notice the PARTITION BY RANGE clause. This defines the partition key. Each partition is then named specifying the LESS THAN value, which dictates the data that will be stored in this partition.

TIP
Each partition can be accessed by its partition name (in place of the table name in the SQL statement). This would give the application the ability to function on other partitions when one partition is having a recovery issue.

Listing 17-5: A range partitioning syntax example

```
CREATE TABLE sales
      ( invoice_no     NUMBER,
        sales_amount   NUMBER(7,2),
        sales_date     DATE)
    PARTITION BY RANGE (sales_date)
      ((PARTITION sales_q1_03 VALUES LESS THAN ('01-APR-2003')
            TABLESPACE ts_sales_q1_03,
          PARTITION sales_q2_03 VALUES LESS THAN ('01-JUL-2003')
            TABLESPACE ts_sales_q2_03,
          PARTITION sales_q3_03 VALUES LESS THAN ('01-OCT-2000')
            TABLESPACE ts_sales_q3_03,
          PARTITION sales_q4_03 VALUES LESS THAN (MAXVALUE)
            TABLESPACE ts_sales_q4_03);
```

NOTE
*Each partition can have its own storage clause
parameters.*

The MAXVALUE clause specifies the default partition for values that do not meet the other partitions' requirements. If an application will be adding partitions with a new range (for example, data organized in partitions by a quarterly date), don't use the MAXVALUE clause.

NOTE
*If the MAXVALUE clause is not used, an error is
returned if the data does not match the requirements
for any of the partitions.*

Hash Partitioning

Hash partitioning takes the partition key and applies a mathematical calculation to derive a unique number known as the *hash value*. Hash values are randomly distributed throughout the range of all possible values, so this value can be used to evenly distribute the rows across the assigned tablespaces. Listing 17-6 illustrates the hash partitioning syntax. The MAXVALUE clause is not applicable to hash partitioning.

Listing 17-6: A hash partitioning syntax example

```
CREATE TABLE sales
      ( invoice_no     NUMBER,
        sales_amount   NUMBER(7,2),
        sales_date     DATE)
```

```
PARTITION BY HASH (invoice_no)
     (PARTITION p1 TABLESPACE SALES_p1,
      PARTITION p2 TABLESPACE SALES_p2,
      PARTITION p3 TABLESPACE SALES_p3,
      PARTITION p4 TABLESPACE SALES_p4);
```

Composite Partitioning

Composite partitioning is a combination of both range and hash partitioning. Listing 17-7 illustrates the syntax for composite partitioning. Notice that there is a RANGE clause and then the SUBPARTITION BY HASH. The table will be partitioned by the range partition key, and then evenly distributed across the subpartitions using the hash value of the key. In this example, the STORE IN clause identifies the tablespaces, and within each tablespace there will be four partitions. This example shows four partitions (P1–P4), each of which has four subpartitions.

Listing 17-7: A composite partitioning syntax example

```
CREATE TABLE sales
     ( invoice_no      NUMBER,
       sales_amount    NUMBER(7,2),
       sales_date      DATE)
    PARTITION BY RANGE(sales_date)
    SUB PARTITION BY HASH (invoice_no)
    SUB PARTITIONS 4
    STORE IN (TS_SALES_P1, TS_SALES_P2, TS_SALES_P3, TS_SALES_P4)
         (PARTITION p1 VALUES LESS THAN ('01-APR-2000'),
          PARTITION p2 VALUES LESS THAN ('01-JUL-2000'),
          PARTITION p3 VALUES LESS THAN ('01-OCT-2000'),
          PARTITION p4 VALUES LESS THAN (MAXVALUE));
```

List Partitioning

List partitioning assigns rows to partitions according to character values. The syntax illustrated in Listing 17-8 looks much like the IN clause of a SQL statement WHERE clause. The OTHER clause is used to define a default tablespace for values that do not meet any of the other partition requirements. If this option is omitted, then an error will be returned to the application/user if a value is presented that is not in one of the partition's lists.

Listing 17-8: A list partitioning syntax example

```
CREATE TABLE sales
     (invoice_no       NUMBER(6),
      sales_amt        NUMBER(7,2),
      sales_state      VARCHAR(2),
      sales_date       DATE)
```

```
PARTITION BY LIST(sales_state)
   (PARTITION sales_north VALUES ('ME','VT','NH','MA','RI','CN')
        TABLESPACE ts_sales_north
   (PARTITION sales_east VALUES ('NJ','NY','PA','VA','NC','WV')
        TABLESPACE ts_sales_east,
    PARTITION sales_west VALUES ('CA','UT','NM','CO','MT','OR','WA')
        TABLESPACE ts_sales_west,
    PARTITION sales_south VALUES ('FL','TX','SC','AR','TN','KY')
        TABLESPACE ts_sales_south,
    PARTITION sales_midwest VALUES ('IA','IL','IN','MN','MO','NE','OH')
        TABLESPACE ts_sales_midwest
   PARTITION others VALUES (DEFAULT ) TABLESPACE ts_default);
```

NOTE
*List partitioning can have only one partitioning
column.*

Index Partitioning Options

Index partitioning allows for indexes on larger table structures to be broken into
smaller units and distributed across multiple tablespaces. There are two types of
partitioned indexes: locally partitioned and globally partitioned indexes.

Indexes that use the table's partitioning parameters are called *locally partitioned*
indexes. These indexes have the same partitioning key, number of tablespaces, and
partitioning parameters as the table the index is associated with. They can index the
partitioning key value or one or more (composite key) different columns in the table,
and still follow the partitioning and tablespace assignment rules used by the underlying
table. Listing 17-9 illustrates the syntax for a locally partitioned index. Notice the
LOCAL syntax and that there is no PARTITION BY RANGE or PARITION BY LIST
clause. Listing 17-10 illustrates a nonprefixed locally partitioned index syntax
example. Note that the index is being built on a different key value than the
partitioning key of the underlying table. Both of these indexes would be on any of
the preceding partitioned table examples (those in Listing 17-5). Notice that these
syntax examples have the same number of partitions as in the syntax in Listing 17-5.

Listing 17-9: A local prefix partition index syntax example

```
CREATE INDEX SALES_DATE_PT_IDX on sales (sales_date)
   LOCAL
   (PARTITION sales_idx_q1_03 TABLESPACE ts_sales_idx_q1_03,
    PARTITION sales_idx_q2_03 TABLESPACE ts_sales_idx_q2_03,
    PARTITION sales_idx_q3_03 TABLESPACE ts_sales_idx_q3_03,
    PARTITION sales_idx_q4_03 TABLESPACE ts_sales_idx_q4_03);
```

Listing 17-10: A local nonprefixed partition index syntax example

```
CREATE INDEX SALES_INVOICE_PT_IDX on sales (invoice_no)
    LOCAL
    (PARTITION sales_idx_q1_03 TABLESPACE ts_sales_idx_q1_03,
     PARTITION sales_idx_q2_03 TABLESPACE ts_sales_idx_q2_03,
     PARTITION sales_idx_q3_03 TABLESPACE ts_sales_idx_q3_03,
     PARTITION sales_idx_q4_03 TABLESPACE ts_sales_idx_q4_03);
```

If a partitioned index's key value is the same as its partitioning value, this is known as a *prefixed* partitioned index. A nonprefixed partitioned index key column is not the same column as the partition key.

Local indexes do not have to have a PARTITION clause. If this clause is not used, Oracle will generate partition names and assign the index partitions to the same tablespaces as the underlying table. This might not give the best SQL performance.

NOTE
I would always list the PARTITION clause, since I don't like Oracle taking defaults (they can change with releases) and I like to separate the indexes from the tables.

Globally partitioned indexes can have their own partitioning values (PARTITION BY RANGE or PARTITION BY LIST clause) and their own individual tablespace assignments. Globally partitioned indexes are always prefixed indexes, as Oracle 10g does not support nonprefixed globally partitioned indexes. Listing 17-11 illustrates the syntax of a possible globally partitioned index on any of the earlier table syntax examples, but this illustration uses Listing 17-5 specifically. Notice that this index has its own range clause/list clause.

Listing 17-11: A global partitioned index syntax example

```
CREATE INDEX sales_invoice_pt_idx ON sales (invoice_no)
    GLOBAL
    PARTITION BY RANGE(sales_date)
        (PARTITION sales_idx_p1 VALUES LESS THAN '01-JUL-03'
            TABLESPACE ts_sales_idx_p1,
        PARTITION sales_idx_p2 VALUES LESS THAN '01-JAN-04'
            TABLESPACE ts_sales_idx_p2,
        PARTITION sales_idx_p3 VALUES LESS THAN (MAXVALUE)
            TABLESPACE sales_idx_p3);
```

TIP
You can create partitioned indexes on regular heap tables (nonpartitioned tables). These, of course, would be globally partitioned indexes, since there would be no partitioning options on the underlying table.

IOT Partitioning Options

IOTs can also be partitioned, and the overflow tablespace can be partitioned as well. IOTs support RANGE, HASH, and LIST partitioning, but not composite partitioning. Listing 17-12 illustrates the syntax for a RANGE partitioning example of an IOT. Notice that individual overflow tablespaces can be defined at the partition level.

Listing 17-12: A partitioned IOT syntax example

```
CREATE TABLE sales
    ( invoice_no      NUMBER,
      sales_amount    NUMBER(7,2),
      sales_date      DATE,
    PRIMARY KEY (invoice_no) )
    ORGANIZATION INDEX
          INCLUDING sales_amount
          OVERFLOW TABLESPACE ts_sales_q1_03_overflow
      PARTITION BY RANGE (sales_date)
    ((PARTITION sales_q1_03 VALUES LESS THAN ('01-APR-2003')
          TABLESPACE ts_sales_q1_03,
       PARTITION sales_q2_03 VALUES LESS THAN ('01-JUL-2003')
          TABLESPACE ts_sales_q2_03 OVERFLOW ts_sales_q2_03_overflow,
       PARTITION sales_q3_03 VALUES LESS THAN ('01-OCT-2000')
          TABLESPACE ts_sales_q3_03 OVERFLOW ts_sales_q3_03_overflow,
       PARTITION sales_q4_03 VALUES LESS THAN (MAXVALUE)
          TABLESPACE ts_sales_q4_03 OVERFLOW ts_sales_q4_03_overflow);
```

IOT partitions must all have the same block size. The overflow tablespaces can have a different block size from that used by the IOT itself, but all overflow tablespaces must have the same block size.

Using Partitioned Indexes for Performance

Oracle provides several methods of partitioning for various application needs. There won't be any performance gain with any of the partitioning options if the partitioning key is not referenced in the WHERE clause of the SQL statement. Hash partitioning is useful for single-row lookups using equality or the IN clause syntax (hashed keys cannot be used by range scans) where there is a large volume of rows being processed and where contention would normally be an issue. Hash global indexes can further spread out a large volume of inserts or updates across more blocks.

Range and list partitioning can benefit from partition "pruning" (the elimination of partitions that do not contain data returned by a search) when the SQL is coded to specifically use the partitioning key values. The cost-based optimizer can see the value in the WHERE clause and can also see how many partitions would be involved in satisfying the needs of the SQL. If the SQL is written in such a way that it does not take advantage of the partitioning key, then partitioning pruning does not happen and there is no performance benefit to using a partitioned object. Composite partitions can do some pruning, but the rows will still be distributed across multiple subpartitions and all of these subpartitions will need to be scanned. The more granular the search, the fewer partitions will need to be scanned, and the faster the SQL will return results.

An e-mail application using Oracle 10g as the repository would be an example that might benefit from hash and/or composite partitioning. This kind of application might have a different table for the inbox, outbox, drafts, and so on, and there would be a large volume of DML that would create a sharing contention if everyone were trying to do e-mail from the same tablespace/individual table.

Summary

This chapter has covered Oracle 10g performance-enhancing features of indexing and partitioning. Both of these features depend on database design and coding style. If the data model is defined correctly, it should be obvious which columns to index and whether partitioning would be of benefit to the application. Having to add a variety of indexes in test or in production shows either that no data model existed or that the data model used was inadequate. If SQL is coded poorly (for example, with functions on indexed columns in the WHERE clause), then indexes will be ignored. If the data is not laid out properly, giving a poor internal relationship between the index leaf blocks and the table data blocks (clustering factor), again, the indexes might not be used. If partitioning is utilized and the partitioning keys are ignored, the SQL working against these objects will perform poorly.

Poorly performing SQL caused by a poor database design is a difficult thing to fix.

PART
V

Oracle Products
on Linux

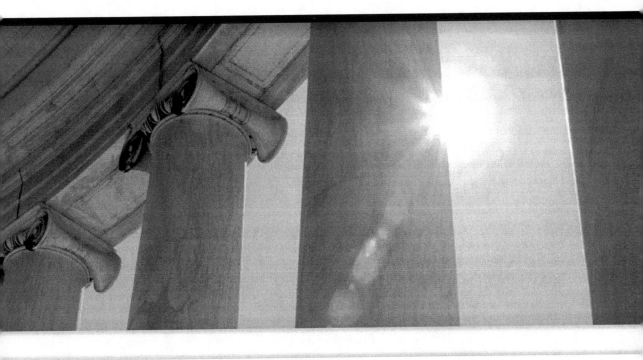

CHAPTER
18

Oracle Application
Server 10g on Linux

o start this chapter, it is necessary to define what OracleAS 10*g* is and of what value it is to the enterprise. OracleAS 10*g* is a standards-based collection of technologies that enable an enterprise to consolidate development, deployment, and delivery of web- and wireless-based applications. What makes OracleAS 10*g* a robust solution is the capacity to expand on basic web-based applications and deliver these applications on wireless devices, provide security while simplifying authentication, integrate with legacy applications, and provide the capacity for business analysis.

With most corporations having an abundance of applications with varying technologies, having the means to integrate, deliver, and analyze the underlying data is an obvious advantage. OracleAS 10*g* provides the infrastructure to centralize application deployments, web configurations, networking, and identity management to meet the expectation of integrated enterprise application sets. In addition, Linux provides a cost-effective, scalable platform for the OracleAS 10*g* technologies. To couple application technology consolidation from OracleAS 10*g* with the cost-effective, scalable deployment method Linux provides yields a great combination for robust, dependable application servers.

Groupings of these servers with like applications form a cluster, which allows for high availability and performance load balancing. These application instances that make up a cluster share a common metadata repository and redundant applications. All application instance types that share a metadata repository are considered to be part of a "farm." All server types that are part of a farm can be centrally managed and monitored. Additional servers can be added or removed from the farm as scalability demands change and service-level agreement demands increase.

What Components Make Up Oracle Application Server 10*g*?

Now that a conceptual understanding of OracleAS 10*g* is established, it is appropriate to break down the various components and describe what they do. The OracleAS 10*g* solution includes components to service the following:

- Java 2 Enterprise Edition
- Management and security
- Portals
- Wireless
- Caching

- Business intelligence

- E-business integration

Java 2 Enterprise Edition

The Java 2 Enterprise Edition (J2EE) provides the industry standard for Java and is the means for developing multitier applications. The advantage for using J2EE is the "write once, run anywhere" paradigm. The benefit to this is obvious to anyone who manages application development and is responsible for its Return On Investment (ROI). J2EE is standardized and modular, allowing a robust service without the need for complicated programming efforts. J2EE generally includes services for Enterprise JavaBeans, JavaServer Pages, XML, and Java Servlets. The key benefit for using the J2EE platform is to quickly develop and deploy enterprise applications that are supported across several platforms and readily available over the Web.

J2EE applications can be rapidly deployed with OracleAS 10*g*, once an EAR file has been created. The EAR file can then be deployed into the J2EE container via a deployment wizard within the Enterprise Manager. This wizard maps all the relevant URLs to the correct web modules, sets up a persistence layer, and assigns a manager to the application.

Administration of J2EE applications is extended with the 10*g* Application Server, as OC4J containers can be added or configured, J2EE resources can be centralized, and applications can be monitored.

Management and Security

This particular aspect of OracleAS 10*g* breaks down into several components that allow complete control and access to various applications within any desired scope. These components are

- **Oracle Enterprise Manager Application Server/Grid Control**   The Oracle 10*g* Enterprise Manager allows for complete deployment and configuration of J2EE application servers. When coupled with Grid Control, the scope of monitoring and control is expanded to include other Oracle products and the host operating system.

- **Oracle Single Sign-On**   With use of the available LDAP database, users can be authenticated from several applications with a single login ID. This makes Enterprise password maintenance much more manageable.

- **Oracle Application Server Certificate Authority**   A centralized server for managing SSL support, this component includes key generation for client-side authentication to provide encrypted information transfer.

- **Java Authentication and Authorization Service (JAAS)** Used to enhance J2EE container security by role-based access control.

- **Oracle Internet Directory** This also uses Oracle's LDAP directory. The LDAP directory uses an Oracle database to store its information. The Oracle Internet Directory is used to allow Single Sign-On and centralized networking.

Portals

Oracle portal technology supports wizard-driven development of enterprise portals. These are self-service by design and allow an individual to manage and deploy content. Following are the components of Oracle Portal technology:

- **Oracle Application Server Portal** With quick setup, Oracle Portal provides a means to rapidly deploy customized content for maximum productivity.

- **Oracle Application Server Portal Developer Kit** Provides the means to rapidly develop enterprise portals.

- **Oracle Ultra Search** This is a robust tool that allows for multirepository searches for information. With OracleAS 10g, this tool allows for integration with Oracle Portal to search across Oracle databases, IMAP mail servers, HTML documents, and Oracle Application Server Portal and system files.

- **Oracle Application Server Syndication Services** This is used with the ICE (Information Content Exchange) to automatically "push" information available to the server to ICE-compliant subscribers.

Wireless

Oracle Wireless technology is used to deliver information via browser, voice applications, J2ME (Java 2 Micro Edition), and two-way messaging.

Business Intelligence

OracleOracleAS 10g provides the means to mine information from various sources and format it in such a way that data can be used to predict and react to quickly changing business conditions. These tools include Oracle Application Server Discoverer, which allows end users to produce reports and graphs from ad hoc queries that can then be published in HTML format.

E-Business Integration

To further streamline the consolidation of disparate business applications, Oracle provides a means of integration with these technologies:

- **Oracle Application Server InterConnect**   Used to integrate enterprise applications. InterConnect uses high-level integration logic and low-level platform services. The integration component consists of an RDBMS Advanced Queuing component and Oracle Workflow. In addition, there are various adapters for applications and protocols that allow for application integration.

- **Oracle Application Server Process Connect**   This is an Oracle metadata business integration tool that transforms, translates, and validates business interactions.

Using Oracle Application Server 10*g*

Using OracleAS 10*g* in its full Enterprise Edition provides an organization the means to fully deploy, secure, and integrate a wide variety of applications. The most efficient way of using OracleAS 10*g* for its designated purpose is by using the command-line utilities of the DCM (Distributed Configuration Management). Enterprise Manager Grid Control is also used for manipulating OracleAS 10*g* instances. The breakdown of these applications is beyond the scope of this chapter but is demonstrated in the section pertaining to configuration of OracleAS 10*g*. An example of the Enterprise Manager Application Server Control is provided in Figure 18-1.

When several instances of OracleAS 10*g* are configured for high availability or clustering, using DCM simplifies the related management. In fact, DCM allows you to

- Keep various instances in sync.

- Back up and recover instance configurations.

- Import and export configurations between instances.

- Start up and shut down instances or subcomponents.

- Verify instance status.

The components the DCM manages include the following:

- OC4J (Oracle Components for Java) (*J2EE*)

- Oracle HTTP Server

- OC4J Applications

- OPMN (Oracle Process Manager and Notification Server)

- JAZN (Oracle Application Server Java Authentication Service)

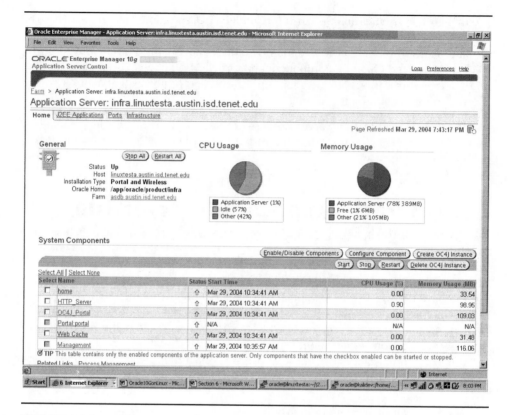

FIGURE 18-1. *Enterprise Manager Application Server Control*

The following tables provide an exhaustive list of DCM line commands grouped by command type and their use:

DCMCTL Shell Commands	Usage
!!	Repeats last command
shell	Invokes dcmctl shell
echo	Places string to output
setLogLevel	Sets level of logging
exit	Exits shell
quit	Quits shell

DCMCTL Archive Commands	**Usage**
applyArchiveTo	Applies configuration archive to instance or cluster
createArchive	Creates cluster/instance archive
exportArchive	Exports archive to/from repository to JAR file
importArchive	Imports archive into repository
listArchives	Lists archives
removeArchive	Deletes archives

DCMCTL Application Commands	**Usage**
deployApplication	Deploys J2EE application
listApplications	Lists OC4J instance applications
redeployApplication	Redeploys J2EE application
undeployApplication	Undeploys J2EE application
validateEarFile	Validates EAR J2EE compliance

DCMCTL Properties Commands	**Usage**
get Error	Displays errors
getReturnStatus	Returns status of last command
getState	Returns state of requested component: OC4J, Oracle HTTP Server, JAZN
help	Lists dcmctl commands
listComponent Types	Lists supported component types
set	Sets dcmctl options

Nonmanaged Cluster Commands	**Usage**
addOPMNLink	Creates nonmanaged OracleAS 10*g* cluster
getOPMNPort	Displays ONS remote port and hostname
listOPMNLinks	Lists nonmanaged AS cluster with local instance
removeOPMLLink	Removes instance from nonmanaged cluster

DCMCTL Process Management Commands	Usage
restart	Restarts application stack
shutdown	Stops application stack
start	Starts application stack
stop	Stops application stack

A simple example of a DCMCTL properties command is shown in Figure 18-2. The command shown in the figure is a general high-level status command that lists the status of all the instance components. To execute the DCMCTL command, you must navigate to $ORACLE_HOME/dcm/bin/dcmctl.

To simplify matters, the dcmctl utility may be placed in your PATH environment variable. In Linux, the default shell is the BASH shell, and in the user's, typically oracle's, home directory is a file named .bash_profile. It is here that the path to the dcmctl command may be placed so that it is sourced into the user environment and run from anywhere in the file system. This removes the need to navigate to the $ORACLE_HOME/dcm/bin directory every time a dcmctl command needs to be executed. As noted, most of what needs to be done to administer an OracleAS 10g server or server clusters can be accommodated by the DCMCTL utility.

An additional tool of great use in managing logs is provided from the Enterprise Manager Application Server Control. This tool, named LogLoader, provides the means to analyze several logs from different areas and group them according to some criteria. LogLoader provides an excellent forensic tool for diagnosing logs according to time/date criteria. This can narrow the search time by consolidating various system logs to coincide with a detected system slowdown or error. The logs are grouped in logical collections according to the scope of the search. For example, when the HTTP_Server component is selected from the LogLoader

```
$ dcmctl getstate -c -v

Current State for Instance:testinst

  Component Type Up Status In Sync Status

================================================
1 home     oc4j Up    True

2 HTTP Server ohs  Up    True

3 OC4j_Demos  oc4j Up    True
```

FIGURE 18-2. *DCMCTL command and output*

application, the error_log and the access_log are searched. If the Database component is included with the HTTP search criteria, then the alert*sid*.log is also searched. The requested logs are then returned to the browser and consolidated for easy review, as shown in Figure 18-3.

Critical logs that need monitoring that should be loaded regularly for review include:

- **Oracle alert log from database**   This will glean information if the database is experiencing any problems. It can also be used to check for any database system changes.

- **Apache access_log**   Lists addresses for incoming requests.

- **Apache error_log**   Lists any error pertaining to HTTP server and loaded modules.

- **DCM logs**   List errors associated with internally managed processes.

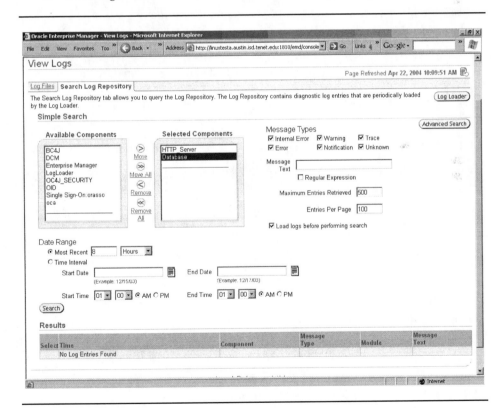

FIGURE 18-3.   *Viewing various logs through Enterprise Manager*

An additional tool for monitoring performance and collecting metrics is the Dynamic Monitoring Service. The intent of this service is to provide a means to instrument J2EE applications based on installing DMS calls into the Java application code. Oracle Application Server 10g has DMS services for instrumenting:

- Oracle HTTP Server
- Java Virtual Machine
- JDBC
- OC4J
- mod_plsql
- Portal
- Jserv
- Oracle Process Manager and Notification Server metrics
- Oracle Application Server Discoverer metrics

Table 18-1 shows samples of metric types that can be collected by the DMS for HTTP Server.

Metric Name	Description	Measurement
connection.active	Number of connections currently open	threads
connection.avg	Average time spent servicing HTTP connections	usecs (microseconds)
connection.maxTime	Maximum time spent servicing any HTTP connection	usecs
connection.minTime	Minimum time spent servicing any HTTP connection	usecs

TABLE 18-1. *Collectable HTTP Server Metrics with DMS*

Metric Name	Description	Measurement
connection.time	Total time spent servicing HTTP connections	usecs
handle.active	Child servers currently in the handle processing phase	threads
handle.avg	Average time spent in module handler	usecs
handle.completed	Number of times the handle processing phase has completed	ops
handle.maxTime	Maximum time spent in module handler	usecs
handle.minTime	Minimum time spent in module handler	usecs
handle.time	Total time spent in module handler	usecs
request.active	Child servers currently in the request processing phase	threads
request.avg	Average time required to service an HTTP request	usecs
request.completed	Number of HTTP request completed	ops
request.maxTime	Maximum time required to service an HTTP request	usecs
request.minTime	Minimum time required to service an HTTP request	usecs
request.time	Total time required to service HTTP requests	usecs

TABLE 18-1.   *Collectable HTTP Server Metrics with DMS* (continued)

Installing and Configuring Oracle Application Server 10*g* on Linux

The following section provides information on how to install and configure OracleAS 10*g* on the Linux platform.

Installation

Installation of OracleAS 10*g* involves acquiring the software, either by requesting the software from http://www.oracle.com or by downloading it from http://otn.oracle .com. Once the media have been staged, make sure that the environment variables $ORACLE_HOME and $ORACLE_SID are set. You will also need to have root, sudo, or easy access to a system administrator to successfully install software, as there are mandatory installation scripts that modify ownership of files and require a privileged account.

Configuration

Configuration of OracleAS 10*g* is contingent upon what instance types are to be installed. The more advanced Application Server configurations require an infrastructure installation. These configurations include both Oracle Internet Directory and an Oracle Metadata Repository. The examples that follow demonstrate the initial configuration of the OracleAS 10*g* using the infrastructure and Oracle Portal. After setting the environment and kernel parameters as prescribed by the *Oracle* 10*g Application Server Quick Installation and Upgrade Guide 10g Release 2 (10.1.2)for Linux x86*, the initial configuration takes place when the Oracle Universal Installer starts up, as shown in Figure 18-4.

After several basic configuration interrogations have taken place, which include determining the Oracle home location, the first major configuration step takes place when declaring the scope of the installation. As mentioned before, the assumption for this example is that of an installation that requires an infrastructure. Figure 18-5 demonstrates initial configuration choices.

The initial configuration interrogation demonstrates the general architecture choices of the application server. Server type choices include an Application Server, which can then be broken down into what type of functional "middle tier" can be installed. These middle tiers include J2EE, Forms and Reports services, and Discoverer. The second type of installation is an Infrastructure, which includes a metadata repository that is required to handle the more sophisticated configurations, such as Oracle Single Sign-On.

If an infrastructure is required, it needs to be installed first as the dependent applications register with the metadata repository. Within the infrastructure configuration, there are two additional parts. One is the metadata repository, which is a 9.0.4 database that contains an LDAP configuration. The second part is Oracle Identity Management, which is a superset of Oracle Internet Directory and Certificate Authority. Oracle Identity Manager is dependent on the installation of the metadata repository.

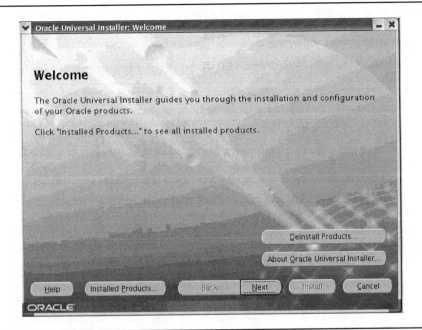

FIGURE 18-4.   *Oracle Universal Installer*

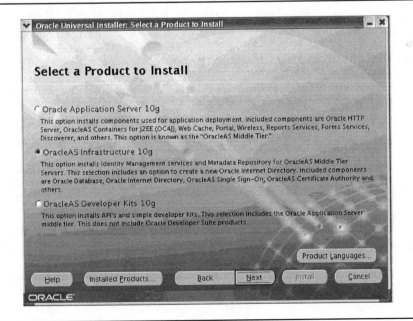

FIGURE 18-5.   *Types of product installations*

Once the base infrastructure has been configured, the accessory configurations can begin. The additional major configurations dependent on an infrastructure include:

■ Oracle Internet Directory

■ Certificate Authority

■ Oracle Single Sign-On

Once the installation has completed, the Enterprise Manager Application Control is used to configure the subcomponents of the Oracle Application Server, as shown in Figure 18-6.

Once the installation has completed, the Enterprise Manager Application Control is used to configure the subcomponents of the Oracle Application Server. Whenever one or more OracleAS 10g installations share a common metadata repository, they are considered to be part of a "farm." The Enterprise Manager Application Control can detect this and lay out the different Oracle home directories in which to configure.

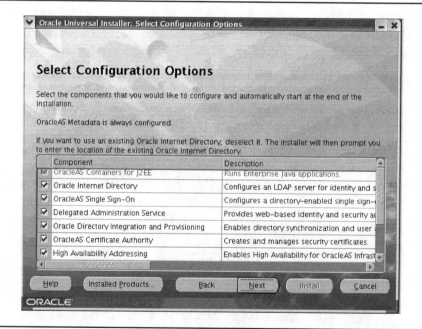

FIGURE 18-6. *Oracle OracleAS 10g subcomponent installation*

Of the subcomponents that need postinstallation configuration, the most important is the httpd.conf file. This file determines everything about how the web pages are served and secured (unless you use HTTPS authentication using SSL, in which case the httpds.conf file is used). The apache httpd.conf file is located in the $ORACLE_HOME/Apache/Apache/conf directory. It is highly suggested that before you make any type of manual configuration changes to this file or any other type of configuration file for the OracleAS 10*g* server, you should back up the server configuration using the dcmctl saveinstance command as follows:

```
$ORACLE_HOME/bin/dcm/bin/dcmctl saveinstance -dir /home/oracle/bkup/
```

The httpd.conf file is configured to

- Enable SSL.

- Create virtual directories.

- Administer security.

- Identify the docroot (directory where web documents are served from).

- Write directives to allow for use of loadable modules for application performance and security, such as mod_perl, mod_plsql, and mod_sso.

- Set up logs and log formats.

- Configure ports.

- Configure directory aliases.

- Add language and character support.

When configuring the apache.conf file, it is recommended that the HTTP_Server Advanced Server Properties from Enterprise Manager be used to edit the httpd.conf file, or any other configuration file defined as Advanced Server Properties. When using Advanced Server Properties to edit configuration files, you can back out and revert the file to its original state. When a change is made to a configuration file through the Advanced Server Properties editor, the administrator is prompted to restart the HTTP server. Figure 18-7 demonstrates the use of the Advanced Server Properties editing tool.

With its many components and services, OracleAS 10*g* provides a method to rapidly and efficiently deploy and integrate Enterprise Application suites. With such rapid deployment of applications, users' immediate concerns should be met. In turn, these evolved applications should help the user community fulfill the daily demands of corporate computing and keep business moving.

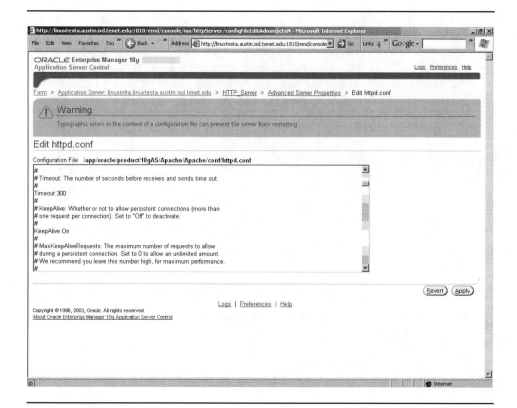

FIGURE 18-7. *Editing the httpd.conf file with Enterprise Manager*

Summary

Linux provides a scalable, robust platform for the OracleAS 10*g* application server. The ability to easily manage and tune the Linux system makes it an ideal platform for application servers. The fact that application servers typically scale well and the affordability of the Linux platform provide a scalable platform where you can easily and quickly add application servers. This, in conjunction with a network strategy that utilizes load-balancing routers, makes it easy to add more application servers.

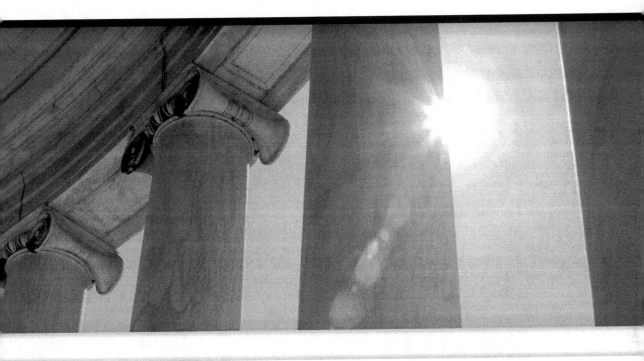

CHAPTER
19

The Oracle E-Business
Suite on Linux

n keeping with the trend of the preceding two chapters, this is an introduction and an overview of the Oracle E-Business Suite (known as Oracle Applications before Release 11*i*). The E-Business Suite runs on the Oracle database server and utilizes the Oracle Application Server, both of which are addressed in this book. The Oracle E-Business Suite is an extremely complicated product with many components that can be tuned and optimized, including the underlying Oracle database server. In this chapter, you will be presented with an overview of the Oracle E-Business Suite and how it integrates and works with Linux. Because of the complexity of the E-Business Suite, this chapter is not an instruction guide to how to install and configure it; rather, it is an introduction to setting it up on Linux.

Overview of the Oracle E-Business Suite on Linux

The Oracle E-Business Suite is an application designed to manage all areas of your business. In fact, the Oracle E-Business Suite now can manage over 100 areas of your business, including:

- Financials
- Contracts
- Business Intelligence
- Human Resources
- Manufacturing
- Marketing
- Procurement
- Order Fulfillment
- Professional Services
- Sales
- Service
- Projects

The E-Business Suite supports 30 different languages. The application tier is available on nine different platforms, including Linux, and the database layer of the Oracle E-Business Suite is available on eight different platforms, also including Linux. It is not necessary that the application tier and the database tier reside on the same operating system. It is also acceptable for the application tier to be on a 32-bit system and the database tier to be on a 64-bit system. Both of these could be Linux systems, or a mix of Linux for the application tier and another operating system for the database tier, or vice versa.

I have personally been involved in migrations of the E-Business Suite from HP-UX and Solaris to Linux where the database tier is converted to Linux at a separate time from the application tier. Conversions can happen on different tiers at different times independently of the other tier.

Because of the complexity of the different modules and their interaction, the E-Business Suite installation includes all available modules. The ones that you use are based on the licensing acquired. Many of the different applications rely on each other. For example, Accounts Payable, Accounts Receivable, and other financials all rely on the General Ledger module.

What Is the Oracle E-Business Suite?

The Oracle E-Business Suite is an integrated set of products designed to run your business, both front-office and back-office. The Oracle E-Business Suite is an extremely complex and huge application. The binaries themselves are in the tens of gigabytes in size. With Oracle E-Business Suite 11*i*, the entire suite is web-based and Forms-based and utilizes the Oracle Application Server 9*i* (OracleAS 9*i*) in order to run. However, since the installation is completely integrated, it is unnecessary to install the Oracle Application Server separately. The entire installation of all components is done through the Oracle E-Business Suite Rapid Installer, or rapidwiz.

The Oracle E-Business Suite is designed for fairly large businesses. The entire application is much too complex and requires too much maintenance for small businesses to utilize. It is necessary to have at least one full-time Oracle E-Business Suite DBA in order to properly maintain the E-Business Suite.

E-Business Suite Architecture

The Oracle E-Business Suite is a multitiered application that can exist on one or more computer systems. There are multiple layers, or *tiers*, to the application, and depending on your needs, they can reside on the same, or multiple, systems. The various tiers consist of the following:

- **Desktop tier** This consists of the web browser used for the newer HTML-based applications, and an add-on Java applet to provide the traditional forms-based user interface.

- **Application tier** This layer, commonly referred to as the middle tier, is made up of a number of different components such as the Web Server,

Forms Server, Concurrent Processing Server, Reports Server, Admin Server, and optional Discoverer Server.

■ **Database tier**   This is the database where the business data and metadata reside.

The application and database tiers can be split up in a number of different ways, depending on the workload on your system. The application tier can run on multiple systems in order to achieve the required performance. It is better to use only a single platform on your application tier to make maintenance easier, since only one set of patches would need to be applied. The database tier can be a stand-alone system or a RAC cluster as required. It is also possible to run both the application and database tiers on the same system.

Desktop Tier
The *desktop* tier, or client layer, is a collection of Java Archive (JAR) files that is downloaded and runs in the client browser. The JAR file is run by the Oracle JInitiator provided by the Oracle Java Virtual Machine (JVM) that is also downloaded to the client system by the application layer. With a Netscape browser, this is implemented as a plug-in, and with the Microsoft Internet Explorer browser, it is implemented as an ActiveX component. Oracle relies on its own JVM because it is not safe to rely on someone else's components.

Application Tier
The *application* tier is the most complicated layer. Here reside the Web Server (based on the Apache web server), the Forms Server, the Concurrent Processing Server, the Reports Server, and the Admin Server. This layer might also contain the optional Discoverer Server as well. It is typical for all of these components to reside on the same system, but they can be split up as well. If they are split up, the Concurrent Processing and Admin Servers are usually run on the same system as the database tier. Let's look at the different components and how they fit into the big picture.

Web Server   The Oracle HTTP Server is based on the Apache web server but has been modified by Oracle to integrate better with the Oracle Application Tier and the Oracle database server. The Web Server includes the Apache web server, the Web Listener, the Java Servlet Engine (JServ), and JavaServer Pages (JSP). If possible, the Web Server services a request itself. But for advanced processing, the Web Listener passes the request on to the Java Servlet Engine, which contacts the database server as needed.

Forms Server   The Forms Server supports the Oracle E-Business Suite forms. This is the traditional Oracle Forms as opposed to the HTML-based (formerly known as

Self-Service) applications. The Forms Server is an Oracle6*i* component that provides communication between the desktop client and the Oracle database server, displaying client screens and initiating changes in the database according to user actions.

The Oracle E-Business Suite supports the use of Socket mode for intranet users, HTTPS for Internet users, and HTTP mode for Forms-based communication. The Forms Listener Servlet allows you to run Oracle Forms applications over HTTP and HTTPS. It creates a Forms Server Runtime process for each client to communicate via the Web Server. The Forms Listener Servlet increases network traffic by approximately 40 percent because the HTTP protocol is more chatty than sockets. But it offers the benefits of reestablishing dropped network connections, requiring fewer machines and ports to be exposed at the firewall, and allowing a more robust and secure deployment over the Internet.

Reports Server   The Reports Server is used to create reports for the Business Intelligence System. The reports services is used, rather than allowing the reports to run unscheduled. With the reports services, you can tune and manage the reports processing, which can be quite resource intensive. When there are a large number of users, reports services can be split out onto several reports servers as necessary. One of the reports servers is designated as the master reports server, which receives the initial request and distributes it to one of the other reports servers.

Concurrent Processing Server   While the Self-Service and Oracle Forms applications run user requests in the foreground, data-intensive operations are run in the background as batch jobs. It is the Concurrent Processing Server that is responsible for running these batch jobs. This specialized server ensures that resource-intensive concurrent processing operations do not interfere with interactive operations. In an Oracle RAC environment, the concurrent processing servers are configured to have various queues defined on different nodes in the cluster, in order to spread the concurrent processing onto the different cluster nodes. This is known as *parallel concurrent processing.* Using parallel concurrent processing in a Linux RAC environment is becoming quite popular.

Admin Server   The Admin (Administration) Server is used to maintain the data model in the Oracle database. The Admin Server runs on only one node in an Oracle RAC cluster, but it is configured to fail over to another node if the primary node becomes unavailable. The Admin Server is used to upgrade the Oracle E-Business Suite, to apply patches, and to maintain data in the database.

Discoverer Server   The Oracle Discoverer Server is a tool designed to help with analysis services and ad hoc query processing. It is also used to perform business projections and is a business analysis tool. The Oracle Discoverer Server is an optional component and might not be deployed in all cases.

Database Layer
The database layer is where the actual data is stored and can be an Oracle8*i*, Oracle9*i*, or Oracle 10*g* database server. For the purposes of this book, we will assume that we are referring to the Oracle10*g* database server. Not only does the database layer store all of your business data, but it stores the metadata that defines the application layer as well. In fact, whenever you run the AutoConfig (adautocfg) utility in order to configure the Oracle E-Business Suite, many metadata tables are updated as part of this process.

What Modules Are Available on Linux
The Oracle E-Business Suite on Linux is fully functional, and all modules that are available in the Oracle E-Business Suite are available on the Linux platform. All tiers of the E-Business Suite (including database applications and client) can run on Linux. Oracle has made a commitment to the Linux platform and has lived up to it by fully supporting 32-bit Linux on the x86 platform. For E-Business Suite support on the Linux operating system for hardware platforms other than the x86 32-bit platform, please visit Oracle MetaLink.

Using the Oracle E-Business Suite on Linux
The Oracle E-Business Suite functions no differently on Linux than on any other platform. Because the Linux platform is less expensive than other platforms, it is more likely that the application layer will be made up of several Linux systems for redundancy and performance. In addition, many Linux E-Business Suite configurations take advantage of the Oracle RAC cluster for the database layer.

The E-Business Suite in a RAC Environment
The Oracle E-Business Suite can be configured to work in a RAC environment by configuring Parallel Concurrent Processing. This allows concurrent managers to run on all nodes in the RAC cluster, thus distributing the workload among those nodes. Parallel Concurrent Processing allows you to specify primary and secondary locations for each of the processing queues. This allows the E-Business Suite processing activity to be distributed among the nodes in the cluster in the manner that you select. The distribution of the workload in the cluster is neither automatic nor transparent. You must select the distribution of the concurrent processing queues and where they run.

As I mentioned, the Oracle E-Business Suite can be configured to run in a RAC environment, but this is not a trivial task to configure. There are a number of tuning steps required, and it must be fine-tuned in order to run optimally.

Installing and Configuring the E-Business Suite on Linux

The difference between installing the Oracle E-Business Suite on Linux and on any other platform arises from the specific Oracle and OS patches and configurations required, including setting and tuning various Linux kernel parameters (see the next section). If you have done this before, it is not extremely difficult to perform the initial installation of the software; however, configuring the Oracle E-Business Suite to perform useful work can be an extremely time-consuming and difficult task, taking many people-months to deploy. Oracle E-Business Suite is very customizable, containing an enormous number of variables that can be configured for currencies, time zones, exchange rates, tax rates, etc.

Installation

The Oracle E-Business Suite is installed using the Rapid Installer program (rapidwiz). The Rapid Installer program is the first component installed, and then it is run in order to install the Oracle technology stack and the applications file system. The technology stack, which provides features common to all Oracle E-Business Suite products, is installed on all systems. Before installing the E-Business Suite, you must plan how you are going to configure the application itself. Since the application is so configurable, particularly for sites needing to customize the applications, considerable functional work is necessary.

The Technical DBA vs. the Functional DBA

In the world of the Oracle E-Business Suite, there are two types of DBAs and consultants: the technical DBA and the functional DBA, or the technical consultant and the functional consultant. The job of the technical DBA is to administer the Oracle database, the concurrent manager, and the queues. In addition, the technical DBA installs the application and applies patches. The job of the functional consultant is to configure the applications from a functional standpoint. The functional consultant makes sure that business functions perform properly and is an expert in certain modules, such as Accounts Payable, Accounts Receivable, and Human Resources. The technical DBA administers the database; the functional DBA administers the applications from a functional standpoint.

Installing the Oracle E-Business Suite application servers, the database server, or the RAC clusters can take on the order of a few weeks. Configuring the Oracle E-Business Suite functionally can take months or even a year or more.

Following are the specific OS and Oracle patches, kernel extensions and parameters, and additional OS configuration required to install the E-Business Suite on Linux. The latest and greatest kernel requirements should be taken from Oracle MetaLink before beginning an Oracle E-Business Suite install. Finding out that a new patch is available after you have already started the installation can be not only time-consuming but costly as well.

A few key requirements for Linux are provided here; however, please check for updates to this list.

OS Patches

There are several patches that must be applied to Linux. This is a current patch list at the time of the writing of this book. Of course, this list might change by the time you read this. Please check MetaLink for the latest list.

For Red Hat Linux 3.0:

- pdksh-5.s.14-13

For (Discoverer) Quarterly Update 2 (QU2):

- compat-db-4.0.14.5
- compat-gcc-7.3-2.96.122
- compat-libstdc7.3-2.96.128
- compat-gcc-c7.3-2.96.122
- compat-libstdcdevel-7.3-2.96.122

Others:

- openmotif21-2.1.30-8
- setarch-1.3-1

After installing these patches, run ldconfig -v.

OS Configuration

There are several things that need to be configured in the OS specifically for Oracle E-Business Suite. These specific tasks must be performed and checked or you will eventually run into problems.

Because Oracle E-Business Suite was built with a specific version of the C libraries, it is necessary to configure the system to use a specific version. There are a few steps necessary to do this.

1. Rename the /usr/bin/gcc and /usr/bin/g++ files.

   ```
   # mv /usr/bin/gcc /usr/bin/gcc323
   # mv /usr/bin/g++ /usr/bin/g++323
   ```

2. Create symbolic links.

   ```
   # ln -s /usr/bin/gcc296 /usr/bin/gcc
   # ln -s /usr/bin/g++296 /usr/bin/g++
   ```

3. Verify that the hostname setting is correct. The command should return a fully qualified hostname. For example: <host_name>.<domain_name>.

   ```
   # hostname
   ```

   This should return hostname.domainname.

4. For the hugemem kernel, install rpm setarch-1.0-2 or higher.

   ```
   # setarch i386
   ```

5. Set the LD_ASSUME_KERNEL environment variable to 2.4.19. Make this setting permanent by entering it in the applmgr and oracle users' shell initialization files (such as $HOME/.bash_profile or $HOME/.profile) or by entering it into the system's global shell initialization file (/etc/profile).

   ```
   LD_ASSUME_KERNEL=2.4.19
   export LD_ASSUME_KERNEL
   ```

6. Apply the pre-installation patch. Once you have set the environment, you must apply a required patch before you begin the installation.

7. Apply one of these OS library patches: 3006854 (for Red Hat 3.0) or 3633386 (for SUSE SLES9). You can download these patches from Oracle MetaLink.

8. Reboot your system.

9. If you are running on Red Hat Linux 3.0, you must also apply post-installation patch 3119415 to the database tier ORACLE_HOME.

Migrating to the E-Business Suite on Linux

Migrating the E-Business Suite to Linux is a fairly complicated process that involves a number of steps. These steps can be broken down into two basic components: migrating the application tier and migrating the database tier. If you are installing the database tier on a RAC server, there is an additional step.

Migrating the Application Tier

Migrating the application tier involves the movement and reconfiguration of the application data files. This involves a lot of copying of data and running AutoConfig to reconfigure the application layer as well as the metadata. This should be done with great care and diligence, since it can be difficult to fix things that have been misconfigured.

Migrating Using the Linux Platform Migration Tool

Linux Platform Migration provides a way to easily move just an existing E-Business Suite middle-tier system (not the database tier) from any platform to Linux, allowing you to use fast, low-cost Linux hardware. The migration utility retains your exact applications patch level so that no APPL_TOP/Database synchronization is necessary. It also allows you to retain many customizations. Instead of installing the E-Business Suite from scratch as outlined previously in this chapter, you would do the following:

1. Prepare the existing system for migration, such as to implement AutoConfig (if on R11.5.8 or earlier). Create and export a current view global snapshot to a text file.

2. Prepare the new system for migration, including applying OS patches, installing Perl and JDK, and setting Linux Kernel parameters (refer to "Installing Oracle Applications: A Guide to Using Rapid Install").

3. Apply the Platform Migration utility patch to the source system. This step creates a custom upload file that is sent to Oracle. Oracle will then create a custom patch that will later be applied. Oracle usually returns this patch very quickly (in a matter of days).

4. Generate and upload the manifest of customer-specific files on the source system.

5. Copy specific middle-tier files from the source to the target system (APPL_TOP, OA_HTML, OA_JAVA, COMMON_TOP/util and COMMON_TOP/_pages, identitydb.obj).

6. Clone the AutoConfig XML application context file.

7. Install the middle-tier technology stack (using rapidwiz) on the target system.

8. Apply the Oracle Interoperability patches for Red Hat (if running this flavor of Linux) to the target system.

9. Run the AutoConfig Setup phase on the target system with the cloned context file.

10. Download and apply the customer-specific update with AutoPatch on the target system.

11. Apply the patch on the target system for migrating from Windows that contains Linux-specific APPL_TOP files that don't exist on Windows.

12. Apply any missing technology stack patches previously applied to your system but not included in new techstack installation.

13. Apply the latest techstack interop patch to the new applications file system.

14. Regenerate file system objects (adgensgn.sh), and then run adadmin to regenerate messages, forms, reports, graphics, and JAR files.

15. Run AutoConfig to complete target system configuration.

16. Perform Finishing Tasks (update third-party extensions; recompile custom code; perform required tasks for UTF8, Discoverer 4*i*, SSO, and Portal; update with new printer and Workflow configuration settings; start all services).

Once the application layer has been moved and the metadata repository has been configured, if you are migrating the database tier to Linux as well, it is time to move the actual data, as is described in the next section.

Migrating the Database Tier

The migration of the database tier involves running a patch at the database on the system that you are migrating from, performing an export, and then importing that data into the target system. The procedure for exporting and importing the data into the new system will vary slightly, depending on whether you are exporting data from an Oracle8*i* database, an Oracle9*i* database, or an Oracle10*g* database. Even the latest version of the Oracle E-Business Suite can utilize an Oracle 9.2 or Oracle 10*g* database (though the application tier still utilizes Oracle 8.0.6 executables). Again, these are the basic steps:

1. Apply the pre-export patch. This patch prepares the database for export. You must perform this step before performing the export or the import will not be successful.

2. Export the database.

3. Copy the export file(s) to the new system.

4. Run the post-import steps. These steps will be described in the interoperability notes.

While migrating the database tier, it is a good time to optimize your database layout and I/O subsystem. Since export and import are going to be used, the underlying data structures of the Oracle database can be modified. If you are not already using them, convert to locally managed tablespaces. If necessary, you can expand tablespaces to span multiple data files. Since the default Oracle E-Business Suite installation as of Release 11.5.10 now creates only 12 consolidated tablespaces with the new Oracle applications Tablespace Model (OATM), whereas older versions included over one hundred tablespaces (two for each module; one for data, one for indexes, plus some extras), this is also a good time to migrate to the OATM.

NOTE
The AutoConfig utility not only configures the application programs but configures the metadata in the database as well. This is important to keep in mind, since a mistake could mean that you need to spend significant time deleting data from the database.

As you can see, there are numerous steps that must be completed for a successful migration. If you have not already done one of these, make sure you are aware of all of the steps required before beginning the migration.

Converting the Database Tier to RAC

Converting the database tier to a RAC cluster is a multiphase project. During the migration or the initial installation of the E-Business Suite, the Oracle database is created. You should not skip this step, since the rapid installer creates the necessary tablespaces and structures that are needed. In order to convert the database tier to RAC, another Oracle installation must be done with the RAC option and the E-Business Suite database must be moved to the new Oracle home. This is due to the fact that the Oracle installer will configure additional components in a RAC environment that are not present in a non-RAC installation. In order for these components to be installed, the Oracle Cluster Ready Services must be running at installation time. The steps are as follows:

1. Install the Oracle instance using the rapid installer as part of the E-Business Suite installation or migration.

2. Install an Oracle RAC cluster.

3. Move the E-Business Suite database to the RAC cluster.

4. Set up Parallel Concurrent Processing (PCP).

These steps are fairly straightforward, but they are time-consuming to perform and require a great deal of attention to detail (and sometimes some debugging skills). The entire process of converting the database to RAC and setting up PCP requires planning and a good check list.

Testing

One of the most important steps in migrating the Oracle E-Business Suite to Linux is the testing phase. Once everything has been configured and all of the data has been migrated, you must perform rigorous functional and performance tests to make sure everything has been properly configured. In addition, it is a good idea to compare row object counts in the new database to those of the original database as it was when the export was done. Carefully check all of the import logs and the Oracle alert log for errors.

Once the testing has been completed, you will be ready for the final conversion and the utilization of the new system by the user community. At this point, the system should be carefully monitored for the next few weeks. Once this has been completed, normal monitoring schedules can be used.

Summary

This chapter has served as an introduction and an overview of how to install, configure, and migrate the Oracle E-Business Suite to Linux. Because the Oracle E-Business Suite is an extremely complicated product, this chapter is not an instruction guide to how to install and configure it, but rather an introduction to setting it up on Linux. Linux is an ideal platform for the Oracle E-Business Suite because of the flexibility, performance, and industry-wide support for Linux. In fact, Oracle itself has adopted Linux as the platform of choice for running its own business.

The Linux platform is rapidly growing in popularity and has been adopted by not only the user community but the hardware and software development community as well. Linux has proved itself to be an ideal platform for web servers, application servers, firewalls, and domain name servers, as well as database servers. The Oracle Application Server and E-Business Suite run very well on the Linux platform. As Linux matures, so will Linux be adopted as the enterprise platform of choice.

Index

GET YOUR FREE SUBSCRIPTION
TO ORACLE MAGAZINE

Oracle Magazine is essential gear for today's information technology professionals. Stay informed and increase your productivity with every issue of *Oracle Magazine*. Inside each free bimonthly issue you'll get:

- Up-to-date information on Oracle Database, Oracle Application Server, Web development, enterprise grid computing, database technology, and business trends
- Third-party vendor news and announcements
- Technical articles on Oracle and partner products, technologies, and operating environments
- Development and administration tips
- Real-world customer stories

IF THERE ARE OTHER ORACLE USERS AT YOUR LOCATION WHO WOULD LIKE TO RECEIVE THEIR OWN SUBSCRIPTION TO ORACLE MAGAZINE, PLEASE PHOTOCOPY THIS FORM AND PASS IT ALONG.

ORACLE
MAGAZINE

Three easy ways to subscribe:

① Web
Visit our Web site at otn.oracle.com/oraclemagazine. You'll find a subscription form there, plus much more!

② Fax
Complete the questionnaire on the back of this card and fax the questionnaire side only to +1.847.763.9638.

③ Mail
Complete the questionnaire on the back of this card and mail it to P.O. Box 1263, Skokie, IL 60076-8263

ORACLE®

FREE SUBSCRIPTION

○ **Yes, please send me a FREE subscription to *Oracle Magazine*.**
To receive a free subscription to *Oracle Magazine*, you must fill out the entire card, sign it, and date it (incomplete cards cannot be processed or acknowledged). You can also fax your application to +1.847.763.9638.
Or subscribe at our Web site at otn.oracle.com/oraclemagazine

○ NO

○ From time to time, Oracle Publishing allows our partners exclusive access to our e-mail addresses for special promotions and announcements. To be included in this program, please check this circle.

signature (required)	date
X	

○ Oracle Publishing allows sharing of our mailing list with selected third parties. If you prefer your mailing address not to be included in this program, please check here. If at any time you would like to be removed from this mailing list, please contact Customer Service at +1.847.647.9630 or send an e-mail to oracle@halldata.com.

name	title
company	e-mail address
street/p.o. box	
city/state/zip or postal code	telephone
country	fax

YOU MUST ANSWER ALL TEN QUESTIONS BELOW.

① WHAT IS THE PRIMARY BUSINESS ACTIVITY OF YOUR FIRM AT THIS LOCATION? (check one only)
- ☐ 01 Aerospace and Defense Manufacturing
- ☐ 02 Application Service Provider
- ☐ 03 Automotive Manufacturing
- ☐ 04 Chemicals, Oil and Gas
- ☐ 05 Communications and Media
- ☐ 06 Construction/Engineering
- ☐ 07 Consumer Sector/Consumer Packaged Goods
- ☐ 08 Education
- ☐ 09 Financial Services/Insurance
- ☐ 10 Government (civil)
- ☐ 11 Government (military)
- ☐ 12 Healthcare
- ☐ 13 High Technology Manufacturing, OEM
- ☐ 14 Integrated Software Vendor
- ☐ 15 Life Sciences (Biotech, Pharmaceuticals)
- ☐ 16 Mining
- ☐ 17 Retail/Wholesale/Distribution
- ☐ 18 Systems Integrator, VAR/VAD
- ☐ 19 Telecommunications
- ☐ 20 Travel and Transportation
- ☐ 21 Utilities (electric, gas, sanitation, water)
- ☐ 98 Other Business and Services

② WHICH OF THE FOLLOWING BEST DESCRIBES YOUR PRIMARY JOB FUNCTION? (check one only)
Corporate Management/Staff
- ☐ 01 Executive Management (President, Chair, CEO, CFO, Owner, Partner, Principal)
- ☐ 02 Finance/Administrative Management (VP/Director/ Manager/Controller, Purchasing, Administration)
- ☐ 03 Sales/Marketing Management (VP/Director/Manager)
- ☐ 04 Computer Systems/Operations Management (CIO/VP/Director/ Manager MIS, Operations)
IS/IT Staff
- ☐ 05 Systems Development/ Programming Management
- ☐ 06 Systems Development/ Programming Staff
- ☐ 07 Consulting
- ☐ 08 DBA/Systems Administrator
- ☐ 09 Education/Training
- ☐ 10 Technical Support Director/Manager
- ☐ 11 Other Technical Management/Staff
- ☐ 98 Other

③ WHAT IS YOUR CURRENT PRIMARY OPERATING PLATFORM? (select all that apply)
- ☐ 01 Digital Equipment UNIX
- ☐ 02 Digital Equipment VAX VMS
- ☐ 03 HP UNIX

- ☐ 04 IBM AIX
- ☐ 05 IBM UNIX
- ☐ 06 Java
- ☐ 07 Linux
- ☐ 08 Macintosh
- ☐ 09 MS-DOS
- ☐ 10 MVS
- ☐ 11 NetWare
- ☐ 12 Network Computing
- ☐ 13 OpenVMS
- ☐ 14 SCO UNIX
- ☐ 15 Sequent DYNIX/ptx
- ☐ 16 Sun Solaris/SunOS
- ☐ 17 SVR4
- ☐ 18 UnixWare
- ☐ 19 Windows
- ☐ 20 Windows NT
- ☐ 21 Other UNIX
- ☐ 98 Other
- 99 ☐ None of the above

④ DO YOU EVALUATE, SPECIFY, RECOMMEND, OR AUTHORIZE THE PURCHASE OF ANY OF THE FOLLOWING? (check all that apply)
- ☐ 01 Hardware
- ☐ 02 Software
- ☐ 03 Application Development Tools
- ☐ 04 Database Products
- ☐ 05 Internet or Intranet Products
- 99 ☐ None of the above

⑤ IN YOUR JOB, DO YOU USE OR PLAN TO PURCHASE ANY OF THE FOLLOWING PRODUCTS? (check all that apply)
Software
- ☐ 01 Business Graphics
- ☐ 02 CAD/CAE/CAM
- ☐ 03 CASE
- ☐ 04 Communications
- ☐ 05 Database Management
- ☐ 06 File Management
- ☐ 07 Finance
- ☐ 08 Java
- ☐ 09 Materials Resource Planning
- ☐ 10 Multimedia Authoring
- ☐ 11 Networking
- ☐ 12 Office Automation
- ☐ 13 Order Entry/Inventory Control
- ☐ 14 Programming
- ☐ 15 Project Management
- ☐ 16 Scientific and Engineering
- ☐ 17 Spreadsheets
- ☐ 18 Systems Management
- ☐ 19 Workflow

Hardware
- ☐ 20 Macintosh
- ☐ 21 Mainframe
- ☐ 22 Massively Parallel Processing
- ☐ 23 Minicomputer
- ☐ 24 PC
- ☐ 25 Network Computer
- ☐ 26 Symmetric Multiprocessing
- ☐ 27 Workstation
Peripherals
- ☐ 28 Bridges/Routers/Hubs/Gateways
- ☐ 29 CD-ROM Drives
- ☐ 30 Disk Drives/Subsystems
- ☐ 31 Modems
- ☐ 32 Tape Drives/Subsystems
- ☐ 33 Video Boards/Multimedia
Services
- ☐ 34 Application Service Provider
- ☐ 35 Consulting
- ☐ 36 Education/Training
- ☐ 37 Maintenance
- ☐ 38 Online Database Services
- ☐ 39 Support
- ☐ 40 Technology-Based Training
- ☐ 98 Other
- 99 ☐ None of the above

⑥ WHAT ORACLE PRODUCTS ARE IN USE AT YOUR SITE? (check all that apply)
Oracle E-Business Suite
- ☐ 01 Oracle Marketing
- ☐ 02 Oracle Sales
- ☐ 03 Oracle Order Fulfillment
- ☐ 04 Oracle Supply Chain Management
- ☐ 05 Oracle Procurement
- ☐ 06 Oracle Manufacturing
- ☐ 07 Oracle Maintenance Management
- ☐ 08 Oracle Service
- ☐ 09 Oracle Contracts
- ☐ 10 Oracle Projects
- ☐ 11 Oracle Financials
- ☐ 12 Oracle Human Resources
- ☐ 13 Oracle Interaction Center
- ☐ 14 Oracle Communications/Utilities (modules)
- ☐ 15 Oracle Public Sector/University (modules)
- ☐ 16 Oracle Financial Services (modules)
Server/Software
- ☐ 17 Oracle9i
- ☐ 18 Oracle9i Lite
- ☐ 19 Oracle8i
- ☐ 20 Other Oracle database
- ☐ 21 Oracle9i Application Server
- ☐ 22 Oracle9i Application Server Wireless
- ☐ 23 Oracle Small Business Suite

Tools
- ☐ 24 Oracle Developer Suite
- ☐ 25 Oracle Discoverer
- ☐ 26 Oracle JDeveloper
- ☐ 27 Oracle Migration Workbench
- ☐ 28 Oracle9i AS Portal
- ☐ 29 Oracle Warehouse Builder
Oracle Services
- ☐ 30 Oracle Outsourcing
- ☐ 31 Oracle Consulting
- ☐ 32 Oracle Education
- ☐ 33 Oracle Support
- ☐ 98 Other
- 99 ☐ None of the above

⑦ WHAT OTHER DATABASE PRODUCTS ARE IN USE AT YOUR SITE? (check all that apply)
- ☐ 01 Access
- ☐ 02 Baan
- ☐ 03 dbase
- ☐ 04 Gupta
- ☐ 05 IBM DB2
- ☐ 06 Informix
- ☐ 07 Ingres
- ☐ 08 Microsoft Access
- ☐ 09 Microsoft SQL Server
- ☐ 10 PeopleSoft
- ☐ 11 Progress
- ☐ 12 SAP
- ☐ 13 Sybase
- ☐ 14 VSAM
- ☐ 98 Other
- 99 ☐ None of the above

⑧ WHAT OTHER APPLICATION SERVER PRODUCTS ARE IN USE AT YOUR SITE? (check all that apply)
- ☐ 01 BEA
- ☐ 02 IBM
- ☐ 03 Sybase
- ☐ 04 Sun
- ☐ 05 Other

⑨ DURING THE NEXT 12 MONTHS, HOW MUCH DO YOU ANTICIPATE YOUR ORGANIZATION WILL SPEND ON COMPUTER HARDWARE, SOFTWARE, PERIPHERALS, AND SERVICES FOR YOUR LOCATION? (check only one)
- ☐ 01 Less than $10,000
- ☐ 02 $10,000 to $49,999
- ☐ 03 $50,000 to $99,999
- ☐ 04 $100,000 to $499,999
- ☐ 05 $500,000 to $999,999
- ☐ 06 $1,000,000 and over

⑩ WHAT IS YOUR COMPANY'S YEARLY SALES REVENUE? (please choose one)
- ☐ 01 $500, 000, 000 and above
- ☐ 02 $100, 000, 000 to $500, 000, 000
- ☐ 03 $50, 000, 000 to $100, 000, 000
- ☐ 04 $5, 000, 000 to $50, 000, 000
- ☐ 05 $1, 000, 000 to $5, 000, 000

100103